THE WILDERNESS OF DREAMS

SUNY Series in Dream Studies
Robert L. Van de Castle, editor

THE WILDERNESS OF DREAMS

Exploring the Religious Meanings of Dreams in Modern Western Culture

Kelly Bulkeley

State University of New York Press

Cover painting by Joshua Adam

Published by
State University of New York Press, Albany

Printed in the United States of America

For information, address State University of New York Press,
State University Plaza, Albany, N.Y., 12246

Production by Marilyn P. Semerad
Marketing by Theresa A. Swierzowski

Library of Congress Cataloging-in-Publication Data

Bulkeley, Kelly, 1962–
The wilderness of dreams : exploring the religious meanings of dreams in modern Western culture / Kelly Bulkeley.
p. cm. — (SUNY series in dream studies)
Includes bibliographical references (p.) and index.
ISBN 0–7914–1745–X (hardcover). — ISBN 0–7914–1746–8 (pbk.)
1. Dreams—Religious aspects. 2. Dream interpretation.
I. Title. II. Series.
BL65.D67B85 1993
291.4'2—dc20

93–9484
CIP

10 9 8 7 6 5 4 3 2 1

To Hilary
for loving a dreamer

CONTENTS

Part 4 Dreams and Religious Meaning

Part 5 Conclusion: Out of The Wilderness

Dreams have a poetic integrity and truth. This limbo and dust-hole of thought is presided over by a certain reason, too. Their extravagance from nature is yet within a higher nature. They seem to us to suggest an abundance and fluency of thought not familiar to the waking experience. They pique us by independence of us, yet we know ourselves in this mad crowd, and owe to dreams a kind of divination and wisdom. My dreams are not me; they are not Nature, or the Not-me; they are both. They have a double consciousness, at once sub- and ob-jective. We call the phantoms that rise, the creation of our fancy, but they act like muntineers, and fire on their commander; showing that every act, every thought, every cause, is bipolar, and in the act is contained the counteraction. If I strike, I am struck; If I chase, I am pursued. Wise and sometimes terrible hints shall in them be thrown to the man out of a quite unknown intelligence. He shall be startled two or three times in his life by the justice as well as the significance of this phantasmagoria. Once or twice the conscious fetters shall seem to be unlocked, and a freer utterance attained.

—Ralph Waldo Emerson, "Demonology" (1844), 7–8

PREFACE

My hope is that at least three different audiences will be interested in joining this exploration of dreams and religious meaning. First would be those who study religion and spirituality. Dreams have played an important role in religious traditions throughout history, and yet they have not received a great deal of sustained scholarly analysis. In particular, there has not been much detailed research on the religious significance of dreams in modern Western culture. My main goal here is to initiate a critical, sophisticated, interdisciplinary study of dreams and religious meaning in the modern West. I believe that the study of dreams can make an important contribution to our understanding of the nature of religion in modern Western culture. As a descriptive enterprise, this work will portray one specific area in which the broader struggles of religion and modernity are being played out. As a practical enterprise, we will try in this work to develop an approach to the religious meaning of dreams that can contribute to the revitalization of religion in the modern West.

The second audience whose interest I hope to spark is the diverse, far-flung group of people who research, investigate, and work with dreams. This group includes psychotherapists, neuroscientists, cognitive psychologists, anthropologists, educators, literary critics, and many, many others. The issue of religious meaning has traditionally been at the very heart of dream study. Our explorations here will show that this issue remains crucial to modern dream study as well. Many contemporary dream researchers have, of course, discussed the religious significance of dreams. However, there have been exceedingly few investigations of dreams that focus *directly* on the issue of religious meaning, using the methodologies of contemporary religious studies—and no investigations, to my knowledge, that apply this focus to the whole multidisciplinary range of fields studying dreams. This work will be unique, I believe, in its use of a religious studies perspective to explore dreams and in its application of that perspective to the full variety of modern dream research.

The third audience I want to address consists of those people, academics or not, professionals or not, who are simply interested in their dreams. It is a curious fact of human existence that we go to sleep each night and have strange, mysterious experiences filled with fantastic images, strong emotions, enigmatic ideas, and bizarre narrative plots. Once in a while, we go to sleep and have *very* strange, mysterious experiences—experiences so vivid, so powerful, so haunting that they dramatically affect our lives. No one, of course, remembers more than a tiny fraction of their dreams, and many people claim that they never remember any dreams at all. I agree with Emerson, however, that almost everyone seems to have had at least one or two dreams during their lives that have stuck with them, dreams whose imagery or emotional power have been so striking that people may still recall them clearly after many years. Our studies here will try to say something about what such vivid, numinous, life-altering dreams might mean.

I believe that this work may also be of interest to certain groups of people outside the studies of religion and of dreams. We will be discussing a number of subjects that are relevant to many other fields of inquiry. For example, we will devote extensive attention to the philosophy of interpretation, and so anyone involved in the fields of literature, art, law, and history—that is, in fields directly concerned with issues of interpretation and meaning—may find our discussions of dream interpretation to be of interest. We will also examine in great detail the conflict-filled relationship between science and religion, a relationship that in many ways has defined the modern West. So people who study the distinctive nature and problems of modern Western culture will find material here relevant to their work. And anyone interested in interdisciplinary studies may take some notice of our efforts to integrate psychological, artistic, neuroscientific, and anthropological approaches to dreams. Many people talk about the virtues of interdisciplinary inquiry, but actual efforts at engaging in such inquiry are much less common. This work, beyond its specific focus on dreams and religious meaning, is in more general terms an attempt to develop an interdisciplinary model of study in the human sciences.

One final note. I am in the process of changing the spelling of my last name, reinserting an "e" that was dropped put of my family's name a few generations back. As a result, works I wrote before 1993 use "Bulkley," while this book and all future writings will use "Bulkeley."

December 21, 1992
Chicago, Illinois

ACKNOWLEDGMENTS

There are many people who helped me create this work, far more than I can thank individually. Nevertheless, I want to thank those friends whose help was especially valuable to me. Don Browning, Wendy Doniger, Bert Cohler, and Peter Homans, all faculty members of the University of Chicago, gave me the warm encouragement and scholarly guidance I needed to transform my dreams into a book. The members of the Association for the Study of Dreams (particularly Jeremy Taylor, Rita Dwyer, Carol Schreier Rupprecht, and Jane White Lewis) helped me realize that I'm not the only dream fanatic on the planet. The editors of *Dream Network Journal* (Linda Magallon and Roberta Ossana) provided me with wonderful opportunities to test out early versions of my ideas. My colleagues and students in the Soc. 2 program at the University of Chicago gave me crucial insights into the relationship between dreams, religion, and culture. Tom "Slim" Traub deserves a medal (or maybe a better nickname) for the countless hours he spent reading and editing early drafts of this book. Josh Adam (the cover artist) and Ed Kelley get the credit for first steering me away from normality; with them I shared my earliest metaphysical journeys into the world of dreams. Throughout my studies I received much-needed moral support from Greg Fukutomi, Ron Rebholz, Harper Martin, Cori Field, Carol Anderson, Emilia Zak, Steve Singer, and Chris Altschuler; good friends all. And of course my family deserves my infinite thanks—Hilary, Dylan, Alex, Michelle, Tish, Ned, Howard, Big Marie and Little Marie. I hope I've made them proud.

PART ONE

INTRODUCTION:
First Steps

1

DREAMS THROUGH THE HISTORY OF RELIGIONS

"Explain all that," said the Mock Turtle.
"No, no! The adventures first," said the Gryphon in an impatient tone: "explanations take such a dreadful time."

—Lewis Carroll, *Alice's Adventures in Wonderland*

Dreams and Religion

The most widespread and longest-standing interest humans have taken in dreams has been in their religious meaning. People in virtually every culture throughout history have reported dreams of gods, spirits, and demons. People have looked to their dream experiences for insights about the soul, the afterlife, and the destiny of both individual and communal existence. They have drawn upon their dreams for spiritual guidance to heal their suffering, to overcome their troubles, and to pursue a good, fulfilling life. Likewise, people from the modern West[1] have also taken a deep interest in the religious meaning of dreams. Many modern Westerners have looked at the ways that dreams can motivate religious belief, either reinforcing adherence to an established religious tradition or spurring the pursuit of new spiritual ideals. Like people from other cultures, modern Westerners have tried to understand how to interpret dreams, how to distinguish dreams that may be religiously meaningful from dreams that are trivial or insignificant, and how to learn from their dreams what makes for a fulfilling life.

In this work we will focus on dreams and religious meaning in modern Western culture, critically examining the most important twentieth-century theories on this subject. As we conduct this examination we will come up against a number of difficulties, problems, and mysteries—as with dreams themselves, nothing in the study of dreams is simple or self-evident. We will therefore need a great deal of patience, a deep capacity for critical self-reflection, and a healthy respect for ambiguity. We will also need the aid of guides from outside the study of dreams to help us overcome the difficulties we will encounter within the areas of dream research. These guides will enable us to pursue the ultimate goal of this work: to develop a new approach to the religious meaning of dreams, an approach that is theoretically sound, practically useful, and appropriate to the distinctive nature of modern Western culture.

To begin, we need to undertake a brief historical review of the various ways that different cultures and traditions have understood the religious meaning of dreams.[2] Such a review could easily expand into a book of its own, so we will have to content ourselves with discussing only a few prominent examples (additional examples and references will be provided in the endnotes to this chapter). I have loosely organized these examples into the following three categories: dreams of the divine and the demonic; dreams influencing religious practices and beliefs; and theories of interpreting religiously meaningful dreams.[3]

Dreams of the Divine and the Demonic

People from countless religious traditions have reported dreams of gods, spirits, saints, and various other divine powers. A religious poem from the ancient Near Eastern kingdom of Akkadia describes a young prince's afflictions, which have brought him near death; the god Marduk comes to him in a series of three dreams and restores the prince to health (Oppenheim 1956, 217, 250). In Homer's *Odyssey* the goddess Athena appears to Penelope in a dream, calming her sorrow and reassuring her that Odysseus will soon return (Homer 4.772ff.). Athena also makes a dream visit to the young princess Nausikaa, just before Nausikaa encounters a naked, bedraggled Odysseus washed up from the sea; in the princess's dream Athena proclaims, "Maidenhood must end!" (Homer 6.1ff.) The Jewish patriarch Jacob has a dream vision of a great ladder spanning heaven and earth, with angels ascending and descending it (Gen. 28.10–22). The Sufi mystic Shamsoddin Lahihi (d. 1506) describes a visionary dream in which he soars into Heaven, "like an arrow shooting forth from the bow" and sees "that the entire universe, in the structure it presents, consists of light" (Corbin 1966, 396–97). Bishop Bruno of Toul, later Pope Leo IX, is reported to have had the following dream:

> [He] saw in his dream a deformed old woman who haunted him with great persistency and treated him with great familiarity. She was

> hideously ugly, clothed in filthy rags, her hair dishevelled and altogether he could scarce recognize in her the human form. Disgusted with her general appearance Bruno tried to avoid her; but the more he shrunk from her the more she clung to him. Annoyed at this importunity, Bruno made the sign of the cross; whereupon she fell to the earth as dead and rose up again lovely as an angel. (Brook 1987, 227)

Many Australian aboriginal tribes believe that the spirits of dead people visit the living in their dreams. These spirits provide dreamers with special knowledge, songs, and magical charms (Howitt 1904, 434–42). Similarly, many Native Americans tell of dreams in which appear the spirits of great ancestors, of animals, and of natural forces like the wind and the sun (Kenton 1929).[4]

People in a number of cultures have also reported frightening, nightmarish dreams of devils, demons, evil spirits, and the more destructive aspects of the divine. The *Rig Veda*, one of the oldest written texts in history, contains a number of hymns that refer to the evil spirits that afflict people in their dreams (O'Flaherty 1981, 218, 288, 292). The Babylonian epic *Gilgamesh* describes a series of harrowing nightmares that plague the hero: in the last of these nightmares,

> The heavens cried out; earth roared.
> Daylight vanished and darkness issued forth.
> Lightning flashed, fire broke out,
> Clouds swelled; it rained death.
> The glow disappeared, the fire went out,
> [And all that] had fallen turned to ashes.
>
> (Gardner and Maier 1984, 140)

In the Old Testament Job is besieged by awful, terrifying dreams; he pleads with God, saying "When I say, 'My bed will comfort me, my couch will ease my complaint,' then thou dost scare me with dreams and terrify me with visions, so that I would choose strangling and death rather than my bones" (Job 7.13–15). The Greek God Zeus sends Agamemnon a "lying dream" in the *Iliad*, a seemingly encouraging dream that convinces the warrior to engage in a battle which actually leads to his death (Homer 1951, 2.5ff.) Through the Middle Ages, Christian convents in Europe were afflicted by epidemics of nightmares, in which demonic succubi attacked nuns in their dreams (Jones 1951, 84). The early Puritan leader John Bunyan tells of recurrent childhood nightmares in which he is haunted by "the apparitions of Devils and wicked spirits, who . . . labored to draw me away with them" (Hill 1967, 100). Contemporary Moroccans often report dreams of jinn (Islamic demons); a frequent dream visitor is the she-demon A'siah Qandisha, a jinn who may take the form of a beauty or a hag but who always has feet of a camel or some other hoofed animal (Crapanzano 1975, 147).[5]

Many times the founder of a new religious movement will describe a dream that had a decisive influence in motivating him or her to lead the new movement. Guatama Buddha is said to have had a series of five dreams that directed him towards the path of enlightenment (Wayman 1967, 7). Muhammed's religious mission, as well as portions of the Koran, were revealed to him in a dream (Bland 1877, 120). The founders of many Melanesian Cargo Cults, nineteenth- and twentieth-century religious movements that anticipate the arrival of gods bearing new wealth, were inspired by their dreams (Burridge 1960; Stephen 1979). The Jamaican prophet Kapo discovered his mission as the leader of a new Afro-Christian religious movement in two dreams when he was twelve years old; in the first dream Jesus takes a bottle and anoints Kapo from head to foot, and in the second seventy-two angels with trumpets tell Kapo to go out and preach to his community (Lanternari 1975, 226–28). Moses Armah, founder of the Action Church among the Nzema people of Southwest Ghana, was inspired by a series of revelatory dreams, in one of which he is instructed to reject a long banana and to eat a short one—meaning, he believed, that he must reject the established churches and found a new one himself (Lanternari 1975, 224–26).[6]

Just as dreams have motivated people to found new religious movements, so dreams have also led people to convert to an established religious tradition. Buddhist monks frequently used the interpretation of an Oriental king's dream as a means of converting the king and his realm to Buddhism (O'Flaherty 1984, 37). Satuq Bughra Khan (d. 955), an Arab tribal chief, led his people into the Islamic community based on a dream in which he was commanded by heaven to convert to Islam (von Grunebaum 1966, 13–14). Emannual Swedenborg initiated his explorations of Christian mysticism after he had a series of revelatory dreams (Toksvig 1948).[7]

Throughout the history of religions a major interest in dreams has been in their prophetic powers. Many religious traditions have stories and legends of dreams that foretell the future, revealing the fates of both individuals and communities.[8] Among the dreams that are prophetic of individual destinies, one of the most common themes is the birth of a great spiritual leader. There are many accounts of pregnant women dreaming of the religiously momentous future of their soon-to-be-born child. In the Jainist tradition the mothers of spiritual heroes are said to dream a series of fourteen special dreams the night of their conception (Sharma and Siegel 1980, 3). Buddha's mother is said to have dreamed of a white elephant entering her womb, the elephant being a common Indian symbol of greatness, stability, and strength (Wayman 1967, 2; Sharma and Siegel 1980, 27–28). The mother of the second Abbasid caliph al-Mansur (d. 775) saw in a dream "a lion come from her loins, crouch with a roar, and beat the ground with its tail. Other lions arose on all sides and pressed towards him, each coming to prostrate himself" (Fahd 1966, 352). Monica, the mother of Augustine of Hippo (d. 430), had the following dream, which preceded not his physical birth but what she saw as his spiritual rebirth as a Christian:

> She dreamed that she was standing on a wooden rule, and coming towards her in a halo of splendour she saw a young man who smiled at her in joy, although she herself was sad and quite consumed with grief. He asked her the reason for her sorrow and her daily tears, not because he did not know, but because he had something to tell her, for this is what happens in visions. Whe she replied that her tears were for the soul I had lost, he told her to take heart for, if she looked carefully, she would see that where she was, there also was I. And when she looked, she saw me standing beside her on the same rule. (Augustine 1961, *Confessions*, bk. 3, chap. 11)[9]

Another common theme of prophetic dreams relates to the other end of the life cycle, namely death. Myths and religious texts from all over the world present dreams in which individual deaths are foretold. In *Gilgamesh* the hero's companion, Enkidu, has a dream in which he is taken to the underworld, "to the house of ashes," presaging his death (Gardner and Maier 1984, 177–82). The Egyptian baker's dream, which Joseph interprets in Genesis, chapter 40, indicates that he will be executed by the Pharaoh. Confucius reportedly received a premonition of his coming death in a dream, in which "he saw himself seated between the two pillars of the platform in front of his house, receiving offerings due to the dead"; he died seven days later (Laufer 1931, 211). Perpetua of Carthage, a third-century Christian martyr, had the following dream while in prison awaiting her execution:

> I saw a ladder of tremendous height, made of bronze, reaching all the way to the heavens, but it was so narrow that only one person could climb up at a time. To the side of the ladder were attached all sorts of metal weapons: swords, spears, hooks, daggers, spikes; so that if anyone tried to climb up carelessly or without paying attention, he would be mangled and his flesh would adhere to the weapons. At the foot of the ladder lay a dragon of enormous size, and it would attack those who tried to climb up and terrify and so discourage them from trying. "He

> will not harm me," I said, "in the name of Christ." Slowly, as though he were afraid of me, the dragon stuck his head out from underneath the ladder. Using it as my first step, I trod on his head and went up. Then I saw an immense garden, and in it a grey-haired man sat in shepherd's clothes. Tall he was, and milking sheep. He called me over to him and gave me a mouthful of the curds he was drawing; and I took it into my cupped hands and ate it. And all those who stood around said, "Amen!" At the sound of this word I woke up, with the taste of something sweet still in my mouth. (Miller 1986, 156)[10]

Dreams have also been seen as prophetic of a community's destiny. Such dreams are reported most often in situations where a community is threatened by some conflict or danger. The book of Genesis shows Abram when he fled from Egypt and was trying to lead the Jewish people through the wilderness to safety; he performed a sacrifice to God, and when the sun went down

> A deep sleep fell on Abram; and lo, a dread and great darkness fell upon him. Then the Lord said to Abram, "Know of a surety that your descendants will be sojourners in a land that is not theirs, and will be slaves there, and they will be oppressed for four hundred years; but I will bring judgement on the nation which they serve, and afterward they shall come out with great possessions." (Gen. 15.12–15)[11]

Often such prophetic dreams come in the midst of war. The Babylonian king Ashburnipal's troops feared crossing a raging river; but the king is said to have had a dream of the goddess Ishtar promising to protect their passage, and his dream served to reassure the troops and to revitalize their campaign (Oppenheim 1956, 209, 249). In the Indian epic the *Mahabharata*, the Pandava brothers have dreams the night before a great battle in which various omens appear, indicating their impending victory (O'Flaherty 1984, 31–35). Muhammed mentions that God sent him a dream before the battle at Badr and that in the dream God had intentionally portrayed the enemy as a small band, so as not to discourage Muhammed and his greatly outnumbered troops (Koran 8.43–46).[12]

The value of dreams in foretelling the future of a community's welfare has led many cultures to institute special dream practices in order to make the most effective use of this prophetic resource. Royal courts throughout the ancient Near East employed dream interpreters to reveal the meanings of the king's dreams (Oppenheim 1956). Each morning after prayers Muhammed asked his assembled followers what they had dreamed, to glean from them any messages from God (Fahd, 1959). In fourteenth-century China dreams were used to guide important political and legal decisions:

> It was obligatory for all officials of higher ranks when entering a walled city to pass the first night in the temple of the city god, in order to receive his instructions in a dream. In case of a difficult point in law judges will spend the night in the city god's temple, in the hope that the god will appear to them in a dream and enlighten them on the case in question. (Laufer 1931, 211)

The Blackfoot people of North America held an annual festival in which they married a young woman, representing the moon, to the Sun god; the day after the festival's climax, the woman was to tell her dreams, which were reported to the whole community (Frazer [1890] 1959, 132). The Iroquois people believed that anyone's dreams could be relevant to the tribe's welfare; significant dreams were reported to the community's leaders, and often the whole tribe was moved to action by the demands of one person's dream (Wallace 1958).[13]

Dreams Influencing Religious Practices and Beliefs

Such dreams of powerful divine beings have had a great impact on the practices and beliefs of many religious traditions. Religious rituals, prayers, myths, and doctrines have all been directly shaped by dream experiences. One of the most direct ties between dreams and religious practice appears in dream incubation rites—rites by which people actively try to evoke visits from the gods in their dreams. Dream incubation rites are found in a wide variety of religious traditions. There is extensive evidence of these rites in Greek and ancient Near Eastern cultures, where temples devoted to dream incubation flourished for hundreds of years (Hamilton 1906; Dodds 1951; Edelstein and Edelstein 1975; Meier 1967). The main concerns at these temples were to incubate dreams that would reveal prophetic knowledge or would promote the religious healing of a physical ailment (often impotence or infertility). People would undergo a series of ritual purifications, recite prayers to the temple's deity, and then sleep in a special sanctuary; in the morning they would report their dreams to temple officials, who would interpret them.

Similar dream incubation rites have been practiced in other religious traditions. Muslim dream incubation is known as *istikhara*; in it, people desiring a prophetic dream are to recite a special prayer, then lie down on their left sides and go to sleep holding onto their left ears (LeCerf 1966;

Fahd 1959). Medieval European Christians believed that on St. Agnes's night (January 21) young people who said a series of Paternosters before sleeping would dream of their future spouse (Seafield 1877, 94). Youths of the Ojibwa people of North America left their villages to undergo "dream fasts," in which they slept on special raised platforms, chanted religious songs, and awaited a dream that would reveal their individual guardian spirit (Radin 1936).[14]

Just as people engaged in various religious rites to cultivate dreams of the divine, they also employed different rites and prayers to avoid having evil dreams or to be rid of the bad influences of such dreams. The *Rig Veda* contains this prayer to the sky god Varuna: "If . . . a friend has spoken of danger to me in a dream to frighten me, or if a thief should waylay us, or a wolf—protect us from that, Varuna" (O'Flaherty 1981, 218). An Egyptian dream book suggests that a person who has suffered a bad dream should say a prayer to the goddess Isis and then rub fresh herbs moistened with beer and myrrh on his face (Lewis 1976, 15). The Islamic dream authority Ibn Sirin taught that evil dreams can be avoided by reciting certain verses of the Koran and saying the following prayer before going to sleep: "O Lord, I fly for refuge unto Thee from the evil of unsound dreams, and from the artifices of Satan in sleeping and waking" (Bland 1856, 129).[15]

Another realm of religious practice in which dreams have historically played a major role is in initiation. Dream experiences have in many cultures been used to initiate people into new religious truths, new stages of spiritual awareness, or new religious vocations. The Hindu Upanishads suggest that recognizing how we create our own dream worlds can be a means of recognizing how we create the world of our waking consciousness—a crucial realization on the path towards Enlightenment (O'Flaherty 1984, 17). Tibetan Buddhists have developed yogic techniques to control or "purify" dreams in order to attain higher stages of consciousness (Wayman 1967, 11). The *Zohar*, one of the major texts in Jewish mysticism, views dreams as spiritual journeys in which the dreamer's soul strives to be united with God; the details of each dream reflects the difficulties, obstacles, and demonic powers that the soul has encountered on its journey towards God (Bilu 1979, 446). Shaikh Ahmad Ahsa'i, founder of a nineteenth-century Islamic reformist movement, had a series of visionary dreams during his adolescence that revealed to him the essentials of Shi'ite theosophy (Corbin 1966, 402–3). Many Sufi mystics began their spiritual pursuits because of a special dream in which a religious guide appears and beckons the dreamer (Corbin 1966, 385–86). Contemporary Pakistanis still have dreams of this type, initiating them into the Sufi brotherhood (Ewing 1989).

Dreams are one of the primary means by which shamans of Siberia and Central Asia are initiated into their vocation; these dreams tend to involve extremely violent bodily dismemberment, followed by a renewal of the organs and a revelation of various shamanic teachings (Eliade 1964). The training of a religious healer among the Diegueno of North America reaches its climax in a series of drug-induced initiatory dreams in which the candidate learns of his secret medicine name (Toffelmier and Luomala 1936, 214). Similar initiatory dream experiences occur among the Arunta of Australia (Spencer and Gillen 1904) and the Ojibwa (Radin 1936), the Iroquois (Wallace 1958), and Mohave (Benedict 1922) of North America.[16]

Dreams have also been a source of countless innovations in religious practice. The creation of new temples, rites, songs, and myths in many different cultures have been inspired by dreams. The Sumerian king Gudea had a dream in which a huge god, reaching from earth to heaven, orders Gudea to build a temple to the god (Oppenheim 1956, 245–46). Thutmose IV, an Egyptian king, fell asleep in the shadow of the Sphinx monument and dreamed that the Sphinx asked him to repair the statue, which had been damaged by the desert sands (Oppenheim 1956, 251). The Shi'ite leader Mir Damad had a dream in which the first Islamic Imam taught him a "prayer of protection" (Corbin 1966, 399–400). Mohave shamans learn of special ritual curing songs and of various other healing powers through their dreams (Devereux 1957, 1036). The Navaho make new variations in their traditional myths based on certain individual dream experiences (Morgan 1932). Melanesian peoples are inspired in their dreams to create new magical charms, ceremonial spirit masks, and ritual dances (Stephen 1979, 8–9).[17]

Along with influencing religious practices, dreams have had a tremendous impact on religious beliefs, such as beliefs about the nature of the soul. Orphic philosophers of Greece believed that dreams freed the soul from its imprisonment in the body and allowed it to roam about the world (Dodds 1951, 135ff.). Similarly, the Christian bishop Synesios states that in dreaming the soul is "disengaged from the tumult of the senses, which only bring to it troubles without end from without" and is thus able to perceive God's truths with special clarity (Lewis 1976, 84). Al Razi, a medieval Islamic dream authority, said that dreaming enables the soul to travel to the realm of the angels and gain knowledge of things concealed from our waking minds (Bland 1856, 145). The Ainu, a people inhabiting a series of islands north of Japan, believe that in dreams the soul is released to visit the spirits of the dead (Ohnuki-Tierney 1987). The Iroquois people believe that dreams are the best means of learning of the soul's true desires, which must be fulfilled immediately (Wallace 1958, 236).[18]

The Interpretation of Religiously Meaningful Dreams

Despite all the valuable contributions dreams have made to religious and spiritual traditions, despite the revelations from divine powers, the prophetic insights into the future, the development of new religious rites and beliefs that dreams have provided, one practical problem has vexed people in virtually every religious tradition: how does one make *sense* of dreams? Dreams tend to be strange, enigmatic, and perplexing; their meanings are rarely plain and straightforward. How then can one learn from good, divinely inspired dreams, protect oneself from evil, demonic dreams, and dispense with trivial, insignificant dreams?[19] How can one accurately *interpret* a dream's true meanings?

The simplest answer to these questions is to reject *all* dreams, no matter how meaningful or religiously significant they may appear to be. For example, Ecclesiastes expresses a deep skepticism toward dreams: "For a dream comes with much business, and a fool's voice with many words . . . For when dreams increase, empty words grow many" (Eccl. 5.3, 7). Aristotle claims in *Prophesying by Dreams* that "it is absurd to combine the idea that the sender of such dreams should be God with the fact that those to whom he sends them are not the best and wisest, but merely commonplace persons" (Aristotle 1941c, 462b). Lucretius, an Epicurean philosopher of Rome (95–55 B.C.), argues that dreams reflect only the preoccupations of the mind and have nothing prophetic or divine about them (Lewis 1976, 32). The Protestant reformer Martin Luther states that "I care nothing about visions and dreams. Although they seem to have meaning, yet I despise them and am content with the sure meaning and trustworthiness of Holy Scripture" (Luther 1945, 7.120). In *Leviathan*, philosopher Thomas Hobbes claims that dreams are caused by "an inward distemper" of the body and that it is impossible ever to verify if a person's dreams really are divinely inspired:

> In a Common-wealth, a subject that has no certain and assured Revelation particularly to himself concerning the Will of God, is to obey for such, the Command of the Common-wealth: for if men were at liberty, to take for God's Commandments, their own dreams, and fancies, or the dreams and fancies of private men; scarce two men would agree upon what is God's Commandment; and yet in respect of them, every man would despise the Commandments of the Common-wealth. (Hobbes [1651] 1968, 90, 333)

A Baptist publication from the early nineteenth century in England rejects religiously meaningful dreams in the following terms:

> If, therefore, we embark on the trackless ocean of dreams and phantoms of the imagination, we may wander far from the truth, and never see land again . . . [W]e are led to the conclusion that evil angels also effect their purposes by having access to the human mind, and if they can find their way to our imagination when the other mental powers are in lively exercise, there can be no doubt respecting their access to an excited imagination when reason and consciousness are not on the alert. (Seafield 1877, 116)[20]

An equally simple answer to the question of how to interpret the religious meaning in dreams is to refer to a "dream book," that is, to a symbol dictionary, compiled by recognized authorities, that will automatically clarify any dream image. Such books, which are found in a wide variety of cultures, try to translate confusing, ambiguous dreams into clear, understandable messages. The *Brahmavaivarta Purana*, an early Hindu text, defines the meaning of various dream images; for example, "If a Brahmana takes some body in a chariot and shows him different strata of heaven in a dream, the seer gets an enhanced life and wealth . . . He, who in a dream, gnashes his teeth or sees some body wandering, suffers loss of health" (Bhattacharyya 1970, 32, 36). An ancient Assyrian dream book offers interpretations such as these:

> If a man ascends to heaven and the gods bless him, this man will die.
> If a man ascends to heaven and the gods curse him, this man will live long.
> If he descends into the nether world and the dead appear, an evil spirit will seize this man; the man has received in the dream a reminder of the gods concerning impending doom.
> If he descends into the nether world and the dead curse him, there is blessing for him upon the command of the deity, long days.
>
> (Lewis 1976, 17–18)

A medieval Persian treatise states that seeing the dead in a dream means the dreamer "will be safe from sorrow and grief"; seeing the Prophet Muhammed indicates that "long and happy will be his [the dreamer's] life; and blessed will he be both in this world and in the next" (Hosain 1932, 570–71).[21]

Simply rejecting all dreams or automatically reducing dream symbols to preordained definitions may be common practices, but they by no means exhaust the views of religious traditions towards dreams. On the contrary, a number of cultures have developed far more thoughtful, sophisticated, and reflective means of dream interpretation. Many religious traditions and spiritual leaders are careful to respect the tremendous complexity of dreams, attending to the wide variety of factors that influence what dreams may mean and using a number of different approaches to interpret them. The following are some examples of relatively more sophisticated means of interpreting the religious meanings of dreams.

The sixty-eighth appendix of the *Athara Veda*, an Indian text from the sixth century A.D., has many of the characteristics of a classically simplistic dream book. However, it actually presents a much more nuanced account of dream interpretation than such symbol dictionaries are generally believed to offer. The *Athara Veda* suggests that different people will have different kinds of dreams according to their distinctive temperaments; thus dreams filled with heat, blood, lightning, and dryness indicate a "fiery" personality, while dreams of cool rivers, moons, and swans point to a "watery" personality. Dreams can come from different sources (some reflect the disturbance of bodily forces, while others are sent by the gods), so their meanings will differ accordingly. The *Athara Veda*'s designation of good and bad omens in dreams is not a random, arbitrary process but rather is directly related to important cultural values, ideals, and restrictions. And dreams are not granted any independent powers over humans; the *Athara Veda* states that if one has dreams but does not become aware of them, the dreams will come to nothing. This suggests that conscious reflection and interpretation of a dream is always necessary for its meanings to emerge (Wayman, 1967; O'Flaherty, 1984).

The Berakhot section of the Babylonian Talmud contains a variety of rabbinic stories, teachings, and reflections on dream interpretation. One common theme throughout this section is that interpreting dreams is an important but very difficult and complex matter. Dreams are always enigmatic and distorted, because "just as there is no wheat without straw, so there is no dream without worthless things" (Ber. 55a). Interpreters must be very careful, then, to separate the genuinely meaningful, revelatory aspects of a dream from the trivial, worthless aspects. A famous aphorism from Berakhot 55a, "A dream that is not interpreted is like a letter that is not read," illustrates the emphasis rabbinic figures put on interpretation—without conscious elaboration, a dream's meaning is lost. Most of the actual interpretations contained in Berakhot focus on language, for language is where divine revelation and personal existence meet. Some dreams are interpreted as verbal puns; for example, a dream in which the dreamer's nose falls off is related to a common verbal expression relating noses and anger, so that the interpretation is that the dreamer has lost his anger (Ber. 56b). Other dreams are tied to Jewish scripture, relating words in dreams to important passages from the Torah (Ber. 56b–57a). The rabbinic interpreters thus make sense of dreams by relating their imagery to the "shared symbolic code" provided by common language, cultural traditions, and sacred texts (Frieden 1990, 84).

Artemidorus of Daldus is perhaps the most famous dream interpreter of the ancient world. His great work the *Oneirocritica*, composed in the second century A.D., has served as the basis for countless popular dream books and symbol dictionaries. However, as Freud recognized (Freud [1900] 1965, 130), Artemidorus presents a surprisingly sophisticated approach to the interpretation of dreams. He insists that knowing the unique character and life circumstances of a dreamer is crucial to interpreting the meaning of his or her dream; the same dream will mean very different things if had by different people. For example, Artemidorus offers the example of a man dreaming that a woman is giving birth to him, and gives different interpretations according to whether the man is rich or poor, is a slave, an athlete, abroad on a trip, ill, involved in a legal dispute, has a wife who is or is not pregnant (23). Along with concentrating on the dreamer's vocation, family relations, and social status, Artimedorus also examines the specific details of each dream; for again, the slightest difference can entirely alter the interpretation. Thus dreams of sexual relations with one's mother are "complex and many-faceted, admitting of many a nice distinction . . . The mere act of intercourse is not enough by itself to indicate what is portended, but the different embraces and positions of the bodies make for different outcomes" (61–64). Furthermore, Artimedorus takes into account the particular customs, religious beliefs, and literary traditions of the dreamer's culture when he interprets a dream.

Synesios, a Christian bishop of Ptolemais in the early fifth century, wrote a brief treatise *On Dreams* in which he discusses the value and importance of divinely-inspired, prophetic dreams. In the imaginative life of our dreams, he says, "we often enter into conversation with the gods: they warn us, answer us, and give us useful advice" (Lewis 1976, 82). Synesios denies the belief that spiritually meaningful dreams come only to the elite; "No one is privileged, either by sex, age, fortune, or profession; Sleep offers itself to all: it is an oracle always ready" (Lewis 1976, 83). Intepreting dreams is difficult, he states, because animal passions and the tumult of sense impressions disturb the imaginative sensitivities of our spirit. Synesios says that dream interpretation requires a calm, tranquil soul, a careful attention to details, and a great deal of experience. He rejects the common use of dream dictionaries—"Personally I ignore these books, and regard them as useless"—and stresses that the uniqueness of each individual soul implies that each person's dreams will have unique meanings. Synesios argues:

> We must not hope then to establish general rules: each one must search for his knowledge within himself. We should inscribe in our memory all that has come to us in our dreams . . . It is a novelty which will perhaps shock received ideas; but nevertheless, wherefore should we not complete the history of our days with that of our nights, and so retain a remembrance of our dual lives? (Lewis 1976, 86)

Islamic tradition contains many works of 'Ilm ul Tabir, or the science of dream interpretation. These works, which often refer to the earlier writings of Artemidorus and other Greek authors, describe in great detail the process of accurately interpreting dreams. Interpreters should be extremely familiar with the Koran, the many commentaries on it, and the traditions on various other religious matters. They should have an extensive knowledge of common proverbs, sayings, literary works, and linguistic usage (Bland 1877, 132). When presented with a dream, interpreters should learn of the dreamer's "age, country, . . . rank and condition in life, his profession, occupation, and habits; of everything related to him personally, and of all the circumstances, even the most trivial, connected with the [dream]" (Bland 1877, 133). The interpreter should then listen to the entire dream, in all its particulars, and examine each detail of the dream with great thoroughness:

> Three things are to be considered with regard to the objects occurring in sleep: *Jins*, the genus or kind, as trees, birds, beasts, animate or inanimate objects, etc.; *Sanf*, the species, as, whether it be a Medlar or a Palm tree, and, of birds, whether a Peacock or an Ostrich; this will lead to a knowledge of the character and country of the dreamer, for, in the first of these two cases, he will be an Arab, ostriches and palms being unknown in Persia; and, in the other, a Persian, as medlars and peacocks are not found in Arabia. Thirdly, *Nua*, or the manner and circumstances of objects seen; how many in number, when, and where; how disposed, and how relating to one another. (Bland 1877, 136)

A modern Pentecostal church in western Uganda presents another case of a more complex approach to the religious meaning of dreams. This church, which merges Christian with traditional African spiritual beliefs, engages in group dream-telling as a regular part of worship—indeed, the dream-telling is "at the heart of [each] service" (Charsley 1973, 247). The church members believe that divine revelations in dreams are available to anyone, and so after a collective prayer the church leader invites people to tell their dreams. Individuals then recount their dreams, often in extensive detail and with great emotional intensity. Many of the dreams concern the given church member's sinful condition, which needs to be revealed and confessed to the congregation. Such dreams are *not* always formally interpreted; rather, a ritual of church forgiving follows the recitation of the dream, serving to reincorporate the troubled individual back into the congregation. Members also recite dreams that address the concerns, problems, and welfare of the church itself. These dreams, which are considered valuable contributions to the vitality of the congregation, are examined by church leaders to discover what special messages from God the dreams reveal. For members of this African-Christian church, then, the "interpretation" of a dream does not focus exclusively on the individual and does not necessarily require an exact, point-by-point analysis. A dream's religious meanings emerge only in the process of the group's worship and prayer and always refer ultimately to the welfare of the congregation as a whole (Charsley 1973, 1987).

A final example of a more reflective, sophisticated approach to interpreting the religious meaning of dreams is provided by the Diegueno people of North America. The religious healers of the Diegueno have, among their other duties, the office of helping tribe members who are afflicted with troublesome dreams (Toffelmier and Luomala, 1936). The Diegueno distinguish among three different types of dream: accidental, common, and important. "Accidental" dreams are due to temporary physical problems and do not merit attention. "Common" dreams do not disturb the dreamer upon awakening and have meanings which anyone in the tribe can interpret. "Important" dreams, however, are both deeply troubling and difficult to understand, and they require the interpretive efforts of the religious healer. The healer will ask the dreamer to describe the dream freely, in as much detail as possible, and to tell of any relevant matters in the dreamer's waking life. The religious healer also considers the stresses Diegueno people face as their culture comes into contact with white American culture and how this is reflected in their dreams (Toffelmier and Luomala's fieldwork was done in southern California in 1934). The interpretations will often guide the dreamer towards traditional cultural and religious resources that can help the dreamer deal with these stresses. Thus for recurrent sexual dreams the healer will emphasize the ways in which the dreams are pointing the dreamer towards marriage with a suitable person in the tribe. For dreams of insistent, angry spirits, the healer will try to identify the spirit and learn which dead relative it represents; then he will determine what object the spirit has left behind and instruct the dreamer to burn that object as an addendum to the traditional Diegueno funeral rite.

2

EXPLORING THE WILDERNESS OF DREAMS

> The clearest way into the Universe is through a forest wilderness.
>
> —John Muir, *John of the Mountains: The Unpublished Journals of John Muir*

Root Metaphors

As limited as the preceding historical review has been, it does substantiate the claim that people in a wide variety of cultures, from ancient times until the present, have drawn religious meaning from their dreams. It should come as no surprise, then, that modern Westerners are also interested in the potential religious meaning of their dreams. We, too, experience numinous, powerful, meaning-rich dreams that deeply affect us. We, too, have developed elaborate theories of how to interpret our dreams. Many of the images, symbols, and themes of our dreams bear a striking resemblance to dream phenomena from other cultures.

But a moment's reflection should prevent us from rushing into hasty, sweeping generalizations about the "universal," "cross-cultural" religious significance of dreams. For modern Western culture is *different* from other cultures, and we treat our dreams *differently* from the ways other cultures have. First, our culture has distinctive social, political, and economic structures that decisively shape all our experiences, including our dreams; we should not assert anything about "universal" meanings without taking these structures into account. Second, modern Western culture has developed a number of new approaches to the study of dreams. The findings of depth psychology, sleep laboratory research, anthropology, and many other fields have thoroughly revolutionized our understanding of dreams. These findings should also be taken into account before we make any broad comparisons. Third and most importantly, our culture has a deeply ambivalent attitude towards religion. Institutional religion has seemingly declined in its political and social power, and it must compete for cultural influence with a variety of secular philosophies and worldviews. Most Western nations have created strict boundaries that limit the role formal religion can play in public life. Nevertheless, religion is still a major force in shaping Western culture, and it continually dashes predictions of its imminent demise. Indeed, many theologians argue that the modern critics of religion are wrong in strictly identifying "religion" with priests, churches, and creeds. These theologians suggest that religion is still playing a powerful role in the modern world. So without an awareness of the very complex status of religion in modern Western culture, *any* statement about the alleged religious meaning of our dreams is bound to be inadequate.

I am trying to raise a question here that I do not believe has been clearly articulated, let alone adequately explored, in the contemporary study of dreams: in what *specific* ways do dreams have religious meaning for people in modern Western culture? If we want to answer this question, we cannot simply say that the dream experiences of modern Westerners have religious meanings *identical* to the dream experiences of people from other cultures; neither can we flatly state that the dreams of modern Westerners do *not* have genuine religious meaning. To answer this question, we must develop a far more sophisticated approach, one that enables us to appreciate the distinctive ways that dreams may have religious meaning in the modern context.

The goal of this work is to explore the question of whether dreams have religious meaning for people in the modern West, study the answers offered by the major dream researchers of the twentieth century, consider their insights, probe their limitations, and work to develop a fuller, more integrated approach. As this study progresses we will develop the following thesis:

> Dreams do have a dimension of religious meaning; this dimension emerges out of the *root metaphors* in dreams. To understand fully the root metaphors of dreams requires an interdisciplinary integration of the different fields of dream study with a theory of interpretation and a theory of religious metaphor.

A few initial words about this thesis may help clarify the precise nature of our work. Dreams have a religious *dimension*: the potential for religious meaning always exists, but it is not always actualized to the same extent in every dream. As we found in the historical review, virtually every culture and religious tradition distinguishes between dreams that are religiously meaningful and dreams that are not. Likewise, we will not be claiming that all dreams are religiously meaningful, only that *some* are to *some* degree. However, we will discover that *all* people's dreams, not just the dreams of churchgoers and other formally "religious" people, have this potential for religious meaning. We will find that a religious dimension is potentially present in *all* people's dreaming.

The central concept we will be using, 'root metaphors', is based on the notion that humans perceive, think, experience, and act in the world by means of metaphors. Metaphorical thinking involves relating to one experience through the categories, concepts, and structures of another experience. For example, the metaphor "time is money" leads us to relate to time in the same ways we relate to money: thus we speak of spending, wasting, or saving time; we treat our time as a precious commodity, as a resource to enjoy or invest; we feel happy when our time is "free," when it is "ours," and we feel upset when our time is used, stolen, or wasted by someone else.[1] We will be following the work of contemporary linguistic philosophers in arguing that metaphorical thinking (as in thinking of time as money) is a crucial element of all human experience, understanding, and behavior.

More specifically, the concept of root metaphors is drawn from the work of philosopher Paul Ricoeur and theologians Don Browning and Sallie McFague. Root metaphors are those metaphors that enable us to understand the ultimate questions of human existence: questions like, What kind of world do we live in? Why are we born? What are good and evil? Why do we suffer, and how do we endure suffering? What happens when we die? How do we live a good, fulfilling, meaningful life?[2] People respond to these ultimate existential questions with metaphors, with images and symbols that shape our perceptions, inspire our ideals, and motivate our behavior.[3] Hence, the experience of the Exodus (Exod. 1–17) serves as a root metaphor to Jewish people, in that God's role in bringing the Jews out of Egypt is taken as a fundamental model for understanding God's role in other situations. The notion of "Mother Earth" serves as a root metaphor to certain Native Americans, in that they take a person's relationship with his or her mother as a fundamental model for their relationship to the natural world.[4] Adam Smith's image of the "invisible hand" (Smith, [1776] 1976) serves as a root metaphor to free market capitalists, in that the reassuring image of a great, benevolent hand carefully tending over our affairs is taken as a fundamental model for perceiving the effects of capitalist economic principles throughout society.[5]

We will fill out this account of root metaphors in much more detail in part 4. For the moment, I want only to note that we will be using "religious meaning" to signify those meanings that pertain to the ultimate existential concerns of human life.[6]

Our root metaphors come to us from a wide variety of sources: our physical bodies, cultural and religious traditions, personal experiences, and the natural environment, among others. Dreams, as the historical review in chapter 1 suggests, have also been one source of insight into our most profound existential concerns, one source of our root metaphors. A full understanding of how deep metaphors emerge in dreams cannot, however, come from any one of the fields of dream research. Only a careful study of the many different approaches to dreams will enable us to understand the emergence of root metaphors in dreams. We will thus look in the following pages to the investigations of depth psychologists, neuroscientists, artists, cognitive psychologists, and anthropologists. Each of these different fields of dream study makes a compelling claim to our attention; each of these fields tells us something important and distinctive about the religious meanings of dreams.

In part 2 we will look at the major figures of twentieth-century dream research and examine their arguments about whether dreams have religious meaning for people in the modern West. Part 3 will address the immediate problems raised by part 2, namely, whether dreams have *any* meaning at all, religious or otherwise, and if so how we can interpret that meaning. Modern dream researchers disagree so radically over how to interpret dreams that we cannot resolve these problems without guidance from outside the study of dreams. We will thus bring in a philosophical theory of interpretation to help us critically evaluate the arguments of the dream investigators and understand how best to interpret dreams. The philosopher Hans-Georg Gadamer will serve as our guide in this critique, for he can offer us some sophisticated and very insightful ideas about meaning, truth, and interpretation that will enable us to overcome these initial problems.

Part 4 will be where we address our primary question, namely how to understand and interpret the religious meaning of dreams. We will elaborate in greater detail the concept of root metaphors and look at a series of dreams in which root metaphors emerge. Then we will use this concept to help us evaluate the views of major dream researchers, develop a fuller, more integrated theoretical understanding of dreams and religious meaning, and offer suggestions on the practical investigation of the religious dimension of dreams.

As we explore all these different fields, we will find it necessary to try and bridge a gaping divide in the study of dreams. On one side of this divide are those dream investigators who deny that the natural sciences have anything of importance to say about the meaning of dreams and who concern themselves only with interpreting the language, imagery, and emotional qualities of dreams. On the other side are those who reject such interpretive approaches as imprecise and arbitrary and who concentrate solely on analyzing the physiological aspects of dreams. We will try to do justice to *both* sides of this divide and work to develop an approach to dreams that accounts for both the interpretive and the natural scientific aspects of dreams. Indeed, we will find that we *must* find a way to bridge the divide, for it is one of the unique qualities of dreams that they are at once narrative texts and somatic phenomena—dreams are tales emerging from the neural activities of the brain, and they are physiological events creating meaningful, imaginative, richly emotional stories.

The Wilderness of Dreams

The brief description earlier of root metaphors makes it clear, I hope, that a sensitivity to metaphors is crucial to our understanding of the religious meanings of dreams. I would also suggest, however, that a sensitivity to metaphors is equally crucial to our methodological orientation in this study. The specific images and models we use will have a subtle but important influence on the approach we take to our subject. We need, then, to reflect briefly on what metaphors will guide our work here.

One common metaphor used to orient research such as ours is that of an architectural project. According to this image, our study would be modeled on the construction of a building: we would begin by gathering the resources we need (i.e., summarizing theories and concepts), then process them from their raw state into more refined, workable materials (i.e., critique the theories and concepts), use the strongest, most solid materials as the basic building blocks (i.e., identify the simplest, most essential ideas to stand as the basis of a new theory), and then construct the rest of the building upwards from that foundation, story by story (i.e., develop the new theory from that initial basis, with each new concept being "higher" than the previous one).

The architectural metaphor serves effectively for many scholarly contexts, but I do not think it will be of help to us. The discord among the different areas of dream research is too rancorous, and the variety of theories and concepts too widespread. The use of architectural images of building blocks, foundations, and frameworks puts us in danger of distorting rather than clarifying our subject. The most striking feature of the modern study of dreams is the tremendous diversity of disciplines involved in it. The richness of this diversity would inevitably be lost in the hierarchical imagery of a building metaphor.

Instead of constructing a multistory building, then, I would propose a different metaphor for the orientation of our work: the metaphor of exploring an expanse of wilderness. We will imagine the subject of dreams as a wilderness region, what we may call "the wilderness of dreams."

According to the terms of this metaphor, we could say the wilderness of dreams is a dark, mysterious region, a region about which little is known but much is fancied. The researchers who have journeyed there have brought back fantastic tales of strange beings, breathtaking wonders, and paralyzing terrors. Many of these tales speak of the wilderness as a sacred refuge, a sanctuary where many religious insights may be discovered. Others, though, speak of the wilderness as a place where religious superstitions may be exposed in all their foolishness and where valuable resources lie waiting to be used to fuel the progress of Western science.[7]

A wilderness metaphor provides us with a very different methodological model for our study. Exploring an expanse of wilderness requires following every path available, in the recognition that each different route may reveal some new, distinctive feature of the region (i.e., making an initial effort to learn of the full range of different theories, and not automatically privileging one over the others). It requires moving in many different directions over time, backtracking again and again (i.e., studying the different theories from a number of perspectives, comparing and analyzing them in a variety of ways). And it is an open-ended process, with the goal being an ever-deepening familiarity with the region (i.e., an ever-deepening familiarity with the object of study).

There are a number of advantages to the use of a wilderness metaphor as a way of orienting our study of dreams and religious meaning. It will encourage us to appreciate how the various approaches to dreams and religious meaning—the various "paths" into the wilderness of dreams—may all lead to important areas, even though they do not all lead to the *same* areas by the *same* means. This metaphor highlights the need for us to study carefully the interrelations between the different paths of research in order to gain the fullest understanding of the dream wilderness. And, the metaphor motivates us to study this wilderness from many perspectives. Just as we would study the geology of a region, then its vegetation, and then its animal life, each time going over the same terrain with a different set of questions, so in this work we will explore the wilderness of dreams with the guidance first of different dream theories, then of a philosophical theory of interpretation, and then of a theory of religious metaphor.[8]

If we adopt the wilderness metaphor, the first step we should take is to make an initial survey of the region, a survey of the various modern approaches to dreams and religious meaning. Such a survey will give us a feeling for what paths have been taken into what fields of dream research. We immediately encounter a problem, however, in that there are so many different fields involved in the study of dreams and so many different figures working within each of these fields—as soon as we start trying to survey the wilderness we are in danger of getting thoroughly lost.[9] My proposal is to focus on those fields that seem to have made the most important contributions to the modern study of dreams and then to focus within each of those fields on one particular figure who has done the most to develop the findings from that field. In this way we will get a sense for the variety of approaches to dreams and yet also have some one figure whose work we can take as a guide. We will explore these fields according to their chronological development, starting with those that were studied earliest, so that we may see how the knowledge of one field influenced later ventures in other fields:

1. Psychoanalysis: Sigmund Freud
2. Surrealism: Andre Breton
3. Analytical Psychology: Carl Jung
4. Content Analysis: Calvin Hall
5. Neuroscience: J. Allan Hobson
6. Lucid Dreaming: Stephen LaBerge
7. Anthropology: Barbara Tedlock
8. Cognitive Psychology: Harry Hunt

There are drawbacks to this approach, of course. We will not be able to consider certain fields that some people may argue are important in the study of dreams, and we will have to pass by the many alternative paths taken within each field (see appendix 1 for a discussion of various other paths). Nevertheless, this seems the best way to initiate our explorations given the goals, and limitations, of our work. If we pass by some important fields or paths, perhaps our failure will inspire the future explorations of others.

PART TWO

EIGHT PATHS INTO THE WILDERNESS OF DREAMS

3

PSYCHOANALYSIS: SIGMUND FREUD

> When, after passing through a narrow defile, we suddenly emerge upon a piece of high ground, where the path divides and the finest prospects open up on every side, we may pause for a moment and consider in which direction we shall first turn our steps. Such is the case with us, now that we have surmounted the first interpretation of a dream. We find ourselves in the full daylight of a sudden discovery.
>
> —Sigmund Freud, *The Interpretation of Dreams*

I wish there were some way we could avoid starting this survey with Freud. Practically every book on dreams that provides any sort of historical background begins with an obligatory outline of Freud's dream theories. I have grown accustomed to skimming over such outlines, and I imagine that most other readers of books on dreams do as well. However, now that I am setting out to survey modern approaches to dreams and religious meaning I find that I, too, must give an outline of Freud's dream theories. Freud is the first great modern explorer of the wilderness of dreams: by means of that solitary, perilous foray through the "narrow defile" of his "specimen dream" interpretation in chapter 2 of *The Interpretation of Dreams*, Freud did reach a vista overlooking a huge expanse of terrain never before investigated with such rigor and honesty.[1]

Even though we shall range far beyond the first trails Freud marked out and explore areas he never reached, we too cannot avoid taking our first steps along his well-trodden path. However, while the next few pages may be tedious to some readers, I will make two promises. One, this initial outline will be brief; we will not dwell excessively on such familiar grounds. And two, our later discussions of Freud will, I believe, lead us beyond the conventional evaluations of his work. After exploring the other paths of dream study and after drawing upon the insights of different philosophical and theological guides, we will come back to Freud: we will find new reasons for challenging Freud, and we will also find many new values in his work.

The principal source for this assessment of Freud will be *The Interpretation of Dreams*. Although the book was written early in Freud's career, he made very few substantive changes in his theory of dream interpretation in later years and kept the work up to date through numerous minor refinements in its successive editions. We will, however, also draw on other writings of Freud in those places where they can help illustrate particular features of his theory.

In the early stages of his career, Freud concerned himself with the treatment of hysterical symptoms in his patients. He tried a variety of different therapeutic techniques, but was not satisfied with their success.[2] Freud also set himself the goal of grounding psychology on a firm, rational, scientific basis, as firm as that of any of the natural sciences.[3] *The Interpretation of Dreams*, published in 1900, reflects both of these concerns. Freud found that dreams could be of great help both in revealing the deepest unconscious conflicts of his patients and in portraying the fundamental dynamics of the human psyche.

The first words of chapter 1 of *The Interpretation of Dreams* announce Freud's basic approach to dreams:

> In the pages that follow I shall bring forward proof that there is a psychological technique which makes it possible to interpret dreams, and that, if that procedure is employed, every dream reveals itself as a psychical structure which has a meaning and which can be inserted at an assignable point in the mental activities of waking life. (Freud [1900] 1965, 35)

Freud devotes the first chapter to a review of the various theories that have been proposed to account for the existence of dreams. He finds that almost all of these theories dismiss dreams as arbitrary, nonsensical phenomena devoid of psychological meaning. Freud, however, devotes the rest of his book to proving that dreams *do* have meaning, that they are governed by identifiable laws, that they occupy a distinctive place in the psychic economy, and that their meaning can be determined by the employment of certain analytic techniques. Freud is, in short, bringing a new and hitherto untamed realm of human experience under the reign of scientific knowledge: the concern with laws, structures, causality, method, and technical control characterizes the agenda of nineteenth-century natural science. Freud sees the interpretation of dreams as an extension of that empiricist project. He asks in his *Introductory Lectures on Psychoanalysis*,

> What is it actually that we want to arrive at? What is our work aiming at? We want something that is sought for in all scientific work—to understand the phenomena, to establish a correlation between them and, in the latter end, if it is possible, to enlarge our power over them. (Freud [1917a] 1966, 100)

Freud describes the process of dream formation in the following way. When we fall asleep, a conflict soon arises between two different desires: on the one hand, we need the rest that a peaceful sleep brings us; on the other, various unconscious urges, which we repress while awake, take advantage of the weakened powers of consciousness in sleep to assert themselves. In order to accommodate both the wish to sleep and the wish to satisfy unconscious urges, the "psychic apparatus" creates dreams as a compromise. When the unconscious urges rise up they cannot be allowed to enter consciousness as they are, because their objectionable nature would disturb the sleeper and inhibit his or her rest. Thus the psychic apparatus transforms the unconscious urges by means of the four mechanisms of the dreamwork (condensation, displacement, regard for representability, and secondary elaboration). The unconscious urges are thus allowed a hallucinatory satisfaction that prevents their real, disturbing character from reaching conscious attention.[4]

This account of dream formation provides the basis for Freud's famous claim that every dream "is a (disguised) fulfillment of a (suppressed or repressed) wish" ([1900] 1965, 194). The motive force of a dream is always an unconscious wish, and the dream itself represents the satisfaction, in a masked form, of this wish ([1917a] 1966, 129). Freud thus distinguishes between the dream's *manifest* content, that is, the distorted, masked dream narrative remembered by consciousness, and its *latent* content, that is, the original wishes, urges, and thoughts that the dream-work transforms ([1900] 1965, 311).

Interpreting a dream, in Freud's view, requires a *reversal* of the process by which dreams are formed. He says in the *Introductory Lectures on Psychoanalysis*,

> And let me remind you once again that the work which transforms the latent dream into the manifest one is called the *dream-work*. The work which proceeds in the contrary direction, which endeavors to arrive at the latent dream from the manifest one, is our *work of interpretation*. This work of interpretation seeks to undo the dream-work. ([1917a] 1966, 170)[5]

The dream-work has destroyed the coherence of the dream-thoughts, has condensed many different meanings into one image, has displaced meanings from one image onto another, and has deliberately hidden the original, true content of the dream. Freud's interpretation tries to recover that original coherence, to unpack and sort out the condensed thoughts, to restore meanings to their proper sources, and to reach back to that original content.[6] Freud states that we must always disregard the structure and coherence of the manifest dream;[7] after carefully gathering the dreamer's personal associations,[8] we must reestablish the broken connections, remove the disguises, and discover the original dream-thoughts. Once this is done, once the latent content emerges, the manifest dream itself is of no use and can be discarded.[9]

Freud argues that dreams are a special kind of text, because they were never meant to be understood ([1900] 1965, 377). A dream is a text that intentionally tries to deceive us, and thus unusual interpretive measures have to be taken. Sometimes an image must be taken in its positive meaning, sometimes in its negative. Sometimes its meaning refers to events in the dreamer's personal history, sometimes to universal symbols, and sometimes to plays on words.[10] Freud admits that all this ambiguity gives dream interpretation an appearance of arbitrariness. However, he argues in his own defense that his dream interpretations reveal many surprising and impressive connections of meanings, that they offer nearly exhaustive accounts of the contents of given dreams, and that this procedure is the same as that followed in the successful psychoanalytic treatment of hysterical symptoms.[11] The objection that the seeming ambiguity of his dream interpretations undermines Freud's basic hypotheses "is invalidated by pointing out that on the contrary ambiguity or indefiniteness is a characteristic of dreams which was necessarily to be anticipated" ([1917a] 1966, 229).

The great value of dreams for Freud, then, is their capacity to display to the canny interpreter all the deepest conflicts of the individual unconscious. Dreams can be tremendously useful in therapy, as Freud demonstrates in his later case studies.[12] Even more importantly, the study of dreams gives insights into the basic structures of the human psyche—hence Freud's grand assertion that "the interpretation of dreams is the royal road to a knowledge of the unconscious activities of the mind" ([1900] 1966, 647). Dreams reveal the most archaic strata of the mind; Freud says that in dreams we discover "mental antiquities" that tell us about the very beginnings of human thought.[13] Thus dreams bear not only on the study of individuals and their illnesses: the analysis of dreams also contributes significantly to our knowledge of human culture. Throughout *The Interpretation of Dreams* Freud points to the relevance of his discoveries about dreams for the understanding of art, mythology, morality, politics, and a host of other cultural phenomena. The study of dreams is in Freud's view one of the newest frontiers in the scientific study of culture.

And what does Freud make of any possible *religious* meaning of dreams? He does credit ancient dream prophets with being closer to the truth about the nature of dream symbolism than were nineteenth-century scientists. However, Freud ultimately rejects all religious claims that dreams reflect any mysterious, prophetic, or supernatural powers.[14] Dreams contain thoughts just like any others; Freud flatly denies that dreams have a special creativity or spiritual potency of their own.[15] Freud's dismissive attitude towards the religious meaning of dreams is in keeping with his understanding of religion in general. He argues in *The Future of an Illusion* (1927) that religion reflects an infantile desire for security and comfort. Religion's absurd illusions must be overcome, Freud believes, if individuals are ever to leave psychological childhood and become mature, rational adults.[16] Indeed, it could be said that the goal of Freud's psychoanalysis is to help the individual do *without* religion: by gaining insight into such debilitating, irrational illusions the individual is able to develop a stronger, more autonomous, more rational ego that can stand on its own, without the aid of crutches built from childish superstitions. Interpreting dreams is one of the primary means Freud uses to gain such critical insights into the unconscious and to strengthen the individual ego.[17] Ultimately, then, Freud's dream interpretation is part of a larger project of *eliminating* the need for religion.

4

SURREALISM: ANDRE BRETON

> How can we even believe ourselves capable of seeing, of hearing, of touching anything if we take no account of these innumerable possibilities, which, for most people, cease to be available at the first sounds of the milkman. The general essence of subjectivity, this immense and richest of all terrains, is left uncultivated . . . The poet to come will surmount the depressing idea of the irreparable divorce between action and dream. He will hold out the magnificent fruit of the tree with those entwined roots and will know how to persuade those who taste of it that it has nothing bitter about it.
>
> —Andre Breton, *Communicating Vessels*

> I believe in the future resolution of these two states—outwardly so contradictory—which are dream and reality, into a sort of absolute reality, a *surreality*, so to speak.
>
> —Andre Breton, *The First Surrealist Manifesto*

An intimate relationship between dreams and artistic expression can be found in cultures throughout history.[1] Chapter 1 touched on this briefly, in the many reports of dreams inspiring the creation of religious songs, dances, masks, and charms. Artistic interest in dreams remains strong in modern Western culture as well. Many of the leading fiction writers of the twentieth century (such as Franz Kafka, James Joyce, Jorge Louis Borges, Gabriel Garcia Marquez, Thomas Pynchon, and Salman Rushdie) weave together waking and dreaming realities in their works.[2] Both film and television productions create, either directly or indirectly, a dream-like experience in their audiences.[3] Countless modern writers, musicians, painters, sculptors, dancers, and actors draw on their dreams for the images that they subsequently transform into artistic creations.[4] The relationship between dreams and art, while generally neglected in surveys of modern dream research, is in fact a field of rich, distinctive, and important insights regarding the nature and meaning of dreams. It is vital for our explorations that we recognize this field and try to integrate its insights with the findings of other fields of dream study.

The focus here will be on the surrealist movement, which began in Europe in the early 1920s and thrived for about two decades. Surrealism is a particularly good example of how artists have explored dreams, and a study of the surrealist movement (as opposed to any of the many other artistic approaches to dreams) has special advantages for our project. First, surrealism draws directly upon Freud's ideas about dreams and the unconscious, while at the same time using those ideas to explore radically different terrain than that covered by psychoanalysis. Surrealism will thus show how one path of dream study can suddenly split and lead off in two different directions. And second, surrealism is an excellent area to explore, given our specific interest in modern Western views of dreams and religious meaning. Surrealism is an avowedly "modern" movement, a direct artistic response to twentieth-century Western culture, and it explicitly connects its approach to dreams, creativity, and the unconscious to that particular cultural context.

We will concentrate specifically on the writings of Andre Breton, the early theorist and champion of the surrealist movement. We will look not so much at the artistic works of the surrealists as at the beliefs, ideals, and goals that surrealist artists tried to express and develop in their works. Breton gives an especially forceful and extensive account of the motivating principles of the surrealists, particularly in his two surrealist manifestos (1924 and 1929) and his philosophical essay *Communicating Vessels* (1932).

Surrealism arose out of the same cultural climate as did the other pioneering modern art movements, such as dadaism, primitivism, cubism, and fauvism. The surrealists shared with these movements a profound dissatisfaction with traditional Western culture. They rejected the strictures of conventional rationality, morality, Christianity, and bourgeois social behavior. Breton opens the *First Surrealist Manifesto* by stating, "The absolute rationalism which remains in fashion allows for the consideration of only those facts narrowly relevant to our experience . . . Boundaries have been assigned even to experience. It revolves in a cage from which release is becoming increasingly difficult" (Breton [1924] 1965, 66). The various movements of modern art were joined in a quest for ways to challenge those boundaries, to escape their stifling effects, and to discover new possibilities of human perception, experience, and creativity.

Surrealism differed from the other movements in its turn to the unconscious as its primary resource for the fight against the oppressive limitations of Western civilization. As Breton immediately acknowledges, Freud is the one who brought the strange nature of the unconscious to the modern world's attention: "Credit for this must go to Freud. On the evidence of his discoveries a current of opinion is at last developing which will enable the explorer of the human mind to extend his investigations" (Breton [1924] 1965, 66). Freud's work reveals how the mental outlook of the modern Westerner is a woefully constricted one, and Breton took the surrealist mission to be the integration of this narrow perspective with the vast potentials of the unconscious mind—the "future resolution" of dreaming and waking realities into a "surreality."[5]

As that mission suggests, Breton and the surrealists were particularly interested in dreams, those expressions of the unconscious regions of the mind so shunned by conventional Western culture. Indeed, to take any interest at all in dreams represents a departure from a rationalistic outlook, as Breton comments, "I have always been astounded by the extreme disproportion in the importance and seriousness assigned to events of the waking moments and to those of sleep by the ordinary observer . . . The dream finds itself relegated to a parenthesis, like the night. And in general it gives no more counsel than the night" (Breton [1924] 1965, 67). The surrealists turned this conventional attitude on its head by granting dreams as much authority as waking rationality in matters of perception, knowledge, and aesthetics.

Surrealists venerated dreams above all for the powerful sense of freedom they give. In stark contrast to the rigid limits imposed by bourgeois society, dreams open up to us a world of possibilities—the editorial of the first issue of *The Surrealist Revolution* states, "the dream alone entrusts to man all his rights to freedom" (Waldberg 1965, 47). The possibilities we discover in dreams often include images and experiences that are bizarre, fantastic, absurd, and disturbing, and the surrealists sought in their art to bring forth the power of the fantastic as a way of directly challenging what we take to be ordinary and normal. The surrealist poet Apollinaire took as his motto "I astonish!" while Breton wrote in the "First Surrealist Manifesto" "The Marvellous is always beautiful, everything marvellous is beautiful. Nothing but the Marvellous is beautiful" (Breton [1924] 1965, 70). Thus the review *Litterature*, an early surrealist publication, included many accounts of dreams and how poets and painters sought to express their dream experiences in their art (Waldenberg 1965, 13–15).

In *Communicating Vessels* Breton presents a detailed analysis of one of his own dreams, and this analysis illuminates very well some key surrealist notions regarding dreams. Exactly as Freud does with his "specimen dream" in chapter 2 of *The Interpretation of Dreams*, Breton first gives the text of his dream, then some comments on the "day residue," and then a line-by-line analysis of the images. His examination uses Freud's psychoanalytic methods to identify instances of condensation and displacement and to connect particular dream images with intimate personal associations. Breton argues that his interpretation of the dream is complete and exhaustive; nothing remains unexplained. Furthermore, he claims that his interpretation proves that there is *no* transcendental, divine force at work in the production of dreams:

> I insist emphatically on the fact that for me it [the interpretation] *exhausts* the dream's content and contradicts the diverse allegations that have been made about the "unknowable" character of the dream, or its incoherence. No mystery in the final analysis, nothing that could provoke any belief in some transcendent intervention occurring in human thought during the night. I see nothing in the whole working of the oneiric function that does not borrow clearly from the elements of lived life, provided one takes the trouble to examine it: nothing (I cannot state this strongly enough), except for those elements that the imagination uses poetically, that would contain any appreciable residue held to be irreducible. From the point of view of the poetic marvelous, something perhaps; from the point of view of the religious marvelous, absolutely nothing. (Breton [1932] 1990, 45)

This example enables Breton to argue that dreams are *not* unfathomable, mysterious utterances from transcendent beings that humans can never understand. Dreams *can* be understood, Breton claims, if we devote ourselves to a careful interpretation of them. His polemic against "the religious marvelous" is a polemic against the barriers erected by the mystifications of traditional religion, barriers that separate humans from the creative powers of their dreams.

What also interests Breton here is that this example shows "the need inherent in the dream to *magnify* and to *dramatize*" (47), and thus to challenge forcefully our ordinary concepts of space, time, and causality. It is precisely this kind of challenging power, so abundantly realized in dreams, that Breton and the surrealists want to bring to bear on the waking consciousness of conventional Western culture.[6] Breton says his goal in *Communicating Vessels* is "to prosecute materialistic knowledge by means of the dream" (55).

Despite their immersion in the world of dreams and the unconscious, the surrealists believed that their art served a practical, revolutionary purpose: their creations were aimed at transforming the waking world of bourgeois culture. Breton begins the "Second Surrealist Manifesto" with the statement, "in the end Surrealism's overall tendency will be readily admitted to have been nothing so much as the provocation, from an intellectual and moral point of view, of the most universal and serious kind of *crisis of conscience*" (Breton [1929] 1965, 76). On an aesthetic level, surrealism sought to create new views of artistic expression, initiating reforms in technique, style, and criteria of beauty. On an intellectual level, the surrealists tried to develop a new way of knowing the world, a way beyond the ordinary polarities that structure Western epistemology—as Breton says, "undertaking the investigation of the elements of reality and unreality, reason and unreason, reflection and impulse" (Breton [1929] 1965, 78). On a religious level, the surrealists rejected traditional Christianity and looked for spiritual inspiration in the occult, in primitive religions, in any form of spirituality condemned by Western society as heretical or demonic (Waldberg 1965, 17, 23). And on a political level, the surrealists's goal was nothing less than the overthrow of bourgeois society (indeed, some surrealists actively aligned themselves with anarchist and Marxist groups).

These revolutionary impulses were never integrated very well with each other, and the lofty goals of surrealism remained largely unachieved. But the important point for us to note is that surrealism did not simply flee into the unconscious, there to surrender to the wonders of dreaming. On the contrary, the surrealists tried to relate their dream experiences to waking reality so as to transform the whole of life. Breton stated as the surrealist ideal, not the denial of waking reality, nor the establishment of a new tyranny of dreams, but rather a new and creative fusion of the two states:

> There is every reason to believe that there exists a certain point in the mind at which life and death, real and imaginary, past and future, communicable and incommunicable, high and low, cease to be perceived in terms of contradiction. Surrealist activity would be searched in vain for a motive other than the hope to determine this point. (Breton [1929] 1965, 76)

It should be clear, then, that surrealism was more than an art movement, more than a particular way of painting or writing poetry. It was explicitly an entire philosophy of life that emerged in reaction against the conventional world view of the modern West. Surrealism sought to integrate waking and dreaming realities into a new means of knowing and experiencing life, a means that would have implications for aesthetics, epistemology, ethics, politics, and spirituality.

5

ANALYTICAL PSYCHOLOGY: CARL JUNG

> In dream-analysis we must never forget, even for a moment, that we move on treacherous ground where nothing is certain but uncertainty.
>
> —Carl Jung, *The Practical Use of Dream-Analysis*

Most books on dreams offer, in addition to a routine outline of Freud's theory of dreams, a correspondingly ritualized summary of Jung's ideas. The argument tends to run: Freud said this about dreams, and Jung said that; now a new *third* kind of dream theory will be proposed.[1] Again, I imagine that readers familiar with such books are accustomed to passing over the summaries in order to get to the (allegedly) new material. But I want to emphasize that this project will follow a very different course: not only will we devote equal attention to many other theories of dreams besides those of Freud and Jung, we will also develop an understanding of dreams and religious meaning directly *out of* our reflections on the approaches of Freud, Jung, and others. The following presentation of Jung's dream theory is thus not simply a rote exercise we must endure before we get to the *real* stuff. Rather, a careful and detailed examination of Jung's ideas (like the preceding examination of Freud's ideas) is the indispensible starting point for all of our subsequent explorations. We cannot develop any understanding of the wilderness of dreams without first becoming intimately familiar with these major pathways.

Carl Jung was a Swiss doctor who in 1904 encountered some of Freud's early writings, among which was *The Interpretation of Dreams*. Jung initiated a correspondence with Freud that culminated in their meeting in 1906. They soon became close friends and colleagues, with Jung assuming a virtually official position as Freud's chief disciple and heir.[2] Jung's interest in dreams began well before his meeting with Freud, as he had been deeply affected in childhood by a number of powerful and mystifying dreams (as Jung describes in his autobiography *Memories, Dreams, Reflections* [1965]). But under Freud's tutelage, Jung directed this interest into the development of psychoanalytic theory. Among his first writings were two papers that gave spirited defenses of Freud's wish-fulfillment theory of dreams (1909, 1910–11).

Freud and Jung had a painful, bitter falling out in 1914, the reasons for which are to this day hotly debated. Jung claimed that Freud's theory had become overly rigid and dogmatic; Freud said Jung's ambition had become dangerously inflated. Whatever the reasons for their break, its effects on Jung were profound and lasting. The subsequent development of his thought is intimately related to Freud's theories, and a full understanding of Jung is possible only when set in this context of his relationship with Freud.[3] This is particularly true of Jung's theory of dreams, so we will keep Freud's views in mind as we review the many writings in which Jung describes his approach.[4]

Like Freud, Jung adopts the model of the natural sciences as his methodological guide in exploring dreams. Jung is tireless in reciting the principles of this method: we must set our theories and prejudices aside, focus on the empirical facts, describe the phenomena as they are, and offer only the most hypothetical interpretations of these facts. He says in "The Psychological Aspects of the Kore,"

> In view of the enormous complexity of psychic phenomena, a purely phenomeological point of view is, and will be for a long time, the only possible one . . . Psychic phenomena occasioned by unconscious processes are so rich and so multifarious that I prefer to *describe* my findings and observations and, where possible, to classify them—that is, to arrange them under certain definite types. That is the method of natural science. (Jung [1951b] 1969, 182–83)[5]

The chief disagreement between Freud and Jung lies in their understandings of how consciousness and the unconscious relate to each other. Whereas Freud (in Jung's view) puts too much emphasis on the development of consciousness, the ego, and rationality, Jung believes that psychological development and health involves a progressive *balancing* of these with the unconscious, the id, and irrationality. Jung argues that the *compensatory* relationship between consciousness and the unconscious is a decisive feature of human psychology: "we can take the theory of compensation as a basic law of psychic behavior" (Jung [1934] 1974, 101). Ordinarily this balanced relationship between consciousness and the unconscious develops naturally, even automatically over the course of a person's life. Jung describes it as an essentially self-regulating process.[6]

Dreams reveal this process with particular clarity: dreams are accurate, honest portrayals of the "actual situation in the psyche," showing how conscious and unconscious forces are interacting.[7] Jung thus denies Freud's sharp distinction between a dream's manifest and latent contents. Dreams appear strange *not* due to the machinations of any deceitful censor, but because our conscious minds do not always understand the special symbolic language of the unconscious.[8] In *Two Essays on Analytical Psychology* Jung states

> Misled by the so-called dream mechanisms of Freudian manufacture, such as displacement, inversion, etc., people have imagined they could make themselves independent of the "facade" of the dream by supposing that the true dream-thoughts lay hidden behind it. As against this I have long maintained that we have no right to accuse the dream of, so to speak, a deliberate manoeuvre calculated to deceive. Nature is often obscure or impenetrable, but she is not, like man, deceitful. We must therefore take it that the dream is just what it pretends to be, neither more nor less . . . The dream itself wants nothing: it is a self-evident content, a plain natural fact like the sugar in the blood of a diabetic or the fever in a patient with typhus. It is only we who, if we are clever and can unriddle the signs of nature, turn it into a warning. (Jung 1966, 100–1)

Among the many functions that dreams serve (and he acknowledges that there are a number of different ones[9]), there are two that Jung considers especially important. The first relates to that essential *compensatory* process of the psyche's development. Dreams have the function of balancing the psyche as a whole, bringing forth unconscious contents that consciousness has either ignored, not valued sufficiently, or actively repressed (Jung [1948a] 1974, 30–31, 36, 38). The second valuable function of dreams is to provide *prospective* visions of the future. Jung agrees with Freud that dreams may look backward to past experiences, but he argues that dreams also look forward to anticipate what the individual's future developments may be.[10] Ultimately, dreams serve to promote the basic developmental process of bringing consciousness and the unconscious into wholeness, the process Jung calls "individuation": "The way of successive assimilations goes far beyond the curative results that specifically concern the doctor. It leads in the end to that distant goal which may perhaps have been the first urge to life: the complete actualization of the whole human being, that is, individuation" (Jung [1934] 1974, 108).[11]

All of this talk of natural courses, automatic processes, and self-regulation might suggest that Jung would not see any need ever to *interpret* dreams. To an extent, this is true; but at the same time, Jung does believe that interpreting dreams can be a very helpful way of assisting the natural process of individuation, especially when it has become obstructed.[12] He says an analyst must start the interpretation of any dream with an admission of ignorance and with a willingness to find something new.[13] At the same time, however, Jung also claims that a great deal of experience and knowledge about comparative religions, mythology, and folk-lore are all required to make an accurate interpretation of a dream.[14] The first step in an interpretation is to seek the dreamer's associations, to establish the conscious context with as much care and detail as possible.[15] Also, Jung prefers to work with series of dreams, for these provide a broader picture of the dreamer's psychic life than can be gained from a single dream.[16] Using the associations as guides, Jung then asks if any meanings come "naturally," of their own accord; any interpretations he offers are tentative hypotheses.[17] We should be suspicious, he says, if any meanings accord too easily with our expectations, "for as a rule the standpoint of the unconscious is complementary or compensatory to consciousness and thus unexpectedly 'different'" (Jung [1952] 1974, 118).

The interpretation of dream symbols is central to Jung's approach to dreams. On the one hand he says that all dream symbols must be related to the dreamer's conscious situation and that there are no fixed meanings to any symbols (Jung [1934] 1974, 105). But on the other, Jung believes that dreams frequently express *archetypal* images, which are collective and transcend the individual's own consciousness. Archetypes, Jung says, are universal psychic structures that underlie all human thought.[18] Thus his interpretations of dreams often leave the realm of the individual's associations entirely when he believes the dream's symbols touch on these universal structures.

One important question Jung asks in interpreting a dream is whether the dream's images and symbols relate primarily to the *objective* level of meaning or the *subjective* level:

> I call every interpretation which equates the dream images with real objects an *interpretation on the objective level.* In contrast to this is the interpretation which refers every part of the dream and all the actors in it back to the dreamer himself. This I call *interpretation on the subjective level.* (Jung 1966, 84)[19]

Ultimately, Jung says that the process of interpreting a dream, of determining whether the meaning is more objective or more subjective, whether the symbols are more personal or more archetypal, is a matter of "joint reflection," a "dialectical process" like the Socratic dialogues, in which both the analyst and the dreamer participate.[20] The key criterion for a valid interpretation is its therapeutic value: if the interpretation brings forth meanings that help the dreamer, it is a valid interpretation. Jung says in "The Aims of Psychotherapy,"

> It ought not matter to me whether the result of my musings on the dream is scientifically verifiable or tenable, otherwise I am pursuing an ulterior—and therefore autoerotic—aim. I must content myself wholly with the fact that the result means something to the patient and sets his life in motion again. I may allow myself only one criterion for the result of my labors: Does it work? (Jung [1931] 1966, 42–43)

The fact that dreams reveal so clearly and with such power the nature of the unconscious makes them of interest to the cultural critic as well as the psychotherapist, Jung believes, for the psychology of the individual exactly parallels the psychology of humanity.[21] Thus the fact that the dreams of so many individuals involves a painful split between consciousness and the unconscious has significance beyond their personal lives. Jung says such dreams also represent

> A broadly human conflict manifesting itself in the individual, for disunity with oneself is the hall-mark of civilized man. The neurotic is only a special instance of the disunited man who ought to harmonize nature and culture within himself. (Jung 1966, 19)

The exploration of the unconscious by such means as dream interpretation has a tremendous cultural value, Jung claims, because it can reveal to people the unconscious forces that they tend to deny or repress: "if people can be educated to see the shadow-side of their nature clearly, it may be hoped that they will also learn to understand and love their fellow men better" (Jung 1966, 26).

Religions have always served, Jung says, to effect the union between consciousness and the unconscious. The individuation process, i.e., the growth of the psyche towards balance and wholeness, is the core of all religious and spiritual traditions.[22] But in the modern age, with so much skepticism about religion, the traditional faiths and rites no longer "work" for people. This is why depth psychology has become so important, in Jung's view, because it can offer a practical, effective means of promoting the individuation process without arousing the modern suspiciousness of religious illusions and superstition.[23] In one of his case studies Jung engages in a lengthy analysis of the patient's dreams, drawing out voluminous parallels with gnostic, alchemical, and mystical symbolism, in order to show how the unconscious of the modern individual is still connected to essentially religious yearnings and how the psychological approach to dreams can help modern people satisfy these yearnings: "the case before us proves that even if the conscious mind is miles away from the ancient conceptions of the rites of renewal, the unconscious still strives to bring them closer in dreams" (Jung [1952] 1974, 211).[24]

Indeed, Jung believes it is precisely because modern Westerners have such a rational, materialistic worldview that "religious compensations" come to play an especially significant role in our dreams in order to balance that one-sided conscious outlook (Jung [1948a] 1974, 36). While such dreams of "religious compensation" are not necessarily frequent, their power and influence is nevertheless tremendous: these "'big' dreams . . . are often remembered for a lifetime, and not infrequently prove to be the richest jewel in the treasure-house of psychic experience" (Jung [1948b] 1974, 36).[25]

6

CONTENT ANALYSIS: CALVIN HALL

> Dreams, in effect, provide us with maps of regions which are inaccessible in waking consciousness. With these maps we are better able to follow the course of man's behavior, to understand why he selects one road rather than another, to anticipate the difficulties and obstacles he will encounter, and to predict his destinations.
>
> —Calvin Hall, *The Meaning of Dreams*

Calvin Hall was an American psychologist whose prolific dream research began in the 1940s and continued on until his death in 1985. Hall's work was initially motivated by a frustration with the theories of Freud and Jung, which appeared to him to be murky, subjective, and difficult to apply practically. He developed a means of studying dreams, the content analysis method, that soon became one of the most influential and widely practiced techniques for studying dreams. Halls' research methods and general views on the nature and meaning of dreams are to this day major forces guiding contemporary dream study.[1] In the following brief survey we will focus on three of Hall's major works: *The Meaning of Dreams*, first published in 1953 and slightly revised in 1966; *The Content Analysis of Dreams*, coauthored with Robert L. Van de Castle in 1966; and *The Individual and his Dreams*, coauthored with Vernon J. Nordby in 1972. These three works give a good sense of both the method Hall used in studying dreams and the ideas he formed about what dreams mean.

Hall describes how the human fascination with dreams has led to many attempts to explain their mysterious messages. The origin of dreams has, for example, "been attributed to such diverse sources as the absence of bed covers or the presence of spirits" (Hall and Van de Castle 1966, ix). Hall believes that Freud's psychoanalytic dream theory went a long way towards demystifying dreams, but since the time of Freud's work little real progress has been made: "it is true that others have advanced different theoretical interpretations of what constitutes the hidden message within dreams, but the methodology of investigating dreams has remained fixated at a qualititative stage of development" (Hall and Van de Castle 1966, ix). This comment indicates the goal of Hall's approach to dreams, namely to provide a *quantitative* method of studying dreams in order to promote objective, empirical knowledge of dreams.

The method Hall develops is quantitative content analysis, which involves taking a written dream report and breaking its contents down into certain structural elements (the basic categories Hall uses are setting, characters, interactions, objects, and emotions); adding this data to a larger body of data collected from other dream analyses; and using a variety of statistical equations with the data to obtain frequencies on the appearance of the different elements. Hall claims that the content analysis method has been applied with great success in many different areas, such as the study of literary material and personality tests. By converting "verbal or other symbolic material into numbers in order that statistical operations may be performed on such material," researchers may study the given material with a minimum of subjective bias and may establish conclusions that are sound, easily replicated, and clearly communicable (Hall and Van de Castle 1966, 1–2). Hall's conviction is that bringing the content analysis method to bear on dreams can yield equally valuable results for modern dream research.

Hall devotes the first chapter of *The Content Analysis of Dreams* to a refutation of the various objections raised against this method. The problem of reductionism, that is, of forcing the material to fit the predetermined categories set by the researcher, can be avoided by a selective, flexible use of the method and by a deep familiarity with the material. The researcher, Hall says, should "be thoroughly conversant with the theory from which he is to derive his categories, for it is out of the dialogue between observation and hypothesis that a useful classificatory system will emerge" (Hall and Van de Castle 1966, 10–11). The application of objective, quantitative methods to such materials as dreams does not, Hall emphasizes, *necessarily* distort those materials; as long as the investigator remains "sensitive, intuitive, and empathic" and respects "the inherent properties of the material with which he is working," the rewards in precise, objective knowledge can be great (Hall and Van de Castle 1966, 26).[2]

The primary data for the content analysis method of dream study are verbal dream reports. Hall distinguishes between these and the actual dream experience:

> A dream is a private experience, and private experiences, until they are objectified, cannot be studied scientifically. Dreams have to be reported before they can be studied. Therefore, a dream may be operationally defined as that which a person reports when he is asked to relate a dream, excluding statements which are comments upon or interpretations of the dream. (Hall and Van de Castle 1966, 18)

Hall acknowledges that this definition raises an important issue in the study of dreams, for Freud insists that it is not the reported or manifest dream but the *latent* dream-content that is of value. However, Hall insists that "the reported dream possesses great psychological significance and that the content analysis of reported dreams is an important tool in personality research" (Hall and Van de Castle 1966, 20). Hall goes on make an even stronger claim that challenges the very legitimacy of Freud's distinction between manifest and latent contents of dreams:

> As a matter of fact, it could be said that there is no such thing as the latent content of a dream. A dream is a manifest experience, and what is latent lies outside the dream and in the verbal material that the dreamer reports when he is asked to free associate to features of the reported dream. How the psychoanalyst arrives at the "true meaning" or interpretation of the dream from the verbalized associations is more of an art than a technique. This art may be of the utmost value in the therapeutic situation, but being a private, subjective type of activity it is of no direct value for research. (Hall and Van de Castle 1966, 20)[3]

Hall thus allows for the possible therapeutic use of psychoanalytic interpretation, but firmly sets it aside when the time comes for objective scientific research into the nature and meaning of dreams.[4]

Hall's main efforts are devoted to the study of dream *series*, a process which he likens both to reading the chapters of a book and to putting a puzzle together (Hall 1966, 2, 71, 82, 84; Hall and Nordby 1972, 188). He believes the method is eminently straightforward and requires no special theoretical knowledge or unique abilities. In any analysis of a dream series,

> The dreams read like chapters in a book. When put together in order as we have done there is organization, unity, and coherence among the dreams. Each dream complements or supplements the other dreams of the series. There is very little left to guesswork since what may seem ambiguous or hidden in one dream is revealed in another dream. Dream interpretations based upon a series of dreams can be very precise and objective if one approaches the task in a scientific manner. (Hall 1966, 84–85)[5]

The interpretation of dreams brings forward the question about the nature of dream symbols, and here again Hall disputes Freud's account. He rejects Freud's claim that symbols serve to hide distasteful or painful meanings. There are so many dreams in which such obnoxious meanings are plainly represented, and so many dreams in which we may "see right through" the symbol to the real meaning, that Freud's theory of dream censorship cannot be right. In Hall's view dream symbols are "a kind of mental shorthand . . . [that] convey in terse and concise language complex and abstruse conceptions" (Hall 1966, 96).[6] Symbols in dreams "are there to express something, not to hide it"; and what the symbols express are our thoughts (Hall 1966, 95). Hall explains the process of symbol formation in dreams as follows:

> Dreaming is a form of thinking and thinking consists of formulating conceptions or ideas. When one dreams, his conceptions are turned into pictures. The images of a dream are the concrete embodiments of the dreamer's thoughts; these images give visible expression to that which is invisible, namely, conceptions. Accordingly the true referent of any dream symbol is not an object or activity, it is always an idea in the mind of a dreamer. (Hall 1966, 95)[7]

Symbols thus "clothe" our conceptions in those "garments" that make them economical and concise containers of meaning.[8] The process of interpreting symbols, then, is a matter of translating one form of expression back into the other, turning the pictures back into ideas: "the goal of dream interpretation is to discover the meaning of a dream by translating images into ideas" (Hall 1966, 214).[9] In fact, there is often little need to interpret a dream at all because the meaning is "transparent," requiring no free associations or lengthy exegetical efforts to make it clear.[10]

We may turn now from the proper methods of studying dreams to the knowledge we thereby gain of what dreams mean. Hall states in *The Meaning of Dreams* that dreams are essentially "projections of the mind" representing not objective reality, but the subjective reality of the dreamer (Hall 1966, 7, 12–14, 86). Once again, Hall distinguishes his views from those of Freud: while Freud claims dreams reveal our unconscious, instinctual impulses, Hall believes the real significance of dreams consists in the way they reveal what we *think* of our impulses. He says,

> Dreams tell us more about a person than that he is sexually and aggressively driven. They tell us what a person thinks about these basic impulses, what people they are directed against, and how they can best be satisfied. (Hall 1966, 70)[11]

Furthermore, dreams reveal the general "conception of the world" a person holds, the worldview (*Weltanschauung*) by which a person understands the total nature of his or her surrounding environment (Hall 1966, 14, 220–21, 226). Dreams can show the many ways in which such a worldview influences waking behavior: in our interpersonal relationships, our work, our politics, our religious beliefs, "in every department of life man reacts selectively to his world in terms of his conceptual systems" (Hall 1966, 220–30).

In *The Individual and his Dreams* Hall says that content analysis has demonstrated a simple truth about dreams. There is a close correspondence between people's dreams and their acts and thoughts in waking life. He presents this as the "continuity hypothesis" of dreams.

> These facts and many others obtained from the content analysis of many dream series have led us to formulate what we call the *continuity hypothesis*. This hypothesis states that dreams are continuous with waking life; the world of dreaming and the world of waking are one. The dream world is neither discontinuous nor inverse in its relationship to the conscious world. We remain the same person, the same personality with the same characteristics, and the same basic beliefs and convictions whether awake or asleep. The wishes and fears that determine our actions and thoughts in everyday life also determine what we will dream about. (Hall and Nordby 1972, 104)[12]

By studying dreams, then, we gain a clear view of the fundamental fears, wishes, beliefs, and ideals that govern the individual in his or her waking life.

Hall argues that the content analysis of dreams has significance beyond the furthering of individual self-knowledge. A scientific approach to dream study, such as Hall provides, can also promote a better understanding of human society by revealing the various conflicts that afflict human beings.[13] The more we know of those conflicts, Hall believes, the better able we will be to deal with them; "after all, man cannot solve his problems unless he recognizes them for what they are and then tries to think his way through to rational solutions." (Hall 1966, 233)[14] Too many of society's problems—war, crime, and mental disease, to name a few—are due in Hall's estimation to our "abject ignorance of the human mind" (Hall 1966, 220). Dreams are an outstanding means of relieving this ignorance, of learning why humans behave as they do, and thus of helping to solve the troubles that ail our society.

In this sense, Hall sets his approach to dreams squarely within the broader context of the progress of modern Western science. He says,

> Throughout history man has displayed considerable creativity in mastering problems of existence and in discovering the secrets of the physical world . . . The accomplishments of science and technology are among the most notable achievements of the human mind. (Hall 1966, 233)[15]

Unfortunately, Hall believes, the scientific method has never been applied to the study of the psychological world (he calls it, in what we would consider very apt terms, "the vast wilderness within" [Hall 1966, 217]). In large part this failure is due to the regrettable human tendency to fear new knowledge. Hall notes that both astronomers and biologists have battled against this prejudice in the past, and now psychologists must struggle against the same stubborn fears.[16] As a result of this ignorance, people have believed that dreams originate in the supernatural, that they are messages from gods, devils, or other supernatural beings. Such views were inevitable, Hall believes, when people relied only upon "rhetoric or speculation"; but the application of the scientific method, in the form of content analysis, will finally enable us to establish "a dependable body of knowledge about dreams" (Hall and Van de Castle 1966, 24). In fact, Hall's research already gives him a sound basis for dismissing the prescientific superstitions about the religious origins and meanings of dreams:

> Dreams are not mysterious, supernatural, or esoteric phenomena. They are not messages from the gods nor are they prophecies of the future. They are not due to something we ate nor are they merely responses to alarm clocks, changes in temperature or bodily movements of the sleeper. They are pictures of what the mind is thinking. Anyone who can look at a picture and say what it means ought to be able to look at his dream pictures and say what they mean. The meaning of a dream will not be found in some theory about dreams; it is right there in the dream itself. One does not read into a dream a meaning that he has learned from some book; rather he reads out of the dream what is there to be read. Any clear-headed person should be able to interpret dreams. (Hall 1966, 120)[17]

7

NEUROSCIENCE: J. ALLAN HOBSON

> This neuronal activity is a sort of continuous war whose effects spread from the brain stem throughout the brain, taking the mind hostage. This battle for the mind occurs regularly—and silently—every night in our sleep . . . The brain stem is the nightly battleground of warring neuronal factions, and REM sleep and dreaming are the result of temporary domination of one neuronal population over another."
>
> —J. Allan Hobson, *The Dreaming Brain*

Many people believe the single most important avenue of dream study in the twentieth century is neuroscience. For decades Freud, the surrealists, Jung, and Hall (among many others) explored the wilderness of dreams with great determination and insight. But the discovery of rapid eye movements (REMs) in the 1950s by scientists at the University of Chicago set off a rush of sleep laboratory experiments—rather like the discovery of gold in a previously ignored region sets off a rush of mining expeditions—that sought to discover the neurological bases of the mental experience of dreaming.[1] Now the neuroscientific approach, with its technological sophistication and its grounding in the methodology of the natural sciences, is widely considered to give the most authoritative knowledge on the nature and meaning of dreams.

The leading neuroscientist active at present is J. Allan Hobson. In 1977, the article "The Brain as a Dream-State Generator: An Activation-Synthesis Hypothesis of the Dream Process," which Hobson coauthored with Robert W. McCarley, offered a powerful assertion of the neurological basis of dreaming and an aggressive challenge to Freud's view of dream formation and interpretation. Hobson refined and expanded his theory in a book, *The Dreaming Brain*, in which he seeks to persuade not only dream researchers but also a "wide lay audience" of the validity of his views (Hobson 1988, xv). Given Hobson's tremendous influence on the modern study of dreams, it will be very important for us to understand his ideas and to consider carefully his arguments about dreams and religious meaning. We will focus on *The Dreaming Brain* as the major statement of his views, drawing on other articles by and about him when helpful.

It is clear from the opening pages of *The Dreaming Brain* that Hobson is writing directly against Freud—the book is a passionately argued polemic against the psychoanalytic account of dreams. But Hobson is not attacking Freud alone, for he sees psychoanalysis as the culmination of a long history of dream interpretation. The real enemy is "the prophetic tradition," generally appearing in a religious guise, in which dreams are seen as caused by external agencies (principally gods or spirits), as containing secret, coded messages, and as requiring elaborate interpretations by special authorities (10–11). In Hobson's view, psychoanalysis is but the latest carrier of this "time-honored" tradition:

> The prophetic tradition of dream study can be seen in its modern as well as its antique form. The wise man, the priest, or the psychoanalyst knows the dream code and can thus predict the future while deciphering both the past and the present . . . The most modern manifestation of this interpretive tradition is the theory of dreams advanced by psychoanalysis. (10, 11)[2]

Rather than obeying this "prophetic tradition," stretching from the Bible to Freud, Hobson will follow the scientific tradition "in which experimental accomplices or instrumentation have been used to make the study of dreams more systematic and more objective" (12). His purpose in *The Dreaming Brain* is to provide a solid psychophysiological account of how dreams are *formed*. With that account as a basis, he will show how we may better understand what dreams *mean* (13–15).

Hobson rejects the prophetic/psychoanalytic tradition for its arbitrariness, its speculative excesses, its irrationality, and its denial of human responsibility (in locating the origins of dreams outside human agency) (9–12). His approach to dreams will refute that tradition on each of these points and will provide a firm, scientifically legitimate understanding of dreams. Indeed, in Hobson's view the greatest crime committed by Freud is that his theory succeeded for half a century in suppressing the scientific study of dreams.[3] Hobson's book is "firmly dedicated to a scientific resuscitation of the 'medical theory of dream life' which Freud disdained" (51).

Rather than speculating about the mind and then using those speculations to speculate further about the brain, as Freud did, Hobson argues that we should take what we *know*, what neuroscience can *prove* about the brain, and use that to make hypotheses about the workings of the mind.[4] He thus turns to his neuroscientific research and presents his model of the brain, which he terms "the reciprocal-interaction model of REM-sleep generation." According to this model, a constant competition between groups of neurons leads to the cycles of waking, sleeping, and dreaming.[5] Hobson likens this process to a "continuous war":

> REM sleep and dreaming are the result of temporary domination of one neuronal population over another. Victorious is a troop of reticular-formation neurons concentrated mainly in the pontine portion of the brain stem; owing to their fusillades of firing in association with REM-sleep events, these pontine reticular neurons are likely to play the executive role in the generation of REM sleep and dreaming. Sharing the white flag of temporary surrender is a population of aminergic neurons located in the locus ceruleus, the raphe nuclei, and the peribrachial regions of the anterior pontine brain stem; hardly a shot is fired by this neuronal phalanx during REM sleep. (183)[6]

The key conclusion that Hobson draws from this reciprocal-interaction model is that dreams are *caused* by neurological processes that are regular, random, involuntary, and rooted in our physiological nature. Dreams are thus *generated* by brain neurology (202). To account for how the activity of neuronal populations can lead to the psychological experience of a dream, Hobson offers the "activation-synthesis hypothesis of dreaming." This hypothesis suggests that after neuronal processes have activated REM sleep, higher brain functions work to synthesize the essentially random input as well as it can:

> The activation-synthesis hypothesis assumes that dreams are as meaningful as they can be under the adverse working conditions of the brain in REM sleep. The activated brain-mind does its best to attribute meaning to the internally generated signals. (214)[7]

In the synthesis stage of dream formation, the brain-mind *adds* meaning to the neurological activity, *creating* meanings where there were none before. Although Hobson admits that we still know far too little about how the synthetic processes work,[8] he claims that his activation-synthesis hypothesis can account for the most important features of dreaming: for example, for its predominantly visual nature (because the neuronal processes stimulate visual systems in particular, the mind "uses its own eye movement data in dream scene elaboration" [211]), for its distortion (despite the best efforts of the synthetic processes, the neurologically generated data are so bizarre that most dream syntheses remain very distorted [212–13][9]), and for its frequently strong emotional content (due, like the visual content, to the neurological activation of emotional systems in the brain [213]).

The role of synthesis in dream formation reflects, Hobson believes, an "essentially human" capacity to imagine and create:

> Activation-synthesis thus includes creativity among its assumptions. This theory sees the brain as so inexorably bent upon the quest for meaning that it attributes and even creates meaning when there is little or none to be found in the data it is asked to process. (15)

Hobson says the brain labors, in sleeping as in waking, to create a meaningful integration of its experience, "even if it must resort to creative storytelling" (219). Indeed, the utterly chaotic and random data that bombard us in our sleep often confound all ordinary means of organizing our perceptions, leading to extraordinary attempts at synthesis:

> It may be that their [dreams'] symbolic, prophetic character arises from the integrative strain of this synthetic effort. The brain-mind may need to call upon its deepest myths to find a narrative frame that can contain the data. (214)

Thus the neurologically generated data are so random and bizarre, and yet the human need for meaning is so profound, that we must resort to stories, symbols, and even myths in order to synthesize the intrinsically inchoate matter of REM sleep into meaningful dreams.

Hobson claims that neuroscientific research devastates Freud's psychoanalytic theories and, by implication, all prophetic or religious theories about dreams as well. He has shown that dreams are caused ("activated") by neuronal activity and not by unconscious wishes, spirits, or gods. He has also shown that the bizarreness of dreams is due to the brain's imperfect attempts at synthesizing intrinsically random data rather than to a censor mechanism or to scheming deities (215, 246). A crucial consequence is that the meaning of dreams is not hidden or coded, but rather "transparent," "clear," "naked," present right on the "surface" of the dream: "for activation synthesis the dream as reported is the transparent and directly legible product of an unusual mode of information processing" (217). Whatever meaning there is to a dream, it comes during the process of synthesis, with no masks, subterfuges, or codings. Once we have proven that dreams have their origins in purely random neurological activity, Hobson believes we are liberated from the shackles of the prophetic tradition's demand for complex interpretative procedures administered by authoritative specialists. We are then able to understand that dreams have meanings that are plain and transparent.

Hobson presents his own dreams and the dreams of "The Engine Man" (an individual who kept a detailed dream journal) as evidence of how the meanings of dreams are in fact clear, undistorted, and transparent. With his own dreams, Hobson finds that his feelings, wishes, perceptions, and thoughts are all easily recognized; "this all seems very transparent to me. Almost naked." (233). Activation-synthesis can account for many of the strange features of his dreams, and his own common sense explains the rest. Hence there is no need for authorities, experts, prophets, or analysts to interpret dreams, Hobson concludes. While he agrees with Freud that dreams *are* meaningful, he strongly disagrees with Freud that the meanings are disguised (on this, he allies himself with Jung[10]):

> I wish again to emphasize strongly that I am not asserting that dreams are either meaningless or unworthy of clinical attention. On the contrary . . . the meaning of dreams is for me transparent rather than concealed, since fundamentally incoherent cognitive elements are synthesized in a personally meaningful way. This "meaning-added" process is the exact opposite of that envisaged by psychoanalysis, which asserts that fully coherent and deeply meaningful ideas (the latent dream content) must be degraded and disguised (by the dream work), resulting in an incoherent product (the manifest dream content) acceptable to consciousness. For me, the manifest content is the dream: there is no other dream. (258)[11]

As he makes clear in his first chapter, Hobson does see his research as bearing on the issue of the religious meaning of dreams in the modern West. He says

> The time-honored approach to understanding dreams is to regard them as communications from external agencies: gods, angels, or spirits. This fundamentally religious idea can never be either proved or disproved. The best that science can do is to examine the evidence for it and try to account for that evidence with propositions that may be capable of verification. (9)

Having examined the evidence, Hobson leaves us with little doubt that he believes this "fundamentally religious idea" about dreams is false: dreams are caused by the automatic neuronal activity of the brain in REM sleep, not by gods, and we don't need priests (or psychoanalysts) to interpret them for us.[12] The following quote is instructive in indicating how Hobson understands the import of his work for the debate about the religious meaning of dreams:

> For the student of consciousness, the development of the polygraph [used to measure REM sleep cycles] is no less portentous than was the discovery of the telescope for the student of the heavens. Numerous myths that we hold about ourselves may come to seem as outlandish as the pre-Copernican idea that the sun moves around the earth. (139)[13]

Just as religious explanations had to retreat in the face of Copernicus's research in astronomy, so Hobson believes that religious explanations are now driven to retreat in the face of advancing neuroscientific research in dreams.

8

LUCID DREAMING: STEPHEN LABERGE

> It can be estimated that in the course of our lives, we enter our dream worlds half a million times. This state of affairs presents us all with a challenge: as we neglect or cultivate the world of our dreams, so will this realm become a wasteland or a garden. As we sow, so shall we reap our dreams. With the universe of experience thus open to you, if you must sleep through a third of your life, as it seems you must, are you willing to sleep through your dreams too?
>
> —Stephen LaBerge, *Lucid Dreaming*

Stephen LaBerge's work *Lucid Dreaming* is certainly one of the most influential books on modern dream research since Freud's *The Interpretation of Dreams*, and while Freud had to wait years for his book to stimulate any sort of response, LaBerge's work created an immediate sensation. His account of the nature and implications of lucid dreaming has generated a tremendous amount of further research[1] as well as a great deal of controversy. Some researchers have argued that actively seeking lucidity in dreams is a violation of the integrity of the dreaming process; others have claimed that lucid dreaming actually represents a higher evolution of our potentials for consciousness; still others have questioned how the focus on lucid dreaming distracts researchers from exploring other important areas of dream study.

In a number of different ways, then, LaBerge's work marks a major turning point in twentieth-century dream study. We will focus our explorations on the book *Lucid Dreaming*, for it is the clearest, most concise statement of what the discovery of lucid dreaming means for the modern study of dreams.

The phenomenon of lucid dreaming involves the achievement, within the dreaming state, of a degree of consciousness that one is dreaming.[2] As LaBerge notes in a historical review, there have been accounts of lucid dreaming experiences dating back centuries, from many different cultures. He cites comments by Augustine, eighth century Tibetan Buddhists, and the Spanish Sufi Ibn al-'Arabi about having lucid dreams (LaBerge 1985, 21–25). In more modern times, LaBerge notes the 1867 book *Dreams and How to Guide Them* by the Marquis d'Hervey de Saint-Denys, the 1968 book *Lucid Dreams* by English parapsychologist Celia Green, and Patricia Garfield's 1974 work *Creative Dreaming* as providing detailed personal accounts of lucid dreaming.

Yet, LaBerge goes on, these accounts were almost entirely ignored by Western scholars and researchers. The analytic philosopher Norman Malcolm declared that being conscious in a dream was a logical contradiction; the sleep and dream researcher Allan Rechtschaffen stated that "single-mindedness," that is, nonreflectiveness, was one of the constant attributes of dreams; and the psychophysiologists B. A. Schwartz and A. Lefebvre argued that apparently "lucid" dreams were actually partial arousals or "microawakenings" during sleep (LaBerge 1985, 60–64). But LaBerge would not abide by these skeptical views. He had himself experienced lucid dreams, he knew of the others who said they had lucid dreams too, and so he became determined to prove that lucid dreaming does truly occur.

LaBerge initiated a set of experiments at Stanford University's sleep laboratory in which he tried to devise a way to communicate "from the lucid dream to the outside world, *while* the dream was happening" (68). His plan was to go to sleep while attached to an EEG recording device, and once he entered REM sleep (the commonly accepted scientific definition of "real" dreaming) he would become lucid and then make a distinctive, prearranged set of eye movements within the dream. The hope was that the eye movements would then show up "outside" on the EEG recordings. After a number of trials, LaBerge finally succeeded:

> We observed two large eye movements on the polygraph record just before I awakened from a thirteen-minute REM period. Here, finally, was objective evidence that at least one lucid dream had taken place during what was clearly REM sleep! (70)

Since that initial success LaBerge's experiment has been widely replicated, and lucid dreaming is now recognized as a legitimate, scientifically verifiable phenomenon.

As he reflects on the process by which he proved that lucid dreaming is "real," Laberge says:

> One can see a parallel with electricity: the Greeks knew of it, but for thousands of years no one regarded it as more than a curiosity. The scientific study of electricity gave rise to remarkable technological developments and an astonishing variety of unexpected applications. (41)

In the same way, LaBerge quickly moves in *Lucid Dreaming* from the scientific discovery of lucid dreaming to a study of how to develop and apply it. He devotes a great deal of his book to discussing how people can learn to dream lucidly, for lucid dreaming, like conscious thought, "is an ability that can be gained or improved by training" (139). LaBerge describes various techniques for inducing lucidity in dreams, and he frequently refers to Buddhist meditation exercises as helping in this regard (144–49). More recently, LaBerge has been developing a special set of goggles that can signal to a sleeping person when he or she has entered REM sleep.[3]

Continuing with the electricity analogy, LaBerge says lucid dreaming has the potential for many exciting applications:

> Though for the moment we can only speculate, our work at Stanford and the accounts of other lucid dreamers suggest that, like electricity, lucid dreaming could also be harnessed to aid us in performing a variety of tasks with far greater ease. (167)

For example, lucid dreaming can make major contributions to the scientific study of the nature and function of dreaming. LaBerge looks in particular at the implications of lucid dreaming for Hobson's activation-synthesis hypothesis of dreams. While many researchers have criticized Hobson for depreciating the role of higher mental processes in forming dreams, LaBerge claims that his lucid dreaming research offers solid proof on this point:

> The phenomenon of lucid dreaming suggests even more strongly the influence of the cerebral cortex on the construction of dreams. For if your dreams were nothing more than the results of your forebrain producing 'partially coherent dream imagery from the relatively noisy signals sent up to it', how would you be able to exercise volitional choice in a lucid dream? (207)

Lucid dreaming thus offers an excellent means of studying how higher cortical functions such as thinking and deliberate action influence the formation of dreams, showing that dream formation is a "two-way street" between brainstem and forebrain and not the one-directional process envisioned by Hobson (203–10).

LaBerge also discusses a variety of practical applications of lucid dreaming for bettering people's personal lives. For example, lucid dreaming can provide us with access to valuable unconscious knowledge.[4] It can enable us to gain more control over our physiological processes and thus work to improve our physical health.[5] Along psychotherapeutic lines, it can promote the psychological integration of ignored parts of one's personality.[6] It can be especially helpful in treating nightmare sufferers,[7] and it can enable us to rehearse future actions and gain visions of what our behavior will bring so that we may make more informed choices.[8] Here, LaBerge believes that the application of lucid dreaming goes beyond personal betterment to make an potentially important contribution to social progress:

> The ecological and political situation of this planet will force enormous changes upon humanity within the next century . . . Certainly the planetary situation is one of unprecedented complexity. And just as certainly, what is needed is unprecedented vision: both to avoid the abysmal catastrophe of nuclear war, and to find the path to true humanity. With the future to gain, and nothing to lose, we shouldn't fear to take our heads out of the sand and into the dream, for dreams may have much to contribute here (for example, novel and creative solutions not thought of during waking life). But before this dream comes true, we will certainly need to increase our understanding of dream control greatly. Since lucidity seems to provide the key to dream control, it seems reasonable to expect that attaining the goal of intentional dreaming will require considerable advances in the art and science of lucid dreaming. (193)

Along with these more worldly applications, LaBerge also believes the individual can pursue a spiritual "path of inner growth through lucid dreaming" (264). Here, he draws again on the Tibetan Buddhist yogic practices that involve lucid dreaming. LaBerge describes the process and ultimate goals of Buddhist dream yoga as involving a "comprehension" of the nature of the dream state. This spiritual "comprehension" begins with lucid dreaming and the realization that the dream state is illusory. It then involves generalizing this insight to all of reality and recognizing that the world and all its phenomena are illusory. And then,

> A final step brings [one] to "the Great Realization" that nothing within the experience of his mind "can be other than unreal like dreams." In this light, "the Universal Creation . . . and every phenomenal thing therein" are seen to be "but the content of the Supreme Dream." (261–64)

Western lucid dreamers gain these insights through their direct dream experiences, LaBerge says; in lucid dreams "they know that the persons they appear to be in the dream are not who they really are" (267). This discovery leads people along that same yogic path of Enlightenment. Ultimately, LaBerge claims, "the fully lucid dreams we have been discussing are instances of transcendental experiences, experiences in which you go beyond your current level of consciousness" (268).[9]

The greatest potential of lucid dreaming, LaBerge believes, is its power to promote an attitude of "lucid living" (273). Just as we can learn to recognize in our dreams that we are dreaming, that what we are experiencing is not "really real" and that *we* are creating the reality of the dream—exactly so, LaBerge says, we can learn to recognize that we create our own models of the *waking* world and that we can change those models and create new ones when new challenges arise. He states,

> It is a traditional doctrine of esoteric psychologies that the ordinary state or consciousness we call "waking" is so far from seeing things as they are in "objective reality" that it could be more accurately called "sleep" or "dreaming." (276)

Lucid dreams provide the opportunity to *practice* this doctrine, to discover its truth as we become conscious within our dreams that we are dreaming. LaBerge concludes his book by saying,

> Lucid dreaming can be a point of departure from which to understand how we might not be fully awake—for as ordinary dreaming is to lucid dreaming, so the ordinary waking state might be to the fully awakened state. This capacity of lucid dreams, to prepare us for a fuller awakening, may prove to be lucid dreaming's most significant potential for helping us become more alive in our lives. (279)

For LaBerge, then, lucid dreaming represents an opportunity for modern Westerners to experience the same spiritual insights, to move along the same path of Enlightenment, as Buddhists have followed for centuries. In LaBerge's hands the technology of the sleep laboratory, far from disproving the belief that dreams have religious meaning, actually becomes a powerful tool for cultivating our dreams as a source of religious discovery.

9

ANTHROPOLOGY: BARBARA TEDLOCK

> The problems with comparing the phenomenology of dreaming between cultures begin even before the telling and interpretation of the dream, at the level of dream sorting, or classification, which is linguistically coded and symbolically rooted in local epistemology and metapsychology. And the problems do not end when the dream comes to be talked about or performed; the outward dimensions of the performance may take nonverbal forms, and the meaning may be questioned all over again at a later time. From the perspective of possibilities like these, any attempt at counting and comparing the manifest content of verbal dream reports that have been deprived of their social and symbolic contexts appears groundless . . . We need to find a way to move not from surface to surface, but from depth to depth.
>
> —Barbara Tedlock,
> *Dreaming: Anthropological and Psychological Interpretations*

The anthropological study of dreams has until recently had a less than distinguished history. The earliest research at the end of the nineteenth and the beginning of the twentieth centuries considered the dream beliefs and practices of other cultures as evidence of their primitivity, in contrast to the West's "civilized" disinterest in dreams (Frazer [1890] 1959; Hastings 1912; Lincoln 1935). Then, with the spread of psychoanalytic ideas, some anthropologists attempted to prove the accuracy of Freud's dream theories by scrounging about for instances of censorship, resistance, and wish fulfillment in the dreams of non-Western tribespeople (Toffelmier and Luomala 1936; Roheim 1945; Wallace 1958; Devereux 1957, 1966, 1969).

Still other anthropologists provided romantic idealizations of the dream practices of non-Western cultures. The most extreme case of this was Kilton Stewart's studies of the Senoi, a Malaysian people who reportedly lived an almost trouble-free life based principally on their cultural reverence for dreams (Stewart, 1951). When the validity of Stewart's research on the Senoi was seriously challenged, the anthropological approach to dreams as a whole suffered a deep loss of credibility (Domhoff, 1985).

From the start, then, the anthropological study of dreams has done little more than provide evidence for other debates. Whether it was to support an evolutionary theory of culture or dispute it, defend Freud's views or refute them, promote the human potential movement or critique it, the studies of anthropology served primarily as a source of cheap labor to be used in the cultivation of theories in other fields.

In 1982 anthropologist Barbara Tedlock organized a seminar entitled "Dreams in Cross-Cultural Perspective" in the hope of opening up some new directions in anthropological study of dreams and trying to bring it "out of its marginal position" in both anthropology and dream research (Tedlock 1987, xi). She invited researchers from a number of different backgrounds, all having extensive fieldwork experience but also having the ability to discuss various theoretical issues such as psychoanalysis, linguistics, and symbolic analysis. After the conclusion of the seminar Tedlock gathered the papers presented and discussed into the book *Dreaming: Anthropological and Psychological Interpretations* (1987). The appearance of this book not only revived the anthropological study of dreams, as Tedlock had intended; it also signaled the full emergence of anthropology as a major field of dream research in its own right, with important and distinctive insights to contribute to the modern study of dreams. Their findings have come to profoundly challenge researchers in all other fields of dream study.

Although *Dreaming* is an anthology of articles, a number of common themes run through the work of all the authors, and in the introduction Tedlock carefully reviews the group's discussions and conclusions. Thus we will take Tedlock as our main figure, but at the same time recognize that she is speaking on behalf of a group of researchers that developed their ideas in concert with one another.

In her introductory chapter Tedlock looks at the history of Western views of dreaming and finds that Western people have tended to make a sharp distinction between dreaming and objective reality. Reaching as far back as Aristotle, this dichotomy finds its most radical statement in the mechanistic dualism of Descartes in the seventeenth century (2). Yet at the same time, Tedlock notes that there is also a long tradition in the West of naive veneration for dreaming, as seen in various literary and artistic movements. Tedlock's seminar directly addresses the issue of how this split in approaching dreams has severely limited anthropological explorations of dreams. She and her colleagues take it as their goal to find ways to move beyond those limits.[1]

The primary conclusion the seminar reaches is that dream reports and dream interpretations are inseparable from the cultural contexts in which they occur. In other words, to understand how other people experience, share, interpret, and act upon their dreams requires a full understanding of their culture. We must carefully study their language, their social institutions, and the psychological, philosophical, and religious beliefs that shape those people's world. Many of the papers in *Dreaming* focus specifically on the "communicative context" of dream sharing and interpretation (21). Thus Waud Kracke insists that we recognize how a dream "report" is a complex synthesis of spatial-sensory experience, language, and cultural discourse. This implies that dreams are not simple "texts" with plain, self-evident contents to them (22). Gilbert Herdt argues that "it is not enough to know what people dream about; we must also know how and what parts of their dreaming experiences they communicate to others" (22–23). In her own paper on the dream sharing and interpreting of the Zuni and Quiche peoples of the Guatemalan highlands, Tedlock shows how their practices represent "distinct culturally constituted communication systems . . . [in which] lower-level symbolic systems are nested within higher-level ontological and psychological systems" (28). The Zuni and Quiche approaches to dreaming derive, Tedlock argues, from deeply embedded cultural structures:

> Differences in dream sharing and interpreting between Zunis and Quiches are traceable to a combination of ontological and psychological differences . . . [For the Zuni] dreaming is a deathlike breach of the fragile boundary between daylight or cooked persons and raw persons. For the Quiche it is merely the free-soul that wanders in the first place, which makes dreaming a less threatening experience; animals, whether encountered in dreams or in the waking state, are never persons, while the dead, although they lose their corporeality, retain their personal names, thoughts, memories, emotions, and their membership in the human category of being. When a living Zuni recognizes the individuality of a dead person in a dream, it implies that the dreamer is as good as dead, whereas for the Quiche this dream would be a meeting of free-souls that might provide an opportunity to learn something of importance from the dead person. (126–27)

A number of other members of the seminar support this idea that broader psychological and spiritual conceptions profoundly shape the experience, sharing, and interpretation of dreams. Basso reverses Tylor's famous dictum (1874) that dreams are the ultimate origin of religion and says that "we see in Kalapalo [a small indigenous people of central Brazil] dreaming theory and its implications that religion, or rather the basic ontological propositions of a people's world view, can just as easily govern the manner of dream interpretation" (102). Benjamin Kilborne shows how the ways in which various peoples classify dreams into different categories stem directly from broader cultural structures: "distinctions made between categories of dreams tend to reflect ideals and values, not simply to describe realities" (185).

At the same time, still other members of the seminar describe how dream sharing and interpretation often has important effects on the cultural structures—and thus how there is a *mutual* influence between dreaming and culture, with formative powers moving in *both* directions. John Homiak refers to the Rastafarian movement of Jamaica as an example of how "dreaming has always been a key source of religious inspiration in prophetic and millenarian movements" (220). Michael Brown describes the uses of dreams by the Aguaruna people of the Andean foothills in Peru to shape their waking world and, in particular, to establish authority and leadership relations:

> Rather than viewing dreams as subjective mental phenomena bearing little relation to events outside of the dreamer's mind, the Aguaruna use dreams and altered states of consciousness as bridges between self and other, as sources of imagery that can be consciously appropriated to alter the dreamer's world. (168)

And Merrill provides details about how communal dream sharing among the Raramuri people of Northern Mexico works as a means of transmitting cultural ideology:

> Dreams are a subject of considerable interest to the Raramuri, often being the first topic of conversation within a household as well as among the members of different households during morning visits. In fact, because they tend to sleep for a few hours, awaken, and then sleep again, they frequently discuss dreams during the course of the night. The role of dream interpreter is not institutionalized within the society, but children are encouraged from an early age to remember their dreams and to recount them to older members of their households, who aid in interpreting them. Such discussions, combined with those among members of different households, are an important means of transmitting and standardizing ideology in the absence of formal institutions, such as schools, for doing so. (203–4)[2]

Having agreed on this basic conclusion regarding the mutual relations of dreaming and culture, Tedlock's seminar discusses some further implications of their work for the general study of dreams. She reports that "we agreed that the concept of manifest content should be expanded to include more than the dream report. Ideally it should include dream theory or theories and ways of sharing, including the relevant discourse frames, and the cultural code for dream interpretation" (25). Also, the seminar decided that the psychoanalytic distinction between primary process and secondary process thought is no longer tenable:

> We were in agreement with Kracke that the distinction between primary process (unconscious and preconscious dream thoughts) and secondary process (conscious dream reports) is much too rigid and not nearly fluid enough to accommodate subtle interchanges of dream and reality that occur in the so-called "dream cultures" in which so many of us have worked. (27)

Tedlock says the seminar came to shift its focus from *dreams* as objects to *dreaming* as an activity in order to avoid reifying dream reports and to acknowledge the continuum between waking and dreaming states, which includes dreams, visions, omens, artistic creativity, and active imagination (29). However, there was also an effort made to avoid blurring some important distinctions between these states. Mannheim argues that the psychoanalytic tendency to interpret myths in the same way as we interpret dreams is mistaken. Tedlock says that

> As an alternative he advocates studying the precise nature of the linkage between dreams and myths by treating dreaming as a "cultural system," or organized by conventional set of signs, which is articulated with but structurally autonomous with respect to other systems, such as narrative. (27)

With these reflections, Tedlock's seminar fundamentally reorients the anthropological study of dreams.[3] By combining their detailed understanding of other cultures with a thorough familiarity with the leading issues of modern dream study, these anthropologists offer insights that are not subservient to the theories of any other field. On the contrary, their explorations take them into new realms of the wilderness of dreams, realms that the other paths of dream research have misunderstood if they have known of them at all.

10

COGNITIVE PSYCHOLOGY: HARRY HUNT

> Perhaps current dream psychology can be likened to puzzling over the physical features of a duck in an immaculate laboratory, when only in its natural setting can the duck demonstrate their function . . . Dream psychology, in haste for its own Darwin, has bypassed the necessary foundations of a Linnaeus. The various available systems of quantitative content analysis are complex and reliable, and they correlate to a degree with cognitive, physiological, and personality variables, but they are still reminiscent of attempting to classify the natural order of species by first, ever so precisely, measuring length of limb, size of tooth, body weight, and so on—disregarding whether the animal is a reptile, fish, bird, or mammal. Dream researchers should rely instead on the initial basis of science: observation, judgement, and classification . . . It is remarkable to me that dream psychology, like cognitive psychology generally, has largely avoided the fundamental observation and ordering of its materials in their natural context.
>
> —Harry Hunt, *The Multiplicity of Dreams*

Cognitive psychology studies the mental processes of memory, reasoning, communication, and imagination—all the various aspects of human intelligence. Dreams have long been of interest to cognitive psychologists as phenomena revealing some of the basic functions of the mind. Jean Piaget's seminal work in cognitive psychology included a number of studies of how children come to understand and reason about their dream experiences (1962, 1963, 1973). David Foulkes has written the most prominent works in this area, most recently *Dreaming: A Cognitive-Psycho-*

logical Analysis (Foulkes 1985; see also 1978, 1982, 1983). Foulkes has long championed the argument that it is impossible to understand dreams without knowing how the cognitive structures of memory, grammar, and logic shape our experiences and our expressions. He denounces those approaches to dreams that try to interpret their meanings without bothering to look at how those meanings are cognitively formed, expressed, and understood by the human mind.

The latest work in the cognitive psychological study of dreams is Harry Hunt's *The Multiplicity of Dreams* (1989), and this is the book on which we shall concentrate. Moving beyond both Piaget and Foulkes in significant ways, Hunt has made great efforts to integrate the research of cognitive psychology with the research of other fields studying dreams. Although Hunt does not have (as yet) the historical stature of his predecessors, his work represents the most advanced statement of the cognitive psychology of dreams and the most stimulating assertion of the relevance of this approach for the modern understanding of dreams. Piaget and Foulkes created the major path into this area of the wilderness, and now Hunt has pushed it on even farther, in directions that are of special interest to us.[1]

Hunt's introductory review of the recent history of dream study, in cognitive psychology and other fields, reveals numerous conflicts, debates, and antinomies. He calls the current situation "a post-modern 'self-deconstruction' of dream psychology" (Hunt 1989, 4). In response to this, Hunt says he is aiming to mediate between what he sees as the two major theories of dreaming. The one, common to researchers like Freud, Hobson, and Foulkes,

> Holds that dreams result from a competition between a coherent organizing system . . . and a more primitive and ultimately disruptive tendency . . . The resultant compromise is then seen as semantically meaningful or randomized nonsense depending on one's understanding of the disrupting agent. (ix–x)

The other theory, found in the works of Jung and James Hillman (a prominent analytical psychologist),

> Holds that the emergent sources of dreaming, at least much of the time, are not "primitive" or "disruptive" at all. Rather they constitute the spontaneous expressions of a symbolic intelligence alternative to standard representational thought and variously termed "imagistic," "affective," or "presentational." (x)

Hunt seeks in *The Multiplicity of Dreams* to develop a cognitive psychology that can describe the formation of dreams in such a way as to do justice to the insights of both theoretical positions. To begin with, he argues that *any* theory of dreams must acknowledge and account for the full range of different dream types. Hunt says,

> If, as most authors believed before psychoanalysis and the laboratory era, there *are* relatively distinct types of dreams, then only by means of their juxtaposition and comparison can we shed light on a dreaming process—whether we conclude that such a process is ultimately unitary or as diverse as the forms it generates. (76)

He emphasizes that among these types of dreams must be included all those rare, "intensified" dream forms which, although they occur infrequently if ever in the sleep lab or in clinical practice, are nevertheless real, distinct, and significant for the study of dreams (45–46).

It is towards this end of describing and categorizing the various types of dreams (and thus following the procedure of the great Swedish naturalist Linnaeus) that Hunt reviews many different sources of dream accounts: texts from the ancient world, anthropological studies, clinical case studies, sleep laboratory research, and the personal experiences of himself and his acquaintances. With this broad array of data in front of him, Hunt offers the following classification of dream types:

- *Personal-mnemic dreams*, regarding common, quotidian matters in the dreamer's life
- *Medical-somatic dreams*, regarding physiological processes of the dreamer's body
- *Prophetic dreams*, presenting omens or images of the future that may come true
- *Archetypal-spiritual dreams*, with vivid, subjectively powerful encounters with numinous forces; often also including extremely strong physical or "titanic" sensations
- *Nightmares*, with upsetting or terrifying images and affects
- *Lucid dreams*, involving consciousness within the dream that one is dreaming

Hunt says that these different forms of dreams do not necessarily occur with equal frequency; on the contrary, some of them occur very rarely

(95–96).[2] But the key point, he argues, is that we recognize that such a range of different forms does in fact exist:

> We find in each historical era and phase of culture a shift in relative importance across a common spectrum of dream typologies. But despite these shifts in the predominant definition and theory of dreaming, despite the contrasting ontological assumptions of these cultures, there is evidence that the same forms of dream experience continue to recur . . . Despite cultural and historical diversity and our own scientific urge toward parsimony, there is a natural order of dream forms. This is our most significant finding. Its implications for a cognitive psychology of dreaming have hitherto not been addressed—let alone its implications for a cognitive science. (90)

Hunt challenges all dream theories (such as those of Freud and Foulkes) that are based solely on the characteristics of one, and only one, of these dream types. At the same time, he rejects any "empty eclecticism" that admits everything and explains nothing (91–92). Rather, Hunt wants to develop a cognitive psychological understanding that can account for processes that generate all the different dream forms, that can give us "insight into a deeper unity of dream formation" (92).

The fundamental problem for such an understanding is how to reconcile those two opposing theories, the one (of Freud, Foulkes, and Hobson) that sees dreams as "stories" organized by propositional structures and the other (of Jung and Hillman) that views dreams as "imagery," spontaneously generated and able to govern narrative development.[3] Hunt's argument is that dreams can be *both*: either of these cognitive processes can take the lead in dream formation. He claims,

> If in fact we have correctly located different types of dreams and if all dreams necessarily mix and match the same dimensions of formation that, separated and exaggerated, produce these types, it follows that narrative structure and visual-spatial imagery will interact variously in dream formation—each will be capable of leading and entraining the other. The dream is an imagistic experience occurring in a creature who structures its ongoing experience in the form of "stories" to be told and understood. (160)

So according to Hunt's argument, Foulkes is right in his assertion that narrative and grammatical structures, the "story lines," can constrain the visual-spatial imagery of dreams (161–62). However, Jung and others are right, too, in believing that unexpected, bizarre imagery often emerges that shapes and even fulfills the narrative course of a dream, rather than disrupting the dream.[4] *Both* of these cognitive modes are at work in dreams:

> We arrive then at a picture of two systems, both self-referential and creatively recombinatory expressions of the human symbolic capacity, interacting in different measures to produce both normative dreaming and its imagistically predominant variations. (168)

Hunt claims that the cognitive processes involved in propositional grammar and in visual-spatial imagery are different from and independent of one another. The different types of dreams would thus reflect different syntheses of these cognitive processes.[5] The more grammar-oriented processes underlie the relatively ordinary personal-mnemic dreams; the more imagistic-oriented processes underlie the rarer "intensified" dreams.[6]

In the final sections of *The Multiplicity of Dreams* Hunt focuses on the latter dream forms, which received far less attention from cognitive psychologists. As an independent cognitive process, Hunt says visual-spatial imagery can generate novel meanings that were not known or understood before and which are not reducible to any underlying verbal processes (108–9). These novel meanings tend to be expressed in metaphorical forms, this being the primary way in which the visual-spatial mode operates:

> Dreams associated with creative discoveries in science, art, and personal dilemmas express an autonomous capacity for visual metaphor that becomes "insight" only when finally articulated. The shock of discovery that accompanies first verbalization of these visual structures suggests that such imagistic thinking can be relatively independent of preceding verbal formulations . . . It is central for a cognitive psychology of dreams that the fantastic transformations of experience in dreams show metaphoric activity *within* dream formation. (100, 216)

Again, Hunt is denying any attempt to reduce all visual and metaphorical images of dreams into preexisting propositional structures. In other words, linguistic expressions of a dream (such as waking dream reports and interpretations) involve a *separate* process from the formation of the dream itself. Although he does not explicitly make the point, Hunt is directly refuting Freud and Hall here. They assert that a dream is at base a verbal proposition that is transformed into imagery—that is, words come first, dream imagery second. Hunt says in some types of dreams, the imagery comes first, and the linguistic expression second (108–9).

The most important reason why the processes of visual-spatial imagery are of such interest is, according to Hunt, that they are often engaged in a sophisticated process of "self-reference," a process of the psyche reflecting upon itself: reflecting on our perceptions, ideas, values, hopes, relations with others and with the world (188–89). Hunt cites "many examples of dreams seemingly based on an autonomous visual-kinesthetic imaginative faculty, whose features, once verbalized, generate novel metaphors for problematic life situations" (109). Among these examples he refers to his own dreams and to the dreams of Jung, of patients of existential psychoanalyst Medard Boss, and of scientific innovators (108–11, 128–40). Such dreams, Hunt claims, "can at times rival works of art in their profound depictions of basic existential issues in human life . . . Such dreams manage to present fundamental life issues in immediate visual-spatial structures that clearly exceed one's conceptual-verbal grasp" (110–11).

Hunt is arguing for a cognitive psychology that recognizes a distinct line of development for visual-spatial imagery, as experienced in dreams and other forms of human symbolic expression (195–202). However, he asserts that the actual ways in which this imagistic capacity are *realized* depends directly on the given cultural context. The key question, he believes, is, does a given culture *encourage* the development of such cognitive capacities or does it *discourage* them? It is important for the purposes of our project to note how Hunt sets his work within a particular vision of modern Western culture. As he studies the history of the various dream types, Hunt shows how different cultures have valued different types (77–92). In past cultures, more emphasis was put on the archetypal-spiritual type of dreams, while in our culture there is much more concern with the personal-mnemic type. Hunt argues that *all* the different types *do* still occur in the dream lives of modern Westerners. However, the nature of modern Western culture is such that certain dream types receive more attention and appreciation, while other dream types are ignored, discouraged, or rejected (87–90). Hunt believes that the modern West focuses more on personal-mnemic dreams and less on imagistic, "intensified" dreams because of the requirements of our technologically oriented society:

> Complex society and urban living will mitigate against the natural development of a self-referential imagistic faculty as surely as they require verbal and technological intelligence. We find here a sociocultural basis for the mnemic and linguistic emphasis of orthodox dream theories and for the tendency of very young children and especially imaginative-intuitive adults to dream in a fashion more reminiscent of tribal peoples. (155)[7]

This poses a problem for modern Western culture, Hunt believes, because it means that we are leaving undeveloped important aspects of human intelligence and are thus significantly limiting our own capacities to know and understand the world.

Hunt's work suggests that modern Westerners, like all humans, have the cognitive capacities to experience religiously meaningful dreams. However, our culture has not encouraged the development of those capacities. As a result, we tend to have a very narrow and highly secularized understanding of the wilderness of dreams.

PART THREE

DREAMS AND INTERPRETATION

11

THE CRISIS OF DREAM INTERPRETATION: GADAMER TO THE RESCUE

What?

—Richard Nixon

Do Dreams Have Meaning?

The foregoing survey reveals to us the work of a number of figures who assert strong claims about the interpretation, the religious meaning, and the cultural relevance of dreams. However, the survey also reveals a dizzying array of approaches, an array so diverse and wide ranging that it seems questionable to treat them as a unified group. Are these figures really studying the same thing? That is the first issue that presents itself to us, well before we study their views on dreams and religious meaning: are these eight explorers even on the same continent?

Yes, they are. One primary concern shared by all these figures is how to understand what dreams *mean* and how dreams may be *interpreted*. However, the eight dream explorers propose many different ideas on this matter, often radically different ideas that directly conflict with one another. Hence comes my claim that the study of dreams is suffering from a "crisis" of interpretation, in the sense that there is so much unresolved debate about what is perhaps *the* most basic issue in all the fields of dream study.

We need, then, to devote our first critical efforts to the resolution of this crisis. Our ability to answer the question, do dreams have religious meaning? directly depends on how we respond to this preliminary question, do dreams have any meaning at all?

Divisive Questions

If we review part 2 with an eye for how the eight figures portray the interpretation of dreams, we find that their disagreements revolve around the following questions.

1. Do dreams have *meaning*, and if so in what degree? Practically all modern dream researchers agree that dreams are meaningful to some extent. Crick and Mitchison's (1983) theory of "reverse learning," the strongest recent denial of dreams having any meaning whatsoever, is generally dismissed as being extreme and without verifiable foundations (Moffitt and Hoffman, 1987, Levin 1990). However, there is no agreement about *how* meaningful dreams are. Freud, for example, claims that *all* dreams are meaningful, even the most "innocent" (Freud [1900] 1965, 215–21). Other figures, however, see some dreams as more and some dreams as less meaningful. Jung distinguishes between "big" and "little" dreams, and Tedlock's anthropological research indicates that many other cultures also draw lines between more and less meaningful dreams. LaBerge suggests that lucid dreams are more meaningful than nonlucid dreams, while Hunt proposes that all the "intensified" forms of dreaming (including lucid dreams, nightmares, and archetypal dreams) are more meaning rich than ordinary, "normative" forms of dreaming are. Hobson goes the farthest on this point, as he claims that while some dreams are meaningful, others are totally meaning*less*—some dreams or parts of dreams truly are nonsense, without any meaning at all.

2. Do dreams have *one* meaning, or *many*? There is a surprising amount of waffling on this issue, with many of the eight figures suggesting first one, then another answer. Freud asserts that dreams have many meanings and that the discovery of one meaning does not mean that others may not still be lurking in the latent content. But then, he compares dream interpretation to translating a hieroglyphic text and to solving a jigsaw puzzle—comparisons that Freud uses to indicate that there is one, and only one, meaning to a dream. Breton believes that a careful analysis can determine *all* the meanings contained in a dream. Hall, like Freud, uses the images of translating texts from foreign languages and of fitting together jigsaw puzzles, and he at times is even more unabashed than Freud is in asserting that there is one meaning to a dream. But then again, he also says at a number of points that dreams often contain many meanings. Jung consistently states that all dreams have many meanings, while Tedlock and Hunt both stress this point very forcefully: Tedlock argues that the many meanings of dreams relate to the many different contexts

(e.g., linguistic, social, interpersonal, metaphysical) in which humans live their lives, and Hunt claims that the many different cognitive processes involved in dreaming lead to many different kinds of meaning.

3. Why are dreams so *strange* in the way they express their meanings? This question refer to the difficulty the waking, conscious mind has in understanding the often bizarre imagery and experiences of dreams. Freud explains this difficulty with his concept of censorship: a psychic censor transforms the disturbing latent thoughts into the manifest content of the dream, intentionally distorting those thoughts so the conscious mind will not be able to understand them. However, almost all subsequent dream researchers reject Freud's reasoning on this issue. Most of them believe that the strangeness of dreams is due to the distinctive way the unconscious expresses itself. The waking mind has difficulty understanding dreams, not because of intentional deception, but because they are expressed in an unusual language. Thus Breton sees dreams speaking in a free, natural form unpolluted by bourgeois values. Jung views dreams as "natural facts," pure expressions of the "objective psyche." Hall believes the unconscious uses a special form of "mental shorthand" to communicate its ideas (note, however, that Hall retains Freud's notion that dreams "translate" thoughts into pictures). Hobson claims dreams are "transparent" in their meaning, the strangeness being due to the only partial success that our higher mental processes have in transforming the random neuronal activity into a coherent story. But Tedlock challenges these post-Freudian claims—she denies that there is any simple, "natural" meaning expressed in dreams and argues instead that dreams are complex products of psychological, linguistic, and social forces.

4. Is there a *cultural* dimension to the meaning(s) of dreams? This question has two aspects: is there any way in which culture influences the meaning of dreams? and, is there any way in which dreams are meaningful, not just for the dreamer, but for the dreamer's culture? Freud believes that in many cases the dream-work makes use of certain "universal symbols," scattered through culture, that have meanings apart from the dreamer's associations. Thus he freely draws on cultural phenomena as resources to use in interpreting dreams. However, he denies that dreams have any meaning *for* culture, as he insists that dreams are purely egoistical and point inwards to the wishes of the dreamer. On this latter point Hall firmly agrees, stating that the meaning of dreams relates to the "subjective reality" of the dreamer and has nothing to do with the "objective reality" of the external world. Breton and the surrealists, however, do see dreams as having meanings for culture: for them dreams reveal the qualities of human life that have been stifled by Western civilization. Jung, like

Freud, identifies the influence of universal cultural symbols in the formation of individual dreams. But unlike Freud and more in line with Breton, Jung also believes that individual dreams can have "collective" meanings that relate to the wider society. LaBerge, too, claims that certain dreams may have, in addition to personal meanings, further meanings that are relevant to broader cultural issues. Hunt argues that cultural attitudes directly influence what forms of dreams we do and do not find meaningful. Tedlock is of course the strongest of our eight explorers in asserting the role of culture in the meanings of dreams. She and her anthropological colleagues show how dream experiences are deeply shaped by cultural factors and also how dreams in turn have meanings which come to influence cultural processes.

5. What are the criteria to determine whether or not a dream interpretation is *valid*? Or, more simply, how do we know if an interpretation is *right*? This is a remarkably vexing question, one that has spurred intense debate among dream explorers. Freud asserts that an interpretation must be cohesive, comprehensive, and clinically useful to be considered valid. Jung, however, denounces Freud for imposing rigid theoretical structures on a dream in order to make his interpretations *appear* cohesive and comprehensive. Jung states flatly that the single criterion is therapeutic value, that is, does the interpretation *work*? Hall rejects both Freud and Jung; he says their standard of therapeutic value is far too subjective, arbitrary, and open to manipulation. Hall's solution is to use a quantitative analysis of dream series, with the criterion being a more rigorous and empirically testable degree of cohesiveness. But then Tedlock claims that Hall's own allegedly objective approach itself suffers from a number of grave anthropological limitations (Tedlock 1987, 20–30; see also Rupprecht, 1985). She argues that only an interpretive approach that includes a detailed understanding of the dreamer's cultural setting can be valid. Hobson attacks Freud's approach with a vengeance, denouncing him for interpretations that are speculative, unwarranted, and reductionistic. However, Hobson himself provides perhaps the weakest criterion of all for knowing when an interpretation is right: he simply asserts that plain "common sense" suffices to recognize the clear, transparent meanings of a dream. It seems appropriate that Hunt, the last of our eight figures, challenges the legitimacy of every preceding set of criteria for interpreting dreams. He claims that a dream interpretation may be valid only if there is an understanding of the cognitive processes underlying each of the different forms of dreaming, for otherwise we may (as most of the other figures do) use the criteria from one dream form to judge—or misjudge, rather—the interpretation of another type of dream.

6. Can dream interpretation be *objective*? More specifically, can dream interpretation be as precise, as certain, and as unambiguous as is research in the natural sciences? Many of the eight figures give yes-and-no answers here. For Freud, the answer is yes, in that with sufficient training, experience, and self-control an analyst can discover the meaning of a dream with objective certainty—Freud sees psychoanalysis, after all, as the newest branch of the natural sciences. But he also answers no, in that dreams are inherently ambivalent phenomena and thus are impossible to analyze with perfect precision. For Breton the answer is yes, because by suspending his or her rational consciousness the artist may express a dream in an objective, unadulterated form; but he also answers no, since the whole surrealist project aims at transcending the limitations of such dichotomies as objectivity versus subjectivity. Jung believes dreams may be studied objectively, according to the "phenomenological" method of the natural sciences, but his emphasis on the interpersonal context in which dream interpretation occurs—the "dialectical" dialogue between patient and analyst—suggests that it cannot be a strictly impersonal, exact process. Hall and Hobson are the closest to giving unambiguously affirmative answers to this question. Hall, with his structuralist dream series method, and Hobson, with his "plain" common sense untainted by psychoanalytic mystifications, both claim that their interpretations are clear, certain, and objective. By contrast, Tedlock and Hunt give the most forcefully negative responses, as they insist that a dream's meaning is inextricably related to a whole host of personal and cultural factors that can never be analyzed with the sort of objective precision found among the natural sciences.

Turning to the Hermeneutics of Gadamer

It is important for us to recognize that these questions lead us to consider issues that extend far beyond the fields of dreams research. The problems of meaning, interpretation, cultural context, and scientific objectivity are all central to what may be called the "modern hermeneutical debate"—the debate over how we should interpret the meaning of various texts. The exact questions that we have just considered in the study of dreams are also being vigorously discussed in many other fields of inquiry. For example, Christian, Islamic, and Jewish theologians are arguing about the extent to which the meaning of sacred texts needs to be adapted to modern circumstances. Judges, politicians, and legal scholars are battling over how to interpret the U.S. Constitution. In American secondary schools and universities, controversy rages about how to teach the "classic" works of Western culture in the light of twentieth-century attitudes towards class, race, ethnicity, and gender. In the social sciences, the debate centers on whether the interpretations of sociology, anthropology, and history can be as exact and as "value-neutral" as the research of the natural sciences. And, ironically enough, discoveries in quantum physics and research by historians of science are calling into question the extent to which the natural sciences themselves are as unambiguous as they have generally claimed to be.

The modern hermeneutic debate is a debate about how to interpret texts, be they legal documents, sacred scriptures, classic books, or scientific data—a debate about how to determine what these texts *mean*. When we look back at our initial survey from this wider perspective, we suddenly realize that the variety of different and often conflicting claims about how to interpret dreams is but one instance of a much broader debate that is raging in the modern West.

Two implications emerge once we recognize the historical and cultural context of the "crisis" of dream interpretation. First, we may find it very helpful to draw upon the works of others who are engaged in the modern hermeneutic debate and to use their ideas as guides in our study of dreams. Second, once we have developed a better understanding of dream interpretation we may be able to contribute some worthwhile insights of our own towards the resolution of that broader debate. We will pursue this second possibility in the conclusion. For now, we will follow the path opened up by the first implication. My proposal is to use the hermeneutic philosophy of Hans-Georg Gadamer to help us address the issues mentioned above. Gadamer's ideas will enrich our understanding of what dreams mean and of how we interpret them. He will help us develop a philosophically sound set of guidelines for dream interpretation. We will then be well prepared for exploring the particular issue of whether dreams have religious meaning.

This proposal may, at first sight, seem excessively troublesome. Must we go outside the fields of dream study and draw upon a complex philosophical theory to help us understand how to interpret dreams? I believe that yes, we must. As we have seen, the disagreements over the meaning and the interpretation of dreams are very strong—and yet, no one *within* the various fields of dream study seems to be having any real success in resolving the disagreements. Dream study is to a remarkable degree a hermeneutically backwards area of inquiry. The simple fact that the 1980s saw the publication of the works of Crick and Mitchison, LaBerge, Hobson, Tedlock, and Hunt, all so important and yet all so radically divergent in their answers to the six key questions we just considered, shows that the disagreements are not going to go away by themselves.

Another, perhaps more whimsical reason why it is especially appropriate for us to turn to hermeneutics has to do with the etymology of that term. Hermes was the messenger god of the Greeks, flying down from Mount Olympus on his winged sandals to deliver the gods' messages to humans. "Hermeneutics" was originally conceived as the practice of interpreting sacred texts, texts in which the will of the gods could be discerned. Only in the last couple of centuries has hermeneutics been generalized to the practice of all interpretation. But we will note with special interest that Hermes was also the deliverer of dreams, particularly those dreams in which the gods engaged in some particular communication with humans (Brown, 1969). We may be reassured, then, that it is mythologically and etymologically legitimate for us to turn to hermeneutics to understand how to interpret the meanings of dreams.

Truth and Method: Gadamer on Interpretation

Hans-Georg Gadamer is a contemporary German philosopher working in the phenomenological tradition of Edmund Husserl and Martin Heidegger. He shares with that tradition concerns about the conditions that shape human existence, about language as a fundamental influence on our experiences, and about the epistemological status of science (Palmer 1969; Bleicher 1980; Bubner 1981). In particular, phenomenology focuses on hermeneutics, on the processes involved in the interpretation of experience.

Gadamer's magnum opus, *Truth and Method*, is one of the most important works written in this tradition. It is a massive study of the philosophy of interpretation, rich with insights for a variety of disciplines. If we take the time to develop an understanding of Gadamer's views on meaning, interpretation, truth, and objectivity, we will, I believe, find him to be an excellent guide in helping us to resolve the "crisis" of dream interpretation.

Is Art Knowledge?

Gadamer starts *Truth and Method* with a consideration of truth as it emerges in the experience of art: he asks, what sort of *knowledge* is involved in our encounter with a work of art? As he looks at the history of the philosophy of art, Gadamer sees a progressive tendency to reduce aesthetics to a matter of purely subjective, personal experience. As a result, Western philosophy has come to believe that art has no relationship with truth, no relationship with objective knowledge of the world. Art is seen as having no purpose or function beyond the sheer expression of beauty—an expression that each individual appreciates subjectively.[1] But Gadamer argues that this view is illegitimate, because it assumes there can be "abstracted" perception, i.e., perception that is pure and immediate, untainted by any preconceptions: "Abstraction until only the 'purely aesthetic' is left is obviously a self-contradictory process . . . Pure seeing and pure hearing are dogmatic abstractions which artificially reduce phenomena. *Perception always includes meaning*" (Gadamer 1975, 80, 82; emphasis added). All perception, Gadamer says, whether it be in the realm of science, philosophy, everyday experience, or art, involves the active participation of the perceiver: whenever we perceive *anything* we make discriminations, note relations, and form tentative judgements. Our perception is never a pure mirroring, "never a simple reflection of what is presented to the senses" (81). We always perceive something *as* something; we always draw what we perceive into a relationship with our world.

Based on this criticism of the theory of pure perception, Gadamer is moved to ask, "must we not also allow of aesthetic experience what we say of perception, namely that it perceives truth, i.e. remains related to knowledge?" (81). The experience of art is *knowledge*, he claims, because it is a mode of understanding our world:

> Inasmuch as we encounter the work of art in the world and a world in the individual work of art, this does not remain a strange universe into which we are magically transported for a time. Rather, we learn to understand ourselves in it, and that means that we preserve the discontinuity of the experience in the continuity of our existence. (86)

The tension between the discontinuity and the continuity of the experience of art with our world is central to Gadamer's understanding of the truth of art. At this point in his argument, he emphasizes the continuity of art and world. While "aesthetic differentiation" strictly separates the two, Gadamer claims that the experience of art involves exactly the same basic characteristics of making discriminations, connections, and judgements involved in every one of our perceptual experiences. These characteristics are all part of the process of relating what we perceive to our world, and thus of *knowing* what we perceive. To the extent, then, that it partakes of the key features common to all perception, the experience of art is indeed a genuine mode of knowing our world.[2]

Art as Play

Having established that art is a means to knowledge, Gadamer turns to consider what *kind* of knowledge it is. He takes the concept of 'play' as the starting point for his reflections on the truth of art. We may gain some understanding of Gadamer's rather dry and convoluted exposition of the main features of play by considering an example of our own—a group of children "playing house."[3] With little more than a couple of small plates, some used clothing, and a chunk of play-dough, a group of children can easily develop an elaborate and engrossing game of house. Each child will adopt a particular role—mommy, daddy, baby, kitty, and so on—and play with the others according to the "rules" of the game. In this case the rules involve the general behaviors expected of each of the characters in each given situation. Thus when it is "dinner time," the mommy and daddy will prepare and serve the food, the baby will cry with hunger, and the kitty will try to sneak food off of the table. The rules are structured enough so that each character has an overall sense of what to do, but they are flexible enough so that each character may freely express him or herself.

We can see all the principal qualities that Gadamer identifies in the philosophical concept of play in this example of children playing house. To begin with, he says all play requires that "the player lose himself in his play . . . The mode of being of play does not allow the player to behave towards play as if it were an object" (92). The children playing house do in an important sense *become* the characters they are playing; the enjoyment of the game directly depends on how much the children can "lose" themselves in the playing. A negative confirmation of this occurs when another child from outside the game comes by and says scornfully, "you're not *really* a daddy just because you've put an old tie around your neck." At best, this shows that this child is not a player of the game; at worst, such a comment can ruin the whole game for the other children because it shatters the self-forgetfulness of the children in their play—it forces them to confront their game as an "object."

A second characteristic Gadamer notes about play is its "medial nature": having surrendered ourselves *in* play, we also surrender ourselves *to* the play, to its movement, its spirit, its flow.[4] He says "in order for there to be a game, there always has to be, not necessarily literally another player, but something else with which the player plays and which automatically responds to his move with a counter-move" (95). In the example of playing house, the game flows to the extent that the children interact back and forth with each other. The greatest fun comes when the unfolding of the game produces a novel situation to which the children must respond creatively. The mommy starts serving dinner, and suddenly the baby throws the food on the floor; now the mommy must come up with an appropriate response to the baby. Again, a negative confirmation of the importance of this characteristic occurs when one particular child dominates the game. If one of the children assumes control over all the others by dictating behavior and dialogue to them, the game is ruined; without the to-and-fro movement in which *all* the children actively and freely participate, there is no play. Gadamer summarizes this quality by saying "*all playing is a being-played*" (95).

A third feature of play, which has already been anticipated in Gadamer's discussion of knowledge in art, is the transformative tension between self-forgetfulness and a continuity with one's self and world. Far from being a discontinuous escape from ourselves, play is fundamentally a process by which we forget ourselves and then *regain* a richer understanding of ourselves. Consider again the playing house game. Anyone who has watched children play such a game knows that, while they are certainly having fun, the children are also engaging in a serious exploration of the nature of the different roles they are playing. What is it like to be a mommy? To be a daddy? How do parents and children get along? When the playing ends, the children emerge from the game transformed; precisely by means of a surrender of their ordinary selves in and to the playing, the children leave the play with a deeper understanding of their selves in the world of their families.

These characteristics of losing oneself, of an interactional, to-and-fro movement, and of a continuity with one's self are, Gadamer claims, common to all forms of play—from playing with a ball, to participating in a religious ritual, to encountering a work of art (95, 98).

The key point of this lengthy reflection on the nature of play is to describe a kind of truth that we come to know in a way *other* than by means of the detached, impersonal, objective method of the natural sciences. The truths we learn in play come only through an active engagement with that which we would know; we enter into a relationship with the object of knowledge and allow ourselves to follow the unfolding of that relationship. Again, what we learn is genuine knowledge, because like all knowledge we relate it back to our world. Gadamer does not deny that natural scientific method yields knowledge. His principal concern is to show that in *addition* to the natural scientific method there are other means of discovering truth, other ways of genuinely knowing the world.

The Human Sciences and the Historicality of Understanding

Gadamer next considers the implications of his ideas about art, play, and knowledge for the research of the human sciences—all those fields of inquiry (in American universities, spanning across the humanities and the social sciences) that examine human life and experience. He wants to describe how the human sciences provide us with genuine knowledge,

knowledge that is distinct from but not inferior to the knowledge gained in the natural sciences.[5]

Gadamer begins by considering the key characteristic of understanding in the human sciences, namely its *historicality*. The study of human life and experience cannot ignore the fact that we are *historical* beings, always shaped by the special circumstances of our particular time and place in history. Thus researchers in the human sciences need to recognize that their work is profoundly influenced by their *own* historical context, by the forces of their particular world. However, the inescapable fact of this influence raises one enormously challenging question: how is it that the historicality of the human sciences does not render all of their findings merely relative, subjective, and contingent? Put more bluntly, is all research in the human sciences nothing more than personal opinion, interesting perhaps but never *true*?

Gadamer answers this question by drawing upon the phenomenological concept of the 'fore-structure of understanding' (235).[6] The fact that the interpreter of a given text is an historical being with a fore-structure, that is, with expectations, assumptions, and interests, is not a fact to be avoided or denied, as it is in the methodology of the natural sciences. Rather, this fore-structure has a *positive* significance, in that it orients the interpreter towards the text.[7] What Gadamer calls the "hermeneutical circle" (a term first used by Wilhelm Dilthey) is the process of moving from the interpreter's fore-structure to the text and back again:

> A person who is trying to understand a text is always performing an act of *projecting*. He projects before himself a meaning for the text as a whole as soon as some initial meaning emerges in the text. Again, the latter emerges only because he is reading the text with particular expectations in regard to a certain meaning. The working out of its fore-project, which is constantly revised in terms of what emerges as he penetrates into the meaning, is understanding what is there . . . This constant process of new projection is the movement of understanding and interpretation. (236)

In this way, then, it is precisely our historicality that makes understanding in the human sciences *possible*. The essential point is that our personal and historically situated expectations, assumptions, and interests do not obscure our interpretations or render them merely subjective. Rather, Gadamer argues, in the human sciences our subjective views are the very conditions of our understanding anything at all.

The Revival of the Concept of Prejudice

Gadamer recognizes the boldness of his claims here, for what he is in effect proposing is the legitimacy of prejudices, of judgements made prior to an encounter with something. The term *prejudice* has an almost exclusively negative connotation in modern usage, suggesting attitudes that are unwarranted, narrow, and destructive to open encounters with others. Gadamer recalls, however, that in its *original* usage the term prejudice meant "a judgement that is given before all the elements that determine a situation have been finally examined" (240); such judgements could be false, but they could also be true—only in the course of further examination could this be decided. Thus "prejudice" properly means "a *provisional* judgement," not necessarily "a *false* judgement."

The later, negative connotation to the term *prejudice* emerged in the time of the Enlightenment. Beginning with Descartes's method of accepting nothing as certain which can in any way be doubted, the spirit of autonomous rationality came to challenge the validity of all prejudices. It became the cardinal principle of the Enlightenment, and later of modern science, to exclude completely all such provisional judgements, so that the light of "pure reason" could determine the true nature of the given phenomenon. The Enlightenment certainly succeeded in exploding many of the false, unwarranted judgements that had restricted human inquiry for centuries (241). However, Gadamer's claim is that in this process the Enlightenment went too far, to the point of denying the possibility that there are *legitimate* prejudices, prejudices which *help* in understanding the world.[8] The Enlightenment and its heir, modern science, thus came to assert that the only legitimate knowledge was that gained by a method of strict, objective rationality unconditioned by any historical circumstances.

Gadamer's studies of art, play, and the human sciences has led him to the contrary conclusion, that "all understanding inevitably involves some prejudices" (239; see also 247). Thus he challenges the Enlightenment by turning its method on itself: "there is one prejudice of the Enlightenment that is essential to it: the fundamental prejudice of the Enlightenment is the prejudice against prejudice itself" (239–40).

Gadamer has argued that the principles of modern science are not the ultimate arbiters of knowledge, that the experience of art and the interpretations of the human sciences are fundamentally "playful" and do involve legitimate discoveries of truth, and that the historicality of human existence is both inescapable and potentially positive. If we accept these claims, then we must agree with Gadamer that the "prejudice against prejudice itself" distorts understanding in all spheres of human inquiry. The quest for a purely objective, unprejudiced attitude has the result of severely impoverishing our experience and knowledge of the world.

Criteria for Valid Interpretations

However, we may follow Gadamer this far and yet still raise a critical question—how do we know that our "prejudices," that is, our expectations, assumptions, and interests, are *not* false? Granted that there may be "legitimate" or "productive" prejudices that open up meanings for us, how do we distinguish these from illegitimate prejudices that distort meanings? (266) To begin with, Gadamer emphasizes that we must remain *open* to a text: we must adopt an attitude of questioning, of sensitivity to the newness of the text, of being prepared for the text to tell us something; "the important thing is to be aware of one's own bias, so that the text may present itself in all its newness and thus be able to assert its own truth against one's own fore-meanings" (238). Again, Gadamer stresses that this is not the same as the modern scientific ideal of strict neutrality and objectivity, for "this openness always includes our placing the other meaning in a relation with the whole of our own meanings or ourselves in a relation to it" (238). It is an openness from *within* a relationship, not from a detached position *outside* the relationship.[9]

But this is still not enough, for merely being aware of our biases does not yet help us determine which of them promote understanding and which of them distort it. Gadamer agrees that we cannot distinguish true from false fore-meanings in the abstract (263). We can accomplish this only, he says, in the very *activity* of interpretation itself. Thus,

> It is impossible to make ourselves aware of it [a given prejudice] while it is constantly operating unnoticed, but only when it is, so to speak, *stimulated* . . . Understanding begins, as we have already said above, when something addresses us . . . In fact our own prejudice is properly brought into play through its being at risk. Only through its being given full play is it able to experience the other's claim to truth and make it possible for he himself to have full play. (266; emphasis added)

So it is in the process of interpretation itself that we learn to distinguish legitimate from illegitimate fore-meanings. A primary criterion for making this distinction is that our interpretation achieves a high degree of consistency, coherency, and comprehensiveness with regards to the text as a whole:

> Thus the movement of understanding is constantly from the whole to the part and back to the whole. Our task is to extend in concentric circles the unity of the understood meaning. The harmony of all the details with the whole is the criterion of correct understanding. The failure to achieve this harmony means that understanding has failed. (259)

A further criterion for confirming that a prejudice or bias is legitimate is how well the interpretation "works-out," that is, how well it helps us achieve the practical tasks that motivated us to approach the given text in the first place. Arbitrary or inappropriate prejudices, Gadamer says, "come to nothing in the working-out" (237).

Gadamer acknowledges that this process of understanding has in principle no final point, no ultimate conclusion; "the discovery of the true meaning of a text or a work of art is never finished; it is in fact an infinite process" (265). To the charge that this leaves Gadamer's whole interpretive approach devoid of any objective grounding, Gadamer responds that such a charge betrays the continued dominance of the Enlightenment prejudice: the demand for knowledge that is always certain, universal, and purely objective. This demand is vain, Gadamer argues throughout *Truth and Method*, and the expectation that such knowledge is even possible can no longer be upheld as the supreme standard by which all interpretations are measured.

While we may grant Gadamer's major point, that the traditional Enlightenment criteria of objectivity, universality, and certainty are no longer valid for the evaluation of all interpretations, we may nevertheless remain unsatisfied with his characterization of the new, more appropriate criteria. For example, what would allow us to decide which of two interpretations, both of which seem to "work-out," is better? How do we adjudicate between interpretations that directly conflict? How, with such reliance on our already-existent prejudices, can we ever recognize meanings that might radically differ from and challenge our conventional views? Such questions persist even after we finish *Truth and Method*. We will want to remember these questions and see if we cannot provide answers to them in our later reflections.

The Fusion of Horizons

Gadamer stresses the importance of being *conscious* of the ways our historical context affects our interpretations.[10] To illustrate the nature of this consciousness, Gadamer uses the image of a horizon. A horizon is the "range of vision that includes everything that can be seen from a particular vantage point" (269). This image indicates that all our experiences occur within a particular historical situation that influences or effects how we come to know our experiences. The process of interpretation does not involve rising above all horizons (as it does in the natural scientific model) nor leaving one's own horizon and entering that of the other (as it does in the romantic model of interpretation[11]). Rather, Gadamer asserts that the process is one of a *fusion* of horizons, that "understanding, rather, is always the *fusion of these horizons* which we imagine to exist by themselves" (273).

The *fusing* of horizons is crucial because it emphasizes the playful tension involved in any interpretive encounter between the horizon of the text and the horizon of the interpreter. The important theme of discontinuity and continuity, first raised in relation to the nature of art and play, reappears here. Gadamer argues that interpretation as a fusion of horizons involves both a moment of "distinguishing" and a moment of "recombining." "Distinguishing" involves the recognition of the text as other, as different, thereby resisting "the overhasty assimilation of the [text] to our own expectations of meaning" (272). "Recombining" is bringing the encounter back into relation with the horizon of the interpreter; the consciousness of the interpreter "recombines what it has distinguished in order, in the unity of the historical horizon that it thus acquires, to become again one with itself" (273). The playful tension between these two moments propels the hermeneutic process. Gadamer says,

> The hermeneutic task consists in not covering up this tension by attempting a naive assimilation but consciously bringing it out . . . In the process of understanding there takes place a real fusing of horizons, which means that as the historical horizon is projected, it is simultaneously removed. (273)

Interpretation as Dialogue

The best model for all these characteristics of the hermeneutic process is the dialogue. The essence of a dialogue, Gadamer believes, consists in the shared inquiry into a question. To inquire into a question requires the recognition that one does *not know*; "in order to be able to ask, one must want to know, which involves knowing that one does not know . . . Discourse that is intended to reveal something requires that that thing be opened up by the question" (326).

The model of the dialogue indicates a further important aspect of the process of interpretation. We must not only become aware of our *own* questions as we interpret a text—we must also discover the questions asked of us by the text itself. When we bring our particular views and interests to a text, we invite the text to *respond to* those views and interests. For example, in constitutional law we bring our questions about, say, flag burning to the interpretation of the first amendment; and then we listen as the constitution *responds to* us, raising questions of its own about how we understand free speech, national symbols, and political protest. In such a process we engage in a genuine dialogue with the text, a two-way conversation in which we question the text, then listen as the text questions *us*, and then ask new questions of our own, on and on. Gadamer stresses that such a dialogue is more than simply determining what the text's alleged "original meaning" once was. Rather, it is the process of bringing the text into relation to our world, to our questions—it is the process, in Gadamer's words, of a fusion of horizons (see 336–37, 355–57).

Gadamer admits that such a view of interpretation implies that what appears to *us* as a text's meaning will not be the same as that which appears to *others* from a different perspective; "it is part of the historical finiteness of our being that we are aware that after us others will understand in a different way" (336). But this is not to surrender to any relativism or arbitrariness in interpretation. The fundamental point here is that only by relating the text to our world may the text "be understood as an answer to a real question"—that is, to a question that is vital, alive, and meaningful to the world of the interpreters (337).[12]

Truth

So what, after all of this, is now to be made of the concept of truth? If we do not always determine truth according to the methods of scientific rationality, how else do we warrant the validity of our knowledge? Gadamer offers two thoughts in the concluding pages of *Truth and Method*. First, he suggests that poetry furnishes a good illustration of how truth emerges in language. He says "what comes into language in a poem moves, as it were, into *relationships of order* that support and guarantee the 'truth' of what is said" (445; emphasis added). These "relationships of order" indicate that we seek to root poetic utterance, and language in general, in the social and historical circumstances of our situation. Truth is not a matter of matching a word or proposition to some fixed, eternal standard but rather a *relating* of the claim to the world of human experience. Gadamer is thus suggesting that our interpretations are true because they make sense in the broader context of what we already know and believe.[13]

Second, Gadamer returns to the notion of play. Understanding is a process of play in the sense of requiring us to enter into a relationship with the given claim. The same characteristics of self-forgetfulness, surrender to the movement of the encounter, and relating of the self-forgetfulness with one's world are as essential in understanding truth, Gadamer believes, as they are in the process of play. The equation of understanding with play reaffirms his central thesis that the truths of art and the human sciences involve us fully in a relationship with that which we would know; "someone who understands is *always already* drawn into an event through which meaning asserts itself" (446; emphasis added). Gadamer concludes *Truth and Method* with the following:

> Thus there is undoubtedly no understanding that is free of all prejudices, however much the will of our knowledge must be directed towards escaping their thrall. It has emerged throughout our investigation that the certainty that is imparted by the use of scientific methods does not suffice to guarantee truth . . . Rather, what the tool of method does not achieve must—and effectively can—be achieved by a *discipline of questioning and research*, a discipline that guarantees truth. (446–47; emphasis added)

So even in making the strongest case he can against the hegemony of modern science, Gadamer nevertheless believes that genuine truth and knowledge are indeed possible. The point of emphasizing the inevitable historicality of all our experiences is by no means to surrender all hopes of truth. On the contrary, we try to "escape the thrall" of our prejudices to the extent that our unconsciousness of them allows them to narrow our vision and thus to close us off from the claims of new experiences. That "discipline of questioning and research," a concise description of the hermeneutic process, is the best means of broadening our horizons and developing our understanding of the world.

Such, in a very abbreviated form, is Gadamer's philosophy of interpretation. It is not a simple approach to interpreting texts. But then again, if we look back at the ideas of the different dream explorers, we see that none of the allegedly simple approaches stand up to critical scrutiny. It may be better, therefore, to surrender the quest for a simple means of interpreting dreams, and to see what comes with a more complex, philosophically sophisticated approach.

12

A HERMENEUTIC CRITIQUE OF MODERN DREAM INTERPRETATION THEORIES

> At dawn my lover comes to me
> And tells me of her dreams,
> With no attempts to shovel the glimpse
> Into the ditch of what each one means
>
> —Bob Dylan, "Gates of Eden"

Is a Dream a Text?

In this chapter we will use Gadamer's ideas to evaluate critically the different dream interpretation theories we have reviewed and thus to help us make some sense of the various insights presented in those theories. However, we must first consider an issue that we did not address as we reviewed the different dream theories: to what extent can a dream be considered a text? Many dream explorers object to characterizing dreams as texts. For example, anthropologist Waud Kracke, a participant in Tedlock's seminar, argues that regarding dreams as texts neglects the fact that the dreamer has direct access to the spatial-sensory aspects of the dream experience, while other interpreters do not (Tedlock 1987, 22).[1] Psychotherapists like Robert Bosnak (1988, 1989), Eugene Gendlin (1986), and Arnold Mindell (1982, 1985) condemn overly intellectual and linguistic approaches to dreams, and focus instead on the physical and emotional experiences of dreams. Existential analysts like Medard Boss (1958) and Erik Craig (1988) question whether the drive to "interpret" dream texts may not violate the integrity of dreaming existence. Similarly, analytical psychologist James Hillman (1979) believes that we should not insist on raising the dream into the waking world, but rather should bring consciousness down into the "underworld" of the dream. For all these dream explorers, the notion that dreams are "texts" is very troubling. We must spend a moment reflecting on this issue, because if we are unsure about the legitimacy of treating dreams as texts, then perhaps we cannot justifiably apply Gadamer's hermeneutic philosophy to the study of dreams.

I believe we can acknowledge these concerns and still legitimately consider dreams as texts. For the purposes of our project, I propose we take a broad view of what a "text" is: a text is that which we interpret; whatever we can fruitfully interpret is a text.

Many people think the term is applied excessively in current usage, that the whole world is being "textualized" by modern critics: the U.S. Constitution and the Bible may be texts, but is the human body a text? Are TV sitcoms, hairstyles, graffiti-covered walls all to be considered "texts"?[2] We do not need to become involved in such questions, interesting as they may be, in order to assert that dreams may legitimately be treated as texts. This assertion simply means that dreams are *interpretable*. Consequently, studying how other kinds of texts are interpreted (e.g., studying Gadamer's ideas on interpretation in art and the human sciences) may teach us something about interpreting dreams.

What this assertion does *not* mean is that dreams must be recorded in some permanent, fixed linguistic form before we can interpret them properly. The broad view of texts I am proposing includes much more than pieces of paper with writing on them. Thus, legitimate dream texts may take the form of written narratives, but they may *also* take the forms of oral communications, artistic expressions, or the private bodily sensations and emotional experiences remembered by the dreamer.[3] It is true, as Kracke notes, that the dreamer is the only person having access to the sensory-spatial aspects of the dream. But this does *not* render dreams entirely opaque to interpretation. On the contrary, it marks a special quality of dream texts that interpreters must account for in their work.

Two further problems arise with this characterization of dreams as texts. One is that some of these forms may change (unlike allegedly "fixed" texts like constitutions and bibles). But the fact that oral dream reports and privately remembered dream experiences may change over time does not automatically disqualify them as texts. It only means that we must take special measures in interpreting them, recognizing that they are especially sensitive to alterations in the dreamer's emotional state, in the context of the reporting, in the temporal distance from the dream experience, and so forth.

A second problem seems even more vexing. Any dream text is inevitably mediated by the dreamer's consciousness—it is never a "pure," "unaltered" product. Freud calls this mediating process "secondary elaboration." Given this inevitable influence of the dreamer's consciousness, any attempt we make to examine a dream text, whether written, oral, artistically expressed, or privately remembered would seem to be nothing but an interpretation of second-hand goods. Most pessimistically, this problem appears to invalidate the whole project of dream interpretation, for we can never get beyond our conscious alterations to reach the true, "original" dream. It would thus be better, perhaps, to call our project "conscious dream report interpretation."

The key to resolving this problem comes in challenging the assumption that there is in fact a true, original dream underlying the consciously influenced dream we remember and express when awake. A number of the dream theorists we have studied give us persuasive reasons for rejecting that assumption and for believing instead that dreams are in their very formation thoroughly influenced by the consciousness of the dreamer. Freud states that the process of secondary elaboration occurs not only after we awake from a dream, but also *within* the dream itself; the categories, conceptions, and attitudes of consciousness are directly and inevitably involved in the dream's "original" formation (Freud [1900] 1965, 526–46). Hobson describes how a dream results from the random neuronal activities being shaped by higher mental processes into some semblance of a coherent story. According to him, there is no dream before these mental processes literally "interpret" the neuronal activities. And LaBerge's research into lucid dreaming offers perhaps the most striking evidence that consciousness may play a direct role in the dream formation process.

Rather than pursuing a quixotic search for an original dream text that many dream researchers suggest simply does not exist, we are better off directing our interpretive energies towards the dream texts we have: remembered images, oral reports, written narratives, and artistic expressions.[4] We certainly do not want to ignore the fact that these texts have been influenced by the dreamer's consciousness to varying degrees, for this is a matter we must always take into account in our interpretations. But we should no longer be misled by the idea that our interpretations are legitimate only if we have somehow managed to grasp an alleged "ur-dream."[5]

We may now, therefore, return to those divisive issues that generate so much controversy among dream interpreters and see if Gadamer's hermeneutic theories help us understand matters better.

The Meaningfulness of Dreams

Gadamer argues that the meaning of a text emerges out of a process of dialogue, where the interpreter's questions initiate a back-and-forth exchange between the interpreter and the text. Accordingly, it is nonsensical to speak of a text's having or not having meaning apart from the active engagement in this process—the only way we can tell if a text has meaning is by trying to interpret it. If we apply these points to the debate over whether dreams have meaning at all, we find first of all that Gadamer's ideas challenge any strong "anti-meaning" position such as that held by Crick and Mitchison (1983): it is senseless to make a blanket statement about dreams having *no* meaning without ever actively trying to interpret them. Gadamer's work also calls into question Hobson's claim that some dreams are truly nonsensical. Hobson's neurological research has given us reason to question whether everything in a dream is meaningful; but it nevertheless remains necessary to engage in the interpretation process before we can know *which* specific aspects are meaningful and *which* are nonsensical.

Gadamer also helps us understand better the varying ideas of Freud, Breton, Jung, Hall, LaBerge, Tedlock, and Hunt about how some dreams are more meaningful than others. His work shows that what is missing in this debate is any explicit awareness of how the specific questions we ask influence the meanings we encounter: dreams may be more or less meaningful according to the different questions we ask of them. For example, Freud asks the question of whether a given dream relates in some way to the dreamer's unconscious life; he finds in every case that the dream does. Thus his claim that all dreams are meaningful, in relation to this particular question, is legitimate. Jung asks the question of whether a given dream is "big" in the sense of presenting a numinous vision of archetypal powers; he finds that this occurs only rarely. Thus his claim that there are "big" dreams and "little" dreams, according to the criteria provided by this particular question, is legitimate.

The resolution of this debate comes when we stop asking the question in an abstract form.[6] We cannot say, a priori, whether dreams are or are not meaningful apart from actively engaging in the process of interpretation itself, apart from asking particular questions of actual dreams and seeing what comes of them.

Rejecting the "One Meaning" View

To the second divisive question we encountered, that is, the question of whether dreams have one meaning or many meanings, Gadamer provides us with emphatic arguments against the "one meaning" view. The metaphors of solving a puzzle and of translating a text from a foreign language, both used by Freud and Hall, appear in the light of Gadamer's hermeneutics to be thoroughly misleading accounts of the process of dream interpretation. Freud and Hall alike offer these metaphors to suggest that a successful interpretation yields one true, certain meaning for a dream, with no other meanings being possible—a puzzle has but one solution, and a translation is but a reproduction of the original text's meaning in a new language. But Gadamer specifically cites the example of translating texts in foreign languages to show that interpretations *never* produce one simple, conclusive meaning. He says,

> The translator must translate the meaning to be understood into the context in which the other speaker lives. This does not, of course, mean that he is at liberty to falsify the meaning of what the other person says. Rather, the meaning must be preserved, but since it must be understood within a new linguistic world, it must be expressed within it in a new way. Thus every translation is at the same time an interpretation . . . [T]he translation of a text, however much the translator may have felt himself into his author, cannot be simply a re-awakening of the original event in the mind of the writer, but a recreation of the text that is guided by the way the translator understands what is said in it. No one can doubt that we are dealing here with interpretation, and not simply with reproduction. (Gadamer 1975, 346–47)

Gadamer believes that the situation of the translator of a foreign language text is paradigmatic of all interpretation, in the sense that every interpretation involves some degree of "re-creation," some degree of adaptation of the text's meaning to the world of the interpreter.[7] Ironically, then, Freud and Hall undercut their own positions by comparing dream interpretation to the translation of foreign language texts. Whereas they intend the comparison to turn on the *singularity* of the meaning being translated, Gadamer helps us see that the similarity derives from the *multiplicity* of meanings that inevitably, and legitimately, emerge from the efforts of different interpreters working out of different contexts.

The basic point we may draw from Gadamer's ideas on translation and meaning is that there may be as many meanings to a text as there are interpreters who ask questions of it, who try to "translate" it. Gadamer thus supports Jung, Tedlock, and Hunt in their claims that dreams have not one but many levels of meaning. If nothing else, a hermeneutic perspective should put to rest forever the idea that a dream has only one meaning.

A corollary to this point is that there is no final meaning of a text, nor any definitive, absolute end to the interpretation of a dream, because new questions can always be asked of it. The interpretation of a dream may have a *practical* end, in that we may find in a given dream sufficient meanings for our purposes. But this practical end should not be confused with any absolute end—as, for example, Breton claims to have reached in the interpretation of his dream. The fact that an interpreter has discovered certain meanings in a dream can never justify the conclusion that there are no *other* meanings to the dream.

Dream Texts as Strange

Gadamer says that in almost every encounter with a text there is a moment of strangeness, of surprise at the distance of the text from our world. This is the moment when the interpreter recognizes that he or she does not know what the text means and that work must be done to make the text familiar enough so that some meaning may emerge. This recognition spurs the asking of questions and the initiation of a dialogue that can bring the interpreter into a relationship with the text.

Our attempts to interpret dreams are virtually always characterized by this moment of strangeness. We wake up in the morning and are amazed by the extraordinary, often bizarre occurrences of our dreams. Dream explorers, as we have seen, hold very different ideas about why dreams are so strange. Gadamer is not a psychologist or a neuroscientist and thus cannot say much about the processes by which dreams are formed. But as a hermeneutic philosopher he does propose two ideas that have direct bearing on the ways dream interpreters address this particular issue. First, Gadamer cautions interpreters against assuming that the initial strangeness of a text is a permanent characteristic. Some degree of strangeness is inevitable at the beginning of any interpretive work, and it will diminish as that work proceeds. Second, Gadamer stresses the need to respect this strangeness, to remain open to the possibility that even after a great deal of interpretation we still will not know the text fully. The danger here is that we may assimilate the text too quickly to our expectations of understanding and thus fail to discover as many new, unexpected meanings from the text as we otherwise might have.

On this first point, we find that Freud has severe troubles. He simply assumes that dreams are by their very nature strange, and he attributes this strangeness to the intentional actions of a psychological censor mechanism. But as other dream interpreters point out, Freud ignores the possibility that he might not have spent enough time listening to the dreams themselves. If he had, he would have found that dreams are not as incomprehensibly garbled as he insists they are, and he would not have had to postulate psychic censors to account for their formation. Dreams remain strange to Freud because he makes a permanent feature out of a temporary condition: in Gadamer's terms, Freud mistakes the initial strangeness of dreams (a characteristic of the initial encounter with any text) for an essential, defining feature of them.

Tedlock also has some troubles in the light of Gadamer's first point here. She suggests that we cannot fully understand a dream's meaning without intimate, detailed knowledge of the linguistic, historical, and sociological features of the dreamer's culture. Tedlock's comments about moving from "depth to depth" in dream interpretation are certainly well taken, for most modern dream interpreters have extremely poor understandings of the influence of culture on dreams. Yet she puts her argument in such strong terms that it renders the dream so strange as to seem virtually unknowable. In a way similar to Freud, Tedlock makes the almost insurmountable strangeness of dreams a first principle of interpretation.

Gadamer provides a way to balance Tedlock's approach. He emphasizes that *all* understandings, even the most thorough and sophisticated, are partial, and that every text will always remain "strange" to some degree. In the case of dream interpretation, no matter how much linguistic and sociological awareness we have we will still not understand everything in the dream—and yet, and this is the crucial point, we may nevertheless understand *something* of it. The fact that all dream interpretations are inevitably partial thus tempers to an extent Tedlock's critique. This is not to sanction interpretations that blithely ignore linguistic and sociological aspects of dreams. Instead, it is to recognize that we may achieve some degree of genuine understanding of a dream even if we have an imperfect apprehension of those aspects, even if we fall short of Tedlock's high standards.[8]

Many of the dream interpreters we have considered encounter problems with Gadamer's second point, that we not assimilate a text too quickly to our expectations of meaning. Breton, Jung, Hall, and Hobson each claim that dreams are not strange at all but are, in fact, entirely clear in their meanings, once we have learned to understand the special language in which they speak. Breton insists that there is no mystery to a dream's meaning; Jung describes dreams as "pure psychic products"; Hall states that many dreams bear messages that are completely "obvious" expressions; and Hobson asserts that dreams are thoroughly "transparent" in their meaning. All four suggest that if we learn the distinctive means of expression used by dreams, it requires little interpretive work to understand them.

The trouble with such claims, from a hermeneutic perspective, is that they suggest that the strangeness of dreams is only apparent and can be overcome completely. Yet as Gadamer has stressed, there is no "pure" perception, no understanding of meaning without some process of interpretation. At best, Breton, Jung, Hall, and Hobson naively mistake their own particular interpretations for the "pure," "natural," or "obvious" meaning of a dream; at worst, they allow their own interpretations to block the emergence of other possible meanings. In either case, the problem stems from a belief that dreams really are not "strange" at all and can be completely understood.

Gadamer's ideas about the critical tension between continuity and discontinuity in our interpretive work with a text are decisive here. In the interpretation of dreams, Freud and Tedlock stress the discontinuity, while Breton, Jung, Hall, and Hobson stress the continuity. Freud and Tedlock remind us that dreams are very strange, are very different from our ordinary world of knowledge, and are very difficult to understand. Freud stresses the continual danger of self-deception as a limiting factor in dream interpretation, and Tedlock shows how the pervasive influence of language and social structure undermines any culturally naive attempts at interpreting dreams. But on the other hand, Breton, Jung, Hall, and Hobson emphasize that dreams are also familiar in many ways, that they *do* have connections to our waking life, and that we *can* achieve some measure of understanding of them. Each of them demonstrates that, despite the strangeness of dreams, we can discover valuable meanings in them. What at first appears as an insurmountably wide chasm between the dream wilderness and the realms of waking consciousness can, in places, be bridged.

The Role of Culture in Dream Interpretation

The fourth divisive question we discussed concerns the extent to which there is a cultural dimension to the meaning of dreams. We found that dream interpreters had two understandings of the issue: how cultural forces influence dreams and how dreams can have meanings for culture. Gadamer's hermeneutics provide a strong basis for affirming the first of these understandings, in that he emphasizes the need to take historical and social circumstances into account in all interpretations. The interpreter of a text must be aware of the historical forces that are shaping his or her encounter with the text: forces that are influencing the way the text is read, the questions the interpreter asks of it, and the meanings that will be of greatest interest to the interpreter.

Gadamer's work most clearly supports Tedlock's and Hunt's assertions about the need for extensive cultural awareness in dream interpretation. His work also provides the grounds for challenging many of the other dream researchers we have studied. This critique is most striking in those cases where the claims for objectivity are boldest: with Hall, Hobson, and LaBerge. Hall argues that his dream series method provides certain, objective information on what dreams mean, and yet his conclusions simply mirror many of the distinctive cultural values of mid-twentieth-century America. For example, Hall is not aware of how his culture's views of male-female relations are coloring his "objective" findings. *The Meaning of Dreams* is (from a late-twentieth century perspective) likely the most sexist book on dreams ever written, presenting numerous culturally specific notions about gender as self-evident, objective fact.[9] Turning to Hobson, we find that he argues that dreams are transparent in their meaning and that plain common sense is sufficient to understand them; yet it is clear that his interpretations are, ironically enough, thoroughly influenced by the very distinctive notions of psychoanalysis.[10] He never considers that what appears transparent to *him* might not be so self-evident to someone from another perspective. And LaBerge claims that his research on lucid dreaming has demonstrated the objective validity of certain Buddhist epistemological notions, such as the ultimately illusory nature of the waking world. But like Hall and Hobson, LaBerge does not account sufficiently for how his own psychological and cultural presuppositions are influencing what he takes to be the meaning of dreams. In his case, LaBerge relies on a particular reading of Buddhist mysticism that inclines his characterization of lucid dreaming to focus on certain features and ignore others.[11]

The point of this hermeneutic critique is not that these dream explorers are wrong. On the contrary, Hall, Hobson, and LaBerge have many interesting and legitimate ideas to offer about what dreams mean. Rather, a hemeneutic critique suggests that their interpretations are, despite all the trappings of natural scientific objectivity, still conditioned by the particular circumstances of their cultural worlds. A hermeneutic critique further suggests that the less awareness there is of this inevitable cultural influence, and the more their particular interpretations masquerade as universal, objective truths, the greater the danger is that these dream interpreters will distort our overall understanding of dreams.

Regarding the other aspect of this issue, that is, whether dreams have meanings *for* culture, we find that Gadamer's work supports the same position we took on the question of whether dreams have meaning at all: there is no way to know if a text is meaningful or not in any particular way until we actually start asking questions of it. From a hermeneutic perspective, then, there is nothing in principle against dreams having meanings for culture. The only way to tell is to ask the questions and see what happens. Breton, Jung, LaBerge, Hunt, and Tedlock all show how the asking of such questions (e.g., What does this dream say to the problems of my culture? Does this dream offer any visions of how to resolve my culture's troubles?) does lead to interesting and meaningful answers. Freud and Hall, who deny this dimension of meaning in dreams, would have stronger cases if their claim was that *few* dreams have significant cultural meaning. However, if they try to argue flatly that *no* dreams whatsoever have cultural meaning, they violate a fundamental hermeneutic principle: meanings cannot be known a priori; they can be known only within the actual process of questioning and interpretation itself.

Criteria for Valid Dream Interpretations

Gadamer offers a number of criteria by which we can judge whether or not an interpretation is valid. One is an internal criterion: the "harmony with the whole," how well an interpretation integrates and makes sense of all the aspects of a text. Another is an external criterion: the "relationships of order," the degree to which the interpretation accords with the rest of our knowledge. A third is an essentially practical criterion: how well the interpretation "works-out," whether it "comes to something" or not, whether it satisfies the practical needs that motivated us to interpret the text in the first place. To the question of what exactly determines how an interpretation has "worked-out," Gadamer presents his ideal of the fusion of horizons. Thus, an interpretation "comes to something" if it opens up new horizons for us, if it expands our understanding, if it reveals new ideas and calls forth new questions. This criterion stands in sharp contrast to any insistence that there must be one final, right interpretation. The best interpretation of a text, Gadamer argues, is the one that opens the most to us, not the one that is most unambiguous and definite.

All of the dream interpreters we have considered agree with the first two hermeneutic criteria for a valid interpretation. They all seek to account for as many aspects of a given dream as they can, reckoning no interpretation legitimate that does not at least try to integrate every detail of the dream into its overall meaning. Furthermore, they all seek to relate their interpretations to "relationships of order," to the other kinds of understanding we have. Thus, for example, Freud relates his dream interpretations to his understandings of neurotic symptoms, jokes, and slips of the tongue; Jung connects his findings about dream symbolism to the religious and mythological symbolism of other cultures; Hobson grounds his analysis of dream bizarreness in his knowledge of neuroscience; and Hunt links his ideas about the multiplicity of dream forms to the recent findings of cognitive psychology.

But this relative unanimity on the first two criteria evaporates when we come to Gadamer's third criterion, for dream explorers do not agree on how to tell whether or not an interpretation has "worked-out" in a practical sense. Freud and Jung claim that an interpretation is valid if it helps the dreamer make psychotherapeutic progress. Hall and Hobson, however, reject that claim as excessively subjective and arbitrary. They argue that Freud's and Jung's reports of psychotherapeutic progress are carefully tailored to prove the interpretations right. But as we have seen, Hall's and Hobson's own ways of determining the practical value of a dream interpretation are also influenced by their "subjective" interests and goals.

The essential point of contention in this debate over the criteria that should guide dream interpretation is this: to what extent do the subjective biases of an interpreter *invalidate* his or her interpretations? Gadamer has argued that the sheer fact of having subjective biases does not matter. *All* interpreters have biases, and it is the vain pursuit of the natural sciences to seek to eliminate them entirely. Rather, our concern should be about how *aware* we are of those biases and whether they help *clarify* our interpretations or *obscure* our interpretations. With our dream explorers, then, it is not a legitimate criticism to say their work is invalid because their subjectivity intrudes on their interpretations. The legitimate criticism would be that their subjective biases are a negative, narrowing force rather than a positive, broadening one.

The Objectivity of Dream Interpretation

The final issue of dispute among dream researchers takes us right to the heart of Gadamer's project, namely to show that those phenomena that do not lend themselves to natural scientific study nevertheless can be known objectively. Dreams can, of course, be studied by natural scientific methods, and the results often are tremendously interesting and important. However, we have seen that the *interpretation* of dreams cannot be conducted according to the standards applied in the natural sciences. Even the strongest proponents of the natural scientific method admit to the virtually insurmountable difficulties of approaching dreams in this way.

The time has long come when we should abandon the Procrustean effort of forcing dream interpretation to lie in a natural scientific bed. The persistence of this effort has been motivated, it seems, by the concern that abandoning it would leave dream interpretation open (even more than it already is) to the charges of arbitrariness, randomness, and vagueness. Without the clear standards of the natural sciences, it appears that we have nothing that can firmly guide our attempts at understanding dreams.

Gadamer addresses exactly the same concerns with the interpretations of art and of the human sciences. In these areas, too, the charge is made that without a natural scientific approach the interpretations are arbitrary and inconclusive—in short, they are not "objective." Gadamer's response is that the objectivity of interpretation in such areas comes not through natural scientific method but through a "discipline of questioning and research," that is, a careful, patient, focused examination that both follows the question-and-answer dialogue wherever it goes and yet continually relates the process back to the initial situation that motivated the interpretation.[12] If an interpreter engages in such a discipline, Gadamer argues that his or her work may be legitimately regarded as "objective" in its results.

Almost all of the dream explorers we have considered show evidence in their practices (if not always in their theoretical formulations) of that "discipline of questioning and research." For example, Jung's method of amplification involves a continual interplay between the dream and imagery from religious and mythological sources. Hall "immerses" himself in his material and tirelessly sifts through a dream series for additional nuances of meaning. And Tedlock moves with great care, insight, and sophistication from her experiences of dream-sharing with the Quiche and Zuni people to examinations of their cultural structures and back to their dream-sharing again.

The objectivity of their dream interpretations is not an objectivity of detached, impersonal neutrality, for all of the dream explorers we have studied are guided by their subjective preconceptions and biases. Rather, their work is, at its best, characterized by an objectivity born of determination, openness, and self-reflection. As Gadamer helps us to see, their objectivity is a matter of disciplined questioning, of using subjective biases to ask questions of the dream texts and to listen for the answers. Dream interpretation *is* a science, not a mysterious, irrational process of Romantic inspiration. But at the same time, it is not a natural science; it is a *human* science, depending in a *positive* way on the subjectivity of its practitioners.

13

THE INTERPRETATION OF DREAMS: HERMENEUTIC PRINCIPLES

> The most skillful interpreter of dreams is he who has the faculty of observing resemblances.
>
> —Aristotle, *Prophesying By Dreams*

Having used Gadamer's hermeneutic philosophy to critique the different theories of dream interpretation, we may now engage in a more positive endeavor: we may draw on Gadamer to develop a philosophically sound approach to the interpretation of dreams. Such an approach can, I believe, validate the key insights of the various dream theories we have studied and yet also overcome their problems and limitations. In short, we can make an attempt here to resolve the "crisis of dream interpretation" outlined in chapter 11. This will provide us with the important philosophical orientation we need to resume our exploration of the question of dreams and religious meaning.

We can best develop the hermeneutic principles of dream interpretation if we refer back to the specific interpretive practices Gadamer discusses and relate the principles of those practices to our subject of dream interpretation.

Dream Interpretation is Like the Experience of Art

Gadamer's primary argument about the experience of art is that it brings us genuine knowledge. He claims that art reveals new aspects of our world to us. Art does not take us away to an utterly alien realm that has no connections whatsoever with the rest of our existence; rather, it opens up different, previously unknown dimensions of life that we then learn to relate back to our ordinary world of knowledge. No matter how strange the art, no matter how distant it may seem from the rest of our existence, our experience and our interpretations of it always involve a process of *relating* it to our world.

There is, of course, a long association between art and dreams. Artists have often been inspired to particular creative efforts by dreams. We saw some evidence of this in chapter 1, and we studied in some detail the role of dreams in surrealist art. Art and dreams have also frequently been associated in negative ways. In *The Republic* Plato condemns both art and dreams as being mere appearances that lead people astray from the proper pursuit of the real and the true (see book 10 on art, and book 9 on dreams). In his essay "The Relation of the Poet to Day-Dreaming," Freud ([1908] 1963) argues that both poetry and daydreaming (which in his view is not fundamentally different from night dreaming) are defensive, wish-fulfilling processes that substitute pleasure for reality.[1]

Gadamer gives us a new basis for making this association of art and dreams and for appreciating (*pace* Plato and Freud) the legitimate, positive knowledge both bring us.[2] The interpretation of dreams, like the interpretation of art, involves a process of active perception: discriminating details, relating different elements to each other, comparing what we know with what we do not know, and trying to bring the strange aspects of the experience into connection with our ordinary world. Just as art does, dreams take us to distant, alien realms and thereby reveal to us surprising, previously unknown features of our familiar existence—providing us with genuine knowledge.

Dream Interpretation is Like Play

Gadamer says the particular kind of knowledge we gain in the experience and interpretation of art is one of the kinds that fall under the general heading of play. There are things we learn in play, Gadamer claims, that we cannot learn from outside the playing. Some knowledge can be gained only through entering a relationship with that which we want to know (the kind of relationship, Gadamer emphasizes, that the natural sciences deliberately avoid). This, I would argue, is true of dream interpretation as well. We cannot understand the meanings of a dream except by entering into a relationship with it, except by "playing" with it.

The main characteristics of play, Gadamer suggests, are the losing of one's self in the play, the surrendering to the play's movement, and the tension of discontinuity and continuity between the play and our world. Gadamer claims that these characteristics guide the best, most enriching interpretations of art. I would extend that claim and argue that these are the characteristics that appear in the best interpretations of dreams. We gain the fullest understanding of a dream when we play with it in these ways: when we leave behind a strict subject-object distinction and enter into a relationship with the dream; when we follow the movement of the interpretation as it unfolds, asking questions, listening for answers, and then formulating new questions based on those answers; and when, in the process of "losing" our selves in the play, we come to find a new understanding of our selves.

Perhaps the preeminent example of how dream interpretation is like play in this positive hermeneutic sense is Jung's account of active imagination. Jung describes this therapeutic process as follows:

> In [active imagination] you choose a dream, or some other fantasy-image, and concentrate on it by simply catching hold of it and looking at it . . . You then fix this image in the mind by concentrating your attention. Usually it will alter, as the mere fact of contemplating it animates it. A chain of fantasy ideas develops and gradually takes on a dramatic character: the passive process becomes an action. At first it consists of projected figures, and these images are observed like scenes in the theater. In other words, you dream with open eyes . . . The piece that is being played does not want merely to be watched impartially, it wants to compel his participation. If the observer understands that his own drama is being performed on this inner stage, he cannot remain indifferent to the plot and its denouement. He will notice, as the actors appear one by one and the plot thickens, that they all have some purposeful relationship to his conscious situation, that he is being addressed by the unconscious, and that *it* causes these fantasy-images to appear before him. He therefore feels compelled, or is encouraged by his analyst, to take part in the play and, instead of just sitting in a theater, really having it out with his alter ego . . . This process of coming to terms with the Other in us is well worth while, because in this way we get to know aspects of our nature which we would not allow anybody else to show us and which we ourselves would never have admitted. (Jung [1955–56] 1970, 495–96)

All of the key elements of play are present in Jung's active imagination process. The dreamer enters into a relationship with the dream, surrenders to the flow of that relationship, and thereby discovers new aspects of his or her own nature. Jung's use of theater metaphors only strengthens the connection with Gadamer, for Gadamer himself uses the example of the theater to illustrate the theoretical aspects of the process of interpretation he has been discussing (Gadamer 1975, 99, 114–18).

Dream Interpretation is Like Interpretation in the Human Sciences

The distinguishing feature of interpretation in the human sciences, as opposed to the interpretive methods of the natural sciences, is the *positive* role of our subjectivity—the way our personal expectations, assumptions, and biases may open up meanings to us. The positive role of subjectivity is equally as central, I believe, to the interpretation of dreams. In the previous chapter we saw the negative consequences of this. We found that all interpreters, even those who claim to be most "objective" and impersonal, are in fact guided by personal biases that often limit what they discover in a dream. However, we now need to recognize that our subjectivity also has *positive* consequences in dream interpretation: that our particular expectations and assumptions can serve as helpful guides, leading us to meanings we would not otherwise have encountered.

Freud suffers from a great deal of criticism over the limiting effect of his personal biases in his dream interpretations. But in this regard, Gadamer's hermeneutics rescues Freud from his critics. Yes, the critics are right, Freud's subjective biases did profoundly influence his dream interpretations. But as Gadamer helps us to see, the crucial question is whether this bias was a *positive* or a *negative* force in Freud's work. The answer to this question, I believe, is that Freud's biases had both effects. Freud's childhood sexual experiences, his troubled relationship with his father, and his ambivalent attitude towards Judaism all focused his attention on certain psychological issues that he explored with incredible insight.[3] These subjective biases had the *positive* effect of motivating Freud to investigate dreams in a particular way, leading to new discoveries about the potential meanings of dreams.

It may be true, of course, that by focusing on these specific issues Freud ignored or depreciated other issues, such as the nature of female sexuality, the significance of relationships with mothers, and the potentially creative, adaptive powers of religion. To the extent that his biases had the negative effect of preventing Freud from appreciating these issues in his interpretations, he deserves the mountains of criticism that have been heaped upon him. But this criticism is legitimate only to the extent that it attacks those instances where Freud's subjective biases prevented him from appreciating other aspects of meaning. The mere fact that Freud *had* subjective biases does not distinguish him from any other dream interpreter and is not itself a basis for special criticism. The revolutionary discoveries Freud did make, discoveries that were thoroughly influenced by his personal, subjective experiences, represent an excellent example of what Gadamer means by the positive value of "productive" prejudices.

Despite such an example of the positive effects of subjectivity, there still may remain a concern over how exactly to tell when our subjectivity is a positive, path-opening influence and when it is a negative, constricting influence in dream interpretation. Indeed, from this concern comes the continual temptation to find a safe, solid, "objective" standpoint, beyond all personal biases, to ground our dream interpretations. But as we saw in the previous chapter, such a quest for objectivity is a vain fantasy, the product of an illegitimate expansion of natural scientific methodology beyond its proper realm. The real question for dream interpretation is, not how to be rid of our personal biases, but how to make the most positive, creative, horizon-expanding use of them.

Gadamer's notion of the hermeneutic circle addresses the concern about how to distinguish negative from positive biases. The only way we can ever make this distinction is by bringing our biases into play: we use them in the interpretation, moving back and forth between the biases and the dream, and see what happens. Thus, for example, Breton asks, how does the given dream challenge modern bourgeois culture? Thus Hall asks, how does the dream reveal the basic dilemmas of human life? Thus Hunt asks, how does the dream display certain syntheses of cognitive functions? These dream interpreters ask their "biased" questions, questions based on their subjective expectations and assumptions, and then watch to see what comes.

We have already considered the criteria Gadamer offers as standards to judge what has "come" of the interpretation and whether our biases are productive or not—the criteria of internal consistency, coherence with other knowledge, and "working-out" in a practical sense. Using these criteria, we are able to determine how much the biases of Breton, Hall, Hunt, and other dream interpreters help open up meanings and how much their biases close off our understanding of the dream. These are very broad criteria, criteria that still do not allow for clear, certain judgements about an interpretation's being right or not. But again, this is the nature of interpretation in the human sciences and the nature, in my view, of dream interpretation as well: we ultimately judge an interpretation not by how certain it is but by how much it opens up to us, by the new horizons it enables us to see.

Dream Interpretation is Like Dialogue

Gadamer states that the best model for the characteristics of interpretation is the dialogue. A dialogue is a shared inquiry into a question, governed by nothing more than a willingness to learn something new and a sensitivity to the perspectives of the others in the dialogue. The goal of a dialogue is the development of a richer, broader understanding of the question, not the grasping of a simple, exact, definitive answer.

We can see three different ways in which these qualities of dialogue characterize dream interpretation. The first is how the interpretation of dreams is a dialogue between the dreamer and his or her unconscious. Jung, for example, describes dream interpretation as a "conversation" between the dreamer and the unconscious. The interpretation is productive, Jung claims, only to the extent that the dreamer is able to maintain an open dialogue with the unconscious. LaBerge's study of the potentials of lucid dreaming also accords well with this characterization of dream interpretation as dialogue. He suggests that the greatest value of lucid dreaming lies in the way it enables the dreamer to react to the dream more consciously, deliberately, and openly. Lucid dreaming thus appears as an experience in which the dialogue between the dreamer and his or her unconscious can reach a special degrees of openness and intensity.

Dream interpretation is also like a dialogue in the sense that it often occurs in an interpersonal setting: with a therapist or analyst, with a dream discussion group, with friends, or with family members. Indeed, Gadamer and other hermeneutic philosophers have taken a special interest in Freud's psychoanalytic therapy as a prime example of how dialogue lies at the heart of interpretation (Palmer 1969; Bleicher 1980; Gadamer 1981; Habermas 1968; Ricoeur 1970, 1974, 1981). The great virtue of engaging in dream interpretation in an interpersonal context is that the other people bring a different set of views into play with the dream. The therapist, group, or family members provide alternative perspectives on the dream that may open up new possibilities of meaning for the dreamer (Ullman and Zimmerman, 1979; Taylor 1983).

The third way that dream interpretation involves dialogue is in the way the different fields of dream study enter into discussions about the meaning of dreams. We can see the fruitfulness of such interdisciplinary dialogues in the work of Hobson, Tedlock, and Hunt. Hobson brings together neuroscientific and psychoanalytic perspectives in a very thought-provoking (if not always well-reasoned) fashion. Tedlock initiates a dialogue between psychological and anthropological approaches to dreams that promises to have a powerful influence on all future dream research. And Hunt draws together the work of depth psychology, neuroscience, anthropology, and cognitive psychology in an ambitious attempt to understand the "multiplicity" of dreams. Unfortunately, such interdisciplinary dialogues remain more the exception than the rule in dream studies. A primary goal of *The Wilderness of Dreams* is to encourage more dialogue among the various fields studying dreams.

One further point should be emphasized about the dialogical nature of dream interpretation. The model of dialogue should not be taken as indicating a strictly *linguistic* process, as being synonymous with verbally asking questions and verbally giving answers.[4] An interpretive dialogue can take place in many different, and *non*verbal, ways: in Jung's active imagination, in Perls's Gestalt therapy, in Gendlin's reflections on the "felt sense" of the dream, in the various forms of dream art, dance, and theater. These are all interpretive "dialogues" with the dream in Gadamer's sense of the term, even though the main focus is not directly on verbal, rationally comprehensible meanings. Just as we found it necessary to broaden the conventional meaning of "text" to account for dreams, so we must broaden our definition of "dialogue" to understand the basic processes involved in dream interpretation.

Beyond Gadamer: Radically New Meanings

Gadamer has been criticized by other hermeneutic philosophers for a tendency towards conservativism. The critics contend that he puts too much stress on relating a text to "tradition," to conventional ideas and beliefs. As a result, Gadamer's hermeneutics renders us incapable of appreciating meanings that may challenge traditions and conventions and that may represent radically new visions of the world. Gadamer has responded that he *does* appreciate the possibility of radically new meanings, as demonstrated by his emphasis on how the interpreter must remain open to the new horizons revealed by the text (Palmer 1969; Bleicher 1980).

We do not need to dwell on the intricate details of this debate. What is important for us is that an openness to radically new meanings be firmly integrated into our understanding of dream interpretation. Many of the dream explorers we have studied strongly assert that dreams often present utterly surprising meanings to us, meanings we have never encountered before. Freud, for example, insists that we should be suspicious if a dream seems too obvious in its meaning—dreams, in his view, rarely tell us what we already know. The surrealists are primarily interested in dreams as a source of astonishment, surprise, and marvel. Jung describes many cases in which his patients have dreams with meanings that completely upset their prior understandings of themselves. Hunt shows how special cognitive processes combine to create entirely novel dream imagery. It is crucial, then, for dream interpreters to have a sensitivity for radically new meanings, for meanings that are shockingly, dramatically different from our common understanding of ourselves and our world.[5]

The Hermeneutic Principles of Dream Interpretation

To sum up, then, we may outline the various hermeneutic principles of dream interpretation in the following way:

1. We encounter a dream as a *text*, as something that is both strange and yet related to us, as something that is not immediately understood, and thus as something that requires interpretation. We recognize that dream "texts" have distinctive qualities, which we must take into account in our interpretations.[6]
2. The interpreter has a preliminary awareness of his or her own *subjective biases* (personal and cultural) and of how those biases will influence the meanings that the interpreter discovers in the dream.
3. At the same time, the interpreter admits to *not knowing* what exactly will come of the dream interpretation; the interpreter is open to the dream, and is open in particular to the possibility that startling, radically new meanings may emerge from the dream.
4. The interpreter *plays* with the dream, surrendering to a back-and-forth dialogue of questioning, answering, and questioning anew; of distinguishing, recombining, and distinguishing again. This play is free, in following its own course of unfolding, yet it is also structured by a self-reflective "discipline of questioning and research."
5. The criteria for a *valid interpretation* are how well it harmonizes the parts of the dream with the whole dream or with a series of dreams (internal criterion); how well it coheres with the rest of our knowledge (external criterion); and how well it "works-out" according to our practical needs and interests (practical criterion).
6. The *ultimate goal* of dream interpretation is to open up areas of understanding, to broaden horizons, to raise new questions, and to widen awareness. The interpretation of dreams thus has no definitive end; it is evaluated according to the particular questions we ask.

14

DORA'S DREAM: THE HERMENEUTIC PRINCIPLES IN ACTION

"Why," said the Dodo, "the best way to explain it is to do it."

—Lewis Carroll, *Alice's Adventures in Wonderland*

Dora's Dream and Freud's Interpretation

It may be helpful at this point to illustrate how these hermeneutic principles operate in an actual dream interpretation. Books on dreams always face two dangers: one is concentrating too much on abstract models, thus allowing their theoretical maps to obscure the actual dream terrain itself; the other is focusing too closely on specific dream examples, looking so intently at the ground at their feet that they never try to reach a vantage overlooking the dream wilderness as a whole. My sense is that, after a lengthy examination of Gadamer's hermeneutic philosophy, the time has come to discuss an actual dream—to see how the hermeneutic principles presented in the last chapter play out in practice.

We will look at Freud's interpretation of one of the dreams of Ida Brauer, the "Dora" of his famous case study *Fragment of an Analysis of a Case of Hysteria* (1905). We will be concerned with Freud's interpretive method, with *how* Freud conducts the interpretation, and not so much with *what* his interpretation results in.[1]

In the fall of 1900, Dora (Freud's pseudonym for Ida Bauer[2]) was brought by her father to Freud for treatment. Dora's family was well known to Freud, and he was already familiar with her long history of mental and physical afflictions: attacks of nervous coughing, loss of voice, and migraine headaches. She had been brought to Freud two years earlier because of an inexplicable cough and hoarseness, but when the attack suddenly disappeared she ended the treatment. Now, in addition to her physical maladies, Dora had become chronically depressed, took no interest in social activities, and was very hostile to both her mother and father. Her parents had a found a suicide note in which she said, "she could no longer endure her life." This alarming discovery motivated Dora's parents to deliver her, despite her reluctance, to Freud a second time.

Dora's father told Freud that her depression and suicidal ideas might be due to an unpleasant incident two years earlier between Dora and a family friend Freud refers to as Herr K. Dora and her father had joined Herr K. and his wife for a vacation at a lake resort. Dora claimed that Herr K. had made a romantic proposal to her during a walk together along the lakeshore. Herr K., when confronted with this charge, vehemently denied it. He said that Dora had probably been overexcited by surreptitiously reading medical texts on sexuality (a piece of information his wife, Frau K., had given to him) and that the girl had simply imagined the whole scene. Dora's father agreed with Herr K. that Dora's story was likely a fantasy, and he asked Freud to "please try and bring her to reason" (Freud [1905] 1963, 26).

Freud remarks at the outset that Dora's case is not a very interesting or unusual instance of hysteria (23–24). He is writing about the case, not because of any unique features of Dora, but rather because he wants to supplement his theoretical descriptions in *The Interpretation of Dreams*: "The following fragment from the history of the treatment of a hysterical girl is intended to show the way in which the interpretation of dreams plays a part in the work of analysis"(15).[3]

Freud begins by presenting "the clinical picture," the extremely intricate pattern of relationships that govern Dora's life. Dora's father had been ill for some time (the result of syphilis contracted during an extramarital affair), so the family had moved to a small town with a milder climate. They soon became good friends with Herr and Frau K. Dora's father and Frau K. formed an especially close relationship, and she took to nursing him during his illness. The romantic nature of this arrangement was obvious to everyone. Dora, who had also developed an intimate friendship with Frau K., began caring for the K.'s two children, acting "almost as a mother to them" (25). Herr K. demonstrated an energetic fondness for Dora, giving her flowers and small gifts and continually seeking to spend time alone with her.

At the start of her treatment with Freud, Dora describes an earlier incident with Herr K. When she was fourteen Herr K. had contrived to be alone with Dora in his office. He closed the window shutters and "suddenly clasped the girl to him and pressed a kiss upon her lips" (28). Freud believes that Dora felt the pressure of Herr K.'s erection against her body.

Dora struggled free and ran out of the office, overcome by "a violent feeling of disgust" (28). Freud wants to pursue the underlying causes of Dora's reaction to Herr K., but Dora insists on expressing her anger towards her father. She has concluded that Herr K. and her father tacitly agreed on a sexual *quid pro quo*: her father would be free to carry on his affair with Frau K. if he allowed Herr K. to seduce Dora.

Dora soon reports a dream, one that she had dreamed many times before.

> A house was on fire. My father was standing beside my bed and woke me up. I dressed quickly. Mother wanted to stop and save her jewel-case; but Father said: "I refuse to let myself and my two children be burnt for the sake of your jewel-case." We hurried downstairs, and as soon as I was outside I woke up. (64)

Freud begins his interpretation by asking Dora to tell him anything that occurs to her in connection to the dream.[4] She describes a dispute between her parents over the locking of certain doors in their home after everyone had gone to sleep. Her father was worried, she says, that "something might happen in the night so that it might be necessary to leave the room" (65). Freud tells Dora to "pay close attention to the exact words you used," for they might be important later in the interpretation. He says in a footnote that "I laid stress on these words because they took me aback. They seemed to have an ambiguous ring about them. Are not certain physical needs referred to in the same words?" (65).

Dora goes on to mention the trip she and her father had taken to the lake resort. Her father was worried that their small wooden cabin had no lightning rod and so could catch fire during a thunderstorm. Freud asks Dora about the relation of the dream to Herr K.'s lakeshore proposal, and he coaxes Dora to admit that the dream first occurred the night after that incident. Furthermore, she tells of how she had taken a nap that afternoon in the cabin and had awoken to find Herr K. standing next to her bed. Frightened and angry, she told him to leave. Dora realized that she could not be guaranteed of her privacy in the house, especially when she discovered that the key to her room's lock was missing. She began dressing very quickly every time she changed clothes, worried that Herr K. might burst in and try once again to press his affections upon her.

Freud tells Dora that the dream portrays the danger she felt at the resort and her conscious intention to flee from that danger as soon as possible. The dream repeated itself each night until she finally did leave. However, Freud digresses briefly to note that, according to his theory in *The Interpretation of Dreams*, dreams do not simply express intentions;

rather, dreams as a rule represent the fulfillment of unconscious infantile wishes. He says, "it is therefore of special importance to me to show that apparent exceptions—such as this dream of Dora's, which has shown itself in the first instance to be the continuation into sleep of an intention formed during the day—nevertheless lend fresh support to the rule which is in dispute" (68). When Freud returns to Dora's dream, then, it is with this goal of discovering the infantile wishes hidden behind the dream's manifest facade.[5]

He asks Dora a number of questions about the jewel case, pointing out that that particular word (*Schmuckkastchen* in German) is also a slang term for the female genitals. Further questioning by Freud leads Dora to recall that Herr K. had once given her a jewel case as a gift and that her mother had rejected a piece of jewelry Dora's father had given her. Freud deduces from these associations the following: that Dora wished her father had given her the jewelry that her mother had rejected, because Dora would have gladly accepted it; that the double meaning of "jewel case" suggests that Dora wanted (unconsciously) to satisfy her father sexually and not leave him frustrated, as her mother has done; that the dream image of her father also refers to Herr K., whom Dora likewise once found standing next to her bed; and thus that Dora also wants (again, unconsciously) to "give to Herr K. what his wife withholds from him," namely her sexual love (70). Freud sums up the interpretation by saying to her,

> "The dream confirms once more what I had already told you before you dreamt it—that you are summoning up your old love for your father in order to protect yourself against your love for Herr K. But what do all these efforts show? Not only that you are afraid of Herr K., but that you are still more afraid of yourself, and of the temptation you feel to yield to him. In short, these efforts prove once more how deeply you loved him." Naturally Dora would not follow me in this part of the interpretation. (70)

Freud says that despite this progress in the interpretation, he is still curious about the ambiguous words Dora used regarding the danger that "something might happen in the night." And, he still has not found the childhood wish that was motivating the dream.[6] But a little more reflection on Freud's part soon resolves these questions. In their next session he explains to Dora how the symbolic connection between fire and water reveals the infantile wish at the core of her dream. Freud notes that Dora's mother tries to save her jewel case from burning, clearly a sexual allusion to the "heat" of love. But, Freud says, the symbolism of fire calls forth its opposite, the symbolism of water, because dreams frequently change one thing into its opposite when repression is especially strong. So another line of meaning suggests that the jewel case is in danger of being *wetted*, another allusion to sexual excitement. And this line of meaning ultimately leads back to Dora's childhood—for in childhood the fear that "something might happen in the night," that something might be wetted, can refer only to bed-wetting. Freud thus concludes that Dora must have been "addicted to bed-wetting up to a later age than is usual with children" (72) and that her father must have frequently awoken her at night to prevent this problem from occurring. Freud finishes his explanation by directly challenging Dora: "And now, what have your recollections to say to this?" (72).

At first Dora says she can remember nothing about it. But then, she finally does recall that she was a bed-wetter up until the age of seven or eight and that her family had to call a doctor to help with the problem. Freud states contentedly that "the interpretation of the dream now seemed to me to be complete." He says the underlying wish producing the dream could be "translated into words such as these: 'The temptation is so strong. Dear Father, protect me as you used to in my childhood, and prevent my bed from being wetted!'" (73).

But then, Dora brings in an "addendum" to the dream, the memory that each time she woke up from the dream she had smelled smoke. Freud believes that such additions to a dream, which are first forgotten and only later recalled, are highly significant; they must have overcome especially strong resistances to reach conscious (73, 100). In Dora's case, Freud believes the addendum probably refers to the most forcefully repressed thoughts in the dream, "to the thoughts, that is, concerned with the temptation to show herself willing to yield to the man" (73). To kiss a smoker, Freud notes, would certainly smell like smoke. Herr K. was a smoker, so the addendum points once again to Dora's unconscious desire for Herr K. But Freud too is a smoker, and so he also concludes that Dora has probably fantasized about kissing him as well. Her resistance to this wish is the basis for her resistance to Freud's treatment, and it explains why Dora's dream has repeated itself now—she feels both tempted and threatened by Freud. He finishes the interpretation by concluding, "everything fits together very satisfactorily upon this view" (74).

A few weeks later, Dora broke off the treatment. Freud believes the analysis did not succeed in helping Dora because he failed to master the transference, that is, Dora's projection of unconscious feelings related to her father and Herr K. onto the person of Freud. Before Freud could bring these unconscious feelings to light, Dora vengefully rejected him just as she had rejected her father and Herr K.

A Hermeneutic Approach to Dora's Dream

Freud's analysis, with its wild contortions, dizzying leaps of reasoning, and outrageous mix of genius and absurdity, may seem intended to prove that dream interpretation really is an arbitrary, utterly subjective process, guided by no principles whatsoever. But this example actually demonstrates in a very clear fashion the six hermeneutic principles of dream interpretation we laid out at the end of chapter 13. We can see that Freud is most effective when his interpretive approach corresponds to those principles and that he gets into the greatest trouble when his approach strays from them.

1. Does Freud treat Dora's dream as a text, as something both strange and yet potentially understandable, as something requiring interpretation? Yes, he does. Freud does not grasp the dream's meaning in an instant; he determines to "make an especially careful investigation of it" (64), recognizing that a process of interpretation is necessary to understand the dream. He also recognizes that the dream is a special kind of text, with distinctive features that must be accounted for. For example, he gives close attention to the addendum Dora makes to her dream, as he has found that such additions are crucial to illuminating the rest of the dream text.

2. Does Freud have a preliminary awareness of his own biases, and of how those biases will shape his questions and expectations? Clearly not. Freud admits that he wants to show that Dora's dream confirms his theory, yet he fails to take into account how such an intention will decisively shape what he finds, and does *not* find, in her dream. He also claims that his interpretation has proved his prior conviction that Dora really loves Herr K.; but again, Freud does not ask whether his prior conviction may unduly influence his interpretation of the dream.

And as virtually all later critics point out, Freud does not address the *counter*transference at work in the case, the unconscious projections *he* is making onto Dora. Some critics of the Dora case argue that Freud's personal and cultural assumptions about "normal" male-female relations intrude upon his interpretation of her dreams. Other critics point out that Freud was sexually molested by a governess as a child and that this experience gave Freud a deep hostility towards governesses; the fact that Dora was essentially a governess for the children of Herr and Frau K. may thus have contributed (unconsciously) to Freud's aggressive treatment of Dora (see Bernheimer and Kahane, 1985).

3. Is Freud open to the dream, to the possibility that new, and perhaps radically new meanings may emerge from the interpretation? No; on

the contrary, Freud finds exactly what he expected to find. The interpretation simply confirms that his dream theories are correct and his beliefs about Dora's unconscious desires have been valid. There is never a moment's hesitation on Freud's part that he knows, or will know soon, precisely what the dream means.

4. Does Freud's interpretation have the character of play, of a back-and-forth dialogue of questioning and answering? Hardly. Freud and Dora are at war with each other, fighting tooth and nail over every detail of the dream. Freud does begin the interpretation with some relatively open questioning, but he soon takes control of the analysis and devotes all his skills to forcing Dora into submission. Freud quickly concludes that *he* knows what the dream means, and his primary interest is making it all as clear, comprehensive, and satisfactory to himself as possible. Regarding Dora, Freud seems to want little more than to break down her resistance to his interpretations. He is content when "she no longer disputed my contention," when she is rendered mute by his aggressive arguments. We would be hard pressed to find a more violent, one-directional, *anti*dialogical process of dream interpretation than this.[7]

5. Do Freud's interpretations meet the three hermeneutic criteria of a valid interpretation, that is, harmonizing the parts with the whole of the dream, fitting in well with other knowledge, and "working-out" in a practical sense? With the first criterion, Freud's interpretation does possess an impressive degree of internal consistency. He weaves the details of Dora's dream with her associations into a remarkably tight, well integrated whole. Freud also tries to meet the second criterion, as he makes numerous references to external sources of knowledge that he believes support his interpretation. For example, he claims previous analyses have demonstrated that the words his patients use can have additional meanings hidden behind their literal sense. This supports Freud in his questioning of Dora's "exact words" and his drawing on the slang meanings of "jewel case." Another example is Freud's claim that opposite concepts tend to be connected symbolically. He bases this claim not only on his therapeutic work with neurotics but also on his study of folklore and mythology. This external knowledge supports Freud's interpretive move from the symbolism of fire in Dora's dream to the symbolism of water.

But at other points, Freud's reference to external sources of knowledge undermines his interpretation. One prominent instance is Freud's assumptions regarding female sexuality—that it is, in its normal form, a matter of "yielding" or "surrendering" to a man (87, 100). Freud derives these assumptions from both clinical practice and from certain notions common in his culture, and he believes they support his view that Dora's dream demonstrates her desire to yield to Herr K.'s proposals. But as many of Freud's critics point out, these assumptions are highly suspect, if not wholly false (Gearhart 1985; Rose 1985; Ramas 1985; Moi 1985; Gallop 1985; Sprengnether 1985). The legitimacy of his interpretation of Dora's dream, then, suffers to the extent that he bases it on these problematic assumptions derived from external sources.[8]

With regards to our third criterion, that of "working-out" in a practical sense, Freud admits that it appears he failed: Dora does not seem to get better as a result of the treatment. Freud defends himself by noting Dora's "vengeful" nature, by imagining that if the treatment had been allowed to proceed he certainly would have cured her and by suggesting that perhaps Dora's condition did improve somewhat after all. All of this may be true, but the simple facts remain that Dora bitterly resisted Freud throughout the treatment and that she ultimately broke off the treatment without having made any clear progress against her ills. These facts must call into question the validity of Freud's interpretations. Dora's resistance is *not*, to be sure, sufficient cause for dismissing his interpretations entirely. Freud has spoken too persuasively about the unconscious roots of resistance to his theories and about difficulties of truly curing psychological ills for us to accept Dora's resistance uncritically. Nevertheless, the dreamer's views must count for *something*; the practical value to the dreamer must give *some* indication of an interpretation's validity.

6. Does Freud's interpretation open up new areas of understanding, raise new questions, and broaden horizons? It doesn't for Freud. He ultimately fixes the dream within the bounds of his previously elaborated theory of dreams. No new questions, possibilities, or understandings emerge for him out of the dream (recall his comment that this case is not interesting in itself but noteworthy only for the theoretical principles it illustrates).[9] Dora, on the other hand, may well have discovered a number of surprising new meanings in her dream. Although it is hard to sense Dora's own experiences and reactions through Freud's highly partisan account of her story, we can imagine that the dream may well have helped her understand better her feelings about Herr K., her anger towards her father, and her antagonism towards Freud. In this sense, Freud's interpretations are not the *total* disaster some of his critics suggest they are. As narrow minded, unreflective, and oppressive as Freud is in this case, it is still possible that he may have helped Dora discover some important new meanings in her dream—he may have promoted a broadening of her emotional horizons. This again is where we must (as Gadamer exhorts us) recognize the potentially valuable nature of subjective biases. Freud is oriented by certain biases, presuppositions, and assumptions, all of which *enable* him

to discern certain meanings of her dream. It is also true, of course, that Freud's biases *prevent* him from recognizing other meanings of Dora's dream, meanings that would likely have been much more valuable in healing her sufferings.

Other Interpretations of Dora's Dream

Since Freud's publication of the Dora case in 1905 there have been numerous rereadings of the case and numerous reinterpretations of Dora's dreams. Erik Erikson ([1962] 1985), for example, argues that Freud failed to appreciate the developmental aspects of the case and ignored the distinctive developmental concerns that an adolescent like Dora was facing. According to Erikson, adolescents are trying to develop a firm sense of identity, an identity that is continuous with the adolescent's childhood experience and yet is also capable of sustaining the adolescent as a young adult, independent of his or her family. Erikson believes that Dora's first dream reflects this developmental theme:

> In Dora's first dream the *house* and the *jewel case*, besides being symbols of the female body and its contents, represent the adolescent quandry: if there is a fire in "our house" (that is, in our family), then what "valuables" (that is, values) shall be saved first? (Erikson [1962] 1985, 54)

Another alternative reading of Dora's dream comes from the literary critic Steven Marcus. Marcus sees Freud's rendering of the Dora case as a work of literature—and more specifically, as a work of modernist fiction. The fragmentary narrative, the incessant digressions and interruptions, the ambiguous use of time, and Freud's attempts to undermine the reader's critical perspective are all characteristics that the Dora case shares with the modern experimental novel. Marcus notes that Freud frequently appears unsure about how well he grasps the case, sometimes expressing arrogant confidence and other times revealing deep doubts about his adequacy—just like the "unreliable narrator" so common in modernist fiction. Marcus claims that Freud's status as an "unreliable narrator," as a narrator who is unsure and/or unaware of his own role in the story he is telling, offers a new insight into Dora's first dream:

> [Freud] is only dimly and marginally aware of his central place in it (he is clearly incorporated into the figure of Dora's father), comments on it only as an addition to Dora's own addendum to the dream, and does nothing to exploit it. Instead of analyzing his own part in what he has

> done and what he is writing, Freud continues to behave like an unreliable narrator, treating the material about which he is writing as if it were literature but excluding himself from both that treatment and that material. (Marcus 1985, 80)

Yet another reworking of Dora's dream comes from the feminist historian Maria Ramas. She argues that Freud constructs the whole Dora case "around a fantasy of femininity and female sexuality that remains misunderstood, unconscious if you will" (Ramas 1985, 150). Freud's belief that female sexuality is a matter of submitting to an aggressive male is, in Ramas's view, the ideological reflection of a patriarchal culture. Ramas agrees with Freud that Dora's hysteria is due to her repudiation of the sexual advances of Herr K. But whereas Freud sees that repudiation as a deviant resistance to normal female sexuality, Ramas sees it as a justified revolt against what Dora's culture has presented to her as "normal" female sexuality. Thus Ramas takes a very different view of the meaning of Dora's first dream. She focuses on Dora's mother, whose obsessional cleanliness was evidently due to having contracted syphilis from Dora's father, a disease which had badly "dirtied" her genitals:[10]

> The fact that the mother is trying to save her jewel case in the dream needs further explanation. If we consider this phrase in light of the suggestion that for Kathe Bauer, as for Ida, heterosexuality equaled contamination and destruction, the dream takes on another meaning. The mother's attempt to save her "jewel case" can have no other meaning—given this shared fantasy—than an attempt to escape heterosexuality and annihilation. Beneath Ida's wish that her father save her jewel case lies the recognition that he, in fact, demands its destruction, as he demands the destruction of her mother's . . . At the deepest level of meaning in the dream, Ida's father is represented as the enforcer of the (hetero)sexual laws and fantasies of Ida Bauer's culture. (Ramas 1985, 168)

There have been many other critical rereadings of Dora's first dream and Freud's interpretation of it (see Decker 1991), but these three suffice to raise an important question: What do we make of all these different interpretations? Such a wide-ranging variety of accounts of what Dora's dream means would seem to raise new doubts about the whole process of dream interpretation. Can Dora's dream mean *all* of these things? On what basis can we judge which of these interpretations are *better* and which are *worse*?

Modern dream interpreters have not offered very good answers to these questions. As a result, their work has been vulnerable to the charges of being unprincipled, relativistic, and subjective. But, as I have been arguing throughout this section, a hermeneutic perspective enables dream interpreters to refute these charges. From a hermeneutic perspective, it makes complete sense that there are a number of different, yet potentially legitimate, interpretations of the same dream. Different interpreters bring different questions to a dream and will almost certainly find different meanings in it. This does not, however, require us to say that all the different interpretations are equally true or valuable. On the contrary, a hermeneutic perspective encourages us to look at which interpretations have generated the most fruitful dialogues with the text; at which ones fit best with the rest of our knowledge; at which ones do the most to widen the horizons of our understanding with new meanings. These standards enable us to evaluate, compare, and judge different interpretations—to give clear reasons why one interpretation is more valid than another.

The many readings of Dora's first dream, far from demonstrating the indeterminacy of dream interpretation, in fact illustrate perfectly how dream interpretation is always an open-ended process. It is a process that we evaluate, not by measuring how close it brings us to a single, unambiguous answer, but rather by reflecting on how much it opens up for us. This study of Dora's dream has, I hope, shown that there *are* clear principles that can effectively guide dream interpretation and that we *do* have sound criteria to judge the validity of our interpretations. The hermeneutic principles we have developed give the practice of dream interpretation a sound philosophical orientation that justifies—indeed, *celebrates*—the diversity of our work without abandoning us to a relativistic chaos.

PART FOUR

DREAMS AND RELIGIOUS MEANING

15

THE CONCEPT OF ROOT METAPHORS

It was so, it was not.

—Salman Rushdie, *The Satanic Verses*

The Two Camps

Hans-Georg Gadamer's hermeneutic philosophy has given us an initial orientation in the wilderness of dreams. He has helped us understand how the various paths relate to each other and how they all provide helpful, but partial, perspectives on the terrain. At the outset of this exploration, we were besieged by a clamor of different claims about what dreams mean and how to interpret them. With Gadamer's guidance, we have managed to distinguish what is legitimate and valuable in these claims from what is exaggerated, distracting, or invalid. Now we may ask our main question: do dreams have *religious* meaning? Once again, the dream explorers we have been studying meet us with a babble of conflicting assertions. Each of them argues that his or her path into the wilderness of dreams leads to *the* key truths about the religious meaning of dreams. What are we to do with these different claims?

We can immediately, if crudely, divide the eight figures we have been following into two camps: Freud, Hall, and Hobson say no, dreams do *not* have religious meaning; while Breton (to an extent), Jung, LaBerge, Tedlock, and Hunt argue that yes, dreams *do* have religious meaning. But we are interested in much more than bald yes-or-no answers; we are seeking a fuller understanding of the question, the sort of understanding that will emerge only after we have overcome the various disagreements among the individual dream explorers, examined their shortcomings, and synthesized their insights. To accomplish this, we will need another external guide, a guide that can help us to explore and then integrate the important nuances of each of the eight dream interpreter's approaches to the religious meaning of dreams.

In this section, the guide will be not a single person (like Gadamer) but rather a concept: the concept of 'root metaphors'. As stated in the introduction, I am proposing the following thesis:

> Dreams do have a dimension of religious meaning; this dimension emerges out of the *root metaphors* in dreams. To understand fully the root metaphors of dreams requires an interdisciplinary integration of the different fields of dream study with a theory of interpretation and a theory of religious metaphor.

Part 3 provided a theory of interpretation, helping us to clarify the process that is involved in understanding the meanings of dreams. Here, in part 4, we will develop a theory of religious metaphor. Our main resources in this effort will be the linguistic philosophers George Lakoff and Mark Johnson, who have described the metaphorical nature of human thought; the theologian Don Browning and his studies of how "metaphors of ultimacy" influence modern psychological thinking; the theologian Sallie McFague, who has examined the primacy of metaphor in modern religious language; and the philosopher Paul Ricoeur, whose ideas about symbols and self-reflection can guide us in the interpretation of religious meanings. The concept of root metaphors represents a way of summarizing the work of these philosophers and theologians and of focusing their views into a powerful guide that can help us to explore the different fields of dream study. This concept will enable us to integrate the insights of our eight dream interpreters and to develop a sound understanding of the religious meaning of dreams.

Metaphorical Thinking

The basis of the root metaphor concept is the idea that all human thinking is fundamentally metaphorical in nature. Many contemporary linguists, philosophers, and literary critics have provided excellent accounts of metaphorical thinking.[1] Here, we will look to George Lakoff and Mark Johnson's work *Metaphors We Live By*, which is remarkable among these accounts for its clarity and directness.

The book opens with a straightforward definition: "The essence of metaphor is understanding and experiencing one kind of thing in terms of another" (Lakoff and Johnson 1980, 5). Metaphors are most obviously at work in cases where we try to understand things that are not concrete or clear by using structures from those things that are more concrete or clear. For example, love is an emotion that often defies easy description, so we use metaphors of physical force to talk about it—speaking of the "electricity" between people, feeling "sparks," "gravitating" towards someone, and so forth. We use our more tangible experiences with physical force as metaphors to structure and thus to understand our less tangible experiences with love.

But Lakoff and Johnson argue that metaphors are not mere decorations to our language. On the contrary, they claim that metaphorical thinking is basic to *all* human conceptual thinking. There is no such thing as "direct" or "immediate" experience that does not ultimately involve our metaphorically relating the given experience to other kinds of experience (56–60).

The metaphors that ground our thinking have a profound influence on our lives. Metaphors shape our perceptions, our experiences, our attitudes, our goals, and our behavior. An example Lakoff and Johnson offer is the common metaphor "rational argument is war." They comment, "this metaphor allows us to conceptualize what a rational argument is in terms of something that we understand more readily, namely, physical conflict" (61–68). According to this metaphor, rational arguments involve "taking positions" to "establish" and "defend"; "attacking" and "destroying" an "opponent's stronghold"; using various "tactics and strategies" to "defeat the enemy" and "gain victory" for one's own side. Lakoff and Johnson's point here is that the metaphor shapes not only how we think of rational arguments, but also how we *act* in them. The clear, concrete imagery of war influences the way we experience rational arguments ("are we defending our position well enough?"), the plans we make in them ("we need to counter-attack that argument"), and the ways we evaluate our behavior ("we wiped them out"). Lakoff and Johnson claim that this widespread influence of metaphorical thinking is pervasive in our lives:

> In all aspects of life, not just in politics or in love, we define our reality in terms of metaphors and then proceed to act on the basis of the metaphors. We draw inferences, set goals, make commitments, and execute plans, all on the basis of how we in part structure our experience, consciously and unconsciously, by means of metaphor. (158)

The metaphors we use are not arbitrary, appearing suddenly out of thin air. Rather, they always have some basis in our experiences—our experiences as creatures with certain kinds of bodies, living in a certain kind of natural environment, belonging to a certain kind of culture. Lakoff and Johnson argue that our metaphors reflect our *interactions* with our bodies, our physical world, and our culture. This seemingly straightforward point has three important consequences for understanding the role of metaphorical thinking in human life. First, there is a vital connection between our metaphors and the culture we live in. Each culture must define a social reality that can enable its members to get along with each other and with the environment. Cultures use metaphors to establish, promote, and defend their social realities, and these cultural metaphors work to orient each individual's perceptions, attitudes, and ideals within the given social reality.[2]

The second important implication of the interactional origins of our metaphors is that all metaphors are *partial*: when we understand one thing in terms of another, we engage in a process of highlighting some aspects and obscuring others. Lakoff and Johnson examine how the metaphor "time is money" (see the preceding note) highlights the ways in which time can be quantified, assigned a value per unit, and used for purposeful ends (66). However, they also note how this metaphor obscures the possibilities that time can be leisurely, that work can be play, and that inactivity can be productive (67). It is inevitable that metaphors provide only partial understandings; this becomes problematic, however, if we adhere to one set of metaphors so strictly that we are unable to recognize the *other* possible ways of metaphorically structuring our lives. Lakoff and Johnson argue that we must always use many different metaphors:

> There is a good reason why our conceptual systems have inconsistent metaphors for a single concept. The reason is that there is no one metaphor that will do. Each one gives a certain comprehension of one aspect of the concept and hides others. To operate only in terms of a consistent set of metaphors is to hide many aspects of reality. Successful functioning in our daily lives seems to require a constant shifting of metaphors. The use of many metaphors that are inconsistent with one another seems necessary for us if we are to comprehend the details of our daily existence. (221)

The third implication here has to do with the "truth" of metaphors. Since the metaphors we use derive from our relations with our bodies, our environment, and our culture, they reflect what Lakoff and Johnson call "interactional properties," rather than any inherent, permanent qualities in things (163–64).[3] Thus the truth of a metaphor depends on how well it fits with the circumstances of our situation and the nature of our purposes. Lakoff and Johnson state, "since the truth of a statement depends on whether the categories employed in the statement fit, the truth of a statement will always be relative to the way the category is understood for our purposes in a given context" (164–65).[4]

Lakoff and Johnson say that one of the main reasons they are so interested in metaphorical thinking is because it enables us to see how reason and imagination are united. Most philosophical accounts of human understanding insist either on the power of objective reason or on the richness of individual imagination. On the one side, understanding must overcome emotion and imagination to be objectively, rationally true; on the other side, understanding must draw on human feelings and values, and not simply on pure, abstract rationality. Lakoff and Johnson's theory of metaphorical thinking enables us to move beyond this philosophical dichotomy. They argue,

> Reason, at the very least, involves categorization, entailment, and inference. Imagination, in one of its many aspects, involves seeing one kind of thing in terms of another kind of thing—what we have called metaphorical thought. Metaphor is thus *imaginative rationality*. (193)

Metaphorical thought is a product of *both* rationality and imagination, and we miss something important about human understanding if we overemphasize either one or the other of these aspects.

Towards the end of their book, Lakoff and Johnson comment that "metaphor is one of our most important tools for trying to comprehend partially what cannot be comprehended totally: our feelings, aesthetic experiences, moral practices, and spiritual awareness" (193). To understand in greater detail how metaphorical thinking underlies our spiritual awareness, we will draw on the reflections of Don Browning, Sallie McFague, and Paul Ricoeur.

Don Browning on Metaphor and Religious Meaning

Theologian Don Browning elaborates on Lakoff and Johnson's insights into the metaphorical nature of thought and looks at the ways we draw on metaphor to respond to basic existential issues of human life. He investigates people's responses to the following question: "What kind of world or universe constitutes the ultimate context of our action?" (Browning 1983, 53). He claims that we all ask this question—whether consciously or unconsciously, silently or with others, in a religious or a secular language—in the process of trying to determine how to live a good, meaningful life. Our answers, Browning argues, take the form of "metaphors of ultimacy":

> When it comes to speaking about the most ultimate (in the sense of most determinative) aspect of our experience, we do it in metaphorical language. None of us knows directly the ultimate context of experience; therefore we take more familiar and tangible aspects of experience and

> apply them metaphorically to the intangible and mysterious ultimate features of experience. The metaphors we use to represent the ultimate context of experience function to orient us toward that context, form our expectations, teach us to see the world in a certain way, and give us the basic vision by which we live. Through our metaphors we thus learn to see the world at its foundations as either warm or cold, responsive or indifferent, predictable or capricious, demanding or permissive, for us or against us. (Browning 1983, 58)[5]

Browning studies the metaphors of ultimacy underlying the approaches of modern psychologists in his book *Religious Thought and the Modern Psychologies*. His principal goal in this work is to show how modern psychologies are serving the essentially religious purpose of providing comprehensive understandings of life, of guiding people in what they should do and how they should look at the world. Browning seeks to show "how the deep metaphors of the psychologists studied here color their implicit moral ideas. We will see how the function of deep metaphors in theology and psychology tends to put both on an equal footing; both disciplines rest their conceptual worlds on assumptions which fundamentally have the logical status of faith" (Browning 1987, 26–27).

For example, Browning finds that Freud's works are grounded in the deep metaphors of *eros and thanatos*, the instincts of life and death. While these instincts begin as psychological working hypotheses, they are soon "elevated into a cosmology and inflated into metaphors which represent the ultimate context of experience" (Browning 1987, 43). Browning describes how Freud's conception of the life and death instincts directly influences his understanding of the duties, the ideals, and the possibilities of human life. Browning comments,

> Freud does not quite comprehend, however, that by taking the position that the psychobiological realm is the only relevant context for human action he has indeed elevated eros and death to metaphors of ultimacy, that is, to metaphors which represent the only effective and relevant ultimate context of experience. To the extent that Freud apotheosized the metaphors of life and death, he used them in ways analogous to the way more explicitly religious people metaphorically represent the ultimate context of experience. Hence, Freud was making his own kind of *faith judgement*. None of us, including Freud, really knows in any direct, tangible, and sensory way what the ultimate context of experience is. What intimations that we have of this ultimate context, we represent, and even investigate, through more concrete metaphors taken from ordinary experience. (Browning 1987, 43–44)

As another example, Browning finds in the humanistic psychology of Carl Rogers that the deep metaphor of *organic growth* colors not only Rogers's psychotherapeutic practice, but also his accounts of moral action, social relations, and the highest goals of human life (Browning 1987, 61–93).[6] And in the behaviorism of B. F. Skinner, Browning sees the concept of *natural selection* serving Skinner as a metaphor of ultimacy. This deep metaphor leads Skinner not only to envision human psychology in a certain way, but also to reject the moral ideal of human freedom and to promote the social engineering of incentives and reinforcements as best hope for a just society (Browning 1987, 94–116).[7]

Browning argues that the deep metaphors of these and other modern psychologists reveal the fundamentally religious qualities of their systems. While they may *begin* with issues of emotion, anxiety, and adaptation, these psychologists inevitably come to describe their visions of the ultimate context of human life—visions that are expressed in metaphorical language and that deeply influence their attitudes about morality, society, and the nature of a good, meaningful life.

Sallie McFague on Metaphors and Religious Meaning

Theologian Sallie McFague offers an approach to metaphorical language in religion that can help us fill out our concept of root metaphors.[8] McFague's writings complement Browning's in important ways. While Browning claims that the modern psychologies, despite their secular appearance, have genuine religious insights, McFague argues that modern theology, despite its tenuous status in a secular culture, continues to provide vital religious meanings for us. Just as Browning looks at the metaphorical language of modern psychology to illuminate its religious foundations, so McFague studies metaphorical language in religion to demonstrate that modern theology's teachings still have enduring religious value.

McFague starts her book *Metaphorical Theology* by admitting that modern Judeo-Christian theology is in trouble. Western society, with its secular governments, its powerful science and technology, and its plurality of peoples and beliefs, appears to have little use any more for religion. The traditional language of religion seems distant, archaic, useless. McFague is concerned that if theology does not address itself to the special circumstances of the modern context, it will suffer the two grave problems of idolatry and irrelevance: theology "will become idolatrous, for we will absolutize one tradition of images for God; it will become irrelevant, for the experiences of many people will not be included within the canonized tradition" (McFague 1982, 3).

In order to overcome the threats of idolatry and irrelevance, McFague turns to contemporary theories of metaphor. She, like Browning, believes that a study of metaphor holds the key to renewing religion's vitality in the modern world. Philosophers of language, she notes, have concluded that metaphor is "the way language and, more basically, thought works" (37); McFague's argument is that metaphor is also the way that religion works. Metaphors in religion—which McFague calls "root metaphors"— differ from other metaphors in the following ways: they seek to account for all of reality, providing a comprehensive vision of the world; they tend to be numerous, complex, rich, and ambiguous; they deal with meanings, values, and feelings (although this does not mean that root metaphors are merely "subjective"—McFague claims they provide true *knowledge* about human valuation, a point supported by Lakoff and Johnson's notion of "imaginative rationality"); and they have a broad influence on us, shaping our perceptions, thoughts, ideals, and practices (103–7).

McFague claims that religious thought and language is *not* fundamentally different from any other kind of thought and language—the same metaphorical processes underlie both "ordinary" and "religious" understandings. In this way she rejects the notion that religion is an outmoded, outdated kind of thought for modern people. McFague argues that anytime we use metaphorical language to describe a comprehensive vision of the meaning and value of human life, we are engaged in religious thinking, whether or not we are using formally "religious" terminology.

But still, what to make of the problems of idolatry and irrelevance in modern theology? McFague believes that we can overcome these problems by emphasizing how living metaphorical language is always *tense*, *jarring*, and *shocking*. A powerful metaphor brings two previously unrelated things into sudden relation with each other, forcing us to grapple with the ways the two things *are*, and are *not* like each other; McFague says

> A metaphor is an assertion or judgement of similarity and difference between two thoughts in permanent tension with one another, which redescribes reality in an open-ended way . . . [G]ood metaphors shock, they bring unlikes together, they upset conventions, they involve tension, and they are implicitly revolutionary. (42, 17)

By emphasizing this shocking, "is/is not" quality of metaphorical language, McFague believes that modern theology may avoid the tendency to fix its notions of God into rigid, narrow images. For example, many feminists claim that the Judeo-Christian tradition has fallen prey to this tendency in its exclusive use of masculine imagery to portray God: "God the Father" appears to be the root metaphor of this tradition. But McFague argues that the metaphor of "God the Father" has become absolutist and idolatrous and that people have forgotten how this metaphor (like any metaphor) *is*, and yet is *not* an accurate description of God. The tension in this metaphor has been lost, and consequently our understanding of God has become narrow and rigid. McFague shows how the Judeo-Christian tradition in fact presents *many* metaphors to describe the divine-human relationship—some masculine, some feminine, and some non-gendered (167–92). When we rediscover this rich diversity of metaphors, and when we remember that each is but a partial rendering of our relationship with God, we avoid the threat of idolatry.[9]

McFague meets the problem of irrelevance in much the same way. She notes again how feminists have challenged the Judeo-Christian tradition, charging that its emphasis on male virtues makes it irrelevant to the experiences of women. McFague responds that the Judeo-Christian tradition does carry metaphors and images that, while underdeveloped by male church authorities, can speak to women's experience—for example, metaphors of God as a mother and as a woman (167–92). The dominant institutions of this religious tradition *appear* irrelevant to the modern world because they have highlighted only a few of its root metaphors and ignored or downplayed others; but McFague argues that the religious tradition *itself* is not irrelevant. She claims that if we recognize how religious language is at base metaphorical, we can overcome the danger of irrelevance: if we regard all root metaphors as partial, we are free to seek new ones that are fresher, richer, and more relevant to our lives.

We should note how McFague refers to Gadamer in discussing root metaphors and religious meaning. She cites his hermeneutic guidelines for the interpretation of texts as a crucial source for her approach:

> We have reviewed Gadamer's hermeneutics in detail because he, better than any other contemporary philosopher of interpretation, sees the connection between interpretation and metaphor; that is, that interpretation is a movement from a familiar base—one's own "prejudices"—to a new, changed perspective through interaction with another and unfamiliar base which is the text . . . What this means, of course, is that metaphorical thinking, as we have described it, is not something alien, esoteric, or "poetic," but simply a precise way of describing what we do when we interpret: we see "this" as "that," we find the thread of similarity with the familiar in the unfamiliar situation and move beyond where we were before as we work through the process of "is and is not" toward new understanding. (57–59)

McFague finds Gadamer's own metaphors of "game" and "dialogue" to be especially accurate descriptions of the open, mobile, playful nature of human thought when it is understanding something new. She sees a direct tie between her account of metaphorical thinking and Gadamer's hermeneutics in the idea that "growing" human thought "has no closure and is radically relative: no judgement is final, no interpretation absolute, no perspective exclusive" (58).

Paul Ricoeur on Symbols and Reflection

Paul Ricoeur is a philosopher whose writings on language, symbolism, and self-reflection have had a major influence on contemporary religious studies (Ricoeur is, for example, a primary inspiration for both Browning and McFague). In his two books *The Symbolism of Evil* (1967) and *Freud and Philosophy: An Essay on Interpretation* (1970) Ricoeur explores the relationship between symbols and philosophical self-reflection. His study of this relationship bears directly on our discussion of root metaphors. Ricoeur can help us understand how to *interpret* root metaphors—what questions to ask of them and what kinds of meaning we may discover in them.

What role, Ricoeur asks, do symbolic or metaphorical images play in the process of developing self-consciousness? Do these images contribute anything of genuine value to a philosophical reflection on the nature of the self? Ricoeur begins to answer these questions by describing the three areas in which symbolic images appear. First is the *cosmic* realm, the realm of primal religious symbols; second is the *poetic* realm of the artistic imagination; and third is the *oneiric* realm, that is, our dreams.

> It is in dreams that one can catch sight of the most fundamental and stable symbolisms of humanity passing from the "cosmic" function to the "psychic" function . . . To manifest the "sacred" *on* the "cosmos" and to manifest it *in* the "psyche" are the same thing. (Ricoeur 1967, 12)

Symbols from these three realms open up dimensions of experience that would otherwise remain closed or hidden, that humans cannot reach through more rational means. Symbolic images express important meanings that are crucial to the development of self-consciousness. Ricoeur argues that without these symbols and the vital meanings they bear, the human self becomes a barren, lifeless abstraction.

Western philosophy has, in Ricoeur's view, generally misunderstood the relationship between symbols and reflection. Either symbols and philosophical reflection are separated into different spheres, each legitimate but neither having any real influence on the other; or, symbols are taken as "primitive" philosophy, as fanciful images that can be stripped of their outer garb to reveal the rational truths lying underneath. Ricoeur rejects both of these views and proposes an alternative: "Between these two impasses, we are going to explore a third way—a *creative interpretation of meaning*, faithful to the impulsion, to the gift of meaning from the symbol, and faithful also to the philosopher's oath to seek understanding" (1967, 348). Ricoeur wants to do justice to both the valuable meanings expressed by symbols and to the philosophical demand for critical rationality. The turn to symbols, he emphasizes, does not mean we surrender our hard-won powers of reason; it does not imply any simple-minded return to the romantic's paradise of an innocent, prerational faith.

> Does [the turn to symbols] mean that we could go back to a primitive naivete? Not at all. In every way, something has been lost, irremediably lost: immediacy of belief. But if we can no longer live the great symbolisms of the sacred in accordance with the original belief in them, we can, we modern men, aim at a *second naivete* in and through criticism. In short, it is by *interpreting* that we can *hear* again. (Ricoeur 1967, 351)

Ricoeur recognizes, however, that this project of developing a "restorative interpretation" (Ricoeur 1967, 349–51), an interpretation that approaches primal symbols with a "second naivete" in order to hear their important meanings, is likely to be rejected by many modern critics. Modern thought is dominated by a "hermeneutics of suspicion" (Ricoeur 1970, 32–33); Feuerbach, Marx, Nietzsche, and Freud have taught us to attack symbols, to demolish their illusions and chastise the "false consciousness" that lies behind them. But Ricoeur argues that such a ruthlessly critical, suspicious approach to symbols is in fact absolutely crucial to a restorative interpretation: only if we subject symbols to the most rigorous rational criticism can we discover the rich, valuable meanings they express.[10]

Ricoeur devotes special attention to Freud, for he sees in Freud's work two valuable contributions to a restorative interpretation of symbols. First, Freud provides what Ricoeur calls an "archeology" and a "teleology" of the self. The "archeology" involves a deep and probing insight into our past. Freud is the great pioneer in discovering the origins of our self in our childhood, in our unconscious, and in our instincts. This archeology, Ricoeur argues, is related to a "teleology," to Freud's vision of what the self can become in the future. The teleology of the self's development is, for Freud, "the process of becoming conscious" (Ricoeur 1970, 492). His psychoanalytic therapy is guided by this teleological vision, as it uses an analysis of one's past to work progressively towards a full, cohesive, thoroughly self-reflective consciousness.[11] Ricoeur believes that Freud's seminal discoveries provide us with a key insight into the nature of symbols: symbols express both the archeology and the teleology of the self.

> We should say that symbols carry two vectors. On the one hand, symbols repeat our childhood in all the senses, chronological and non-chronological, of that childhood. On the other hand, they explore our adult life: "O my prophetic soul," says Hamlet. But these two functions are not external to one another; they constitute the overdetermination of authentic symbols . . . These authentic symbols are truly regressive-progressive; remembrance gives rise to anticipation; archaism gives rise to prophecy. (Ricoeur 1970, 496–97)

A second contribution that Freud makes to the development of a restorative interpretation of symbols is his use of a "mixed discourse" (Ricoeur 1970, 59-158). Ricoeur sees in Freud's theories a mixed language of energetics and meaning—Freud speaks of physical energies, forces, and mechanics, and also of psychological meanings, interpretation, and language. Although many critics accuse Freud of inconsistency and confusion on this point, Ricoeur claims that Freud uses a mixed discourse intentionally, because he recognized that there is an intimate and irreducible relationship between the physiological and the psychological aspects of the self. Freud always speaks of both organic forces and conscious meanings; his genius, Ricoeur argues, is that he

> never confronts one with bare forces, but always with forces in search of meaning; this link between force and meaning makes instinct a psychical reality, or, more exactly, the limit concept at the frontier between the organic and the psychical. (Ricoeur 1970, 151)

Freud reveals not only how the instincts "represent or express the body to the mind" (Ricoeur 1970, 137), but also how we can know the instincts only by interpreting them as they emerge in our dreams, fantasies, and works of culture—that is, in *symbols*. The important point here, Ricoeur claims, is that symbols are always both force *and* meaning: symbols are deeply rooted in our organic, physiological nature, and yet they are known to us only through the interpretations we make of their meanings.

Ricoeur's work, while difficult to explain in so short a space, nevertheless adds a great deal to our understanding of root metaphors. He points directly to dreams as a primary source for the expression of religious meanings, meanings that are indispensible for the full development of the human self. Most importantly, Ricoeur offers us an extremely helpful approach to the interpretation of root metaphors. He encourages us to look to root metaphors for insights into both the past and the future—into both the archeology and the teleology of the self. He prompts us to explore both the physiological and the psychological dimensions of root metaphors, to discover how root metaphors may reflect both organic force and psychic meaning. And, Ricoeur describes an attitude of "second naivete," which can guide our interpretation of root metaphors: we subject root metaphors to a thorough, critical, highly "suspicious" analysis, and then we *listen* to what the root metaphors have to say to us, allowing our critical rationality to be renewed and revitalized by their rich, primal meanings. Ricoeur emphasizes that "the second naivete is not the first naivete; it is postcritical and not precritical; it is an informed naivete" (Ricoeur 1970, 496).

Summary: The Key Characteristics of Root Metaphors

We may now draw together these different linguistic, theological, and philosophical theories, describe concisely the concept of root metaphors, and explain how this concept will help us to understand the religious meaning of dreams. With the ideas of Lakoff and Johnson, Browning, McFague, and Ricoeur to support us, we can offer the following definition: *Root metaphors are metaphors that express our ultimate existential concerns; root metaphors provide religious meanings that orient our lives.*

As Browning and McFague suggest, root metaphors reflect our visions of those basic existential questions that every person tries to answer in some way or other: questions like, Why are we alive? Why do we suffer? Why do we die? What happens to us after death? What is good, and what is evil? Is there a God? Is the universe a fundamentally orderly or a fundamentally chaotic place?[12] Historically, these questions have been addressed by the world's religious and spiritual traditions. But as McFague and especially Browning emphasize, the secular philosophies of the modern era also respond to these existential issues in metaphorical languages. Browning comments,

> Even the various sciences have their metaphors of the most determinative context of experience. And insofar as they have been used dogmatically to account *exhaustively* for the most truly determinative aspects of experience, these scientific metaphors function as faithlike statements analogous to the metaphors of creator, governor, and redeemer in Christian theology. We see this happening in some dogmatic and positivistic uses of the metaphors of free variation and natural selection in

> evolutionary theory, in the mechanistic billiard ball analogies in Newtonian physics, . . . and finally in the more romantic metaphors of harmony and "complementarity of excellences" found in . . . free-market economics. (Browning 1983, 58)

These "nonreligious" philosophies are thus religious in function, if not in name, to the extent that they are fundamentally guided by certain root metaphors.

Root metaphors are not, however, the exclusive property of formal religious traditions or secular philosophies. People may develop their own more personal and idiosyncratic root metaphors that respond to the basic existential concerns of their own individual lives. Lakoff and Johnson note that

> Just as we seek out metaphors to highlight and make coherent what we have in common with someone else, so we seek out *personal* metaphors to highlight and make coherent our own pasts, our present activities, and our dreams, hopes, and goals as well. A large part of self-understanding is the search for appropriate personal metaphors that make sense of our lives. Self-understanding requires unending negotiation and renegotiation of the meaning of your experiences to yourself. In therapy, for example, much of self-understanding involves consciously recognizing previously unconscious metaphors and how we live by them. It involves the constant construction of new coherences in your life, coherences that give new meaning to old experiences. The process of self-understanding is the continual development of new life stories for yourself. (Lakoff and Johnson 1980, 232–33)

Such personal metaphors are *root* metaphors when they touch on issues of ultimate meaning and value that have arisen in a person's own particular life: Why am *I* alive? Why do I suffer in *this* particular way? What are the most powerful forces shaping *my* life? There is, of course, no sharp and absolute distinction between "personal" root metaphors and other, more "communal" root metaphors; indeed, all root metaphors have both personal and communal elements, and most people orient their lives with the help of both kinds (See Obeyesekere 1981). The point of making this distinction is to highlight the fact that some root metaphors may respond to the existential concerns of only one person and may provide essentially religious meanings to that one person alone. We will encounter some instances of more personal root metaphors in the following chapter.

To continue with our summary of the characteristics of root metaphors: Lakoff and Johnson claim that all new metaphors have their origins in an "imaginative rationality," and this is certainly true of our root metaphors as well. Root metaphors involve both our powers of imaginative, poetic creativity and our faculties of rational categorization and inference. Lakoff and Johnson would also remind us that root metaphors do not spring right out of our minds, fully formed, but rather emerge out of our interactions with our bodies, our environments, and especially our cultures. Our root metaphors, no matter how original or pure they appear, always bear the influence of these interactions.

The most powerful, most vital root metaphors are characterized by a high degree of tension—what McFague calls their "shocking," "iconoclastic," "revolutionary" quality. Root metaphors challenge us, demanding that we work to make sense of how they both are and are not adequate visions of ultimate meaning and value. McFague further emphasizes that all root metaphors are partial (a point Lakoff and Johnson make as well), that even the most powerful and insightful root metaphors are still only limited expressions of matters that cannot be exhaustively defined.

Lakoff and Johnson, Browning, McFague, and Ricoeur all join to support the point that root metaphors have a tremendously widespread influence in our lives. They shape the ways we perceive, categorize, and reason about the world; the ways we feel emotionally about our experiences; the ways we behave in our daily lives; the ways we make moral judgements about right and wrong; the ways we relate to other members of our community; and the ways we establish ideals, values, and future goals for ourselves.

The concept of root metaphors will now serve us as a guide in the next three chapters, as we return to the wilderness of dreams and ask whether dreams have religious meaning. In chapter 16, we will look at some actual dreams in which root metaphors emerge and consider the extent to which these dreams are religiously meaningful. Then, in chapter 17, we will use the root metaphor concept to evaluate how well the eight dream theories account for the religious meaning of dreams. Finally, chapter 18 will conclude this section with a discussion of how the concept of root metaphors can provide practical guidelines for exploring the religious meaning of dreams.

The Differences between Root Metaphors and Symbols

Before moving on to these other matters, we need to clarify one point of possible confusion: how exactly are the terms *root metaphor* and *symbol* related?[13] Religiously meaningful dreams are most commonly said to have "archetypal symbols," a reference to Jung's concept of 'archetypes'. I believe, however, that the root metaphor concept gives us a better, more precise way of understanding the religious meanings expressed in dreams. To speak of "metaphors" reminds us that in all forms of thinking, waking, and dreaming, we use the categories of what we *know* to try and understand what we do *not* know; it thus reminds us that our understanding is always *partial*, that in highlighting some things we always obscure or neglect other things. In the example McFague presented, the root metaphor of God the Father highlights certain aspects of the relationship of humans to the divine. But because this metaphor portrays the relationship in an exclusively masculine form, it obscures the possibility that we may also relate to the divine as a *mother*, or as a *friend*. Root metaphors are always partial, and remembering this fact prevents us from becoming too attached to our religious insights, no matter how perfect or heaven-sent they seem.

To speak of dream images as metaphors (rather than as symbols) also reminds us that the images are at least partly our *own* creations and thus are always related to our experience and our culture. The term *symbol* too often implies an independent ontological entity floating about in an ideal Platonic realm. This can lead to the rigid fixing of culturally specific meanings onto supposedly "universal" symbols (such as the Freudian tendency to define every elongated object, in every culture through history, as a phallic symbol). Metaphors, by contrast, are always related to actual people and actual cultures. By their very nature metaphors depend on specific, context-bound notions for their meaning. This is not, however, to take away from the often startling novelty of dream images—the emergence of a new, fresh metaphor clearly involves some sort of primal, spontaneous creativity, what Lakoff and Johnson call our "imaginative rationality." Nor is this to deny that people from different cultures and different historical eras frequently use the same metaphors to express virtually identical meanings, as demonstrated by the comparative study of religions and mythologies. The main point here is that we need to *reconnect dream images with cultures*. Referring to dream images as metaphors helps us in this: it helps us avoid the problematic tendency towards a culturally and historically naive universalization of meaning that too often occurs with the use of the term *symbol*.

Yet another virtue of regarding dream images as metaphors is that it highlights the *narrative movement* that so often characterizes powerful dreams. Many contemporary dream interpreters concentrate so much on analyzing particular symbols that they lose sight of the narrative flow and integrity of a dream. This is the great danger of any kind of structuralist analysis of dreams: by breaking a dream into little pieces, we can obscure the dream's overall narrative movement; and yet it is precisely this narrative movement that so often discloses powerful, profound meanings.[14] We avoid this problem if we speak of dreams as metaphors, for metaphors are themselves tiny narratives. At the heart of a metaphor is a verb—an action, a movement, a change. Symbols, by contrast, are nouns, discrete images that come to life only when set within a story. Perhaps this is why symbol dictionaries abound, while a "metaphor dictionary" sounds nonsensical.

The adjective *root* in the root metaphor concept emphasizes three things. First, it reflects the way these particular metaphors reach down into the deepest issues and concerns of human existence. Second, it highlights the *living* nature of these metaphors, the vital, powerful influence they have in our lives. And third, it points to our need for many such metaphors if we are to enjoy a balanced, thriving life. A tree would topple over with the first wind if it had only one root, and it therefore sends many roots into the earth to anchor and nourish it. Just so, we need many root metaphors to orient, nourish, and invigorate our lives.

The term *root metaphor* is, to sum up, not automatically synonymous with the terms *symbol*, *archetypal symbol*, *sacred symbol*, and so forth. These terms may in certain cases be roughly identical with *root metaphor*, to the extent that they denote the same characteristics discussed in this chapter. But the concept of root metaphors has the important advantage of illuminating more clearly, fully, and accurately the religious qualities and potentials of our dream experiences.[15]

16

FLYING WITH GREAT EAGLES AND EATING SHORT BANANAS: EXAMPLES OF ROOT METAPHORS IN DREAMS

Toto, I have a feeling we're not in Kansas anymore.

—Dorothy Gale, in *The Wizard of Oz*

The Emergence of Root Metaphors in Dreams

In the preceding chapter we developed the concept of root metaphors out of the work of Lakoff and Johnson, Browning, McFague, and Ricoeur. But while they helped us understand theoretically the nature and meanings of root metaphors, they said very little about how root metaphors actually appear. We now know what root metaphors *are*, but we still do not know how exactly they *emerge*. In this chapter we will look at some detailed examples of root metaphors appearing in dreams. The goal will be to provide concrete evidence for a central assumption of this project: *dreams are a primary source of root metaphors*.

The following six dreams were all powerful experiences that had deep, transformative effects on the dreamer—and, in some cases, on the dreamer's community as well. I have divided these dreams into two loose groups. The initial three dreams are more explicitly "religious," in the sense of coming to members of a distinct religious tradition and having overt religious imagery. The second group consists of three dreams that are less explicitly religious, involving people who are not members of a formal religion, and/or whose dreams have little or no overt religious imagery.

We will examine these dreams according to the following criteria, drawn from the theoretical definition of root metaphors proposed in the previous chapter:

1. Does the dream involve metaphorical expression, that is, the use of more concrete, tangible images to help express less concrete, tangible meanings?
2. Does the dream touch on fundamental issues of human existence?
3. Is the dream unusually powerful, shocking, challenging, or tension filled? Does it force the dreamer to react to it?
4. Does the dream have deep, transformative effects on the dreamer's life (and, perhaps, on the life of the dreamer's community), shaping his or her thoughts, feelings, values, and actions?

Flying with The Great Eagle

The ritual of the Ojibwa dream fast is frequently cited in order to demonstrate the role of dreams in shaping religious beliefs and worldviews. If the concept of root metaphors has any claim to being useful in explaining the religious meaning of dreams, it should be able to account for the main characteristics of classic dream phenomena like the Ojibwa dream fast.

The Ojibwa are a branch of the Algonquin people of North America, living north of the Great Lakes in what are today the Canadian provinces of Manitoba and Ontario. The following account of the dream fast comes from anthropologist A. Irving Hallowell, who did fieldwork among the Ojibwa from 1930 to 1940.[1]

Dream fasts generally served as initiation rituals for Ojibwa boys (although there are accounts of Ojibwa girls going on dream fasts as well [Radin 1936]). Before leaving for the fast, the boy was given carefully washed clothes and a specially dyed animal skin to sleep on. He would then head into the forest with his father, grandfather, or other male relatives, who would help the boy find a suitable spot to build a *wazison* (a sleeping platform up in the trees). The boy would spend up to ten days and nights on the *wazison*, alone and fasting, until he had a dream in which a *pawagan* (a spirit being or other-than-human being) bestowed a blessing upon him (Hallowell 1966, 282–83).[2]

One particular Ojibwa boy's dream experience was described to Hallowell as follows:

> When I was a boy I went out to an island to fast. My father paddled me there. For several nights I dreamed of an *ogima* [chief, superior person]. Finally he said to me, "Grandson, I think you are now ready to go with me." Then *ogima* began dancing around me as I sat there on a rock and

> when I happened to glance down at my body I noticed that I had grown feathers. Soon I felt just like a bird, a golden eagle. *Ogima* had turned into an eagle also and off he flew towards the south. I spread my wings and flew after him in the same direction. After a while we arrived at a place where there were lots of tents and lots of "people." It was the home of the Summer Birds. (Hallowell 1955, 178)[3]

Hallowell adds that "after returning north again the boy was left at their starting point after his guardian spirit had promised help whenever he wanted it. The boy's father came for him and took him home again" (Hallowell 1955, 178).

Hallowell stresses that Ojibwa relations with *pawaganak* are *not* metaphorical; they are real experiences, as real as any contacts with other humans (Hallowell 1966, 279).[4] But the dream fast experience clearly *becomes* metaphorical, in the sense that it helps the boy understand the many intangible qualities of his self, his tribe, and the world around him. His dream acts as a *known* experience through which he progressively learns about *unknown* realms of reality. The dream thus serves the boy as a metaphorical experience, even though the dream itself is not experienced or initially interpreted as a metaphor.

Through his dream fast experience this particular youth comes to understand better two particular aspects of his culture's religious beliefs. One is the ultimate nature and power of the human self. In his dream the boy sees the eagle, the "Master" of its species or "Great Eagle" (Hallowell 1966, 284), turn from a human into a bird, and then the boy himself turns into a bird. This experience teaches him that *pawaganak* and humans both have the power of metamorphosis; both, as Hallowell comments, have "a similar structure—an inner vital part that is enduring and an outward form which can change" (Hallowell 1961, 42). This similar structure implies that when humans die their inner vital part will endure, just as the *pawaganak* endure: "the human self does not die; it continues its existence in another place, after the body is buried in the grave" (Hallowell 1961, 43). The dream fast thus provides the boy with a concrete experience that helps him understand better the mysterious nature of spirit beings, death, and the afterlife.[5]

The second aspect of Ojibwa religious beliefs the youth learns through his dream is the importance of developing relationships with a *pawagan*. The dream fast provides Ojibwa youths with their first official encounter with the realm of *pawaganak* and enables them to establish a special relationship with members of this realm. The boy's dream experience of flying with the Great Eagle meant that "the Master of the Golden Eagles became one of the boy's tutelaries, or 'guardian spirits', for life"

(Hallowell 1966, 285). Hallowell emphasizes the vital importance of developing such relationships for the Ojibwa to live a "good life." He says it is only within the intricate web of social relations with *pawaganak* that an Ojibwa individual can fare well in life;

> the Ojibwa believe that a good life, free from illness, hunger, and misfortune (i.e., *pimadaziwin*) cannot be achieved through relations with other human beings alone, cooperative as they may be. The help of powerful persons of the other-than-human category is a necessity. (Hallowell 1966, 274)

The boy's dream gives him a tangible experience with a member of this generally intangible spirit community and serves throughout his life as a guide towards the Ojibwa ideal of *pimadiziwin*.

The dramatic setting of the dream fast, with the ritual preparations, isolation, and ascetic practices, insure that the dream experiences will be intense and powerful. The dreams had an unquestionably transformative effect on the Ojibwa youths. Hallowell comments that

> The dream fast was the most crucial experience of a man's life: the personal relations he established with his *pawaganak* determined a great deal of his destiny as an individual. He met the "persons" on whom he could most firmly depend in the future. He also acquired knowledge of the specialized powers that would be of potential benefit to his fellow human beings. The dream fast was recognized as the ultimate source of their validation . . . [Furthermore,] the dream fast introduced a boy to a new set of moral obligations. The full benefit of the power and knowledge obtained was made contingent upon the fulfillment of obligations to other-than-human entities that assumed a primary moral force in his life . . . [T]he commands of *pawaganak* were considered absolute. (Hallowell 1966, 288–89, 287)[6]

In the Ojibwa youth's dream fast experience, imagery that is relatively more concrete (i.e., the boy meeting the "Master" of the eagles, turning into a golden eagle himself, and flying away with the Master) helps him understand meanings that are relatively less concrete (i.e., the nature of the human self and the spirit community). These meanings touch on basic Ojibwa religious beliefs, and the dream fast experience produces a deep, transformative effect on the boy's religious and existential orientation in life.

The Ojibwa dream fast involves experiences that are widely acknowledged to be religiously meaningful. The capacity of the root metaphor concept to account for the main features of these dream experiences is evidence that the concept does provide a legitimate, useful guide to exploring the religious meanings of dreams.

Eating the Short Banana

We will turn now to some more contemporary dream examples and consider how well the root metaphor concept helps us understand the religious meanings of these dreams. First, we will look at the dreams of Moses Armah, a member of the Nzema people of southwest Ghana who founded the Action Church in 1948. The development of new religions, churches, and cults out of one person's revelatory dreams is a phenomenon commonly reported in anthropological literature (Wallace 1956; Stephen 1979; Gregor 1981). Mr. Armah reported his dreams to the Italian anthropologist Vittorio Lanternari, who has investigated many cases of dreams that reflect crises in traditional societies and that have given rise to new socioreligious movements (Lanternari 1975).

Born in 1908, Armah lived in a country suddenly awash with radically conflicting cultural forces: Western economic and political forces, missionaries from a variety of Christian sects, and prophets teaching Hindu doctrines all mixed together with traditional African tribal religions and healing cults. Countless new syncretic religious movements sprouted up all across Ghana (224). Armah had originally been a Methodist, but he was deeply influenced by the cultural ferment around him. He described having the following dream experiences in 1941:

> One night I dreamt and saw Jesus personally. He was walking on something like a bridge. A big house was nearby. I had the house in front of myself, and the bridge on my side. I was standing there. I saw Jesus personally and he was walking like a person. He was a person, and he was clothed with a blue cloth. The wind was blowing; he was walking and his hair were all on his back. I was looking at him, and he was turning slowly. At a moment he gazed at me and I fell down. I put up and saw that he had gone. "This is Christ, he is going." Now Jesus returned again. He looked at me: as soon as my eyes met his, I fell down: three times. After this I could not see him again, and I came out of the dream. At that time I had not yet thought of founding a new Church. This is the first dream I had.
>
> The second dream was that I dreamt that from my hair was growing a bunch of bananas. It grew and became mature. Then I saw somebody cut it down. That banana was "longhands" [two kinds of banana grow in Ghana]. I was on the way come to get them plucking them to eat. But

> the person came and said: "Don't eat!" Then he brought me another kind of banana, the short one, which I ate. He told me: "Don't eat the long one, but eat this." Then I came out from the dream. I was puzzled. From that day I dreamt that long banana, each time I smell it I vomit. I don't touch it at all. At first I did not understand the meaning of the bunch of banana. But now I understand it. I should found this church. The banana bunch was the symbol of the new church. Eat the short one means found the new church. (224–25)

Armah recognizes the metaphorical nature of the banana image in his second dream. Bananas are an important crop in Ghana, both as a foodstuff and as an export product; they are a very concrete element in the people's well-being. In Armah's dream eating bananas serves as a metaphor to express something much less tangible, namely his religious allegience, his participation in a spiritual tradition.[7] The choice in the dream of eating one kind of banana rather than the other kind metaphorically expresses the decision Armah must now make to leave his old church and found a new one.

Armah's metaphorical choice between the two types of banana touches on some of the most fundamental concerns of his life. To leave his old church means leaving his accustomed religious tradition, leaving his faith community, and changing the basic values that have guided him. To start a new church means seeking a new relationship with God, reorienting his whole life, and developing a new community. Armah's dreams represent a transformative religious experience, in the sense that they forcefully propel him into a new relationship with the divine.[8] Yet the power and influence of his dreams is not limited to Armah's individual life, for he went on to develop a new religious movement that attracted many adherents. Lanternari notes that such revelatory dreams often address more than individual concerns alone. In times when foreign influences are rapidly upsetting traditional patterns of living, the revelatory dreams of a new religious leader frequently express the concerns of a whole community: a new church

> helps its followers overcome the feeling of existential precariousness that results from the conditions of underdevelopment, misery, and social subordination in which they live . . . The founder's dream activity acts as an explosive outlet for all the frustrating experiences accumulated by the individual himself and by the group of which he is the exponent and interpreter. (228–29)

Armah's dreams provided him with a root metaphor that motivated a profound spiritual change in his own life and in the lives of many other people in his community.

Finding the Cave beneath the Mother House

The last of this group of more religiously explicit dreams is that of a woman from my home town in California, whom I will call "Mrs. M." Her dreams, which she has described to me both verbally and in writing, illustrate clearly how root metaphors reach back through a wide variety of past experiences and then reach forward to influence numerous aspects of the dreamer's future life.

Mrs. M. (born in 1938 in Los Angeles) married immediately after finishing college. Although she had done very well in school, she did not pursue a career but instead devoted herself to the full-time care of her children. Soon after her marriage, a long-simmering conflict with her parents broke out into an open fight. She cut off contact with all members of her Irish Catholic clan for a number of years and concentrated her energies on creating her own family and home. In her early forties Mrs. M. decided to go back to school. Her interests turned to caring for the aged, the infirm, and the homeless, and she entered a Presbyterian seminary to study for the ministry.

Throughout her life Mrs. M. had recurrent dreams of double houses: she would be in one house and then find that it opened onto another one; she would walk through these houses, trying to figure out how the two related to each other. Towards the end of her seminary training she had the following dream:

> I was going to one meeting after another in the mother house at Domenican College [a nearby Catholic convent]. We were working on the homeless problem. I was tired of the endless talk and doing. Someone said to me that if I really wanted to be near to God and know God that there was a place deep within the heart of the convent where I could do that. I went off in search of this holy place—and found it. It was a dark cave or grotto made of wet drippy rocks. There was a stream coming into the cave that made a small gurgling fountain of water. It was quiet except for the sound of the moving water. It was quite dark. A short nun dressed all in black was quietly shuffling around taking care of the grotto. She told me that if I sat down on the red bench and waited quietly that maybe I would experience God. The red seat was covered with cheap, worn vinyl and there was a tear in the seat that had been repaired with tan tape. I thought it probably wouldn't happen to me but I'd sit quietly and see what would happen.
>
> It was dark and quiet and I began listening to the sound of the little fountain of water. Before long I became aware that the water was rushing faster and then I found myself becoming one with the water and

> being thrust into space. My being became at one with the stars and the suns. I experienced complete peace, complete understanding of how everything in the universe fit into an integrated whole and a total unity with God—not becoming God, but the indescribable feeling of being that I was totally with God. This feeling continued for some time and then I simply found myself back on the red bench. The little nun continued her work but I knew that she knew that I had met God in that cave.

This dream uses the dominant image of Mrs. M.'s life—the image of the home—to express the nature of her path towards a relationship with God. Homes have always been the center of her world; whether in breaking away from them or creating them, looking for them or helping those who do not have them, homes have represented the most concrete, tangible realities in Mrs. M.'s life. The recurring double-house dreams used this image to represent a variety of different conflicts and concerns in her life. In this dream of finding the cave beneath the mother house, the concrete image of the convent home metaphorically addresses the very intangible question of how she can be related to God.

It takes no special insight to see that this dream deals with basic existential issues. Mrs. M. is weary of a life oriented exclusively around "endless talk and doing." She wants "to be near to God and know God," but she is not sure that she can have such a direct, intimate relationship with the divine. She goes down "deep within the heart of the convent," into a place that represents some of the strongest and yet most ambivalent influences on her life. Despite her skepticism, she has an intense visionary experience that reveals to her the harmony of the universe and the living reality of God in her life.

The dream made a powerful and lasting impression on Mrs. M.—she says, "even though this was a dream it was a real experience that has affected my life ever since." In this sense, Mrs. M.'s dream is *real*, not a metaphor for something else. But much like the Ojibwa boy's dream of the Great Eagle, her dream also *becomes* a metaphor in that it provides a clear, concrete experience *through which* she comes to understand less clear, less concrete concerns in her life. For example, the dream renewed Mrs. M.'s conviction to pursue a career in the ministry. The arduous years of seminary training had made her question whether entering the clergy might paradoxically be taking her farther away from God. But this dream metaphorically expressed the real presence of God in her life, and this relieved her doubts about becoming a minister. The dream also led her to reflect anew on her negative feelings about her Catholic upbringing. Finding the cave beneath the Catholic convent is a living image that metaphorically expresses the potential values that Mrs. M. could discover below the surface of Catholicism and that could positively contribute to her present spiritual life.

So Mrs. M.'s dream accords with all our criteria for a root metaphor dream: her dream experience of finding the cave beneath the mother house provides her with a powerful metaphorical image that enables her to deepen her relationship with the divine, to revitalize her commitment to her spiritual ideals, and to revisit the long-standing wounds from her religious upbringing.[9]

Searching for a Sufi Pir in the Telephone Directory

The dream of Ahmad Sahib, a Pakistani businessman with a British education, is an appropriate transition from the first to the second group of dreams in this chapter. As with the first group, Sahib's dream involves a number of overt religious images and characters; and yet unlike the first group, Sahib was not a formal member of any specific religious tradition at the time of his dream. The following account of Sahib's experience appears in anthropologist Katherine Ewing's article "The Dream of Spiritual Initiation and the Organization of Self Representations Among Pakistani Sufis" (1989).

Sahib describes his early life as one of conflict between two cultural identities. On the one hand he was a modern Westerner who was educated in England during World War II and who became a successful businessman. But on the other hand he was a South Asian Muslim who had "a love for the mystical side of Islam" and "a yearning beyond the material aspects of life" (62). He says, "from childhood I had been looking for a teacher, but I couldn't define my thoughts clearly" (62). Then, in 1946, Sahib had this dream:

> I dreamed of a basement room, with a street passing outside at the level of the ventilators. It was a long narrow room with a low table and a carpet. There was food on the table. I was at the door waiting for a guest to arrive, sitting cross-legged in a spirit of great expectation. Then I saw two people coming, and they stood on the stairs. One was my *pir* [a sufi spiritual guide and healer]. I didn't know him. The other was very saintly, tall, fair, with curved eyebrows and a white turban. Both were dressed in white, with black shawls, as the Prophet wore. I suddenly realized that these were the people I had been waiting for. I was awe-struck. I couldn't move. They came and sat at the low table. My *pir* said to the saint, "This is my son. Take a good look at him." The food on the

> table was dal [lentils], curried spinach, and chapatis [flat wheat bread]. The saint took a morsel of chapati, dipped it into the spinach and dal, and then put it into my mouth. I can still taste it, a heavenly taste. It filled me with longing and love. I ate it, and as the morsel went down my throat, both of them disappeared.
>
> I ran up the road, like a madman on the public street, shouting and crying for them. I knew that they were my life. Then I saw a telephone booth and a thick telephone directory. I flipped through it as if I were searching for his number. I was saying Khwaja Muinuddin Chishti [founder of the Chishti order of Sufis in India, d. 1236] over and over again. When I awoke I was actually saying this. (62)

It is very common, Ewing notes, for Pakistani men to begin searching for a spiritual guide because of a dream like Sahib's. She describes the long history in Muslim culture of such "initiation dreams," which have the power of "transforming the life of the dreamer" (60). Ewing argues that Sahib's experience conforms to the traditional pattern of Sufi initiation dreams. We can see how his dream also has all the characteristics involved in the emergence of a root metaphor.

Sahib's dream is a pointed metaphorical expression of the central dilemma in his life: he yearns for a more spiritual existence, but he cannot find it in his modern Western life. The image of Sahib frantically seeking the name of a thirteenth-century Sufi mystic in a modern telephone book is both poignant and arresting. It clearly indicates the folly of trying to satisfy his religious urges by means of conventional Western ideals and values. Before the dream, Sahib says, "I couldn't define my thoughts clearly"; but then the dream comes and presents a direct, vivid image that metaphorically expresses the inchoate feelings Sahib could not previously understand.[10]

His dream certainly reaches to the basic existential issues of Sahib's life. It concerns the nature of his personal identity, his relationship with his Muslim heritage, his struggle with the material and the mystical aspects of life, his sense of the divine, and his future destiny in life. These are not exclusively personal issues, however. As Ewing notes, Sahib's conflict stems directly from the Pakistani colonial experience under British rule, and many of his contemporaries have undergone similar struggles (64). His dream thus weaves together both personal and communal questions about the nature and destiny of Pakistani life in modern Western culture (much as Armah's dream did in reflecting his culture's experiences with the modern West).

Sahib's dream had the powerful effect of thoroughly transforming and refocusing his life; he says "ever after that [having the dream] I searched for the *pir* who told Khwaja Muinuddin, 'This is my son'" (63). Sahib continued his quest for twelve years, determined to find his *pir*. Finally, in 1958, he met a Sufi spiritual guide who greeted him with the words, "You have taken a long time coming, but you are here" (63). Sahib began studying with the man and soon became a *khalifa* (designated spiritual successor) of his *pir*.

Sahib's dream brought his life into sharper focus; it provided a direct, unmistakable picture of his core existential dilemma, and it powerfully motivated him to set out on an entirely new kind of life that would satisfy his deepest longings. As Ewing says of all Sufi initiation dreams, "the dream thus becomes a pivot in terms of which [the dreamer] reorients his life" (60).[11] The image of seeking his pir in a phone book became a root metaphor for Sahib, portraying the most decisive forces in his life and opening the way to a new, more meaningful existence.

Blistering White Paint

The root metaphors that emerge in dreams do not necessarily have to take an explicitly religious form. Often, the imagery is very personal and idiosyncratic, reflecting existential concerns and conflicts that are specific to the individual dreamer (see Obeyesekere 1981). The following example of such a dream expressing a more personal root metaphor is taken from the work of Jeremy Taylor, a dream workshop leader and author of *Where People Fly and Water Runs Uphill: Using Dreams to Tap the Wisdom of the Unconscious.*

In one of Taylor's workshops a woman described dreaming the exact same image, over and over again:

> A disembodied close-up view of a wooden surface painted white. The paint is just beginning to blister and bubble . . .
>
> [Taylor comments,] each time she dreams it, in the fleeting instant she catches sight of the slightest bulges in the white painted surface, she is assaulted by feelings of despair and anguish and terror—feelings far more intense than any similar emotions she experiences in waking life. Invariably, when the dream occurs, she jerks awake with feelings of misery and terror filling her awareness, and clinging to her even on into wakefulness. As these feelings slowly ebb away, they are replaced by anger, confusion, and frustration. " . . . What possible reason could there be for such a seemingly innocuous dream to be so *horrible*?!? *Why* do I keep dreaming it, over and over again, all my life?" . . . She told the group . . . that this particular dream was the bane of her life, and seemed to her to be "totally meaningless and pointless." (Taylor 1992, 282–83)

The woman, whom Taylor refers to as "Mary," had been having this dream in the same basic form for as long as she could remember. As Mary, Taylor, and the group discussed the dream, it suddenly emerged that the dream was referring to terrible incidents of physical abuse and emotional trauma from Mary's childhood, incidents that she had never consciously acknowledged until right then. "Blistering white paint," she realized, was a strikingly accurate image of how she had always covered up or "whitewashed" the painful memories of those incidents. The dreams show that the socially presentable facade of her life could not prevent all the long-repressed suffering from "bubbling up" from underneath.

This recurrent dream metaphorically expresses a whole range of intensely painful emotions that Mary had not been able to understand consciously. The dream draws upon the very concrete, very simple image of a white painted surface beginning to blister to help her understand the vastly more amorphous and complex experiences of being abused as a child. These experiences were among the most powerful forces shaping Mary's life. They were decisive in forming her strong attachment to the value of social respectability and her equally strong fear of social stigma and rejection; they gave her an extreme sensitivity to feelings of shame and guilt; and they created lifelong problems in forming intimate relationships with others.

The concerns and issues expressed in Mary's dream are somewhat different from those in the other dreams we have examined. Mary's dream does not involve God, saints, or any other supernatural beings. However, her dream does touch on fundamental existential issues in her life. Mary's experiences of childhood abuse shaped the way she understood the world, her identity, and her relationships with other people. The dream's profound power is clear from its incessant recurrence and from the uniquely disturbing emotions it always evoked in her. It challenged her to face the reality of her suffering, to acknowledge the still painful wounds lying behind her carefully managed appearance of social acceptability.

When Mary finally did reach a conscious understanding of her dream of blistering white paint, it had a tremendously transformative effect on her life. Taylor comments,

> In Mary's case, the unexpected appearance of the repressed memories of childhood abuse led her to deepen and intensify the course of professional therapy she was already embarked upon . . . Eventually, it led her into more open and candid communication with her adult siblings. In taking this courageous step, Mary helped all her siblings release themselves from terrible blocks and miseries. It turned out that each one had been abused separately, and had been suffering in solitude and silence,

> supposing that the disturbing dreams and occasional flashes of horrible memories were "made up," or that he or she "had been the only one." When Mary found the courage and clarity to speak with her siblings . . . they all experienced tremendous relief, along with shock, grief, sadness, and anger. Their darkest and most confused memories and intuitions were acknowledged and confirmed by other family members, once the terrible fear and silence were broken. With these shared revelations, life-long patterns of confused relating and neurotic avoidance of commitment and intimacy in Mary and other members of her family suddenly began to make more sense. As the amnesia and the denials were lifted through honest communication, the patterns of neurotic behavior in the whole family began to change. (294–95)

The root metaphor of blistering white paint thus inspired Mary not only to change her own life but also to help her brothers and sisters understand the painful experiences that had been among the most fundamental and formative forces in all of their lives.

The Extinguished Candle, Relit

The approach of death is a situation that frequently brings forth powerful, numinous dreams.[12] The vivid imagery and existential meaningfulness typical of these dreams accords very closely with our account of root metaphors. The following dream was described by Dr. Jay Dunn, a British psychoanalyst, in Millie K. Fourtier's work *Dreams and Preparation for Death*.

Dunn's patient was an older woman (we will call her "Margot") in a hospital suffering the final stages of a terminal disease. One morning she reported to the doctor this dream:

> She sees a candle lit on the window sill of the hospital room and finds that the candle suddenly goes out. Fear and anxiety ensue as the darkness envelops her. Suddenly, the candle lights on the other side of the window and she awakens. (Fourtier 1972, 1)

That same day Margot died, "completely at peace" in Dr. Dunn's words (1).

The metaphorical image in Margot's dream is as simple as it is profound. She is about to die, about to end her mortal life. What will happen to her then? Will it be painful? Where will she go? To these basic existential questions Margot's dream responds with the metaphor of a candle extinguished, and relit. The candle goes out in her hospital room, and there is a moment of fear and darkness; but then the candle lights again outside, dispelling Margot's anxious feelings. The simple, tangible image of the candle helps Margot understand the supremely intangible issue of a person's fate after dying.

The imagery of Margot's dream relates to the virtually universal use of light, fire, and flame to express metaphorically the enduring essence of a human being (Eliade, 1965). Many of the world's religious traditions practice funeral rituals involving fires of various sorts (Thomas 1987). Although Margot is lying alone in a hospital room, and the fire comes in the plain form of an ordinary candle, her dream draws on the same metaphorical imagery and touches on the same existential issues as do those religious funeral rites. Furthermore, the dream's powerful effect on Margot, giving her the strength to face death, is identical to the effect sought by most religious funeral rites: to reassure people that death is not something to be feared, that there will be life and light even after our mortal existence is extinguished. Margot's dream presents her with a root metaphor, as simple as it is poetic, that enables her to meet the final existential crisis of human life with peace and contentment.

Filling Out the Root Metaphor Concept

These six examples give some substance to the concept of root metaphors, for which we provided only a theoretical definition in the previous chapter.[13] All of these dreams possess the key characteristics of root metaphors. They are metaphorical expressions that touch on fundamental issues of human existence, that are unusually powerful and challenging, and that have deeply transformative effects on the dreamer. The examination of these six dreams justifies our basic claim: root metaphors *do* emerge in dreams, and dreams in which root metaphors emerge *do* have religious meaning.

We have done more, however, than simply confirm our theoretical understanding of root metaphor dreams. By looking at these actual dream experiences, we have discovered further aspects of root metaphors that we could not see or appreciate fully from a purely theoretical perspective. For one thing, we find in all of these examples that the special dreams appear in a period of *crisis*. With Margot it is the crisis of impending death; with the Ojibwa boy it is the crisis of making the transition from adolescence to adulthood. In these two cases the crisis is of a more personal nature, while in other cases a dimension of communal crisis is also involved. For example, Ahmad Sahib's dream of seeking his *pir* in a telephone directory relates not only to his personal difficulties in establishing a life's identity but also to the difficulties of many Pakistanis in trying to integrate traditional Muslim and modern Western colonial influences. Taken together, the six dreams we have examined suggest that root metaphors appear when the dreamer (and often his or her community) is experiencing a crisis, a profound threat to his or her ordinary, accustomed life or worldview.

A related point is that these root metaphor dreams help the dreamer adapt effectively to the given crisis.[14] Sometimes this adaptation leads to a deeper integration into one's traditional faith or worldview (the Ojibwa boy entering his tribe's society of human and other-than-human beings); sometimes the adaptation involves a transition from one tradition to another (Moses Armah leaving the Methodist Church to found his own Action Church); and sometimes the adaptation produces a forcible rejection of a past faith or worldview (Mary repudiating her "white paint" existence[15]).

And finally, we see in many of these dreams how the root metaphors bear an impulse towards a *moral* response—the dreamer frequently feels a strong need to express gratitude, to help others, to contribute something to the community's welfare. The Ojibwa commonly returned from their dream fasts with new dances, songs, or healing rites to give to the community. Moses Armah's dream motivated him to preach a message of spiritual renewal among his people. Mrs. M.'s mystical dream encounter with God further strengthened her commitment to do God's work in the world. And Mary's discovery of the painful realities behind her "blistering white paint" dreams led her to help her brothers and sisters face those same realities in their own lives.

Now that we have developed a way of understanding the religious meaning of dreams and have successfully applied it to a set of actual dreams, we may return to our study of the leading modern dream explorers. The primary question we will ask in the next chapter is, how well do modern dream explorers account for religiously meaningful dreams?

17

ROOT METAPHORS AND THE EIGHT PATHS INTO THE DREAM WILDERNESS

"And now,' cried Max, "let the wild rumpus start!"
—Maurice Sendak, *Where the Wild Things Are*

The root metaphor concept provides what has always been lacking in the study of the religious or spiritual dimension of dreams: a clear, sound, well-developed notion of religious meaning.[1] The preceding chapter applied this concept to a selection of actual dreams in order to illustrate that root metaphors do emerge in dreams and that such root metaphor dreams do have religious meaning. In this chapter we will, at last, bring all the theories together and engage in a critical "wild rumpus": we will use the root metaphor concept to analyze, compare, and evaluate the eight dream theories we have been studying. We will ask how well these eight theories accord with the understanding of the religious meaning of dreams we have developed in this section. Do these theories cohere with the concept of root metaphors? Do they conflict with it? Do they contribute additional nuances to it?

Evaluating the "Yes" Camp

To begin, we can consider how the root metaphor concept enables us to support those dream explorers who affirm that dreams do have religious or existential meaning.

At first glance, Andre Breton seems to be opposed to the idea that dreams have any religious meaning. After all, he declared that the analysis of his own dream revealed, "from the point of view of the religious marvelous, absolutely nothing" (Breton [1932] 1990, 45). However, this statement must be understood in the specific context of Breton's hostility towards conventional Western culture and particularly towards its Judeo-Christian religious heritage. His dream reveals no religious quality, insofar as "religious" is defined by that monotheistic heritage. However, Breton and the surrealists are tremendously interested in dreams for their transformative power, their power to challenge "normal" reality and to reveal new potentials for human creativity, spirituality, and knowledge. Dreams open up a realm of freedom and "marvel" that surrealists avidly draw upon to overturn our ordinary experiences of reality. According to Breton, surrealism promotes not just a theory of aesthetics but an entire existential vision of life, and dreams are a vital source of creative energy for developing that vision.

Once we appreciate these ideas, we can see that Breton's view of the transformative force of dreams relates closely to our characterization of dreams and religious meaning. His emphasis on the stunningly creative imagery of dreams and on the far-ranging existential meanings of this imagery is an excellent statement of the qualities of root metaphor dreams. In particular, Breton's interest in the tremendous power of dreams to shock us, to challenge our conventions and thrust revolutionary visions of reality at us, is exactly the same as our interest in the iconoclastic force of root metaphor dreams (recall McFague's argument that root metaphors challenge our customary spiritual beliefs, checking our tendencies towards idolatry). Dreams do not, from Breton's perspective, substantiate the Judeo-Christian religious tradition; but they certainly do have a powerful and profound influence on our ultimate spiritual ideals and values.

Our discussion of root metaphors can also help us perceive the excesses of Breton's account of dreams. He attacks the rationalism of Western culture so vigorously that he seems to ignore the important role of rationality in dream imagery. Lakoff and Johnson argue that metaphorical expressions, such as those in dreams, emerge out of a *creative combination* of imagination and rationality. Lakoff and Johnson also help us appreciate how dreams are always shaped to some extent by the dreamer's *culture*. Breton and the surrealists, however, stress the pure, absolute "freedom" of dreams, their utter liberty from *all* rationality and *all* cultural convention. After our discussion of root metaphors, such claims appear to be excessive and untenable.

But on the whole, the root metaphor concept corresponds quite closely to Breton's approach to dreams and religious meaning. Indeed, Breton and the surrealists have much to offer us in return. Most approaches to dreams (e.g., the approaches of depth psychology, sleep laboratory research, content analysis, and anthropology) have the tendency towards the intellectual and the linguistic; they work to bring the meanings of dreams straightaway into rational thought and language. The surrealists, though, develop the meanings of dreams in a more roundabout fashion, through various forms of artistic expression. More than other dream explorers, the surrealists *play* with dreams in the full, Gadamerian sense—experimenting with different means of expression, probing the bounds of ordinary language, moving freely between the absurd and the profound. This approach to dreams is not mere frivolity or escapism; Breton did define surrealism as an attempt to *integrate* dream and reality. Rather, the surrealists offer us a different means of bringing forth the religious meanings of dreams, a means that plays artistically with the creative dimensions of what we are calling root metaphor dreams.

Carl Jung is without a doubt the most influential voice in the "yes" camp. To study the religious meaning of dreams is often considered identical with taking a Jungian approach. Jung's view of dreams and religious meaning stems from his notion of the collective unconscious, the psychic substratum that underlies the mental life of all people. He claims that the forces of the collective unconscious naturally propel humans forward in the process of individuation, that is, the growth of the psyche towards balance and wholeness. Jung sees the collective unconscious as guiding the symbols and teachings of all religious traditions throughout history. In the modern era, however, when formal religions have lost their vitality, people must find their own individual way of relating to the collective unconscious. Depth psychology has arisen to help people in this process. Dream interpretation is a primary means used by depth psychology, for Jung claims that our dreams reveal these forces of the collective unconscious, presenting archetypal symbols that guide us along the path of individuation.

Much of what Jung says about the religious meanings of dreams corresponds exactly with our characterization of dreams and root metaphors. Jung claims that dreams often relate directly to the fundamental process of human life, that is, individuation. Some dreams have an especially powerful influence in promoting this process. Indeed, what Jung calls "big dreams" or "archetypal dreams" can be taken as roughly synonymous with our "root metaphor dreams." Jung's insight that dreams have a "prospective" function of orienting us towards our future agrees exactly with Ricoeur's argument that all symbols have a "teleological vector." Jung emphasizes that dreams tend to jolt our conscious views, offering compensatory meanings to balance our psyche, and that we should be suspicious anytime a dream's meaning seems obvious to us. All of this relates remarkably well with our claim, based on Lakoff and Johnson's and McFague's work, that root metaphors profoundly challenge our ordinary accounts of reality.

The root metaphor concept thus agrees on almost all points with Jung's approach to the religious meanings of dreams, and it provides his psychological theory with strong philosophical support. Perhaps more importantly, the root metaphor concept also enables us to clarify two important problems with Jung's view of dreams.[2]

The first concern is raised by all of Jung's talk of "natural laws," "plain facts," and "pure products of the psyche." It seems that with such language Jung is veering dangerously close to a naive, romantic view of the human unconscious. Much like Breton, Jung appears to be denying the important role of rationality in shaping the expressions of our unconscious. It is one thing to recognize that dreams *challenge* rational structures, and another thing to assert that dreams are *free from* rationality, that dreams are "pure," "natural," and "untainted." To make the latter assertion can blind us to the profoundly creative, growth-enhancing powers of human rationality. Lakoff and Johnson speak of "imaginative rationality," of human thought and experience as emerging out of a metaphorical process of imagination and rationality. This is one reason that the term *metaphor* is preferable to *symbol* in dream studies, because the combination of imagination and rationality is foregrounded in the former term. Dreams do have something primally imaginative, spontaneous, and "irrational" about them. But dreams also always involve comparisons, relations, contrasts, narrative structures—all *rational* processes, and all essential to metaphorical thinking. We seriously misunderstand the creative power of dreams if we fail to appreciate the union of imagination *and* rationality in their formation.

The second concern raised by Jung's views on dreams and religious meaning has to do with the *essentialism* of the collective unconscious and the archetypes. Jung often speaks of the archetypal symbols that emerge in dreams as independent ontological entities with fixed, universal meanings. At times he presents the archetypes as equivalent to Platonic Forms, enjoying their existence in a reality completely separated from any actual human experience. Many critics of Jung have attacked this essentialism, condemning him for elevating his own personal notions to the status of universal psychic realities. Feminists, for example, charge that Jung's characterization of the anima archetype (i.e., the archetype representing feminine qualities in a man's psyche) reflects more his and his culture's particular views of women than anything about the "feminine" in a pure, universal sense (Rupprecht 1985, Wehr 1987). But here again, the root metaphor concept can be of assistance. As Lakoff and Johnson, Browning, and McFague all stress, our metaphors always reflect our cultural context; the experiences we have living in a particular historical and cultural environment directly influence the metaphorical imagery that emerges in our dreams. When we ignore this cultural influence, we become vulnerable to an *idolatry of dreams*—reifying some meanings, ignoring or obscuring other meanings, and becoming imprisoned within the limits of our culture to the exact extent that we are unaware of its influence upon us.

As often as Jung makes statements that sound thoroughly essentialist, he also condemns all suggestions that the archetypes have any fixed meaning or content. We do not need to get involved in Jungian polemics, however, to make our point: we must always be sensitive to the role of culture in shaping the religious meanings of dreams. It is one of the biggest advantages of the root metaphor concept (over the notion of archetypal symbols) that it emphasizes clearly the cultural context of religiously meaningful dreams.

Stephen LaBerge claims that his research on lucid dreaming opens up new spiritual possibilities—people may, he announces, pursue a "path of inner growth through lucid dreaming." He says the experience of lucid dreaming leads us beyond ordinary levels of consciousness, to the point where we realize that the world of our perceptions is ultimately illusory and of our own creation. Lucid dreaming can produce "transcendental experiences" in which we gain fundamental insights into the nature of reality. Such insights, which LaBerge claims are directly related to the enlightenment experiences of Tibetan Buddhists, can profoundly change our ordinary lives, enabling us to be "fully awake" in our daily existence.

LaBerge's affirmation of the religious or spiritual meaning of lucid dreams does in many ways cohere perfectly with our characterization of root metaphor dreams. The special lucid dreams he describes do touch on matters of ultimate existential concern, with a revolutionary power that can transform a person's whole understanding of reality. Furthermore, LaBerge's research gives substance to the idea (which we have derived from Ricoeur) that root metaphor dreams reflect both psychological and physiological aspects of the self. LaBerge has made some provocative suggestions about the physiological aspects of lucid dreams and about the possibility of exploring bodily processes while in the state of lucid dreaming.[3]

In many ways, LaBerge is most interested in the religious meaning of the *form* of lucid dreaming—lucid dreaming itself becomes a root metaphor for LaBerge. The experience in lucid dreaming of creating one's own reality is for him a metaphor for all of life, metaphorically expressing the spiritual belief that we create our own reality in waking life as well. Hence LaBerge suggests that lucid dreaming can help cultivate a spiritual attitude of "lucid living." In using lucid dreaming as a root metaphor, LaBerge is indeed adopting a spiritual view very similar to that of Buddhists. As we found in chapter 1, Buddhist enlightenment is frequently precipitated by the realization that dreaming and waking are not truly distinct from each other. The recognition of dreaming as illusion leads to the recognition that waking life is ultimately an illusion also (see Laufer 1931; Wayman 1967; O'Flaherty 1984).

However, the root metaphor concept enables us to identify an important problem with LaBerge's account of the religious meaning of lucid dreams. This problem regards the *relevance* of lucid dreaming as a root metaphor. Sallie McFague argues that root metaphors become irrelevant when they do not speak to people's lived experience. She says that certain Judeo-Christian root metaphors, for example, are so male oriented that they are irrelevant to the experiences of women. Thus, McFague says, all root metaphors must be evaluated according to their relevance to people's actual experience.

When we consider LaBerge's root metaphor of lucid dreaming in this way, we find that it does not relate well to many people's lived experience, and that it does run the danger of irrelevance. Specifically, the root metaphor of lucid dreaming suggests a radical idealism, that is, an attitude that all reality is utterly illusory, merely a creation of the unenlightened human imagination. Such radical idealism is extremely hard to relate to the actual, day-to-day experience of modern Westerners—does this mean that the ringing of my alarm clock is not "real" and that I don't have to go to work? Does this mean that my sick child is an "illusion" and so I don't need to care for him? Does it mean that societal violence, oppression, and poverty are mere "creations of my mind" and that I don't need to do anything to help others?[4] The root metaphor of lucid dreaming, in LaBerge's formulation of it, seems irrelevant to the important concerns of most people's daily lives.[5] As a result, we must add a note of caution to our appreciation for LaBerge's many important and insightful claims about the spiritual value of lucid dreaming.

Barbara Tedlock, while basically affirming the religious meaning of dreams, is far less exultant in her discussion of the issue than are Breton, Jung, and LaBerge. Tedlock and her anthropological colleagues show that in many non-Western cultures dreaming does have religious meaning, in either of two ways. First, people's dreams may *reflect* their culture's spiritual, metaphysical, and psychological beliefs. The interpretation of dreams can thus give insight into the deepest foundations of a person's worldview. Or second, people's dreams may *create* new religious imagery that can actively influence or transform the dreamer's religious orientation—confirming to a degree E. B. Tylor's theory (1874) that dream experiences are the origin of religion.

Tedlock's anthropological findings on the religious meanings of dreaming in non-Western cultures have many points in common with our account of root metaphor dreams. As we have done, she affirms that dreaming often does involve issues of existential importance, that religiously meaningful dreams can have a challenging, revolutionary power to them, and that they may provoke deep, transformative effects in the dreamer. Furthermore, Tedlock's insights on how dreaming both reflects and creates cultural meanings mark a major contribution to our understanding of the relationship between religiously meaningful dreams and the dreamer's cultural context. Her analysis of Zuni and Quiche dream beliefs illustrates how dreaming can reflect the basic existential values of the dreamer's culture. The Zuni experience dreaming as a "deathlike breach of the fragile boundary" between the living and the dead, while the Quiche believe that in dreaming the dreamer's "free-soul" meets other free-souls and learns valuable teachings from them (Tedlock 1987, 126–27). In both cases, dreaming experience reflects important beliefs about reality, death, the soul, and the boundaries between self and other. Tedlock's work here prompts us to explore dreams not only for the personal root metaphors of the individual dreamer but also for reflections of the root metaphors of the dreamer's culture. This implies that the study of root metaphor dreams can be an important means of understanding the religious ideals and values of a culture and of examining the ways that a culture instills (or partially instills, or fails to instill) these ideals and values in its members.

Tedlock and her colleagues also offer some concrete evidence for the idea that dreams can actively create new religious ideals and values. John Homiak argues that the religious role of dreaming in the Rastafarian movement of Jamaica illustrates how "dreaming has always been a key source of religious inspiration in prophetic and millenarian movements" (Tedlock 1987, 220); and Michael Brown describes how the Aguaruna people of Peru use dreams as a source of imagery to transform creatively their waking ideals, values, and relationships (Tedlock 1987, 168). However, Tedlock seems less interested in the "creation" aspect of dreaming than in the "reflection" aspect. If there is a problem with her work (from our perspective), it is that she does not draw upon the many other anthropological studies that give a fuller account of this aspect of dreams and religious meaning. For example, Thomas Gregor (1981, 1983) has provided us with fascinating studies of the Mehinaku people of Brazil, describing how their dreams are the origin of much of their religious activities. Vittorio Lanternari (1975) has examined the role of dreams as "charismatic significants" inspiring the rise of new religious movements in Africa and the Caribbean. Michele Stephen (1979) has reviewed the many ways that dream experiences have contributed to the transformation of traditional religious beliefs and rituals of Melanesian cultures. Many other anthropologists have also done excellent work investigating the role of dreams in creating new religious meanings. Tedlock's research is but the leading voice in a growing body of anthropolgical studies on dreams and religious meaning.

Harry Hunt, the final member of our "yes" camp, presents a cognitive psychology of dreams that fits very smoothly with our account of the religious meanings of dreams. Hunt argues that there is a genuine cognitive psychological basis for religiously meaningful dreams. He finds that "intensified dreams" such as nightmares, lucid dreams, and dreams with prophetic qualities have their source in certain cognitive capacities for creative visual-spatial imagery. These cognitive capacities enable the emergence of dreams that may express novel images relating to fundamental life problems. While such intensified dreams may be rare, Hunt claims that they "can at times rival works of art in their profound depictions of basic existential issues in human life."

Hunt's work on the "multiplicity of dreams" has many points in common with our exploration of root metaphor dreams. He has a sophisticated appreciation for the role of metaphorical expression in dreams, and he affirms that dreams have the potential to touch on profound existential issues. Hunt's first contribution to our understanding of the religious dimension of dreams is his study of how "intensified dreams" involve special syntheses of the cognitive processes of imagination and rationality—exactly the point that Lakoff and Johnson make in their notion of "imaginative rationality." Hunt gives this crucial notion a solid cognitive psychological basis, demonstrating that what we are calling "root metaphor dreams" emerges out of both imaginative and rational cognitive processes. He thus allows us to accommodate both the romantic claims (as seen in Breton and Jung) that religiously meaningful dreams stem from natural, entirely a-rational sources and the rationalist claims (from Freud, Hall, and Hobson) that dreams are formed by rational, lawful mental processes.

Hunt also provides us with important insights into the cultural influences on religiously meaningful dreams. He agrees with Tedlock that cultural beliefs and structures profoundly shape dreaming experience. But Hunt goes on to describe the cognitive aspects of this shaping influence. Humans have the cognitive capacities to experience a "multiplicity" of dream forms, ranging from personal-mnemic dreams of ordinary, day-to-day activities to "intensified" dreams like nightmares, prophetic dreams, and lucid dreams. Hunt argues that the *actualization* of these cognitive capacities depends on the given cultural context—an individual from a culture that depreciates visual-spatial imagination (as modern Western culture does, in Hunt's view) is less likely to experience the intensified dreams that arise out of such cognitive capacities than is an individual from a culture where visual-spatial imagination is valued and actively cultivated.

Hunt's argument here has important bearing on our understanding of root metaphor dreams. He claims that the experience of intensified dreams can open us up to cognitive capacities that we in modern Western culture have not really tried to develop. If we take Hunt's intensified dreams (like we took Jung's "big dreams") as roughly synonymous with our root metaphor dreams, we find him supporting the notion that root metaphor dreams can creatively transform our fundamental perceptions of reality. Such dreams can bring to life previously uncultivated cognitive capacities that may enable us to develop a fuller, more satisfying orientation towards the ultimate concerns of human existence. Hunt's research gives a cognitive psychological justification for our claims that root metaphor dreams can create new religious meanings.

The "No" Camp

We will now widen our critical "wild rumpus" to include the work of those dream explorers who argue that dreams do *not* have religious meaning. The root metaphor concept can help us identify the weaknesses of their arguments against the possibility of religiously meaningful dreams. But much more importantly, our work on root metaphors will also enable us to recognize many valuable points in these arguments. The legitimate insights of the "no" camp can tremendously strengthen our understanding of the religious meanings of dreams.

Freud of course makes a very energetic argument against the idea that dreams have genuine religious meaning. Actually, Freud makes three distinct arguments. First, he asserts that dreams merely reflect (or, more accurately, disguise) the dreamer's unconscious wishes; these wishes are mediated by entirely ordinary, lawful psychological processes. Thus Freud says that dreams have no special creativity to them and involve no influx of supernatural, prophetic powers. Second, in his writings on religion, Freud states repeatedly that religion is an infantile illusion, prompted by a fear of hard reality. For Freud, the appearance of religion in dreams or anywhere else signals immaturity and weakness. And third, Freud presents his therapeutic practice as a means to help people overcome the need for religious meanings—psychoanalytic therapy aims at overcoming such infantile illusions and strengthening the autonomous, rational ego. In Freud's therapy, dream interpretation is a way to abolish religious belief, not develop it.

Provocative as it is, Freud's attack on the religious meaning of dreams suffers from a number of flaws. His denial that dreams involve genuine creativity has been refuted by many researchers who show convincingly that dreams do indeed involve truly creative processes of reasoning and expression (see Fosshage 1983, Levin 1990). His sharp distinction between infantile (i.e., religious) and mature (i.e., nonreligious) thought does not stand up to Lakoff and Johnson's and McFague's compelling arguments that the same basic metaphorical processes underlie both "religious" and "nonreligious" thought. Freud's condemnation of religion is weakest in his claim that religion is always a childish illusion. He is certainly correct in noting that religious beliefs may be infantile (e.g., the image of God as a big, bearded father up in the sky), but he does not recognize that religious beliefs may also be more mature, sophisticated, and well-attuned to reality.[6] Ricoeur directly challenges Freud on this point:

> Freud's exclusive attention to repetition becomes a refusal to consider a possible epigenesis of religious feeling, that is to say, a transformation or conversion of desire and fear. This refusal does not seem to me to be based upon analysis, but merely expresses Freud's personal unbelief . . . Freud seems to me to exclude without reason, I mean without any psychoanalytic reason, the possibility that faith is a participation in the source of Eros and thus concerns, not the consolation of the child in us, but the power of loving; he excludes the possibility that faith aims at making this power adult in the face of the hatred within us and outside of us—in the face of death. (Ricoeur 1970, 534, 536)

Freud's narrow, unreflective view of religion severely weakens his arguments against the religious meanings of dreams.

However, this is not to say that Freud has nothing to contribute to our understanding of root metaphor dreams. He may be wrong in claiming that *all* religious beliefs are infantile illusions—but he may be right in claiming that *some* of them are. Freud is acutely aware of the human inclination to self-delusion, and he rightly insists that the growth of consciousness depends on an ability to deal honestly with unpleasant, painful realities. The harsh skepticism Freud brings to dreams is an indispensible element of our model for exploring root metaphor dreams, namely Ricoeur's "second naivete." According to this model, we critically analyze our dreams with all the suspicion and wariness that Freud teaches us to have, carefully probing for masks, illusions, and self-deceptions; then, having engaged in such a critique, we go on to listen to whether the dream is speaking to our ultimate existential concerns. If we use Freud's insights in this way, we find that he can make an extremely valuable contribution to our understanding of religiously meaningful dreams.

Like Freud, Calvin Hall has virtually no use for religion. While disagreeing with Freud on many points, Hall does essentially agree with him that twentieth-century dream research has proved that dreams arise from the human psyche, not from any supernatural forces. Hall asserts that the strange symbols in dreams are simply translations of thoughts into pictures—no more divinely inspired or religiously prophetic than any other product of our mental functioning. He does allow that by studying a series of dreams we can discover the dreamer's "Weltanschauung," that is, the overall worldview that orients his or her life and that may have religious aspects to it. But Hall agrees with Freud that the most mature, psychologically developed Weltanschauung is one that values autonomy, rationality, and empiricism and that compared with this a "religious" worldview is essentially inferior.

Hall's appreciation for the religious meanings of dreams is limited by the same mistake that limited Freud: identifying "religion" with infantile, superstitious beliefs. According to this definition of the term, Hall has nothing positive to say about the religious meanings of dreams. But the root metaphor concept enables us to see that religious meanings do not necessarily relate to superstitions, deities, priests, or churches; rather, they have to do with the ultimate concerns of human existence. These ultimate concerns may be expressed in formally "religious" language, or they may emerge in non-religious, "secular" language. When "religion" is understood in this sense, we find that Hall does in fact have some contributions to make to our project. He demonstrates that analyzing a series of dreams can reveal the dreamer's Weltanschauung, showing the core existential values and ideals that are guiding his or her life. This is identical to our claims regarding the root metaphors that emerge in dreams. Thus, Hall's methods for studying dream series (conducting a structural analysis of recurrent themes, patterns, and images) can be of great help in exploring root metaphors and dreams. Much like Tedlock, Hall claims that dreams can directly reflect the fundamental beliefs and values of an individual's life. Despite his inadequate definition of religion, Hall's content analysis approach can aid our understanding of the religious meanings of dreams.[7]

J. Allan Hobson shares with Freud and Hall a deep skepticism towards the idea that dreams have religious meaning. He opens *The Dreaming Brain* with a clamorous attack on what he calls the "prophetic tradition" of dream interpretation—the tradition that claims that dreams are caused by external agencies (like gods or spirits), filled with mysterious messages, and impossible to understand without the aid of special authorities. Against this "prophetic tradition," Hobson promotes a scientific approach that is empirical, systematic, and objective. This approach reveals, he claims, that dreams are indeed produced by important powers of creativity and imagination; sometimes, he admits, dreams reveal our "deepest myths." But Hobson does not believe that the meanings of dreams have anything to do with divine or supernatural realms. The activation-synthesis hypothesis of dreaming, he claims, refutes the prophetic tradition of dreams once and for all. Hobson's account of dreaming differs from those of Freud and Hall in that Hobson believes dreams do display genuine creativity. He says dreams emerge out of creative processes that are an "integral part of healthy brain-mind activity, whether one is asleep or awake" (Hobson 1988, 18). But like Freud and Hall, Hobson denounces any suggestions that dreams might have religious or spiritual meaning. He insists that dreaming is a natural, not supernatural, phenomenon and that the meaning of dreams is simple, plain, and free from the mysterious prophecies that religious authorities have tried to attach to them.

Once again, we find that a condemnation of the religious meaning of dreams turns on a particular (and very faulty) definition of religion. Hobson identifies a religious view of dreams with the claims that dreams are (1) caused by external agencies, (2) filled with complex, mysterious messages, and (3) impossible to understand without the assistance of authorities. But the root metaphor concept has nothing whatsoever to do with either the first or the third of these claims; and as for the second claim, we have already discussed at length (in part 3) why Hobson's view about the "simple, plain" meaning of dreams is untenable. Hobson's attack on the "prophetic tradition" may successfully demolish the dream interpretation practices of certain priests thousands of years ago, but his critique does not affect our study of dreams, root metaphors, and religious meaning.

Hobson's activation-synthesis model does, however, have a great deal to contribute to our understanding of root metaphor dreams. Surprisingly, Hobson can offer us some important insights into the physiological processes involved in the emergence of religiously meaningful dreams. The first hint of this comes in his description of how the mind "synthesizes" the random neural signals that flood the brain during REM sleep. The result of this synthesis is a dream, which orders the random data into a more or less coherent story. The human mind is, Hobson says, so "inexorably bent" on creating meaning that it will go so far as to "call upon its *deepest myths* to find a narrative frame" for the essentially meaningless neural signals (Hobson 1988, 15, 214; emphasis added). Right there, Hobson is suggesting what Tedlock, Hunt, and Hall have described in more explicit terms: dreams can *reflect* the basic existential beliefs and values of the dreamer, the "deepest myths" that frame and orient our lives. Although he may not have intended it, Hobson in fact provides strong scientific evidence for this assertion about the religious meaning of dreams.

There is still more for us to learn from Hobson's work. What Hobson describes as the synthetic process of dream creation is directly related to the processes by which root metaphors are *created* in dreams—in other words, his account of how dreams create meaning may also help explain how dreams create *religious* meaning. We can see this if we examine his analysis of one of the dreams of the "Engine Man" (the person whose dream diary Hobson uses to illustrate his theories). Hobson points to the Engine Man's "Customs Building" dream as an example of how the brain's random neural activity produces an utterly chaotic experience, which the mind then tries to render coherent and meaningful:

> Walking south on 14th St., just south of Pennsylvania Ave. Street was very muddy. A few blocks (about 3) south of the avenue (Pa. Ave.) I turned east, passing behind various buildings none of which seemed large. No one in sight except my companion, a child of perhaps 6 to 8 years, who later turned into Jason [his nephew] but who, at first, seemed like a stranger. I asked him if he knew the location of the Customs Building; he said "no," and I remember thinking that it was very probably in some other part of town. It was at the Customs Building where all the animals (except small ones such as cats) must be registered or declared, weighed, and the proper tax paid . . . Some person we were looking for had brought an animal from the train to the Customs Building. (Hobson 1988, 272)

In this dream the Engine Man wanders about the city streets and building corridors, unsure of his location or his purpose. He is forced, Hobson says, to ask himself, "Where am I? What am I doing here? Who is with me? What is my relationship to that person?" (273). Hobson's analysis of the dream focuses on the Engine Man's attempts to fix his "orientational bearings" (273) in the dream by creating responses to these questions.

But if we listen to those questions again—"*Where* am I? *What* am I doing here? *Who* is with me? *What* is my relationship to that person?"—we realize that they are questions with potentially *existential* connotations; they are questions that *could* relate to a person's religious or spiritual orientation in life. The dreaming mind's responses thus could create new ways of understanding our ultimate existential concerns, could in other words create new root metaphors. Hobson's activation-synthesis model indicates that dreaming involves a process of responding to experiences of disorientation, confusion, and uncertainty, experiences produced by the neural activity of REM sleep. The key point here is that the dreaming mind may well relate the disorienting experiences of REM sleep to the most fundamentally disorienting experiences of human existence—the experiences of suffering, death, moral conflict, meaninglessness, and so on—and creatively respond (with novel metaphorical images) to those disorienting existential experiences.[8]

Looking back to the root metaphor dreams of chapter 16, we can easily apply Hobson's activation-synthesis model to those religiously meaningful dreams. For example, Ahmad Sahib's dream of looking for a Sufi *pir* in a telephone book involves many of the same questions as does the Engine Man's dream: Sahib wonders where he is, whom he is with, and what his relationship is with those people. Likewise, Mrs. M.'s dream of the cave beneath the mother house of the convent also presents her with questions like those faced by the Engine Man. She tries to understand where she is, what she is doing there, and how she is related to the different people she encounters. Hobson's model indicates that such orientational questions may be initially raised ("activated") by the neural activity of REM sleep; our root metaphor concept suggests that the mind's creative response to ("synthesis of") such questions may, in certain circumstances, lead to new religious insights.

The root metaphor concept does not require us to ignore the important insights of skeptics like Freud, Hall, and Hobson. On the contrary, it enables us to appreciate their main ideas, to correct some of their biggest problems, and to develop new, previously unrecognized aspects of their work.

18

TOWARDS INTEGRATION: INTERPRETING "BEING DISSECTED BY THE EVIL ALIEN"

I'll let you be in my dreams
If I can be in yours
—Bob Dylan, "Talking World War III Blues"

The Risk of Interdisciplinary Integration

We are now in a position to correlate the various paths we have studied and develop an integrated approach to dreams and religious meaning. Such an interdisciplinary effort presupposes, of course, that an integration of this sort (1) is possible, (2) is desirable, and (3) is not going to create more problems than it solves. But we have good reasons to hold these presuppositions. Regarding the first, we have repeatedly found evidence that the insights of the different dream explorers can indeed be fruitfully related to each other. Regarding the second, we have found that no one dream explorer has a fully adequate approach to dreams and religious meaning and that some kind of integration of their views is the only means of developing a better understanding of this subject.

It is the third presupposition that should give us greatest pause.[1] Perhaps the various dream theorists hold fundamentally incompatible views—why should we forcibly reconcile their ideas? Wouldn't it be worse to paper over their sharp disagreements and fabricate an artificial, lowest-common-denominator approach that is so all-embracing as to be lifeless? An empty eclecticism is the great danger all interdisciplinary studies face, for when we try to reconcile serious disputes we risk ignoring genuine differences; when we try to synthesize extremely different ideas we risk draining away their critical force. In our particular case, however, this danger can be avoided. There is no question here of a forcible merging of theories, for each of the eight dream explorers we have studied has expressed an eager interest in the findings of other fields of dream study and in the findings of areas outside dream study. An impulse towards interdisciplinary understanding propels each of their efforts. So instead of imposing an alien goal on them, we are working to achieve what they have all clearly announced as their *own* goal: an integration of the various disciplines studying dreams.[2]

Toward a Theoretical Integration

There are three different sources to draw upon in developing a theoretically integrated understanding of the religious meaning of dreams, an understanding that centers on the concept of root metaphors. The first is the work of the philosophers and theologians we considered in chapter 15. Lakoff and Johnson, Browning, McFague, and Ricoeur gave us the initial outlines of the root metaphor concept and provided strong arguments for its validity as a way of understanding the religious meaning of dreams. From their studies we have developed the following definition: root metaphors are metaphors that express our ultimate existential concerns; root metaphors provide religious meanings that orient our lives. Root metaphor *dreams* are dreams that have these characteristics.

The second source is the experience of religiously meaningful dreams, as reported in both historical and contemporary contexts. We looked at six examples of such dreams in chapter 16 and found that the root metaphor concept accounted for the religious meanings of these dreams, even when the dreams did not appear to be conventionally "religious" in form. In particular, the examples highlighted the crucial elements of action, movement, and narrative flow that characterize root metaphor dreams. But more than confirming the initial definition of root metaphors, these dreams also added new aspects to our theoretical understanding. The six examples indicated that root metaphor dreams tend to appear during times of personal and/or cultural crisis, to help the dreamer adapt to such crises, and to motivate moral action.

The third source of theoretical integration is the work of the eight dream explorers we began studying in part 2. As we saw in chapter 17, many aspects of their approaches to the religious meaning of dreams correspond very closely to the root metaphor concept. Breton, Jung, LaBerge, Tedlock, and Hunt (the "yes" camp) all affirm that dream images and experiences may have religious meaning, that dreams may touch on the ultimate exististential concerns of human life. They describe how dreams can reflect the religious beliefs or Weltanschauung of the dreamer and how dreams can also be the creative source of new religious ideals and values.

Most significantly, the root metaphor concept receives strong theoretical support from the explorers who take a natural scientific approach to dreams. Hall's quantitative content analysis confirms the claim that dreams can reveal the most basic existential orientation of an individual. While Breton, Jung, and Tedlock reached the same conclusion by less formally scientific means, Hall uses a structuralist analysis of long dream series to justify this key point regarding the religious meaning of dreams. LaBerge employs the technological equipment of modern sleep laboratories to investigate the spiritual potential of lucid dreams. He has demonstrated that lucid dreaming is a scientifically "real" phenomenon, and he has thus opened up new paths for exploring the physiological aspects of religiously meaningful dreams. Hobson's activation-synthesis model of dreaming provides neuroscientific support for the claims that dreams can reflect religious meaning (in the mind's drawing on our "deepest myths" to make sense of random neural data) and that dreams can create religious meaning (in the mind's creative responses to the disorienting effects of REM sleep). And Hunt gives us a cognitive psychological basis for understanding the religious meanings of dreams. He shows how distinctive cognitive processes relating to our capacities for visual-spatial imagination are involved in the creation of "intensified dreams," that is, dreams that have a numinous and often religious or spiritual quality to them.

This theoretical integration has also involved a critical evaluation of the main problems in the work of these eight dream explorers. We have used the root metaphor concept to challenge Breton's cultural naivete and romantic view of the unconscious, Jung's essentialist claims about the collective unconscious, LaBerge's questionably relevant root metaphor of lucid dreaming, and the narrow, inadequate view of religion held by Freud, Hall, and Hobson. These problems are serious, but seen in the critical light of the root metaphor concept they are not fatal to any of the dream explorers. We have found that even the most skeptical dream explorers (i.e., Freud, Hall, and Hobson) have extremely important insights to contribute to our understanding of dreams and religious meaning. The greatest test of an interdisciplinary approach is its capacity to appreciate the full critical force of conflicting theories and then to integrate them without losing any of that force. The interdisciplinary approach we have developed around the root metaphor concept has, I believe, gone a long way towards meeting this test.

Towards a Practical Integration

Now, we can develop a different kind of integration, one that is oriented less towards theory and more towards *practical* concerns, that is, towards the practical guidance the root metaphor concept provides in exploring the religious meanings of dreams.

Religious meaning is but one of the many kinds of meaning that we can discover in dreams. Thus, the hermeneutic principles we developed in part 3 to guide the *general* practice of dream interpretation apply to this particular area of dream interpretation. Those principles are, to restate them briefly:

1. We encounter a dream as a special kind of text, as something both strange and yet related to us.
2. We have a preliminary awareness of our subjective biases.
3. We are open to the dream and admit to not knowing what exactly will come of the interpretation.
4. We play with the dream, surrendering to a back-and-forth dialogue with it.
5. The criteria for a valid interpretation are how well it harmonizes the parts of the dream with the whole, how well it coheres with the rest of our knowledge, and how well it "works out" according to our practical needs and interests.
6. The ultimate goal of dream interpretation is to broaden horizons, open up new questions, and widen awareness.

The first matter to settle in exploring the religious dimension of dreams is the question of *which* dreams to interpret. Which dream "texts" are most likely to have religious meanings? The initial answer would have to be strikingly powerful, vivid dreams, what Jung calls "big dreams" and what Hunt refers to as "intensified dreams." These would be dreams with numinous divine or mythological beings in them; intensely terrifying nightmares; especially powerful lucid dreams; and dreams so startling or profound that people remember them their whole lives. Such dreams, although rare, would seem to be good candidates for a spiritually oriented interpretation. Another immediate answer would be recurrent dreams. The recurrence of striking themes, figures, or situations often indicates an important structure of meaning that may derive from our basic existential ideals and values. Recurrent dreams are excellent sources for discovering the root metaphors that are orienting our lives.

However, recurrent dreams and spectacular "big dreams" are not the only kinds that have religious potential. What we have been referring to as "root metaphor dreams" are dreams that touch on the basic existential concerns of human life. Sometimes root metaphor dreams have an intensified, numinous power, and sometimes they take much more subtle and shadowy forms. Insights into our existential concerns can often be gained from seemingly quiet, innocuous dreams, from dreams that do not appear at first sight to have any special religious force to them.[3] This is not to say, of course, that *every* dream is religiously meaningful. Rather, it is to suggest that any dreams *may* be religiously meaningful, not just "big" or recurrent dreams. The only way to find out if a dream is religiously meaningful or not is to begin reflecting on the dream and see what comes of it.[4]

In exploring the religious dimension of dreams, our "bias" is that some dreams will have religious meanings; this is our initial presupposition, our hermeneutical prejudice. Such a presupposition leads us to ask certain questions, to initiate a dialogue with the dream. We can draw upon the characteristics of root metaphors discussed earlier to focus this dialogue. The following set of questions, then, reflects an expansion on the hermeneutic principles of dream interpretation (part 3) that draws upon the key elements of root metaphors (part 4).[5]

1. What are the most prominent images in the dream? Any interpretive efforts to understand the religious dimension of a dream must start with the living images of the dream itself—focusing on the immediate, vital, tangible presence of the images, their primary qualities and properties, the dreamer's felt experience of them. We started in this way with the dreams of chapter 16, concentrating on the main characteristics of the frantic searching through the phone book in Ahmad Sahib's dream, the white paint beginning to blister in Mary's dream, and the candle being extinguished and then relit in Margot's dream.

2. Do the images metaphorically express religious or existential concerns? After focusing on the most vital, tangible images, we may ask whether they are metaphorically expressing more amorphous, intangible matters relating to the dreamer's ultimate existential concerns. As we saw in chapter 16, dream images can metaphorically express concerns that are conventionally religious (e.g., Moses Armah and his church affiliation, Mrs. M. and her relationship with God) as well matters that do not appear to be "religious" but in fact touch directly on the dreamer's ultimate existential concerns (e.g., Mary's past experiences of sexual abuse).

3. What is the emotional power of the dream? Religiously meaningful dreams often have an especially powerful emotional impact on the

dreamer. Carefully exploring the nuances of this emotional power can open up many aspects of a dream's religious meaning. Sometimes the dream's emotions are joyful, as in Mrs. M.'s dream, and sometimes they are terrifying, as in Mary's recurrent nightmares; sometimes they are awe-inspiring, like the Ojibwa boy's dream, and sometimes they generate deep spiritual longing, as with Ahmad Sahib's dream. The root metaphors in dreams serve as a means by which the dreamer can discover, experience, and understand these emotions.

4. Does the dream relate to a current life crisis or transition? Religiously meaningful dreams frequently emerge at times of change, of crisis, of suffering, of transformation; the dreams speak to these experiences, setting them in the context of the individual's ultimate existential concerns.[6] The Ojibwa youth's dream addressed the often difficult passage from adolescence to adulthood. Margot's dream occurred as she approached death, the mysterious transition from life to that which lies beyond life.

5. Does the dream relate to both the dreamer's past and the dreamer's future? Ricoeur helped us to see that root metaphor dreams always recall the past (one's "archeology") and point towards the future (one's "teleology"). For example, Mrs. M.'s dream of finding the cave in the heart of the convent looked back to reveal that the source of her current spiritual discontent lay in her troubled relations to her Catholic past. The dream also looked forward to suggest that a reconciliation with her past could lead to a more fulfilling spiritual life in the future.

6. What potentials does the dream have to transform the dreamer's waking life? As McFague emphasized, root metaphors are *challenging*—they force us to reflect, to question and change our waking lives in response to their meanings. The transformative effects can relate primarily to the dreamer's individual life (as, for example, Ahmad Sahib's dream motivated him to become a Sufi); they can also relate to the dreamer's communal life (as Moses Armah's dream led him to form a new church, and Mary's dream prompted her to transform the relationship patterns of her family).

A final point about the practical approach to religiously meaningful dreams regards the general attitude we take in exploring such dreams. We have found that Ricoeur's account of the "second naivete" can be our guide in this process. According to Ricoeur's account, we should not approach dreams as simple, straightforward revelations from the gods—that would be an uncritical "first naivete" that ignores all the demands of critical rationality and leaves us vulnerable to superstition and self-deception. Rather, we should always subject dreams to critical analysis, adopting a "hermeneutics of suspicion" to unmask our deceptions, puncture our illusions, and purify our false consciousness. The dream explorers we have studied have offered valuable aids to this process of critique: for example, Freud's psychoanalytic methods of overcoming resistance, Hall's quantitative content analysis, and Hobson's work on identifying the true "nonsense" of dreams.

But *then*, the model of a second naivete encourages us to go *beyond* the rigorous, suspicious examinations of critical rationality and engage in what Ricoeur calls a "restorative interpretation": returning to the dream itself with a new, *post*critical openness, an openness vastly more sensitive for having undergone a process of skeptical examination.[7] It is at this point that we can most freely *play* with the dream and creatively explore the potential wealth of meanings it expresses relating to our ultimate existential concerns. Here too, some of the dream investigators we have studied can contribute to a restorative interpretation of dreams, to a process of creative playing with them. Breton's account of the role of dreams in surrealist art indicates that a variety of art forms can provide a space in which the religious potentials of dreams may be playfully explored. Jung's methods of dream amplification and active imagination both involve a playful dialogue with the dream, promoting the emergence of the dream's religious meanings. And Tedlock's fieldwork experiences with the Zuni and Quiche peoples indicates that sharing dreams with radically different people can lead to surprising and profound discoveries about their dreams and one's own dreams.

Ricoeur's model of the second naivete helps us to integrate, on a *practical* level, all the different materials we have been studying. It coheres with the hermeneutic principles of dream interpretation, it is consistent with the root metaphor concept, and it does justice to the key insights of the major twentieth-century dream theorists. With such a model to guide us, we may confidently explore the religious potentials of dreams, knowing that we are satisfying the demands of critical rationality and yet also honoring the powerful, insistent, "irrational" calls to religious awareness and growth that emerge in dreams.

A Final Dream: "Being Dissected by the Evil Alien"

To conclude this chapter, devoted as it is to interdisciplinary integration, it seems sensible to attempt an integrated interpretation of a dream—that is, to draw upon *all* the different methods, approaches, and principles we have developed through the preceding chapters to explore a particular dream.

Such an interpretive effort will give us a clearer sense of both the viability and the value of the interdisciplinary integration we have developed.

The dream we will study is one of my own, what I regard as one of the most powerful dreams of my life.[8] Throughout my adolescence I suffered recurrent nightmares of being chased, the dreams sometimes coming as frequently as two or three times a week. The dreams had a fairly common pattern to them: a large, dark, and somehow deformed or mutilated person would be pursuing me; I would try to use a weapon (usually a gun) against my antagonist, but the weapon never worked; I would try to run away, but could never totally escape, and I would awaken in a heart-thumping panic. In a number of dreams I was chased by Darth Vader, the huge, black-masked villain of the *Star Wars* movies.

These nightmares deeply troubled me. Their emotional force and ceaseless recurrence made them impossible to ignore, even though I could see no apparent reason why I kept having them. Then, in the middle of my sophomore year of college, I had this dream:

> I'm a knight of some sort, and a fellow knight and his parents, a king and queen, are fighting about something, something to do with the acceptance of a gift from his brother, the heir apparent, who is outside on the fire escape (outside my room) with all his retinue. I tell the parents to leave (we're all in my room) and try to reason with this knight. There's some sort of precedent for this problem, and I try to convince him to accept the gift. I'm having trouble speaking because I'm really congested.
>
> There's a lot of intrigue involved, and I see a hand with a ball like a pin cushion in it, evidently some sort of poison, come down onto the face of a sleeping man. There are strange shadows about, and as I hear the piercing scream of the man, I see the face of the person who's doing the killing: it's not some faithless wench, as I'd thought, but some sort of extraterrestrial creature with a face like a cloven foot. The dead man seems to alternate between being me and being another guy like on a television show or something.
>
> After killing him/me, the creature proceeds to dissect the body. He takes out the heart, still pumping and attached to the major arteries, and some other vital organs; at that point I'm watching. Now it's me, as I see him taking my sperm, each individual sperm floating from this piece of tissue in the air into some sort of container. I also see the creature picking, like pieces of corn off a cob, these little white pill-like objects off an organ or something of mine, the objects representing my DNA or something like it, whatever it is that makes me *me*. The creature seems to be having trouble getting them all into the container, and as one pops onto the floor I think that maybe there's hope.

> Then I'm watching again as he takes a knife to the head. I get grossed out and look away. At some point Scott, a bald punk-rocker from downstairs comes into the scene. I look back, and either Scott or the creature is opening the head up, which looks like two pie tins holding mashed potatoes between them. I guess it's Scott, because I'm so disgusted that I chase whoever it is away; when I look back, though, some dog has eaten out all the brains like a plate of leftovers. At this point I am the body again, and lash out at Scott in bitter anger, feeling incredibly violent about what's been done to me. Although I realize that my eyes must be gone and that I must be blind, I see Scott by the fireplace, lunge my shoulder at him, and grind my elbow into his groin. I lift him up with my elbow and body slam him, coming down with all my weight on his groin. He doesn't seem hurt really and even kind of laughs; I realize then the futility, as the creature slowly walks off. We're both too weak to go after the creature who caused our misery, so we're beating on each other instead. It's like we're the last two men on earth, and I hear some music, like to a TV show, about the "dying race." (February 28, 1982, Sunday night)

I awoke with overwhelming feelings of horror and disgust, and immediately wrote the dream down (I'd been keeping a dream journal for about a year). The dream is set in my room in a student cooperative dormitory at Stanford University, where I was living at the time. My room was the best in the house, with a fireplace, a big refrigerator, and a door out onto a fire escape landing. Scott lived in the basement of the house, in a little space he had semilegally constructed for himself. He was a big fan of punk rock, a violent, antiauthoritarian form of music; like other punk rockers, he shaved his head bald and wore ripped, militaristic clothing. I thought Scott was a nice guy, and we got along fine, although we weren't particularly close. My friends in the dorm and I read a lot of science fiction, medieval epics, and myths of ancient heroes. We enjoyed using the language and images of those stories to play around with each other. For example, our games of backgammon became epic battles between two knights vying for honor. A week or so before the dream a couple of us had seen the movie *Excalibur*, a Hollywood version of the Arthurian legend. I remember thinking to myself after the movie, I really *wouldn't* want to be a knight in those times; I'd be too afraid of being killed.

In a more general sense, the setting of the dream was my student life at Stanford. I was at one of the best universities in the country and doing very well. My grades were great, I was playing on the school's lacrosse team, and I had lots of friends; frequently I thought to myself, this is the perfect life. But at the same time, I was struggling with two deeper-lying conflicts. One was the confusing nature of my relationship with a woman friend (I'll call her "Loren"). Loren and I had been extremely close for three years, and I valued our friendship very much. She was a passionate feminist, and from her I learned a whole new way of looking at gender relations in our culture. Indeed, she and I were very conscious of how our own relationship ran counter to the normal pattern of male-female relations, as we had an open, equal, intimate, nonsexual friendship. The problem was, I also happened to be very physically attracted to Loren. For a long time I hid those feelings from her in order to preserve the intimacy we had created. But then, a few weeks before this dream, our relationship suddenly (at her instigation) became romantic. Now I was even more confused, because whatever was to happen next, we clearly were not going to have a conventional boyfriend-girlfriend relationship. What would our relationship be, then? I had no idea.[9]

The second conflict regarded my choice of an academic major. I was in the middle of my sophomore year, and the time was approaching when I would have to commit myself to a particular field of study. I had always been interested in economics and political philosophy, and I had frequently thought of going into business or law. I was a hardworking person, proud of my independence and rationality, and I knew I could be successful in those fields. But at the same time, I had become increasingly interested in religion, mysticism, psychology, and mythology, and increasingly dissatisfied with the idea of working in a conventional job. By the time of the dream the latter interests had prevailed, as I had pretty well decided to be a philosophy and religious studies major. But I was deeply worried about what such a decision would mean for my future. My parents would certainly disapprove, and a big split between us seemed inevitable. My father was an insurance broker, from a long line of insurance men, and I would be breaking with that family tradition. I had no idea how I might make a living after graduating, or what exactly I would "do"—there weren't many philosophy and religious studies firms around, hiring recent graduates. For all my increasingly counter-cultural behavior and ideals, I had always managed to be extremely successful in conventional terms. Now, however, I was about to make a decision that would set me down a path with no familial or cultural supports.

These two conflicts, which were my dominant concerns at the time of the Evil Alien dream, shared a common theme. Both of them involved my stepping outside the norms of my family and my culture and suddenly finding myself alone, confused, and overwhelmed by strong, disruptive urges. And with both of them, my reaction was to try controlling the disruptive urges and working hard to succeed—working to maintain my relationship with Loren and working to be a great religion and philosophy student.

Eight Reflections on the Dream

So much for the dream text and its immediate context in my personal life. The next step in appoaching this dream is to draw upon the hermeneutic principles of dream interpretation we developed in part 3, and to see what the eight dream explorers would have to say about it.[10]

Freud, I feel confident, would focus on the Oedipal conflicts that pervade the dream. The first scene, with the "heir apparent" and his family having a fight, reflects my current situation with my parents: would I, the oldest male, carry on the family business tradition, or would I refuse and go my own way? In the dream I am caught in the middle, between these warring factions. The second scene, when the Evil Alien appears and dissects me, could be interpreted as an obscenely elaborate castration fantasy. As punishment for rejecting the family tradition and for disobeying my father's authority my "organs" (many of them with phallic shapes) are cut from me. The wish motivating the dream would be a masochistic wish to be punished by my father—for in punishing me, he is bringing me back *into* the family, something that part of me desperately wants.[11]

Breton would likely be struck by two aspects of the dream. One would be the face of the Alien. When I wrote out the dream I drew a picture of the Alien's face, which was extremely vivid in my mind. Breton's interest in the artistic creativity emerging in dreams leads me to look more carefully at this picture, to see what it suggests. It is cloven, like the devil's foot; it looks like breasts, and also like a vagina; it is reminiscent of Darth Vader's mask, but rounder; it looks like an upside-down heart. Breton's second interest would, I imagine, be in the perverseness of the dream, its graphic portrayal of thoroughly revolting acts of violence. I don't know if I would call anything about the dream "marvelous," but it is certainly shocking, fantastic, and "free" from the constraints of conventional Wesetern morality and decency.

Jung might approach the dream at the "subjective" level—that is, looking at its characters and images as reflections of elements within my own unconscious. The Evil Alien has many qualities of the shadow archetype: he is huge, black, and utterly inhuman. He represents those feelings that I repress or deny; in his image those feelings are twisted them into hideous, destructive urges that turn around and attack me. I try to repress my romantic longings towards Loren, so the Evil Alien violently destroys my sexual organs; I try to deny my need for paternal approval, so the Evil Alien renders me helpless and then abandons me. But Jung might also see the dream as reflecting more than my personal shadow and regard it as an expression of true *evil.* Jung states, "it is quite within the bounds of possibility for a man to recognize the relative evil of his nature, but it is a rare and shattering experience for him to gaze into the face of absolute evil" (Jung [1951c] 1969, 19). Jung, I believe, would see the overwhelmingly numinous power of this dream as indicating that the Evil Alien has its roots in something *beyond* my personal shadow.[12]

A couple of months after the dream I was working on an essay for a Zen Buddhism class and reading some of Jung's writings on eastern religions. I came across the following passage, which Jung quotes from the *Tibetan Book of the Dead*:

> Then the Lord of Death will place round thy neck a rope and drag thee along; he will cut off thy head, tear out thy heart, pull out thy intestines, lick up thy brain, drink thy blood, eat thy flesh, and gnaw thy bone; but thou wilt be incapable of dying. Even when thy body is hacked to pieces, it will revive again. The repeated hacking will cause intense pain and torture. (Jung [1939] 1969, 520)

This neatly synchronistic experience made a powerful impact on me. I was not only struck by the parallel imagery between this passage and my dream but also deeply affected by Jung's comments on the passage:

> These things [exploring the unconscious] really are dangerous and ought not to be meddled with in our typically Western way. It is a meddling with fate, which strikes at the very root of human existence and can let loose a flood of sufferings of which no sane person ever dreamed. (Jung [1939] 1969, 520)

From this perspective the dream can be interpreted as a direct warning about my study of religion and philosophy. I was approaching these subjects in a "typically Western way"—rationally, willfully, with a strong desire for success and acclaim. The dream forced me to stop and ask myself, do I really know what I'm getting myself into?

In accordance with Hall's method of dream interpretation, I conducted a brief content analysis of thirteen of my dreams in the two months surrounding the Evil Alien dream (five dreams before it, seven after it). I am sorry to report that nothing in this series of dreams reads like the chapters of a book, or fit together like a jigsaw puzzle. If anything, I discovered that the Evil Alien dream was *more* complex and involved many *more* themes, fears, desires, and conflicts than I had first perceived.[13] Nevertheless, a couple of themes do stand out. In five of the thirteen dreams I am trying to get away from my present location; twice I am trying to go on a vacation, and three times I am trying to escape someone who is chasing me. In each of those five dreams, however, I fail: I never get to the vacation place, and I never escape my pursuers. In four dreams from this series I am looking for valuable objects (e.g., shells, gold, a little pipelike thing, and a small black object) that are rare and hard to find; in the dreams I never get them. And in four of the dreams the setting is my dorm, with two dreams (immediately preceding the Evil Alien dream) having me try to get out of my room by stairs or the fire escape, but unable to succeed. Following Hall, I would say that this series of dreams establishes a general pattern of desires being frustrated, with my customary reactions to those desires repeatedly failing. The desires touch on almost all of those "basic human conflicts" that Hall describes: desires revolving around Oedipal sexuality, security, morality, aggressiveness, and death.

Hobson would likely begin by focusing on the tremendous disorientation and vagueness that characterizes many parts of the dream. I frequently say "some . . . ," "some kind of . . . ," "something like . . . " in the dream text. At many points I am not sure who is who or what is what. According to Hobson, this would be evidence of the essentially arbitrary nature of the dream, its origin in the random neural activity of my brain (if that's so, my neurons must have been having a block party that night). The radical bodily disintegration I experience could also be tied to the chaotic, fragmented quality of that brain activity. But Hobson might go on to suggest that we analyze the points of greatest clarity, order, and definition in the dream, for those would be the points where my mind had been most successful in imposing ("synthesizing") some sort of meaningful order on the neural chaos. The hand with the poison ball is very clear and distinct in my mind; so is the creature's face. The particular elements of my dissected body are especially well-defined—my heart, my sperm, the white pill-like objects, the pie-tin head. And the sensation of driving my elbow into Scott's groin is sickeningly vivid and clear. Drawing upon Hobson's "broadly psychodynamic" perspective, I see these relatively clear and distinct images as reflecting unconscious themes of aggression, sexuality, and concern over the integrity of my body.

Because the dream was not an overtly lucid one, LaBerge's views would appear to have no relevance here. But that may be too facile a reading of LaBerge's contribution to dream study. My dream contains many shifts of perspective and perception; I am continually moving within the dream from one level of awareness to another. LaBerge's work is, in the broadest sense, about the significance of such shifts of awareness. Although I never move to a point where I say, "I am dreaming," the many different moves I do make are, when I reflect upon them, quite meaningful. The primary locus of shifting perceptions is the dissected body: I am watching the body be killed and dissected, then I *am* the body, then I'm watching it again, back and forth. These shifts enhance the intensity of my horror and disgust. It's being done to me, and I *know* it's being done to me, I *see* it happening. And twice I shift my awareness from experiencing the physical destruction of the body to *thinking* about its meaning. I think about the hope for the future represented by the little pill-like object that escapes, and I think about how meaningless it is for Scott and me to be fighting as the Evil Alien, the true source of our rage, walks away. These reflections strike me as very important, for they are the only positive glimmers in the dream. Even though the Evil Alien has ravaged me, I have the awareness at a certain level that there *is* hope for the future and that I *know* something now about why humans hurt each other. In the face of so much violence and destruction, those reflections are precious to me.

As an anthropologist, Tedlock would probably comment on the parallels with the dream visions experienced by shamans in many different cultures (see Eliade 1964). These dream visions, which have the function of initiating a person as a shaman, typically involve (1) the dreamer's physical and/or spiritual departure from the community; (2) the killing and graphic dismemberment of the dreamer and a harrowing encounter with spiritual beings; and (3) the reintegration of the dreamer back into the community, now with a new, culturally sanctioned role as tribal healer (see also Turner 1969, Van Gennep 1960). My dream follows the first two parts of this cross-cultural pattern, that is, the departure from my community and the killing and dismemberment by spirit beings, but not the third, the reintegration into the community.

Tedlock would also try to understand my dream's cultural context. In particular, she would focus attention on my culture's role in structuring the linguistic expression of this dream. The dream draws upon a number of culturally specific idioms, most directly the idioms of medieval epics and of science fiction. These are literary genres that are generally seen in our culture as trivial, insignificant, and far removed from the mainstream. But that is exactly why I enjoyed them so much, because they helped me envision possibilities, ideals, and truths that transcended the limits of the world in which I grew up. However, the dream also draws upon the idiom of television (the guy who is killed is either me or "like someone on television," and the end of the dream has the television theme song). Television is the supremely mainstream form of cultural expression in the West, powerfully shaping the lives of us all. And yet, I find television to be the supremely trivializing force in our culture, reducing all meanings to bland, trite, commercially acceptable pap. Now when I reflect (with Tedlock's help) on the ways these different cultural idioms structure my dream, I realize that they reveal a fundamental conflict. On the one hand, I believe that the fantasy and science fiction elements of the dream are expressing ideals I hold that are real and important but that my culture tends to dismiss as trivial foolishness. On the other hand, I feel that the television elements are expressing my desperate desire to make all this "mainstream," to make it "commercially acceptable," to frame this experience in such a way as to keep myself in contact with my culture. But in so doing, I risk trivializing those valuable meanings that I have discovered. In short, the clash of linguistic forms is expressing a clash of meanings: the conflict between fantasy/science fiction elements and television elements is expressing my conflict between wanting to transcend my culture and wanting to stay related to it.

In the terms of Hunt's cognitive psychology, there are many aspects of "intensified dreams" in my dream experience. There are strong, vivid images and powerful kinesthetic sensations; there are multiple shifts of perception and awareness as well as intense, overwhelming emotions; and there is a coherent, well-structured narrative framework. I see Hunt as offering insight, much as Tedlock does, into the meaningfulness of the dream's *form*. Hunt argues that modern Western culture has focused its interest on "personal-mnemic" dreams and has made little effort to understand the more "intensified" forms of dreaming. According to Hunt, then, the simple fact of having such a dream might itself have the meaning of challenging the norms of Western culture. That was certainly the way I experienced the dream: the dream made me feel marked, set apart, isolated, and not in an especially pleasant way. Everything around me looked different, because I had experienced something that my world could not explain. Having an "intensified" dream served to intensify the painful distance that was growing between me and the world of my family and culture.

A Dialogue: The Theme of a Conflict with My Culture

This theme of a conflict between me and my family and culture has come up in many of the eight different readings of the dream. From Breton's point of view, such a spectacularly grotesque dream illustrates perfectly the creative power of the unconscious; the dream could thus be seen as evidence of my true freedom from the constraints I felt were being imposed upon me. Similarly, Tedlock's anthropological approach and Hunt's cognitive psychological perspective both suggest that the *form* of the dream signifies a distancing of myself from the mainstream norms of my cultural world.

But Freud's and Jung's perspectives lead me to wonder whether this freedom, this distancing process, is an entirely positive achievement. Freud enables me to see that I am extremely ambivalent about leaving my family's world. I would like to reconcile the knight and the king and queen and have them accept his gift; I would like my parents to continue supporting and approving of me, to accept the "gift" I have for studying religion and philosophy. Jung's notion of the shadow archetype makes me look at the Evil Alien as all that I fear in my relationship with my parents: my fear is that they will become utterly cold, foreign, uncaring, faceless creatures willing to destroy me and then abandon me. According to Jung, the shadow archetype represents (in a warped, twisted form) those feelings we have not been able to integrate into our conscious personalities. From that viewpoint, I can see that the Evil Alien is the result of my demonizing a whole set of feelings I have towards my parents: wanting them to be warm, close, caring, willing to nurture and stay with me. My recognition of the Evil Alien's face as an upside-down heart expresses this shadow dimension very succinctly.[14]

Hall helps me gain some further insights here. As I made the content analysis of my thirteen dreams during the two months surrounding this dream, I noticed that there was a structural parallel *within* the two scenes of the Evil Alien dream. In the first scene I am a knight, shuttling between the knight aligned with inside the room (who is aligned with the king and queen) and the knight outside on the fire escape; at the end of the second scene I am caught between the Alien, who is hurting me, and Scott, whom I am hurting. This structural parallel adds to the meanings already suggested. The knight outside and Scott are both images of freedom, of a rejection of traditional, mainstream values. Their presence in the dream emphasizes the urges I feel to move towards that freedom, to escape the norms and the expectations that are being imposed upon me. But at the same time, the "I" of the dream is standing *in between* the knight and Scott, on one hand, and the king and queen and the Evil Alien, on the other; I am caught between the representatives of freedom and the representatives of parental/conventional authority. My painful, confusing position *between* the two sides is an apt image of the emotional dilemma I was facing at that point in my life.

LaBerge's insights about the shifting levels of awareness within dreaming experience also contribute to my understanding of this issue. I both am and am *not* the body being dissected. I feel it happening from the inside, and yet I also see it happening from the outside. This means, I believe, that the Evil Alien is attacking only a *part* of me, the part that wants to escape it. The *other* part of me is not being attacked, because it does not want to escape the Evil Alien. The shifts in perception within the dream would thus reemphasize the different ways I am related to the Evil Alien—as a victim of its violence and as a passive, and thus compliant, observer of its actions. My perception is clearest in relation to the Evil Alien's specific acts of violence. The one exception is the extremely vivid image of my body-slamming Scott in the fire place, and grinding my elbow into his groin. Hobson leads us to view such points of clarity as the points where my mind is working hardest to create meaning. This suggests another structural parallel, this time between the Evil Alien and myself: just as the Evil Alien attacks me, I attack Scott; it punishes me, and I punish Scott. A third way of relating to the Evil Alien thus emerges—I *identify* with it, hurting others just as it has hurt me. I attack the punk rocker, a representative of those anti-cultural urges I feel within myself. I try to destroy his creative powers and drive him into the fire place (preventing him from "escaping" the fire, as the knight tries to do).[15]

The Religious Dimensions of the Dream

This dialogue could go on for some time, of course. But we should turn now to focus on exploring the religious dimension of this dream. Much as we did in chapter 14, with Dora's dream, we have established in my Evil Alien dream that the hermeneutic principles of dream interpretation developed in part 3 are sound and useful.[16] To this point, the interpretation has certainly succeeded in raising new questions and opening up new horizons of understanding. Now we can explore the religious or spiritual meanings that emerge in the dream. The six questions outlined earlier in this chapter will be our guide in this process.

1. The most prominent image in the dream is undoubtedly the Evil Alien's dissection of my body. The Alien is overwhelmingly powerful and utterly inhuman; I feel there is no way I can communicate with him, influence him, or fight him. I react to the Alien with passivity, simply watching as he takes my body/the body apart. At the end I lash out in rage against Scott, but I realize that such behavior is futile. The Alien has me completely in his control.

2. The dream raises an extremely powerful, and extremely disturbing, religious question for me: what is the nature of evil? This dream has provoked long reflections on evil, its presence within me and its influence on the world. The image of the Alien dissecting my body strikes me as thoroughly evil: an image of violent, inhuman, destructive forces working to annihilate my very being. I feel very strongly that Jung's distinction between the relative evil of the personal shadow and the absolute evil of forces transcending the individual self applies to this dream. And yet, and this is the most disturbing element of the dream, I sense that these evil forces are entering into my life through *human* relationships, through my relation-

ships with my family and my culture. The way absolute evil emerges into human life is *through* the personal and cultural conflicts we suffer.

The differences between the Evil Alien and Darth Vader (my antagonist in previous nightmares) is very significant here. Darth Vader is a perfect image of the personal shadow, for underneath his black mask he is in fact Luke Skywalker's father. At the end of the *Star Wars* film trilogy Luke succeeds in redeeming his father from the "dark side of the Force" and reestablishing a positive relationship with him. Darth Vader's evilness is relative, and it can be transformed. My dream, however, does not present me with Darth Vader, as did many of my past dreams. This dream refers to the image of Darth Vader but goes *beyond* it; there is *more* to the Evil Alien than elements of my personal shadow, *more* than my troubled relations with my parents. The Alien, I believe, is expressing powers far more destructive, more inhuman, more fundamentally *evil* than those embodied by Darth Vader. The unsettling realization I make is that in my struggles with my family and my culture, I have somehow stumbled upon real evil.

3. There are a number of occurrences within the dream that generate tremendous emotional power, a power that I still vividly feel ten years later. As I reflect on these occurrences and the emotions they evoke, I find that each of them enriches my understanding of the nature of evil. To begin with, I am horrified by my first sight of the Alien and by seeing it murder the sleeping man. This horror reflects my shocked realization that evil is right here in front of me, in my supposedly perfect life.[17] The one truly positive emotion in the dream is hope, which I feel when I see the white pill-like object bounce away. This gives me a sense that life, creativity, and growth can survive into the future, that evil's victory is not total. This little object represents only the merest potential of future life, but it is enough to give me real hope.[18] Then, I feel bitter anger and rage about what the Alien has done to me. The fact that I direct this violent rage towards Scott seems to suggest (following Jung's subjective level of interpretation) that I hold the "Scott-like" elements within myself responsible for allowing the evil into my life: if only I had not been so resistant to my family, if only I had been less antagonistic towards my culture, then none of this would have happened. My vicious attack of Scott directly reflected my deep-lying conviction that if I could only *control* my impulses and desires, my Scott-like, anti-cultural urges, then I could protect myself against the onslaught of evil. But the final emotion of the dream, despair, emerges out of my realization that attacking Scott is useless. No matter how violently I try to control my impulses, it will not affect the emergence of evil into my life.

4. The dream certainly relates to a cluster of life crises I was experiencing at the time. I was trying to decide on my future course of studies and thus my future social and economic identity; I was struggling to break away from my family and yet to find a way to maintain their respect and support; and I was trying to understand how to develop an intimate, romantic, yet nontraditional relationship with Loren. To draw upon Erik Erikson's developmental theory (1963), I was struggling to achieve a sense of competency, a firm identity, and a capacity for intimacy, all at once.[19]

From this perspective, the parallels between my dream and the imagery of initiatory dream visions in other cultures are very helpful. Indeed, it is here that the various meanings of the dream start to come together for me. The dream strikes me as representing an *unconsumated initiation.* In my current life I was in the process of leaving my family, its values, traditions, and expectations, and establishing a new identity, a new pattern of intimate relationships, and a new set of abilities. The dream makes use of classic (archetypal?) imagery to express this process: I enter a liminal world of chaos, destruction, and death; I encounter evil, demonic forces that annihilate my being. According to the classic pattern, I would then be *re*constituted, *re*created, integrated into a *new* community. But here, something goes wrong. I meet powers darker and more evil than anything I've ever imagined, and I can't escape them. There is no one to guide me, no new world to move towards, no new community to become a part of. I know that I cannot return to my old world, but I have no idea how to emerge out of this chaotic realm of evil and violence.

I feel that in this dream an initiation of some sort has *begun*; it has destroyed once and for all my ties to the past and taught me more than I ever wanted to know about the evil that can enter into human life. But the initiation is not *consumated.* The process does not lead to any new, creative reintegration of my self. It does not lead me into any new communities or relationships. Rather, it leaves me with an acute sense of isolation, fear, rage, and despair, and a terrible awareness of the reality of evil.

5. The foregoing discussion makes it clear that the dream relates to both my past and my future. The first scene, with the knights and the king and queen, can be viewed as an archeological prologue. It establishes a context of family conflict, separation, and anger, a historical context that frames my encounter with the Evil Alien. The first scene brings forth the question of whether or not I will carry on my family tradition—in other words, how I will relate to my family's past.[20]

The future-oriented, teleological aspects of the dream emerge in the two emotions of hope and despair. The hope is a vision of future potential, an image of the creative new life that may survive the encounter with evil and that may, in some distant time to come, grow and flourish. The despair is a realization of what will be my probable reaction to this experience. My fear of the Evil Alien is likely to make me behave in the future with extreme caution; it is likely to intensify my self-control, often to violent extremes, in an effort to stifle any urges or impulses that might provoke the Evil Alien to return.

Ultimately, the dream has a very weak teleological force to it. That underscores the dilemma I find myself in: there is no real guidance towards the future, no real insight into how I can emerge out of the violent chaos within which I am caught.

6. The dream had many challenging, transforming effects on my life. Most immediately, the dream challenged me to reflect upon evil, to acknowledge its reality and power even if I could not grasp it intellectually. The dream thoroughly transformed my self-image. In a word, it humbled me. It deflated my confidence in the powers of my will, my rationality, my self-control. The dream made me far more willing to admit that there are things I do not understand and cannot master. However, it did not snuff out my curiosity or my desire to understand. On the contrary, the dream convinced me that there really *are* realms far beyond the conventional bounds of my culture, realms I had now seen for myself, realms that I urgently wanted to explore. Perhaps surprisingly, the dream eliminated all my remaining doubts about studying religion and philosophy. I was absolutely sure now that I wanted to devote myself to learning more about those subjects—not, as before, with an eager, energetic desire to "succeed" but with a more tempered desire simply to experience and to understand.[21]

And yet the dream also challenged me to find a way to maintain some sort of relationship with my family and my culture. It would have been too easy simply to reject them, to cast them behind me. I felt very strongly that doing so would be surrendering to the Evil Alien; my encounter with the Evil Alien challenged me to try and create new, better relations where he had destroyed them. I saw in the dream how my present struggles were rooted in my past relationships. Any future growth would have to acknowledge that rootedness, and it would have to evolve out of those relationships.

Again, it was unclear what direction and what form such future growth would take. But that represents, I feel, the ultimate challenge of the dream: the challenge to create a future for myself, to find my own way out of the destructive realm of the Evil Alien, and to become reintegrated into my community.[22]

Conclusion

It should be clear by now that this dream has served as an important root metaphor in my life. "Being Dissected by the Evil Alien" is a root metaphor dream in that it uses tangible, concrete imagery to express intangible existential meanings that have had a powerful, deeply challenging and transformative effect on my life.

As an example illustrating the various principles and methods we have discussed, the interpretation of this dream has demonstrated the following points. First, a variety of different disciplines may be used fruitfully to interpret a dream, and the result is an understanding that is richer than that which any one discipline alone could provide. Second, certain principles of hermeneutic philosophy can help us to integrate the different disciplines and develop a theoretically sound and practically useful interdisciplinary method. Third, an interpretive approach that explores the religious dimensions of a dream is not opposed to other kinds of interpretation but draws upon them and creatively expands upon their insights. Fourth, the religious or spiritual meanings of dreams do not need to be expressed in conventionally "religious" imagery, nor do they emerge only in the dreams of conventionally "religious" people (as we also saw with the last three dreams in chapter 16). Fifth, to explore the religious meanings of a dream does not require us to ignore the insights provided by a rational, critical analysis of the dream; conversely, to engage in such a critical analysis does not require us to ignore the numinous religious meanings that may emerge in the dream. Sixth and finally, the practice of interpreting a dream, especially a dream that seems to have a religious or spiritual dimension to it, is messy. Contrary to what Freud, Breton, Hall, Hobson, and many others have claimed, dream interpretation is rarely a straightforward matter. It is never an objective, "scientific" process in the common meaning of that term. However, it is certainly true that dream interpretation may be pursued in better or in worse ways. As a modern proverb has it, just because an absolutely germ-free environment is impossible does not mean that surgeons perform medical operations in the sewer. You do your best given the conditions that exist. In the interpretation of dreams, doing your best means being patient, playful, open-minded, self-reflective, comfortable with ambiguity, and willing to use many different perspectives and methods. Most importantly, it means adopting as your goal the creation of broader horizons—not final, conclusive answers, but new questions, new sensitivities, and new potentials.

PART FIVE

CONCLUSION:
Out of the Wilderness

19

WHY ALL THE INTEREST *NOW* IN THE RELIGIOUS MEANING OF DREAMS?

You can go to the East
To find your inner hemisphere
You say we're under the same sky,
You're bound to realize, honey, it's not that clear

—Amy Ray, "Land of Canaan"

Our Historical Context

All the recent interest in dreams and religion may, from a certain historical perspective, appear extremely odd. Christopher Evans, author of *Landscapes of the Night*, expresses this puzzlement well:

> Ostensibly it might seem as if the psychical approach to dreams was a product of pre-scientific thinking, arising from a relatively unsophisticated view of the world which failed to distinguish between subjective and objective reality. If so, one might reasonably have expected the idea that during sleep the mind or soul could step through into a supernatural world or acquire supernatural powers to have gently slipped away as it became replaced by new understandings of the nature of the human brain and mind. Unfortunately, or fortunately (depending upon which way you like to look at the universe), the psychical view of dreams failed to disappear conveniently with the advance of science and technology . . . One could indeed argue that the psychical view of dreams is still the most ardently held in many parts of the world today, including the technologically sophisticated West. (Evans 1983, 50)

We can readily appreciate why Evans is so exasperated at the strange historical tenacity of the "psychical" view of dreams. After all, modern Western culture is in many ways based on a profound skepticism towards all things religious. Enlightenment philosophers, whose championing of human reason helped shape the modern West, devoted much of their energies to denouncing the irrationality of religious belief and to liberating people's minds from the control of priests, churches, and dogmas.[1] The American and French revolutions produced new political systems that formally constricted religion's previously powerful and widespread influence on society. Modern scientific advances in biology, astronomy, geology, and many other fields of research revealed the superstitious errors of many religious ideas and offered far more persuasive ways of explaining the world.[2] There can be little doubt that religion's status has radically diminished in the modern era of Western culture.

Given this historical context, the question has to be raised of *why* so many twentieth-century Westerners are interested in the religious or spiritual potentials of dreams. Indeed, the question becomes all the more intriguing when we notice that this interest actually seems to be *growing*: looking beyond our eight dream theorists, we find that a huge number of more popularly oriented books have been published recently that describe methods of exploring the religious dimensions of dreams (e.g., Faraday 1972, 1974; Delaney 1979, 1991; Garfield 1974; Taylor 1983, 1992; Ullman and Zimmerman 1979; Krippner and Dillard 1988; Gackenbach 1989—the list could go on and on). What is the significance of this? How is all this interest in the religious potential of dreams connected to the changed role of religion in modern Western culture? Our study of dreams and religious meaning cannot conclude without reflecting on these questions. We cannot leave the wilderness of dreams without considering where this particular realm of experience lies within the broader landscape of modern Western culture.

Secularization Theories: The "Decline" versus the "Transposition" of Religion

The academic study of religion's place in modern Western culture is known as the study of *secularization*.[3] Generally speaking, theories of secularization tend to take one of two basic forms. The first is the "decline" theory (see Marx 1978; Frazier 1959; Weber 1976; Durkheim 1915; Dewey 1973; Berger 1967; Rieff 1966; Blumenberg 1983). According to decline theorists, religion has gradually been defeated by scientific rationality as a way of ordering and understanding reality. Most of these theorists see religion's decline as an evolutionary process, as a forward advance in the development of human culture: religion was spawned by ignorance, fear, and weakness, but modern science now enables us to do without religion's comforting illusions and to adopt a more mature, realistic view of the world.[4] To continue promoting religion is thus, according to the decline theory, to cling to an outmoded, developmentally inferior worldview that is retarding the progress of human civilization.

The second basic kind of secularization theory sees not a decline, but a "transposition" of religion in the modern West (see Tillich 1948; Mannheim 1936; Eliade 1954, 1957; Maslow 1964; Bellah et al. 1985). Rather than falling into irrelevance, religion has in this view adapted to the modern context, and it has been "transposed" into new, more culturally appropriate forms. These theorists look to psychology in particular as the major new arena where essentially religious concerns may be explored—psychology describes human nature, offers prescriptions for attaining a fulfilling life, and provides therapeutic treatments to cure people's suffering, all functions that formal religions have traditionally served.[5] Transposition theorists assert that humans have an inherent need for religion and that if they cannot satisfy this need in either traditional or modern forms, the vitality of society as a whole is threatened. This is the great danger, some of these theorists believe, of the modern West's skepticism towards religion: the more people's authentic religious needs are depreciated, the more those needs are perverted, finding a warped expression in bigotry, fanaticism, and violence.

If we turn now to reconsider our eight dream explorers, we find that their interests in dreams and religious meaning correspond almost exactly to either one or the other of these secularization theories. On the "decline" side, Freud, Hall, and Hobson assert that the study of dreams is a means of destroying religious superstitions and promoting the progress of science and rationality. Their research is contributing to the evolutionary process of moving beyond religion to a more scientific view of the world. Freud, for example, comments in one of his *New Introductory Lectures on Psychoanalysis* that

> The last contribution to the criticism of the religious Weltanschauung was effected by psychoanalysis, by showing how religion originated from the helplessness of children and by tracing its contents to the survival into maturity of the wishes and needs of childhood . . . If we attempt to assign the place of religion in the evolution of mankind, it appears not as a permanent acquisition but as a counterpart to the neurosis which individual civilized men have to go through in their passage from childhood to maturity. (Freud [1933] 1965, 147–48)

Hobson characterizes his research in a similar way, setting the study of dreams in the great modern tradition of science's victorious battles with religion:

> For the student of consciousness, the development of the polygraph is no less portentous than was the discovery of the telescope for the student of the heavens. Numerous myths that we hold about ourselves may come to seem as outlandish as the pre-Copernican idea that the sun moves around the earth. Already, for example, it is clear that dreaming comes not from angels, nor from incubi, nor even from wishes, but from the automatic activation of our brains in REM sleep . . . In viewing the dream as the subject's own active anticipation of the future rather than as a prophecy sent from a god, we have come full circle from animistic theism—to scientific humanism. (Hobson 1988, 139, 81)

These are classic statements in the decline theory of secularization. Indeed, it is extremely interesting to note how all three of these dream explorers refer to Copernicus, and two of them cite Darwin, in order to frame their work. In the 1917 essay "A Difficulty in the Path of Psychoanalysis," Freud says that just as the collective narcissism of humankind rebelled against astronomy's discovery that the earth is not the center of the universe and biology's discovery that *Homo sapiens* is not distinct from other animal species, so have people rejected the psychoanalytic discovery that the waking ego is not the master of the individual personality (Freud [1917b] 1963, 185–88). Hall claims that the irrational objections to scientific research on dreams is only a fresh instance of the basic pattern of scientific progress: "this resistance against knowledge has been met before in history. The astronomers met it and so have the biologists" (Hall 1966, 218). And Hobson, in the above quotation, directly compares the historical significance of sleep laboratory research on dreams to Copernicus's study of astronomy. All three dream researchers, then, use exactly the same examples to cast the historical nature of their discoveries as part of the ongoing march of scientific progress.

So according to these decline-oriented figures, the wilderness of dreams is one of the last hideouts of religious superstition. Science has rousted religion from almost every realm of knowledge, and dream researchers should aim to complete the job by ferreting out the final remnants of religious belief cowering in the area of dream study.

But Breton, Jung, LaBerge, Tedlock, and Hunt vigorously oppose this "decline theory" approach to dreams and religious meaning. Their views fit perfectly within the transposition theory of secularization. These figures argue that dreams are a legitimate means of regaining contact with spiritual energies whose traditional outlets have been repressed by the scientific rationality of modern Western culture. Jung, for example, says that

> dreams contribute to the self-regulation of the psyche by automatically bringing up everything that is repressed or neglected or unknown . . . It is therefore not surprising that religious compensations play a great role in dreams. That this is increasingly so in our time is a natural consequence of the prevailing materialism of our outlook. (Jung [1948a] 1974, 36)

Hunt expresses a similar view that, despite the modern West's hostility towards religion and spirituality, dreams can be a means of regaining contact with religious energies:

> Liam Hudson [1985] has questioned whether dreaming will survive in a technological, utilitarian world society based on ever increasing materialism and "success." If dreaming becomes more and more mundane and even subjectively ceases in the lives of many modern adults, then could this same fate not become general—as a postmodern but not post-money mentality works its way pervasively through people's lives? Perhaps. Yet given the correlations between vivid dreaming and aesthetic ability, creative imagination, and intuition, and the Ur-relations between dreaming and literature, metaphor, and metaphysical thought, it seems more likely that certain individuals will continue to develop the full multiplicity of dreaming relatively independent of social sanction. (Hunt 1989, 218)

Jung and Hunt are expressing notions directly related to the transposition view of religion's place in the modern West. The wilderness of dreams, from this perspective, is one of the last sanctuaries of true, primal religious energy; dreams can be a powerful source of inspiration to help us resist, and perhaps overthrow, the dominance of scientific rationality and materialism in our culture.

The decline and transposition theories of secularization are, like any pair of diametrically opposed responses to a difficult question, unable by themselves to resolve the issue. Each theory highlights genuine failings in the other but cannot overcome its own weaknesses. The decline theory, as applied to the study of dreams, does make legitimate points about how some dream explorers succumb to simplistic, antiscientific idealizations. Too often people do wax excessively romantic about the pure, pristine spiritual wonders of dreams. This naive yearning has led dream explorers to rush headlong into some very slippery terrain. G. William Domhoff (a student and colleague of Calvin Hall) has written an excellent analysis of this yearning and the troubles dream researchers get into when their desires unduly cloud their critical judgement. Domhoff's book *The Mystique of Dreams* (1985), which documents the rise and the fall of dream researchers' fascination with the Senoi people of Malaya, is one of the strongest and most persuasive calls for a more critically self-reflective and scientifically controlled approach to dreams.[6] Domhoff argues that the Senoi controversy illustrates the problems that are created by an antirationality, antiscience bias in dream study.

Freud, Hall, and Hobson express concerns similar to those raised by Domhoff. Freud decries critics of psychoanalysis who reject his views on dreams simply because they do not like the unpleasant truths he is uncovering. Hall asserts that opponents of content analysis have an unjustified and irrational aversion to all quantitative statistical research. And Hobson denounces those advocates of the "prophetic" tradition of dream study who have dismissed out of hand the important findings of neuroscientific research on dreaming. From the perspective of these dream researchers, the study of dreams and religious meaning is riddled with romantic illusions that may preserve happy, gratifying fantasies but that ultimately retard the progress of genuine knowledge about dreams.[7]

These points are all valid to a large extent. However, those dream explorers who hold a transposition kind of theory have many legitimate objections of their own to make. Against the decline theory, they argue that there *are* valuable insights we can gain by studying the dream beliefs and practices of non-Western cultures. We need not be starry-eyed idealists or rabid science-bashers to recognize that some "primitive," "prescientific" cultures may have much to teach us about the nature, functions, and religious meanings of dreams. For example, at the end of chapter 1 we examined a number of different approaches to religiously meaningful dreams, approaches that are sophisticated, insightful, and well reasoned. These approaches do not partake of modern scientific research, yet they reflect understandings of dreams that we can hardly dismiss as naive, primitive, or inferior to our own. At the very least, such examples suggest that we not assume (as decline theorists do) a simple, linear model of progress in human knowledge of dreams, with *our* knowledge standing alone at the forefront of that progression.

Jung and Hunt make another telling argument against the "decline" theory. They assert that the apparent decline of religion in the modern West has actually involved the rise of a new kind of worldview, that is, the worldview of scientific rationality. This worldview truly functions as a "religion," in the sense of providing an all-embracing account of the most basic, determinative aspects of reality. As we have seen, Jung and Hunt argue that there has been not a *loss* of religion but rather a *shift* to a new kind of religious faith.[8] The crucial problem, according to Jung, Hunt, and others from this perspective, is that this new religious faith is inadequate. Scientific rationality can explain many things, but it cannot provide the sort of existential meaning and spiritual orientation that humans fundamentally need. Freud, for example, dismisses all such desires as mere remnants of infancy, and proposes that the most mature attitude towards life is one of stoic resignation. Hobson at least recognizes that humans do display an "inexorable need for meaning," but he frequently belittles this (to him) stubborn, irrational trait and suggests that humans would be better off not engaging in mystical quests for deep, hidden meanings. Transposition-oriented dream explorers see views like those of Freud and Hobson as clear evidence of the inability of scientific rationalism to recognize, respect, and fulfill the irrepressible human need for religious meaning.

Ricoeur on the "Modern" Mode of Belief in Symbols

The stark polarization between these two different theories of dreams and religion in modern Western culture poses us with a challenge: can we find a way to bridge these widely separated positions? I believe that Ricoeur's reflections on the *cultural* significance of the "second naivete" approach to religious symbols can provide such a bridge. We have already used Ricoeur's ideas to develop a model for the practical exploration of the religious dimension of dreams. However, we can see that Ricoeur's development of the "second naivete" also addresses the cultural conditions of the modern West, and is intended to overcome exactly the sort of gaping divide we are facing here.

In the conclusion to *The Symbolism of Evil*, Ricoeur considers the question of how to integrate rational knowledge with the religious experience of symbols. He emphasizes that this is a *cultural* question, that this question is both raised and determined by the distinctive qualities of modern Western culture:

> This task has a precise meaning *now*, at a certain stage in philosophical discussion, and, more broadly, in connection with certain traits of our "modernity." The historical moment of the philosophy of symbols is that of forgetfulness and restoration. Forgetfulness of hierophanies, forgetfulness of the signs of the sacred, loss of man himself insofar as he belongs to the sacred. The forgetfulness, we know, is the counterpart of the great task of nourishing men . . . It is in the age when our language has become more precise, more univocal, more technical in a word,

> more suited to those integral formalizations which are called precisely symbolic logic, it is in this very age of discourse that we want to recharge our language, that we want to start again from the fullness of language. (Ricoeur 1967, 349)

Ricoeur, like the transposition theorists, is deeply concerned with the negative effects of scientific rationality, with the modern West's loss of nourishing religious meaning. But like the decline theorists, Ricoeur also fully appreciates the gains that have been made by scientific rationality, and he does not propose to dismiss those gains in a headlong romantic quest for past wonders. He says, "It is not regret for the sunken Atlantides that animates us, but hope for a re-creation of language. Beyond the desert of criticism, we wish to be called again" (349).

What we need, Ricoeur argues, is an approach to religious symbols that can *restore* our relationship to these nourishing images by using a *critical* appreciation of them—"we are in every way children of criticism, and we seek to go beyond criticism by means of criticism, by a criticism that is no longer reductive but restorative" (350). The critical reduction of symbols and myths can, he believes, clarify their meanings for us. Through criticism we learn that symbols are not valid explanations of natural phenomena or of history, that they are shaped by social, political, and economic structures, and that they have their psychological roots in our childhood experiences. But these critical discoveries do *not*, Ricoeur claims, destroy religious symbols; on the contrary, such criticism can open up the true, authentic nature of these symbols as "primordial sign[s] of the sacred" (353), as revelations of the human relationship with the cosmos. As such, religious symbols can bring new vitality to modern Westerners who feel trapped within the sterile confines of scientific rationality.[9] Ricoeur stresses that this revitalization of the modern West through a critical restoration of religious symbols is not antiscience and does not mean we deny our modernity:

> Does that mean that we could go back to a primitive naivete? Not at all. In every way, something has been lost, irremediably lost: immediacy of belief. But if we can no longer live the great symbolisms of the sacred in accordance with the original belief in them, we can, we modern men, aim at a second naivete in and through criticism. In short, it is by *interpreting* that we can *hear* again. (351)

The great virtue of the "second naivete" model of approaching religious symbols, Ricoeur believes, is that it is true to our culture—the modern West is remarkable for the critical powers of its philosophies and its sciences, and Ricoeur wants to do full justice to our culture's achievements in those realms. But Ricoeur also wants to find a way to overcome the spiritual limits of our culture, a way to escape the barrenness of scientific rationality and regain a living, nourishing relationship with the sacred. His notion of the "second naivete" represents a distinctively *modern* solution to the impasse between the decline and the transposition views of religion in Western culture:

> For the second immediacy that we seek and the second naivete that we await are no longer accessible to us anywhere else than in a hermeneutics; we can believe only by interpreting. It is the "modern" mode of belief in symbols, an express of the distress of modernity and a remedy for that distress . . . Thus hermeneutics, an acquisition of "modernity," is one of the modes by which that "modernity" transcends itself, insofar as it is forgetfulness of the sacred. I believe that being can still speak to me—no longer, of course, under the precritical form of immediate belief, but as the second immediacy aimed at by hermeneutics. This second naivete aims to be the postcritical equivalent of the precritical hierophany. (352)

If we return now to the question with which we headed this chapter, that is, why all the interest *now* in the religious meaning of dreams? we find that Ricoeur's reflections can help us formulate an answer. The growing interest in the religious dimension of dreams reflects a profound desire, in Ricoeur's words, "to be called again," a belief "that *being* can still speak" to us. Many modern Westerners are dissatisfied with the existential meanings provided by their culture. The rationalism, commercialism, and individualism promoted so vigorously in the modern West do not always lead to a fulfilling, meaningful life. Many people have looked for religious rituals, mythological symbols, and spiritual teachings that can reconnect them with the sacred and provide them with existential meanings to guide their lives. Dreams, as we have abundantly seen, have always been an outstanding source of religious images and symbols. So modern Westerners interested in dreams are simply exploring a realm of religious meaning that humans have been exploring for the same reason throughout history. In this sense, Ricoeur supports the transposition answer to this chapter's question: people are so interested in dreams and religious meaning *now* because they are seeking authentic religious symbols and meanings that they cannot find elsewhere in modern Western culture.

But, Ricoeur's support for the transposition theory has important qualifications. He insists that modern Westerners *cannot* experience religious symbols in the same innocent, prerational way that people from other cultures have. In other words, we cannot become the Senoi. We have learned, through centuries of strenuous efforts, that religious symbols always bear with them nonreligious influences and illusions of all sorts. Ricoeur reminds us that this hard-won knowledge is one of the great achievements of Western culture, enabling us to overcome many forms of ignorance, to open up new realms of discovery, and to cultivate free intellectual inquiry. If, therefore, we are to remain true to the culture that has formed us, we must bring this knowledge with us when we seek a new encounter with religious symbols. Ricoeur argues that we must reject the romantic desire for a "pure" experience of religious symbols and subject them to a critical, rational examination. In this sense, Ricoeur affirms the decline theorists in their suspicion that all the renewed interest in dreams and religious meaning threatens to deny the genuine gains of scientific rationality and to revive the religious superstitions and illusions that proved so destructive in our culture's past.

Ultimately, Ricoeur's reflections all lead to the (deceptively) simple suggestion that we "seek to go beyond criticism by means of criticism, by a criticism that is no longer reductive but restorative" (Ricoeur 1967, 350). We go beyond the critical skepticism towards the religious meanings of dreams by *means* of that critical skepticism: first, by listening carefully to what Freud, Hall, and Hobson have to say and using their methods of reductively analyzing dreams and *then*, by drawing upon the restorative interpretive methods of Breton, Jung, LaBerge, Tedlock, and Hunt to seek, in an attitude of "second naivete," whatever religious meanings our dreams may reveal to us.[10] In this way we remain faithful to our culture and yet are able to explore realms of experience and meaning beyond our culture's boundaries.

20

THE FUTURE OF THE WILDERNESS OF DREAMS

> This world falls on me with dreams of immortality
> Everywhere I turn all the beauty just keeps shaking me
>
> —Amy Ray, "World Falls"

My favorite hikes are those in which I climb up the highest, steepest mountain ridge I can find, and then run back down, dashing in minutes over wilderness terrain it initially took hours to cover. That is essentially what we are going to do here, as we rush back over issues it has taken 19 chapters to explore, touching briefly on some of the many implications and potentials of our study of dreams and religious meaning.

Dream Research

The first area to dash through is that of current and future dream research. Our studies have suggested many new directions for dream researchers to explore. Cognitive psychologists, for example, could follow Hunt's lead in examining the roles of memory, imagination, and reason in the emergence of root metaphor dreams. Content analysts could develop a "religious meaning" scale to use in analyzing dream series, identifying images, themes, and patterns that relate to the dreamer's ultimate existential concerns. Clinicians and psychotherapists could provide case studies detailing the root metaphors orienting a client's life and the emergence of those root metaphors in the client's dreams. Sleep laboratory researchers could help us try to explain in greater detail the processes involved in the "activation" and the "synthesis" of existentially meaningful dreams. Anthropologists could study whether the root metaphor concept is useful in a cross-cultural understanding of the spiritual significance of dreams.

Nightmare researchers could pursue the possibility that nightmares are a special kind of root metaphor dream that reveals fundamentally evil, destructive, or demonic aspects of human existence.

The study of dreams and religious meaning by modern dream researchers has been restricted by the lack of a clear account of what religious meaning is. Lacking a sound theoretical model, dream researchers have apparently been reluctant to get involved in such a seemingly mystical, "New Age" subject as the religious potential of dreams. My hope is that the root metaphor concept will fill this need, providing a clear, critical, theoretically sophisticated understanding of dreams and religious meaning that can be of practical use to dream researchers.

Hermeneutics

The second area in which our explorations may have some valuable implications is that of hermeneutics. As we discussed in part 3, the question of how to interpret texts has become a profoundly important and bitterly divisive issue in our culture. In the American context, debates over legal texts like the U.S. Constitution, over religious texts like the Bible, over artistic texts like rock music lyrics, and over educational texts like the "Great Works" of Western culture have all turned on what people say these texts *mean* and how people say we should *interpret* them. Such debates have motivated philosophers to reflect anew on the age-old discipline of hermeneutics and to see if theories of textual interpretation from past eras can help us reconcile the rancorous debates that wrack contemporary Western culture.

At the least, our studies should suggest that dream interpretation is a legitimate realm of hermeneutics: humans have been reflecting on the interpretation of dream "texts" at least as long as they have been trying to interpret religious, artistic, legal, and historical texts. Dream interpretation is perhaps *the* oldest hermeneutic practice in human history,[1] and thus merits far more serious philosophical attention than it has hitherto received.

But our explorations indicate that the study of dreams can provide more than a source of historical comparisons. The hermeneutic principles of dream interpretation we derived from Gadamer are applications of a prominent hermeneutic philosopher's ideas to a common realm of human experience. While Gadamer's work is so abstract and theoretical as to be inaccessible to virtually anyone but professional scholars, we have applied its key points to dreams, an area of common experience with which everyone is at least somewhat familiar. The point is that dream interpretation is a place where sophisticated hermeneutic ideas about truth, reality, and meaning can be made *accessible*—where the valuable insights of thinkers like Gadamer can begin to reach beyond university philosophy departments into the lives of a wider spectrum of the public. *Any* means of encouraging people to reflect on issues in hermeneutic philosophy marks a genuine contribution to our culture's debates on textual interpretation.

Religion

Third, our reflections can contribute something to the revitalization of religion in modern Western culture. As discussed in the previous chapter, the model we have developed provides an approach to the religious dimension of dreams that does *not* require an antiscience romanticism, that does *not* depend on membership in a church or belief in the Judeo-Christian God, and that enables us to explore *beyond* the spiritual limitations of our culture. According to this model, we can explore dreams in such a way as to affirm the critical methods of scientific rationality and yet look past the all-embracing worldview of scientific rationality to fulfill existential needs that that worldview cannot satisfy.

More specifically, I believe the exploration of dreams can help us cultivate a number of particular religious or spiritual values, values that many contemporary theologians, philosophers, and social commentators have claimed the modern West must develop if we are to grow and flourish as a culture. Exploring the religious dimension of dreams can nurture a respect for the non-rational, imaginative forces that shape our lives, and an awareness of the ultimate interdependence of all experience and all life. It can promote a realism towards evil, as well as a hopefulness towards overcoming evil. It can enrich our appreciation for the religious significance of seemingly small, trivial aspects of life, and it can strengthen our motivation to *act*, to put our religious ideals into practice in our communities.

This is only, of course, my own view of the religious or spiritual values that can be discovered and developed in the course of exploring dreams. Other dream researchers would almost certainly have different perspectives on this issue. Nevertheless, I believe our studies here provide substantial evidence that the exploration of dreams can indeed cultivate important religious or spiritual values. That evidence is sufficient to legitimate the main point here: to the extent that dream exploration does cultivate spiritual values, ideals, insights, and virtues such as those listed above, we may justifiably claim that dreams do have something to contribute to the revitalization of religion in modern Western culture.

Interdisciplinary Research

Our studies have implications for yet another area, namely that of interdisciplinary inquiry. There is a growing trend in Western scholarship towards using the insights from many different disciplines to develop a broader, richer understanding of a given subject. This trend is motivated by the realization that single-discipline approaches at best offer a limited view of the subject and at worst give rise to narrow, reductionistic misreadings of the subject. Our study of the religious meanings of dreams has, I hope, illustrated the wisdom of this trend towards interdisciplinary inquiry. We have drawn not only upon a wide range of different fields of dream research but also upon a variety of philosophical, theological, and sociological theories to help us understand our subject. It is beyond dispute that we have a vastly better understanding of the religious meanings of dreams now than if we had decided to refer only, say, to the research of depth psychologists.

Beyond illustrating the virtues of interdisciplinary inquiry, our explorations may also be of some practical use to researchers who are interested in pursuing other kinds of interdisciplinary study. We have had to overcome some of the most treacherous obstacles any form of interdisciplinary research faces: the clash of the natural sciences and the human sciences, the age-old debate over how the mind and the body interrelate, the hazards of using data from different cultures and from many different eras of history, the demand to integrate theory and practice, and the rancorous conflict between religion and science. Our efforts to surmount these obstacles are certainly not beyond criticism, but we have at least shown the kinds of challenging issues that interdisciplinary inquiries frequently address.

I would make this claim about the value of interdisciplinary research even more strongly when applied to the specific subject of dreams and religious meaning. Dream explorers may dispute the relevance of Gadamer's philosophy, the usefulness of the root metaphor concept, and the viability of Ricoeur's "second naivete"; that would be fine. But I would argue very forcefully that any future study of dreams and religious meaning *must* draw upon *some* theory of interpretation, *some* theory of religious metaphor, and *some* theory of religion and culture. It is one thing to question the particular theories we have used here; it is another thing to question the need for critical, interdisciplinary reflection on these issues. The study of dreams and religious meaning has in the past suffered greatly from a failure to engage in such reflection. My greatest hope is that if our specific arguments in this work do not appeal to dream researchers, at least the general model of critical, interdisciplinary inquiry we have developed for exploring dreams and religious meaning will be of enduring use in dream studies.

Child Education

The final area in which our work may have valuable implications is in child education. As many anthropologists have indicated (see, e.g., Gregor 1981, Tedlock 1987), dream-sharing and dream interpretation play an important role in children's education in many different cultures. This is not currently the case in modern Western culture, of course, where dream-sharing is considered appropriate only in the analyst's office, in the sleep lab, or at cocktail parties (Dombeck 1991). But I believe our studies have raised the intriguing possibility that dreams could make a very valuable contribution to child education in our culture. We have already discussed in this chapter how interpreting dreams is a means of bringing important but abstruse hermeneutic theories into a more accessible realm of ordinary experience open to all people. This suggests that by teaching children about dreams we could teach them, for example, how to appreciate meanings that may be ambiguous or "irrational," how to be open to meanings that are novel or surprising, how to recognize the creative interrelations between rationality and imagination, and how to engage in playful, free-flowing dialogues with "strange" others.[2] We have also discussed how the study of dreams is best done by an interdisciplinary method of relating the findings of different fields of study. This suggests that by studying dreams, children could learn how the mind and the body are interrelated, how people from different cultures are both like us and unlike us, and how science is not necessarily opposed to art and religion.

At the end of *The Multiplicity of Dreams*, Harry Hunt offers some very provocative ideas about using dreams in child education. His research indicates that the cognitive processes involved in "intensified dreams" are the same as those involved in artistic, philosophical, and spiritual creativity. Hunt speculates that if children were encouraged to share and play with their dreams, the effect could be to cultivate the cognitive roots of humanistic reflection:

> While early education for the symbolic frames that "do" and "control"—reading, writing, arithmetic—is excellent, no comparable emphasis exists for the abilities and sensitivities that feed into history, literature, the arts, and spirituality. Indeed, it is commonly held that systematic early education in these more aesthetic-expressive fields is impossible and that such development will take care of itself in the espe-

> cially gifted anyway—despite continuing evidence of a separation between "two cultures" and their chronic imbalance. Given the close relation between dreaming and creative imagination and the centrality of dreamtelling in primitive cultures, it seems to me that there is an equally fundamental way to teach the roots of aesthetics, literature, and philosophy to very young children. The bases of these humanistic disciplines would be truly and soundly laid were elementary teachers to encourage children to tell their dreams, to compare them with those of other children and other possibilities of dreaming, and to listen to the dreams of teachers and parents. I have been especially struck, as have many others, by the enthusiasm and vigor with which children take up such opportunities. Perhaps that is not an accident. (Hunt 1989, 218–19)

Hunt gives a cognitive psychological basis for what anthropologists have found to be true in other cultures and what some dream explorers have found to be possible in our culture, too (Garfield 1985; Wiseman 1986): namely, the values of integrating dream-sharing into the regular curriculum of child education.

The wilderness of dreams has been seen by modern Westerners either as a desolate, uninhabitable wasteland, or as a frontier region overflowing with raw materials to be greedily exploited, or as an exotic nature refuge to be visited (briefly) by tour bus. My proposal here is that we make the wilderness of dreams a part of our regular, day-to-day environment; that we teach people, beginning in childhood, that dreams are a realm where we can learn about our selves and our culture, where we can explore our emotions, our ideas, our bodies, our hopes, our fears, and our most deeply held religious or spiritual concerns. In a culture where concern is mounting about children's lack of strong, trustworthy values, about the inadequacy of our educational system, and about the desperate need for innovative approaches to teaching, the time may have come to explore more fully the educational potentials of dreams.

Appendix One

OTHER PATHS INTO THE DREAM WILDERNESS

It is impossible in a work that seeks anything short of an encyclopedic range to give adequate attention to every modern approach to dreams. However, as we engage in our particular project we need to note at least in passing what fields and paths we are not covering. Doing so will make us aware, first, that there really is a huge variety of different approaches to dreams, extending far beyond the eight I have chosen, and second, that many of these other approaches are also deeply interested in the religious meaning of dreams. In this way I hope to allay any doubts that I have exaggerated the diversity of the fields of dream study or the prominent place in modern dream research of the question of religious meaning.

The surrealists and Jung were not the only ones directly motivated by Freud to pursue the study of dreams. Many psychoanalytically oriented psychologists developed distinctive views of dreams, how to interpret them, and whether they have religious meaning. Among the first of these are Alfred Adler (1956) and Samuel Lowy (1942). Adler sees dreams as expressing the dreamer's "life-style," that is, the dreamer's vision of his or her own self as it exists and relates to the world; in contrast to Freud, he believes that dreams involve adaptive, forward-looking processes of imaginative problem solving. Lowy claims that the fact that we remember so few of our dreams must indicate that whatever meaning they have, it must serve functions that operate at an unconscious level.

In the 1950s and 1960s a new group of psychoanalytic psychologists offered ideas about the nature and meaning of dreams. Among the most prominent of these figures are Erik Erikson (1954), Medard Boss (1958, 1977), and Erik Fromm (1951). Two common themes in their works are that dreams serve adaptive, creative functions and that dreams relate to religious experience and the development of religious values. Some years later another new generation further elaborated on psychoanalytic theories of dreams. Some of these, like Richard Jones (1978), Charles Rycroft (1979), and Liam Hudson (1985), are influenced by the findings of sleep laboratory research and try to relate psychoanalytic concepts to these findings. Others, like Thomas French and Erika Fromm (1964), D. W. Winnicott (1971), and Heinz Kohut (1978), focus more on developing psychoanalytic dream theories within the context of therapeutic practice. Like the preceding generations, these psychoanalytic psychologists are all interested in exploring the positive, creative functions of dreams, functions that many of them believe to be directly related to the religious dimensions of human life.

There have also been many developments in Jung's theory of dreams by later figures in the analytic psychology tradition. The most prominent of these figures is James Hillman (1979), who argues that most depth psychological approaches to dreams concentrate too much on bringing the dream into the light of conscious day; he believes it is more valuable to bring consciousness down into the "underworld" of the dream, to work within the unconscious realm of the symbols themselves rather than trying to interpret them according to the standards of the waking world. Andrew Samuel's work *Jung and the Post-Jungians* (1985) reviews the modifications later analytic psychologists have made to Jung's dream theory.

As with the depth psychologists, there are countless researchers in the natural scientific fields studying dreams that we cannot discuss at any length. It is worth noting, however, two trends in this area of dream research. One is the growing appeal of computer analogies to describe the brain processes involved in dreaming. The most extreme presentation of this view comes in the 1983 article "The Function of Dream Sleep" by Francis Crick and Graham Mitchison. They propose that the function of dream or REM sleep is to "remove certain undesirable modes of interaction in networks of cells in the cerebral cortex," much as a computer must periodically clean out unnecessary and potentially disruptive patterns of functioning. Crick and Mitchison thus suggest that "attempting to remember one's dreams should perhaps not be encouraged, because such remembering may help to retain patterns of thought which are better forgotten. These are the very patterns the organism was attempting to damp down" (Crick and Mitchison 1983, 114; see also Evans 1983)

The other trend is for natural scientific approaches to explore the ways in which dreaming may involve special processes of creativity, problem solving, and mental development (see Haskell 1986 and Levin 1990 for good overviews of this research). Especially noteworthy here are Ernest Hartmann's (1984) research on the relationship between nightmares and creativity and Rosalind Cartwright's (1984) studies of the role of dreams in treating depression.

A number of modern philosophers have tried to understand what *kinds* of experiences dream are, what relations they have with waking experience, what we can *know* of and from our dreams, and how the dream self relates to the waking self. Among the most important of these philosophers are Ludwig Wittgenstein (1966, 1972), who devoted some extremely interesting thought to the philosophical legitimacy of Freud's key concepts; Norman Malcolm, whose monograph *Dreaming* (1959) is certainly the single most important modern work on the philosophical nature of dreams; and Gordon Globus (1987), who brings a phenomenological perspective to bear on the nature and meaning of dreams. Charles Dunlop has edited a collection of essays (1977) that surveys modern philosophical interest in dreams. Again, given our space constraints we are not be able to address many of the issues raised by these philosophers. But our discussion in part 3 of the nature of interpretation did touch on some important points of the philosophy of interpretation.

One of the most frequently neglected areas of modern dream research is that of popular dreamwork, that is, those approaches to dreams which engage in dream discussion, interpretation, and expression in primarily non-therapeutic contexts. Figures like Ann Faraday (1972, 1974), Montague Ullman and Nan Zimmerman (1979), Patricia Garfield (1974, 1979), Gayle Delaney (1979, 1991), and Jeremy Taylor (1983, 1992) all have written numerous books describing their many years of experience in doing "dreamwork" with ordinary people outside the analyst's office and the sleep laboratory. While the work of these figures is generally ignored by scholars and professional psychotherapists, I believe that popular dreamwork in fact makes an important contribution to our understanding of dreams, particularly in our understanding of the religious potentials of dreams. Popular dreamworkers study the dreams of relatively normal, well-adjusted people who are interested in their dreams as sources of personal insight, creativity, and often spiritual guidance. This is an approach that differs from that taken by other dream researchers; thus the ideas and observations of popular dreamworkers deserves at least the sincere and open-minded attention of anyone trying to understand the modern study of dreams. Popular dreamworkers do follow their own distinctive path into the dream wilderness, and although they may take tour buses along with them, that does not invalidate what they discover.

One of the newest and most promising approaches is the use of techniques from literary criticism to study dreams, in effect treating dreams as an imaginative expression distinct from but structurally related to other forms of imaginative expression. Among the leaders in this field are Bert States (1988), Phillip McCaffrey (1984), and Carol Rupprecht (1985, 1993). Their approaches are actually very close in a number of ways to what we are doing as we draw on Gadamer and Ricoeur.

The failure to include the works of historians of religion, like Mircea Eliade (1954, 1957, 1960, 1964, 1965), Joseph Campbell (1949, 1986),

Wendy Doniger O'Flaherty (1984), and others, might seem the greatest omission in our project. Their chief object of study, after all, is the variety of religious phenomena in human life, and they do devote some attention to the ways people have viewed dreams as a source of religious revelation. However, I decided not to add the history of religions to the other fields of dream study we are exploring, because there is no substantial, detailed work on dreams from this perspective that would be appropriate for our project. Eliade, Campbell, and other historians of religion tend to limit their reflections on dreams to isolated comments scattered throughout their works, making it difficult to summarize their ideas with brevity and clarity.

O'Flaherty's work *Dreams, Illusion, and Other Realities* (1984) is the obvious exception to this problem, as it is a well-researched and provocative study of dreams by a leading history of religions scholar. However, O'Flaherty discusses *myths* about dreams as much as she does actual dream experiences, and although the relationship of myths and dreams is very intriguing, it is a subject that takes us far afield from our stated project: trying to understand whether the dream experiences of modern Westerners have religious meaning. Nevertheless, O'Flaherty's book is one of the most challenging modern works on dreams, and her ideas inform many of our discussions in this volume.

Appendix Two

DOES GOD SPEAK IN DREAMS?

All of our efforts in studying the religious dimension of dreams may appear to be dancing around what some people consider *the* key question on this subject: if we say that dreams are religiously meaningful, doesn't that mean we're saying that dreams are inspired by God, by the gods, or by some kind of supernatural power? The historical review of dreams and religion in chapter 1 indicates that many people throughout history have indeed believed that dreams are inspired by divine beings. Modern dream researchers like Freud, Hall, and Hobson argue strenuously, however, that dreams are produced by strictly *natural* processes and that belief in God-inspired dreams is a superstitious relic of prescientific ignorance. But Jung and LaBerge, among others, dispute these researchers. They argue that transcendental forces do in fact inspire certain dreams. And Hunt does not speak of gods, but he believes that the depths of the human imagination are so profound that it is legitimate to speak of divinely inspired dreams.

The question comes down to this: does the claim "dreams may have religious meaning" *necessarily imply* the claim "dreams are caused by God, the gods, or other supernatural powers"? Are the two claims *identical*?

The best way to deal with this important issue is to refer to William James' illuminating discussion of religion and the subconscious in his classic book *The Varieties of Religious Experience*. James' goal in this work is to understand religious experience in terms that people who are not formally religious can make sense of (a goal very similar to our own in this project). The main resource James uses to achieve this goal is the psychological concept of the subconscious. His survey of religious experiences reveals that their manifestations

> frequently connect themselves with the subconscious part of our existence . . . [I]n religion we have a department of human nature with unusually close relations to the transmarginal or subliminal region [i.e., the subconscious] . . . Our intuitions, hypotheses, fancies, superstitions, persuasions, convictions, and in general all our non-rational operations,

> come from it. It is the source of our dreams, and apparently they may return to it . . . It is also the fountain-head of much that feeds our religion. In persons deep in the religious life, as we have now abundantly seen—and this is my conclusion—the door into this region seems unusually wide open; at any rate, experiences making their entrance through that door have had emphatic influence in shaping religious history . . . Let me then propose, as an hypothesis, that whatever it may be on its *farther* side, the "more" with which in religious experience we feel ourselves connected is on its *hither* side the subconscious continuation of our conscious life. (James [1900] 1958, 362, 366, 386)

James aims this argument at skeptics who do not believe that God or the gods really have any role in so-called religious experiences. His response is that such beliefs—"over-beliefs" in his terms—are not necessary in order to appreciate the reality, the power, and the effects of religious experiences. The well-established psychological concept of the subconscious is enough to account for the primary features of such experiences. For James, the "hither" side of religious experience is the human subconscious; that is where we see religious experiences beginning to emerge into our lives. The belief that religious experience may on its "farther" side connect us with God or the gods is a possibility, an "over-belief," that James does not rule out, but does not insist on either.

We can apply this same argument to the debate over whether or not God "really" speaks through our dreams. We have developed the root metaphor concept out of sound, well-reasoned philosophical and theological theories; we have used this concept to understand the authentically religious meanings of some actual dream experiences. Nowhere has our characterization of the religious meanings of dreams depended on an over-belief in the existence of God, the gods, or other supernatural beings. Our explorations have done nothing to *refute* such an over-belief, but neither have they *required* it. The root metaphor concept in no way conflicts with the more skeptical views of dream researchers like Freud, Hall, and Hobson. *Their* over-belief that dreams have no sources beyond the human mind is entirely compatible with a recognition that dreams have genuine religious or spiritual meanings.

Hobson's vehement arguments on this point merit a moment's further consideration. He asserts that the historical evolution of dream theory has been towards a view of dreams as endogenously produced (Hobson and Lavie 1986): in other words, dreams are produced by brain neurons, not gods. But Hobson admits in *The Dreaming Brain* that his activation-synthesis hypothesis gives a very weak account of the process by which dreams are "synthesized" by higher mental functions. Hobson cannot tell us why a dream, once activated by the brain, develops the particular form and meaningfulness it ultimately possesses. He says it is nothing more than "human creativity," but that is simply a statement of Hobson's own over-beliefs. His theory about the brain's role in the generation of dreams does *not* necessarily conflict with an appreciation for their religious meanings. To borrow James' language again, the brain may be the "hither" side of dream generation; what is involved in the "farther" side remains, and perhaps always will remain, beyond the grasp of scientific rationality.

Anyone who is at all interested in dreams should contact the Association for the Study of Dreams (P.O. Box 1600, Vienna, VA 22183; 703-242-8888). The ASD can introduce you to the many different areas of contemporary dream study (both academic and nonacademic), and can put you in contact with people who share your dream interests.

NOTES

Chapter 1. Dreams through the History of Religions

1. Defining "the modern West" is a tricky business. It can refer to a tiny elite (e.g., the faculties at a few English-speaking universities), to a geographically bound group (e.g., the people who live in Western Europe and North America), or to virtually all humankind (e.g., everyone whose life has been influenced by the values and technologies of the United States). For the purposes of this work, "modern Western culture" will mean, in a *geographic* sense, the cultures of North America and Western Europe; in a *temporal* sense, those cultures in the twentieth century; and in an *ideological* sense, the people within those cultures whose views have been primarily shaped by the Enlightenment, by modern science and technology, and by psychological approaches to human nature.

2. Many books on dreams begin in this way, with a brief review of dreams through history. At their best, these reviews simply recite the same well-known examples; at their worst, they present their examples with absolutely no citations or references to other sources. The worst offender in this regard is Norman MacKenzie's *Dreams and Dreaming* (1965), which does not give a single reference for any of the thousands of dream examples it describes (unfortunately, many subsequent books and articles on dreams cite MacKenzie's book as a primary source). Other books suffering from a poor organization of citations are Seafield's *Literature and Curiosities of Dreams* (1877), Hill's *Such Stuff as Dreams* (1967), Coxhead and Hiller's *Dreams* (1976), Stephen Brook's *The Oxford Book of Dreams* (1987), and Krippner and Dillard's *Dreamworking* (1987). In the following pages I will refer to these works with great hesitancy and only in those cases where I have not been able to locate independently the texts they cite.

3. I feel extremely uneasy with typologies of this sort, as they too often establish arbitrary, artificial distinctions that lead to serious misunderstandings of the given material. Nevertheless, the mass of data on dreams in the history of religions is so huge that some sort of categorization is essential to making sense of all this material. The following typological review should, despite its inherent limitations, provide us with a historical context that can help us evaluate accurately the major dream theories of the modern West.

4. The following are references to other examples of dreams of divine beings. In the fourth book of Homer's *Iliad* Rhesus receives a dream visit from the goddess Minerva; in the first book Achilles comments "even a dream comes from Zeus" (i.63). In Genesis 32 Jacob "was left alone; and a man wrestled with him until the breaking of the day" (Gen. 32.24), and Jacob comments "I have seen God face to face, and yet my life is preserved" (Gen. 32.30). The apostle Paul reports a series of dreams that reassure him of God's presence as he engages in his missionary travels (Acts 16.9, 18.9, 23.11, 27.21–26). In his *Confessions* St. Augustine comments that dreams are one way in which we learn that "we did not make ourselves, but he who abides forever made us" (3.6). Henri Corbin describes a variety of dreams of divine beings in his essay "The Visionary Dream in Islamic Spirituality" (1966); for example, the early Islamic mystic al-Hakim at-Tirmidhi (d. 898) would learn of important spiritual matters through his wife, who frequently dreamed of angels visiting her (408). Nathaniel Bland's study "On the Muhammedan Science of Tabir; or, Interpretation of Dreams" (1853) also includes numerous reports of dreams of divine beings in the Islamic tradition. Bland presents a number of dreams of the Tipu of Mysore (an eighteenth-century Persian Sultan) in which the prophet Muhammed appears, giving advice and inspiration (146–49). St. Anselm was "confirmed in the love of God and the contempt of the world" by a dream in which a flood of filth swept countless people away, while above the slime rose a beautiful, silvery cloister (Brook 1987, 227). The early Protestant leader John Bunyan reported a dream of a wonderous, sun-warmed mountain, with an almost impenetrable wall surrounding it; Bunyan interpreted the mountain as the "church of the living God" and his struggle to pass through the wall as the struggle to achieve true faith (Brook 1987, 228–29). John Milton speaks in *Paradise Lost* of divine inspiration for the writing of his great poem coming in his sleep (9:20–23); in the poem itself, a dream comes to Adam and shows him the beauties of Paradise (8:283ff.; Adam's questions about his origins preceding this dream give it the form of an incubation); later, Eve comments, "For God is also in sleep, and dreams advise, which he hath sent propitious, some great good presaging" (12:610–13). In "The Personal Use of Myth in Dreams" Dorothy Eggan presents a selection of a Hopi man's dreams of his guardian spirit (Eggan, 1955, 448).

In numerous cultures and religious traditions, dreams are considered a fundamental means of encountering divine beings. Tertullian, a Christian father from third-century Rome, said that "Just about the majority of people get their knowledge of God from dreams" (Miller 1986, 157). In "Some Aspects of Zulu Religion" African religions scholar D. M'Timkulu comments that "dreams can . . . be very important sources of information and guidance; they provide one situation in which living human beings have contact with the spiritual world" (M'Timkulu, 1977, 17). In "The Meaning of Dreams in Tikopia" anthropologist Raymond Firth says of the Tikopia people of the Solomon Islands that "Dreams are valuable circumstantial evidence for the reality of the spirit world" (Firth 1934, 66). In *The Varieties of Religious Experience* William James presents a letter he received from a Mormon church leader, who states the Mormon belief that revelations from God are received "through dreams of sleep or in waking visions of the mind," among other means (James 1900, 365).

Other good sources on dreams and relationships with divine beings are A. Leo Oppenheim, "The Interpretation of Dreams in the Ancient Near East" (1956); Jackson Stewart Lincoln, *The Dream in Primitive Cultures* (1935); E.R. Dodds, *The Greeks and the Irrational* (1951); G. E. Von Grunebaum, "Introduction: The Cultural Function of the Dream as Illustrated by Classical Islam" (1966) (this is the introductory essay in *The Dream and Human Societies*, which Von Grunebaum edited with Roger Callois; this anthology is perhaps the best single source in English on all forms of dream study); Michele Stephen, "Dreams of Change: The Innovative Role of Altered States of Consciousness in Traditional Melanesian Religion" (1979); Vittorio Lanternari, "Dreams as Charismatic Significants: Their Bearing on the Rise of New Religious Movements" (1975); Clyde Kluckhorn, "Myths and Ritual: A General Theory" (1942); Alex Wayman, "Significance of Dreams in India and Tibet" (1967); Patricia Cox Miller, "'A Dubious Twilight': Reflections on Dreams in Patristic Literature" (1986); Morton Kelsey, *God, Dreams, and Revelation* (1974); Frank Seafield, *Curiosities of Dreams* (1877) (while Seafield's book is filled with interesting dream accounts, his citations are unclear and thus impossible to verify); Richard T. Curley, "Dreams of Power: Social Process in a West African Religious Movement" (1983); Bengt G. M. Sundkuler, *Bantu Prophets in South Africa* (1961); Johannes Fabian, "Dreams and Charisma: Theories of Dreams in the Jamaa Movement (Congo)" (1966); Berthold Laufer, "Inspirational Dreams in Eastern Asia" (1931); Philippe Descola, "Head-Shrinkers versus Shrinks: Jivaroan Dream Analysis" (1989).

5. The following are references to other examples of dreams and nightmares of demons, evil spirits, and other malevolent forces. Job's friend Elihu explains the cause of his nightmares in this way: "For God speaks in one way, and in two, though man does not perceive it. In a dream, in a vision of the night, when deep sleep falls upon men, while they slumber on their beds, then he opens the ears of men, and terrifies them with warnings, that he may turn man aside from his deed, and cut off pride from man; he keeps back his soul from the Pit, his life from perishing by the sword" (Job 33.14–18). The Chaldean king Nebuchadnezzar is troubled by bad dreams, which Daniel interprets as foretelling the king's woeful future (Dan. 2, 4). Eusebius's *Ecclesiastical History* reports that Natalius the Confessor "had real bruises to show for his night-long beating by dream angels" (5.28; quoted in Miller 1986, 154). In *The Odyssey* Penelope suffers many bad dreams (19 459, 20.24); Plato, however, denounces Homer for suggesting that God, who must be conceived of as "simple and true in word and deed," could send a false dream like that of Agamemnon's in *The Iliad*: "when anyone says such things about the gods we shall be angry, and shall not give him a chorus" (*The Republic*, 2.382–83). The Roman general Hannibal was threatened in a dream by the goddess Juno that if he sacked her temple she would blind him (Hill 1967, 97). In *Paradise Lost* Satan sends an evil, tempting dream to Eve; it directly leads to her tasting of the forbidden fruit (Books 4 and 5). St. Augustine complains that he cannot control the unruly dreams that give free reign to his carnal desires and aggressive urges (*Confessions*, 10.30). Members of a Ugandan Christian church believe that all strange, bizarre dreams are caused by Satan (Charseley 1987, 291). The Enlightenment

philosopher Descartes reported having a dream in which he thought "he had been surrounded by evil" (Hill 1967, 150–51). The eighteenth-century mystic and scientist Emanuel Swedenborg had many dreams of grappling with "the Evil one" (Swedenborg 1986). Many figures from the romantic period of European literature described horrifying nightmares: Samuel Taylor Coleridge said he often woke himself up with his own agonized screams over the nightmares that plagued him three nights out of every four (Brook 1987, 189–90); Robert Southey dreamed as a child that the Devil came to visit him and his governess (Hill 1967, 105); Thomas de Quincey had a fantastic nightmare in which horrifying mythological creatures from the Orient attacked him—"I was buried in stone coffins, with mummies and sphinxes, in narrow chambers at the heart of eternal pyramids. I was kissed, with cancerous kisses by crocodiles, and was laid, confounded with all unutterable abortions, amongst reeds and Nilotic mud" (Hill 1967, 106–9); John Keats dreamed of visiting Dante's hell—although he found this dream to be "one of the most delightful enjoyments I ever had in my life" (Hill 1967, 54). The Tikopia people of the Solomon islands believe that nightmares are caused by mischevious spirits that lie to and trick people (Firth 1934). The Azande of Africa see bad dreams as the creations of witchcraft; when witches sleep their souls are freed to go off on missions of evil and destruction (Evans-Pritchard 1937, 230–35).

The best modern sources on nightmares are Ernest Jones's *On The Nightmare* (1951) (despite its relentless Freudian reductionism), John Mack's *The Nightmare and Human Conflict* (1970), and Ernest Hartmann's *The Nightmare: The Psychology and Biology of Terrifying Dreams* (1984). None of these works, however, gives a very satisfying account of nightmares from either a historical and cross-cultural perspective or from a religious studies perspective.

6. The following are references to other examples of dreams that motivated the founding of new religious movements. Curley, in "Dreams of Power: Social Process in a West African Religious Movement" (1983), offers a number of references to modern African religious movements in which dreams served to legitimize the new message of the each movement's founder. Sundkuler, *Bantu Prophets in South Africa* (1961), Fabian, "Dreams and Charisma: Theories of Dream in the Jamaa Movement (Congo)" (1966), and Lincoln, *The Dream in Primitive Cultures* (1935) also provide evidence of dreams inspiring the founding of new religious movements. Anthony Wallace ("Revitalization Movements" [1956]) has made the most sweeping theoretical argument on this point: he claims that all religious revitalization movements throughout history have been shaped by the transformational experiences (such as dreams) of certain individuals, who use those experiences to lead in the development of a new "Gestalt" that enables members of the society to create a more satisfying culture.

7. The following are references to other examples of dreams that led the dreamer to convert to a religious tradition. Frank Seafield describes a revelatory dream by the seventeenth-century philosopher J. B. Van Helmont (involving a glimpse of an intensely beautiful light); it led him "to abandon the philosophy of the Stoics, and to direct his attention to Divine wisdom" (Seafield 1877, 375–76).

Von Grunebaum describes a number of dreams leading people to convert to Islam in his essay "Introduction: The Cultural Function of the Dream as Illustrated by Classical Islam" (1966). Berthold Laufer describes a variant of this kind of dream: a Buddhist Lama is having difficulty converting a Mongol emperor; but the Lama has a dream in which an old man instructs him how to answer the emperor's questions, and he finally succeeds in converting the emperor to Buddhism (Laufer 1931, 209). The most famous Western instance of a conversion dreams is that of the Roman emperor Constantine, who adopted Christianity because of a dream (MacKenzie 1965, 50; I have not been able to verify Mackenzie's uncited reference). Anthropologist Vittorio Lanternari describes a number of conversion dreams, many of which involve images of "Jesus, the light, the burning fire, and the joyous song"; for example, he says a young Puerto Rican man dreamed that a voice spoke to him "from the depths of the flame," an experience that led to the man's becoming a Pentecostal minister (Lanternari 1975, 228–29). Similarly, Sundkuler tells of the important role of conversion dreams in African missionary churches, with these dreams almost always including images of light, shining clothes, and rivers (Sundkuler 1961, 267). In *The Two and the One* Mircea Eliade recounts an American man's dream of "the mystic light," filled with Christian symbolism (Eliade 1965, 19ff.); he goes on to examine at length the imagery of light in other religious traditions. Leaders of the Jamaa movement of the Congo see dreams as an important resource to promote people's conversion to Christianity (Fabian 1966, 557). By far the most interesting single source on conversion dreams of which I know is Richard Curley's "Dreams of Power: Social Process in a West African Religious Movement." Curley describes in detail how members of the Nigerian True Church of God join the church once they have had a special conversion dream: "The conversion dream becomes a personal charter of the church member, and it is often used as a claim to full status in the congregation . . . Conversion dreams are used as validation of a person's religious faith and are retold and cherished by the individual as a part of his own personal charter" (Curley 1983, 29, 36).

8. The following are references to other examples of prophetic dreams foretelling the future of the individual dreamer. According to E. R. Dodds, the famous Delphic oracle of Greece was originally a dream oracle, at which the prophetic meanings of people's dreams were explained (Dodds 1951, 110). Joseph's two dreams of the sheaves of grain and of the sun, moon, and eleven stars foretell his future greatness, much to his brothers' displeasure (Gen. 37.5–11); then, Joseph interprets the prophetic meanings of the Pharaoh's two dreams (Gen. 41). The wise men were warned in a dream that if they went back to the angry King Herod they would be in grave danger (Matt. 2.12). Cicero presents a number of reportedly prophetic dreams in his work *On Divination*. The Trisasti text, an important compilation of Jainist teachings, affirms the prophetic meanings to be found in dreams (Sharma and Siegel 1980, 3, 12). The famous Chinese statesman Tao K'an (d. A.D. 334) had a dream of his future political success (Laufer 1931, 212). René Descartes believed that a dream, in which he saw a dictionary and a collection of poems, was an indication of his future (Hill 1967, 150–51; for an extremely inter-

esting reading of Descartes' dreams, see Francoise Meltzer, "Descartes's Dreams and Freud's Failure, or The Politics of Originality" [1987]). Frank Seafield presents a variety of arguments for and against the prophetic powers of dreams (Seafield 1877, 133–39). Anthropological literature indicates that dreams are seen as prophetic of accidents, illnesses, and success in hunting and fishing among the Azande of Africa (Evans-Pritchard 1937), the Tikopia of the Solomon Islands (Firth 1934), the Achuar of the Upper Amazon (Descola 1989), the Mehinaku of Brazil (Gregor 1981), and the East Cree of Canada (Flannery and Chambers 1985). Jackson Stewart Lincoln (1935) offers other evidence of beliefs in the prophetic powers of dreams among various cultures. Naphtali Lewis's work *Dreams and Portents* (1976) is the best collection of classic Western views on this subject.

9. The following are other examples of religiously significant dreams preceding the birth of a child. An ancient Egyptian text describes a woman praying to the god Imhotep for a son; the god instructs her in a dream to perform certain rites, which result in the woman bearing a male child (Oppenheim 1953, 252). Another Egyptian text tells of how the wife of the famous magician Khamuas had a dream in which an apparition told her to prepare a certain medicine that would insure the birth of a great magician son (Oppenheim 1953, 194). The mother of Zoroaster, the Persian prophet, reportedly dreamed during her pregnancy of a dark cloud raining down terrifying, misshapen creatures; then her infant son appears threatened by the creatures, but God saves him and brings the child to her (Seafield 1877, 289–93). Some Islamic scholars see the revelation made to Moses' mother to give her son to the pharaoh's sister to nurse as a dream (Koran 28.7; discussed in Meier 1967, 422). In the hagiographic *Life of Milarepa*, the sage Marpa and his wife (who will be the Tibetan saint's spiritual "parents") both dream of his imminent arrival in their village (43–44). Alex Wayman describes the anunciation dreams of the parents of Buddha, Mahavira (founder of the Jaina sect), and certain Tibetan religious figures (Wayman 1967, 2). According to some Buddhist traditions, Buddha's father had special dreams before Buddha left the palace for a life of ascetic wandering (Sharma and Siegel 1980, 72). Nathaniel Bland describes various anunciation dreams in Islamic history (Bland 1853, 121). Certain Australian tribespeople practice what ethnographers have called "conception totemism": during pregnancy the parents will have a dream in which is revealed the child's totem (Spencer and Gillen 1904). The most extensive studies of anunciation dreams are Otto Rank's *The Myth of the Birth of the Hero* (1909) and Fred Jeremy Seligson's *Oriental Birth Dreams* (1989).

10. The following are references to other examples of dreams relating to death. Greek tragedies are filled with prophetic dreams that reveal the god-fated doom of the characters (Dodds 1951). Ovid's *Metamorphoses* tells a story of the drowning at sea of King Ceyx and of the goddess Juno sending a dream to his wife Alcyone to inform her of Ceyx's death (book 11). An ancient Near Eastern myth tells of the god Tammuz dreaming of his own death, which he cannot forestall no matter how hard he tries (Oppenheim 1956, 246). Teutonic religious traditions

contain numerous accounts of dreams portending the doom of certain heroes (Hastings 1912, 37–38). The Tibetan Buddhist saint Milarepa, a yogin and poet from the eleventh century, learns in a dream of his family's destruction (*The Life of Milarepa*, 89). David Ryback's book *Dreams That Come True* describes a number of modern dreams in which someone's death is accurately foretold (Ryback 1986, 142–50). See also Marie Louise von Franz, *On Dreams and Death* (1986).

11. The following are references to other examples of prophetic dreams relating to the future of the dreamer's community. Many African missionary churches include dream-telling in their regular worship services in order to learn from people's dreams important information regarding the congregation as a whole (Sundkuler 1961; Charseley 1973, 1987; Curley 1983). A number of Native American peoples believed that the dreams of individuals had significance for the tribe as a whole (Lincoln 1935, Wallace 1958). The history of Islam is replete with dreams foretelling communal and political developments (Von Grunebaum 1966, Fahd 1966).

12. The following are references to other examples of dreams relating to battles or warfare. The Hittite king Hattushili reported many dream of the goddess Ishtar, who guided and reassured him before important battles (Oppenheim 1956, 254). Alexander the Great told of many dreams relating to his military campaigns (Hughes 1987). The Greek general Xenophon had a dream that inspired him to lead his army out of a Persian trap (Hughes 1987). The Jewish military leader Maccabeus told his troops of a dream in which the prophet Jeremiah gave him a golden sword as a gift from God; encouraged by this dream, his troops went on to defeat their enemy (2 Macc. 15.11–19). Theodosius I, emperor of Rome in the fourth century A.D., dreamed that his army won a great victory with the help of two Christian saints (Hill 1967, 8–9). The emperor Charlemagne, in *The Song of Roland*, is visited in a dream by St. Gabriel, who reveals to him the violent horrors of the next day's battle. The fifteenth-century English king Richard III is said to have had a "terrible dream" in which evil spirits haunted and tormented him (Hill 1967, 97–98). Iraqi leader Saddam Hussein's reported dream in late October 1990, in which Muhammed told him his missiles were pointed in the wrong direction, is a recent example of this type of dream (Friedman 1990).

13. The following are other examples of institutionalized use of prophetic dreams. The second book of Daniel describes the Chaldean king Nebuchadnezzar demanding the magicians, sorcerers, and enchanters not only to interpret his dream but also to tell him the dream itself; only Daniel is able to meet this lofty test (Dan. 2). Ancient Chinese government officials made extensive use of the services of dream interpreters (Brennan 1993). The Roman emperor Augustus decreed that all dreams about the state must be reported to the government officials (Mackenzie 1965, 50; I have not been able to verify this example, for which MacKenzie gives no citation).

14. The following are references to other examples of dream incubation rites. The Sumerian epic *Gilgamesh* includes a number of dream incubation prac-

tices, some of which work and some of which do not. Jewish teachers sought special dreams of historical Jewish authorities in order to learn particular points of knowledge (Singer 1904, 656). Laufer describes a medieval Chinese ruler who incubated a dream in order that Shang-ti, the supreme god, would reveal who should be the next prime minister (Laufer 1931, 212). Seafield refers to a source describing how Franciscan monks would perform a mass and then sleep on special mats in anticipation of a revelatory dream (Seafield 1877, 26). Boswell reports in his biography of Samuel Johnson that Dr. Johnson would recite a prayer to God for a dream of his deceased wife: "if Thou hast ordained the souls of the dead to minister to the living, and appointed my departed wife to have care of me, grant that I may enjoy the good effects of her attention and ministration" (Seafield 1877, 117). Both John Keats and Ben Johnson reportedly wrote poems referring to dream incubation practices on St. Agnes's eve (Mackenzie 1965, 75; Seafield 1877, 94). Edward W. Lane reports in his *Account of the Manners and Customs of the Modern Egyptians* (1871) that a contemporary Egyptian student prayed for a dream visit from Muhammed to clarify a confusing religious problem (as presented in LeCerf 1966, 376). The Azande of Africa eat "ngua musumo," i.e., dream medicines, in order to have prophetic dreams (Evans-Pritchard 1937, 174–75). The Achuar of the Upper Amazon use spells and sexual abstinence to incubate dreams of spirits who can help interpret enigmatic dreams from the past (Descola 1989). The Ibans of Borneo sleep on graves to elicit dreams of special spiritual protectors (Woods 1974, 117). Zionist prophets in Africa smear themselves with a mixture of ashes and water to "see clear dreams" (Sundkuler 1961, 272). The East Cree of Canada hang bear skulls above their sleeping mats to bring on helpful dreams (Flannery and Chambers 1985, 15).

Perhaps the longest dream incubation on record is that of the tenth-century Islamic mystic ash-Shah al-Kirmani, who finally received a dream visit from God after forty years of nocturnal vigils in quest of such a dream (Meier 1963, 422).

There is better historical research on dream incubation rituals and practices than on virtually any other type of dream phenomenon. Other good sources on this subject are Walter Jayne's *The Healing Gods of Ancient Civilizations* (1925), Ernest Jones's *On The Nightmare* (1951) (although many of Jones's citations are obscure), A. Leo Oppenheim's "The Interpretation of Dreams in the Ancient Near East" (1957), the entry on dreams in Hastings's, *Encyclopedia of Religion and Ethics* (1912), Toufy Fahd's *Songes et leur Interpretation* (1959), and Naphtali Lewis's *Interpretation of Dreams and Portents* (1976).

15. The following are references to other examples of rites intended to forestall a bad dream or nightmare, or to dispel their evil influences once they have been dreamed. Singer describes how in different times Jewish people have prayed and fasted to avoid bad dreams (Singer 1904, 656). The Roman historian Pliny claimed that aniseed has the power, if "attached to the pillow, so as to be smelt by a person when asleep, of preventing all disagreeable dreams" (Seafield 1877, 61). St. Ambrose reportedly said special prayers to avoid demonic dreams (Krippner and Dillard 1987, 39). Crapanzano (1975) details the measures modern Moroccans take to prevent dreams of demons and jinn. Eggan tells how the Hopi "are

instructed to wake someone, even in the middle of the night, to relate a bad dream, and they must then go outside and spit four times to rid themselves of evil thoughts" (Eggan 1955, 449).

An interesting modern parallel is provided by psychoanalyst Carol Brod, who describes the bedtime prayer of a thirteen-year-old girl who has been suffering terrible nightmares: "Oh God, I will not dream about rape, I will not dream about murder, about mugging, killing, sexual abuse, molesting, anyone touching me, being followed, grave yards, dead bodies, any scary faces, twilight zone, Alfred Hitchcock, sleepaway camp, any movie that's really scary. Also, God, don't let me dream about sharks, being followed, scary faces, murderers. Then [the girl says], I repeat the prayer so I can really get the things out of my mind. Then at the end I always say God, thank you for everything, Amen" (Brod 1991, 3).

16. The following are references to other examples of dreams playing a role in religious initiations. In the Roman tale *The Golden Ass*, the hero Lucius receives a series of dreams urging him to become an initiate in the mysteries of the goddess Isis. The Tibetan mystic Milarepa gained many spiritual insights and developed special psychic powers in his dreams (*Life of Milarepa*). Henri Corbin describes an Islamic student friend of his who has a dream of the mysterious house of the Imam—exactly like the dreams commonly experienced by Shi'ite initiates (Corbin 1966, 405–6). Anthropological literature offers numerous examples of cultures in which special dreams initiate a lifelong relationship with a spiritual guardian among the Achuar of the Upper Amazon (Descola 1989), the Mehinaku of Brazil (Gregor 1981), the East Cree of Canada (Flannery and Chambers 1985), the Zulu of South Africa (Sundkuler 1961), and the Ibans of Borneo (Woods 1976); among the Mehinaku and the Zulu, some dreams also herald the careers of shamans or diviners (Gregor 1981, 712, 715; Sundkuler 1961, 266). Lincoln (1935) gives many examples of other initiatory dreams among Native American peoples.

In this context, we may gain a new perspective on the requirement that trainees in both Freudian and Jungian schools of psychotherapy undergo a supervised analysis of their dreams—a process that effectively functions to "initiate" the trainees into the worldview of the schools.

17. The following are references to other examples of dreams influencing religious practices. Oppenheim (1956) provides a number of examples of such dreams. For instance, the Egyptian king Nektonabos dreams that the goddess Isis comes to him to say that he has been neglecting her temple (253); Ptolemy Soter, another Egyptian king, dreams that a colossal statue tells him to take it back to Alexandria, its original location (250); the Babylonian king Nabonidus has a dream of the gods Marduk and Sin, who instruct him to rebuild a ruined temple (250); and the author of the Akkadian religious poem "Epic of Irra" says he wrote the poem to praise a god who came to him in a dream (193). E. R. Dodds (1951) gives many examples from ancient Greek culture of dreams influencing religious practices. Seafield reports that the early Christian father Cyprian was told in a dream to mix wine with water in the Eucharist (Seafield 1877, 102). Laufer tells of how the medieval Tantra school of Buddhism drew on dream experiences for inspira-

tion in writing of sacred texts in undertaking missionary journeys (Laufer 1931, 209–10). Laufer also tells of the role of dreams in the creative work of Kwan Hiu, a great painter of Buddhist saints (or Arhats); when people admired his strange but moving portraits and asked him how he imagined such unorthodox visions, he replied, "I paint what I see in my dreams" (213). Howitt describes how many Australian peoples get religious songs and charms from their dreams, and how people would perform certain rituals to propitiate dead spirits they had seen in their dreams (Howitt 1904, 434–37). Roheim (1945) also discusses (from a trenchantly psychoanlytic position) the relations of dream experiences to the religious rites and beliefs of Australian tribespeople. Anthony Wallace (1958) gives extensive details on the influence of dreams on Iroquois religious practices. Other anthropological studies find dreams influencing innovations in religious practices and beliefs among the Achuar of the Upper Amazon (Descola 1989), the Mehinaku of Brazil (Gregor 1981), the East Cree of Canada (Flannery and Chambers 1985), and numerous African churches (Sundkuler 1966; Curley 1983; Charseley 1973, 1987). Clyde Kluckhorn proposes in "Myths and Rituals: A General Theory" that myths have their origins in individual dream experiences: "we find Hocart recently asking: 'If there are myths that give rise to ritual where do these myths come from?' . . . Hocart's question can be answered very simply: from a dream or a waking phantasy or a personal habit system of some individual in the society" (Kluckhorn 1942, 50). Kluckhorn goes on to give an example of a Navaho rite having its origin in a dream (61). Karl Abraham's "Dreams and Myths: A Study in Folk Psychology" was the first major psychoanalytic study of the relations of dreams to myths (Abraham [1909] 1955); Ernest Jones cites many other early psychoanalytic studies on the relationship between dreams and myths (Jones 1951, 65–67). Lincoln devotes an entire chapter to dreams that have influenced religious practices and beliefs (Lincoln 1935, 44–99). Vittorio Lanternari (1975) also gives a wide-ranging set of examples of dreams that lead to special religious and cultural creations.

18. The following are references to other examples of dreams relating to religious beliefs about the soul. A number of the Upanishads (e.g., *Brihad Aranyaka*, *Prasna*, and *Chandogya*) describe what dreaming reveals about the soul and about reality. O'Flaherty (1984) discusses the Upanishadic views and sets them in the context of other Hindu and Buddhist dream beliefs. Plato contends that dreams show us the worst parts of the soul—"a terrible, fierce, and lawless class of desires exists in every man, even in those of us who have every appearance of being decent people. Its existence is revealed in dreams"; thus, Plato claims that "the worst of men . . . is surely the man who expresses in waking reality the character we attributed to a man in his dreams" (Plato 1961, book 9). Aristotle states that since the soul of a good man is better ordered than the soul of others, "the dreams of good men are better than those of ordinary people" (Aristotle 1941a, 1102b). Augustine claimed that although unruly carnal desires disturb our sleep, we will be free of them once our bodies die and our souls ascend to heaven (Augustine 1971, 1.25, 19.4); more cryptically, Augustine said that it is not the soul but a "phantom" in each person that is active in our dreams (18.18). Athanasius, however, argues

that dreams in fact prove that the soul is both rational and immortal (Miller 1986, 154). *The Encyclopedia of Religion and Ethics* offers many examples of dreams influencing religious beliefs about the soul; for instance, Orphic and Pythagorean philosophers saw dreams as the free movement of the soul, while Egyptians believed that dreaming indicated a special kind of spiritual awareness rather than the activity of a wandering soul (Hastings, 1912, 31, 32, 37); and Enlightenment philosophers like Descartes, Leibniz, Locke, and Diderot debated on whether or not dreaming proves that the mind is always active (30; for further discussion of Enlightenment philosophers and their views on dreams, see J. Allan Hobson and Peretz Lavie, "Origin of Dreams: Anticipation of Modern Theories in the Philosophy and Physiology of the Eighteenth and Nineteenth Centuries" [1986]). Seafield presents Plutarch's account of how the Stoic philosopher Zeno saw dreams as reflecting the virtue of the soul (Seafield 1877, 141); Seafield also presents the arguments of a number of Christian bishops who claim that dreams demonstrate the immortality of the soul (122). According to Laufer, Chinese dream theory holds that the spiritual soul, or *hun*, leaves the body during sleep (as it does at death) and communicates with other souls and with the gods (Laufer 1931, 210). Other cultures that reportedly hold the same essential notion about the wandering of the soul in dreams are the Achuar of the Upper Amazon (Descola 1989, 440–43), the Azande of Africa (Evans-Pritchard 1937, 230–35), the Tikopia of the Solomon Islands (Firth 1934, 65, 71), the Mehinaku of Brazil (Gregor 1981, 710–11, 717), and numerous Australian peoples (Howitt 1904, 435ff.).

The subject of dreams and religious beliefs in the soul has received extensive historical study. E. B. Tylor's work *Primitive Culture* (1874) is the classic statement of the notion that belief in the soul originates in dreams. Although Durkheim directly disputes Tylor in *The Elementary Forms of Religious Life* (1915), Tylor's view has remained very influential. Ernest Jones (1951) and J. S. Lincoln (1935) wrote influential books on dreams that followed and expanded on Tylor's thesis. Firth argues that his findings on the dream beliefs of the Tikopia refute Durkheim and affirm Tylor (Firth 1934, 73–74).

The striking number of cultures and religious traditions in which it is believed that dreams are the experiences of the soul, freed during sleep to wander about, raises an important question, Is this an instance of a truly universal, even archetypal belief? Or is it a product of the limited viewpoint of modern Western anthropologists and historians, who cannot help but conceptualize other people's dream beliefs in this way? The question is worth pondering.

Dreams have also often been directly related to religious beliefs about the nature of reality. The Greek philosopher Heraclitus sharply distinguished waking and dreaming realities, saying that in dreams we "retreat into our own world" (Heraclitus 1987, frag. 89). Dodds describes other Greek views of the reality, and irreality, of dreams (Dodds 1951, 108ff.). Plato's *Theatetus* contains Socrates' famous discussion on how we can ever know if we are dreaming or not (a discussion continued in the Enlightenment by such philosophers as Hobbes, Descartes, and Pascal). The *Brhadaranyaka Upanishad* suggests that dreams are *between* mortal and immortal existence (See O'Flaherty 1984); the Islamic concept of "Alam al-Mithal" expresses a very similar belief, namely that dreams involve us in a third kind of reality, between physical and spiritual realities (Rahman 1966). O'Flaherty notes, however, that medieval Indian philosophers believed that human reality is but a dream of God (O'Flaherty 1984, 76). Similarly, the early Christian text *The Gospel of Truth* describes a life without faith in God to be a dream, illusory and ephemeral (Miller 1986, 163–64). Some Buddhist philosophers distinguished between the dream images, which are unreal, and the dream emotions, which are real (Wayman 1967, 9). The Jivaro people of South America believe that dreams give us a truer view of reality than we gain in waking life (de Ropp 1987); Descola (1989) also discusses the Jivaro belief on this point. The Tikopia of the Solomon Islands and the Mehinaku of Brazil also believe that dream experiences are genuinely real (Firth 1934, Gregor 1981); Lincoln (1935) gives many examples of Native American peoples who believe dreams are equally as real as waking experiences. The Iroquois (on this score, perhaps the most anti-Platonist people known) believe that dreams are so real that they immediately upon awakening act out what they saw and did in their dreams (Wallace 1958, 238–40). Schweder and Levine (1975) describe the cognitive developmental processes involved in beliefs about the reality of dreams. Schweder's work with the Hausa people of Nigeria leads him to make a very thought-provoking claim regarding the reality of dreams: "By the time they are 10 years old, [Hausa children] believe dreams are mere 'fantasies', unreal and internally located . . . Later, however, as adults, Hausa children change their minds. Adult theory tells them that their 10-year-old understanding of dreams (which, of course, is *our* adult understanding of dreams) was inadequate—that dreams are a type of 'vision' giving access to an external, objective numinous realm of the soul and its wanderings. Hausa are not only capable of a 'subjectivist' view of dreams. They entertain that viewpoint as ten year olds, and reject it!" (Schweder 1982, 362; see discussion of this passage in O'Flaherty 1984, 53–60).

A third area of religious belief in which dreams have historically been an important element is beliefs about death, dying, and the dead. Oppenheim (1956) recounts many ancient Near Eastern dream reports in which the dreamer either visits the land of the dead or is visited by an inhabitant of that realm; the Sumerican epic *Gilgamesh* includes both kinds of dreams. Likewise, numerous ancient Greek texts relate dreams and death. For example, Hesiod's *Theogony* presents dreams and death as children of the same parent—"And Night bore frightful Doom and the black Ker, and Death, and Sleep, and the whole tribe of Dreams" (Hesiod 1973, vv. 211–12); both *The Odyssey* and *The Iliad* involve dreams relating to death; Plato concludes *The Republic* with the story of Er, who makes a dream journey to the underworld (book 10); and many tragedies present dreams in which the characters are visited by the dead (see Dodds 1951). The early Christian father Tertullian said that sleep is the "very mirror of death"; Miller comments that for Tertullian "what the dreams of sleep image is the death that is really life" (Miller 1986, 157). *The Tibetan Book of the Dead* describes the ordeals of the soul after death in terms strikingly reminiscent of dream experiences. O'Flaherty describes the intense interest Indian philosophers and theologians take in dreams in which the dreamer dies (O'Flaherty 1984, 22). Von Grunebaum refers to dreams that shaped Islamic understandings of death and the afterlife (Von Grunebaum 1966, 14). Descola describes how some members of the Achuar of the Upper Amazon have dreams in which the spirits of the dead complain that the dreamers should do more to honor them (Descola 1989, 442–43). Howitt reviews various Australian beliefs about dreams and the dead, and concludes, "It is evident from these facts that there is a universal belief in the existence of the human spirit after death, as a ghost, which is able to communicate with the living when they sleep. It finds its way to the sky-country, where it lives in a land like the earth, only more fertile, better watered, and plentifully supplied with game" (Howitt 1904, 439–40). The Tikopia of the Solomon Islands also believe that dreams enable one to visit the land of the dead (Firth 1934, 65, 68–69). Seafield gives a nineteenth-century Englishman's account of a revelatory dream in which the wonders of the afterlife are shown to him (Seafield 1877, 419–24).

Peter Berger, a sociologist of religion, has noted that both dreams and death are universal experiences of marginality and anomie that all societies must structure and render meaningful: "The sheltering quality of social [and religious] order becomes especially evident if one looks at the marginal situations in the life of the individual, that is, at situations in which he is driven to or beyond the boundaries of the order that determines his routine, everyday existence. Such marginal situations commonly occur in dreams and fantasy . . . The marginal situation *par excellence*, however, is death" (Berger 1967, 22–23; see also 41–43).

Finally, dreams have frequently played a role in the resolution of theological debates over particular points of religious belief. Von Grunebaum describes a number of dreams in which Muhammed appears to elucidate for people difficult points of theological doctrine (Von Grunebaum 1966, 14–16). Seafield reports that the sixteenth-century Protestant reformer John Zwingli resolved an argument over the Eucharist by means of a dream of his (Seafield 1877, 358). On a more ominous note, Todorov describes in *The Conquest of America* how Christian missionaries working to convert the Aztecs were to "track down very vestige of idolatry, even in the Indians' dreams"; one missionary leader demanded that the natives "should be examined [in confession] regarding what they dream; in all of this there may be reminiscences of pagan times. In dealing with these things it would be good to ask them [in confession] 'What do you dream?' and not try to skim over it like a cat walking on hot coals. Our preaching should be dedicated to condemning and abominating all this." (Todorov 1982, 204–5).

19. Not everyone is as intuitive in this regard as Augustine says his mother was: "She always said that by some sense, which she could not describe in words, she was able to distinguish between your [God's] revelations and her own natural dreams" (Augustine 1961, 6.13). People from many religious traditions have wondered about how to distinguish between different kinds of dreams. The classic text is Homer's *Odyssey*, in which Penelope says "Two gates for ghostly dreams there are: one gateway of honest horn, and one of ivory. Issuing by the ivory gate are dreams of glimmering illusion, fantasies, but those that come through solid polished horn may be borne out, if mortals only know them" (Homer 1961, 19.529ff.) Dodds (1951) describes other Greek classifications of true and false dreams. Another renowned text in this regard is the *Commentary on the Dream of Scipio* by Macrobius, in which dreams are classified into five types: enigmatic, prophetic,

oracular, nightmares, and apparitions (Macrobius 1952, 87–88). According to Bland, Islamic works on dream interpretation tended to divide dreams into those caused by God, by Satan, and by natural causes (Bland 1856, 126–27). Wallace quotes an exasperated Jesuit missionary among the Iroquois as saying, "The Iroquois have, properly speaking, only a single Divinity—the dream. To it they render their submission, and follow all its orders with the utmost exactness . . . [This people] would think itself guilty of a great crime if it failed in its observance of a single dream. The people think only of that, they talk about nothing else, and all their cabins are filled with their dreams. They spare no pains, no industry, to show their attachment thereto, and their folly in this particular goes to such an excess as would be hard to imagine" (Wallace 1956, 235). Stephen (1979) says that Melanesian religious traditions do not believe all dreams are religiously significant, and Fabian (1966) says new religious movements in the Congo also differentiate between human and divine dreams. Similar distinctions are made by Tikopia of the Solomon Islands (Firth 1934, 64), the Zulu of South Africa (Sundkuler 1961, 265), and the Achuar of the Upper Amazon (Descola 1989, 441–44). In Milton's *Paradise Lost* Adam is uneasy over the difficulties in distinguishing God-sent from evil dreams (Milton [1667] 1974, book 5). Seafield cites a number of Christian Bishops who argue that some dreams are from God, others are from Satan, and the rest are of no special importance (Seafield 1877, 33–34, 109–14). The eighteenth-century English novelist Daniel Defoe argued that God used to speak to people directly in their dreams; now, however, "our heads are so full of impertinent thoughts in the day, which in proportion crowd the imagination at night, so our dreams are trifling and foolish; how shall we know when they are to be taken notice of, and when not? when there is a real apparition, haunting us, or showing itself to us, and when not? in a word, when an angel, or when a devil, appears to us in a dream?" (Woods 1976, 164).

20. The following are references to other examples of denunciations of dreams and religious meaning. The apocryphal book of Sirach condemns dreams, saying, "As one who catches at a shadow and pursues the wind, so is he who gives heed to dreams" (34.1–8); other Old Testament passages reflecting a similar skepticism towards dreams are Deut. 13.2–5 and 18.9–14; Ecclus. 5.7; and Jer. 29.8). In his book *On Divination* the Roman philosopher Cicero rejects the religious and prophetic meanings so many people claim to derive from their dreams; "Do not the conjectures of the interpreters of dreams rather indicate the subtlety of their own talents, than any natural sympathy and correspondence in the nature of things?" (Cicero 1876, 260). Seafield reports that both St. Basil and St. Bernard of Clairvaux instructed Christians to ignore their dreams and concentrate instead on the doctrines of salvation contained in scripture (Seafield 1877, 102). Malinowski ([1927] 1985) claims that the Trobriand islanders take little interest in their dreams. The seventeenth-century English minister Jeremy Taylor argues that seeking religious meanings is dreams only gives control of your soul to the devil: "if you suffer impressions to be made upon you by dreams, the devil hath the reins in his own hands, and can tempt you by that, which will abuse you, when you can make no resistance" (Woods and Greenhouse 1974, 162–63).

21. The following are references to other examples of dream books. Oppenheim (1956) provides a translation of an Assyrian dream book at the end of his essay on ancient Near Eastern dream interpretation. Lewis (1976) gives selections from dream books used in Egyptian and in early Christian traditions. The Jainist Trisasti text includes a list of what various dream symbols means (Sharma and Siegel 1980, 17). Todorov notes that dream books were used in Aztec culture (Todorov 1982, 78). Fahd (1966) describes various dream books used in medieval Islamic culture.

Chapter 2. Exploring the Wilderness of Dreams

1. For studies on time and on how different cultures structure time in different ways, see Marshall Sahlins, *Stone Age Economics* (1972); E. P. Thompson, "Time, Work-Discipline, and Industrial Capitalism" (1967), Nancy Cott, *The Bonds of Womanhood* (1977), and Juliet B. Schor, *The Overworked American: The Unexpected Decline of Leisure* (1992).

2. Ricoeur, Browning, and McFague each argue that *all* humans seek answers to these questions, in some form or other. The answers may not be completely conscious, they may not be very well reasoned, and they may not take an explicitly "religious" form; but in one way or another, all humans do try to formulate answers to these sorts of ultimate existential questions. Other theologians and religious thinkers who have made this same essential argument are Paul Tillich (1948, 1951–63, 1952), who develops the concept of "Ultimate Concern"; David Tracy (1975), with his notion of the "limit-questions" at the horizon of all human experience; and Mircea Eliade (1957, 1960, 1965), who has explored the fundamental myths and symbols that motivate both religious and secular cultures. Frederick Ferre's article "The Definition of Religion" (1968) is an excellent reflection on the issues involved in this approach to religion.

3. Paul Ricoeur describes how such root metaphors—"cosmic symbols," in his terminology—are the primary material out of which people elaborate myths, theologies, philosophical systems, and worldviews. See *The Symbolism of Evil* (1967) and *Freud and Philosophy* (1970).

4. Sam Gill's work *Mother Earth* (1987) describes how this root metaphor has a surprisingly recent origin—illustrating, from our view, the way that *new* root metaphors may be developed to deal with new personal or communal situations.

5. This example illustrates that root metaphors need not be explicitly "religious" in form in order to serve an essentially religious purpose.

6. I will be using "religious meaning," "spiritual meaning," and "existential meaning" as synonymous terms.

7. In my essay "Telling Stories about Dreaming" (Bulkley 1991a), I discuss

these different narrative renderings of the history of twentieth-century Western dream study. I term the two major accounts the "Self-Actualization" story and the "Triumphant Science" story, and offer my own "Coat of Many Colors" story.

8. Beyond having many promising implications for the methodology of our study, the wilderness metaphor has a number of other qualities that make it especially appropriate for this work. It is a "natural" metaphor in two senses. First, it is a metaphor that many dream researchers choose frequently ("naturally") to describe their work, in their speaking of paths, fields, terrains, natural resources, etc. Second, there are long-standing relations between the wilderness and religion, with mystics, prophets, and shamans from many cultures finding wilderness areas to be particularly evocative of religious experiences. Indeed, as chapter 1 indicated, there are numerous accounts through history of religiously meaningful dreams occurring in wilderness settings. Thus the wilderness metaphor, rather than being a foreign construct arbitrarily imposed on the study of dreams, actually stems from a deep relationship between dreams, nature, and religion. I have explored this relationship in greater detail in the essays "The Quest for Transformational Experience: Dreams and Environmental Ethics" (Bulkley 1991c) and "Dreaming to Heal the Earth" (Bulkley 1991e). See also Roderick Nash, *Wilderness and the American Mind* (1973) and Robert C. Fuller, *Americans and the Unconscious* (1986).

9. I am intentionlly resisting the temptation to say "missing the forest for the trees"; there is a fine line between metaphorical thinking and poor punning.

Chapter 3. Psychoanalysis: Sigmund Freud

1. In a letter Freud wrote to his close friend Wilhelm Fliess (6 Aug. 1899) he describes *The Interpretation of Dreams* as follows: "The whole thing is planned on the model of an imaginary walk. At the beginning, the dark forest of authors (who do not see the trees), hopelessly lost on wrong tracks. Then a concealed pass through which I lead the reader—my specimen dream with its peculiarities, details, indiscretions, bad jokes—and then suddenly the high ground and the view and the question: which way do you wish to go now?" (Masson 1985, 385).

2. Among these techniques were the use of cocaine, electrotherapy, and hypnotism. See Clark 1980, 99.

3. Freud declares his intentions along these lines in his early work *Project for a Scientific Psychology* (Freud [1895] 1954).

4. At times Freud describes this process of the dreamwork as *allegorical*: "Analysis showed that in such cases the dream-work found itself faced with the problem of transforming into a dream a series of highly abstract thoughts from waking life which were incapable of being given any direct representation. It endeavored to solve the problem by getting hold of another group of intellectual material, somewhat loosely related (often in a manner which might be described as

'*allegorical*') to the abstract thoughts, and at the same time capable of being represented with fewer difficulties" (Freud [1900] d1965, 563; emphasis added).

5. See also 1917a, 129: "Thus even in these simple children's dreams a difference remains between the latent and the manifest dream, there is a distortion of the latent dream-thought: ***the transformation of a thought into an experience***. In the process of interpreting a dream this alteration must first be undone."

6. See *Introductory Lectures on Psychoanalysis*: "If we carry over our conception of the separate elements to the whole dream, it follows that the dream as a whole is a distorted substitute for something else, something unconscious, and that the task of interpreting a dream is to discover this unconscious material" (Freud [1917] 1966, 112, 114).

7. See *The Interpretation of Dreams*: "We should disregard the apparent coherence between a dream's constituents as an unessential illusion, and . . . we should trace back the origin of each of its elements on its own account. A dream is a conglomerate which, for purposes of investigation, must be broken up once more into fragments" (Freud [1900] 1965, 486; see also 136, 455. See also *Introductory Lectures on Psychoanalysis* (Freud [1917] 1966), 181.

8. These are gathered through the process of "free association." See *The Interpretation of Dreams* (Freud [1900] 1965), 134–36.

9. See Freud [1900] 1965, 346: "One part of it [the dream] is made up of the essential dream-thoughts—those, that is, which completely replace the dream, and which, if there were no censorship of dreams, would be sufficient in themselves to replace it." See also Freud [1900] 1965, 556: "It is often possible by means of analysis to restore all that has been lost by the forgetting of the dream's content; at least, in quite a number of cases one can reconstruct from a single remaining fragment not, it is true, the dream—*which is in any case a matter of no importance*—but all the dream-thoughts." (Emphasis added.)

10. See Freud [1900] 1965, 376–77.

11. See Freud [1900] 1965, 566. See also 1917a, 228–32. In *The Interpretation of Dreams* Freud comments on the special requirements for the interpretation of one's own dreams, what he considers to be the most difficult type of dream interpretation: any who seeks to do this must "endeavor during the work to refrain from any criticism, any *parti pris*, and any emotional or intellectual bias . . . he [sic] must work, that is, with as much persistence as an animal and with as much disregard of the result" (Freud [1900] 1965, 561). Similarly, he also says in the same work that "it must not be forgotten that in interpreting a dream we are opposed by the psychical forces which were responsible for its distortion. It is thus a question of relative strength whether our intellectual interest, our capacity for self-discipline, our psychological knowledge and our practice in interpreting dreams enable us to master our internal resistances" (563).

12. See the following works by Freud: *Fragment of an Analysis of a Case of Hysteria* ([1905] 1963; a.k.a. the "Dora" case); *Analysis of a Phobia in a Five-Year Old Boy* ([1909a] 1955; a.k.a. the "Little Hans" case); *Notes Upon a Case of Obsessional Neurosis* ([1909b] 1955; a.k.a. the "Rat Man" case); and *From the History of an Infantile Neurosis* ([1918] 1955; a.k.a. the "Wolf Man" case).

13. See Freud [1900] 1965, 587–88, 646–48; See also *Some Additional Notes on Dream-Interpretation as a Whole* (Freud [1925] 1963).

14. See Freud [1900] 1965, 128–32, 464.

15. See Freud [1900] 1965, 347–48, 384–85, 453–54, 481–82, 618–19n. See also 1917a, 181–82, and Freud [1923] 1963, 208. Freud denies the prophetic character of dreams but admits that there may be telepathic forces at work; see Freud [1925] 1963, 226–30.

16. See *The Future of an Illusion*: "Surely infantilism is destined to be surmounted. Men cannot remain children forever; they must in the end go out into 'hostile life'" (Freud [1927] 1963, 49.

17. There are a number of grounds upon which it may be argued that psychoanalysis aims at the elimination of religion. In *The Psychopathology of Everyday Life* Freud observes that "religion is destined to be changed again by science into the psychology of the unconscious" (Freud [1901] 1955, 146). In *Obsessive Acts and Religious Practices* Freud claims that there is an identity between the two phenomena: "one might venture to regard the obsessional neurosis as a pathological counterpart to the formation of a religion, to describe this neurosis as a private religious system, and religion as a universal obsessional neurosis" (Freud [1907] 1963, 11) Thus, to the extent that psychoanalytic therapy works to cure the patient of neurosis, it would also tend to "cure" people of religion as well. This is also the underlying theme of *Totem and Taboo* ([1913] 1955), Freud's first major statement on religion. Here he argues that religion originates in the extremely ambivalent emotions we feel towards our fathers; again, given that psychoanalysis seeks to help individuals overcome difficulties arising from the Oedipal period of development, it also works to overcome religious attachments as well. In "Leonardo Da Vinci and a Memory of his Childhood" Freud notes how Leonardo's last writings "breathe the resignation of the human being who subjects himself to the laws of nature, and who expects no alleviation from the goodness or grace of God. There is scarcely any doubt that Leonardo had prevailed over both dogmatic and personal religion" (124–25). The case study *From the History of an Infantile Neurosis* ([1918] 1955) portrays the development of the neurosis of the "Wolf Man": in his childhood the Wolf Man suffered from an extremely obsessional piety, which later disappeared entirely—evidence, for Freud, that religion is transitional stage between infancy and adulthood. In his later writings, Freud attacks religion with increasingly sharp invective: "when a man has once brought himself to accept uncritically all the absurdities that religious doctrines put before him and even to overlook the contradictions between them, we need not be greatly surprised at the

weakness of his intellect" (Freud [1927] 1963, 48); "The whole thing [religion] is so patently infantile, so foreign to reality, that to anyone with a friendly attitude to humanity it is painful to think that the great majority of mortals will never be able to rise above this view of life" (Freud [1930] 1961, 21). And in lecture 35 of the *New Introductory Lectures on Psychoanalysis*, entitled "The Question of a Weltanschauung," Freud expressly states that religion is the most powerful enemy of modern science; but while the battle still rages, Freud is confident that science will ultimately emerge victorious. The natural sciences have already refuted religion's accounts of the creation of the universe, and now psychoanalysis has inflicted the fatal blow "by showing how religion originated from the helplessness of children" (Freud [1933] 1965, 147).

Chapter 4. Surrealism: Andre Breton

1. See Coxhead and Hiller, *Dreams: Visions of the Night* (1976) and Mackenzie, *Dreams and Dreaming* (1965). These are bad books on dreams, but good books on dream art.

2. See my review of Salman Rushdie, *The Satanic Verses*, (Bulkley 1989a), where I read the controversial novel as a contribution to dream studies.

3. I have written reviews of "Akira Kurusawa's Dreams" (Bulkley 1990a), "Jacob's Ladder" (Bulkley 1990b), and "Freddy's Dead" (Bulkley 1992) in which I discuss dreams in films and films as dreams.

4. *The Dream and the Text: Essays on Language and Literature*, edited by Carol Schreier Rupprecht (1993), is the best collection of essays on dreams and literary creativity. Numerous accounts of the use of dreams in painting, theater, poetry, sculpture, dance, and other artistic media may be found in issues of *Dream Network Bulletin/Journal.*

5. See also *Surrealism*: "A work cannot be considered surrealist unless the artist strains to reach the total psychological scope of which consciousness is only a small part" (Waldberg 1965, 84).

6. In *Communicating Vessels* Breton analyzes a second dream. This second dream contains a dream within a dream, and Breton argues that such dream experiences demonstrate the impossibility of distinguishing waking from dreaming realities (Breton [1932] 1990, 105–9.

Chapter 5. Analytical Psychology: Carl Jung

1. Examples of this are Hadfield 1954, Fromm 1951, Hall 1966, and Ullman and Zimmerman 1979. Actually, this is only one of the two basic patterns for books on dreams. The first reviews Freud and Jung, and then presents new theory

X; the second reviews Freud and sleep laboratory research, and then presents new theory Y. Examples of the second pattern are Hudson 1985, Evans 1983, and Rycroft 1979.

2. For further information on the relationship between Freud and Jung (and on the subsequent break in their relationship), see Jung's autobiography, *Memories, Dreams, Reflections* (1965), *The Freud/Jung Letters* (McGuire 1974), and Peter Homans, *Jung in Context: Modernity and the Making of a Psychology* (1979).

3. This is the principal thesis of Peter Homans in *Jung in Context: Modernity and the Making of a Psychology* (1979).

4. Unlike Freud, Jung did not write a central, definitive statement on his theory of dreams. Indeed, I don't believe Jung wrote a central, definitive statement on anything. His essays tend to be very abstruse, expansive works with endless references, asides, and elliptical comments—always fascinating, but never definitive. The following summary of Jung's ideas about dreams draws on four principle collections of texts, all printed in Princeton University Press editions: *Dreams* (1974), *Two Essays on Analytical Psychology* (1966), *The Archetypes and the Collective Unconscious* (1969), and *The Practice of Psychotherapy* (1966). Although I am aware that Jung said something about dreams in practically everything he wrote, this selection of texts represents, I believe, most of Jung's key ideas on dreams.

5. On analytic psychology and the methodology of the natural sciences, see also the following works by Jung: "Individual Dream Symbolism in Relation to Alchemy" (1952), 294; *Two Essays on Analytical Psychology* (1966), 134, 211, 222; "The Aims of Psychotherapy" ([1931] 1966), 38–40; "Concerning the Archetypes, with Special Reference to the Anima Concept" ([1954] 1969), 54–70; and "The Psychological Aspects of the Kore" ([1951b] 1969), 186.

6. See *Two Essays on Analytical Psychology* (1966), 62–63, 162, 166; also his "Aims of Psychotherapy" ([1931] 1966), 51.

7. See the following works by Jung: "General Aspects of Dream Psychology" (1948a), 31, 49; "On the Nature of Dreams" (1948b), 75; "The Practical Use of Dream-Analysis" (1934), 90–93; *Two Essays on Analytical Psychology* (1966), 100–1, 131.

8. For more on the "symbolic language" spoken by the psyche, see Jung's "General Aspects of Dream Psychology" ([1948a] 1974), 49; "The Practical Use of Dream-Analysis" (1934), 90–93; *Two Essays on Analytical Psychology* (1966), 106, 138; "The Psychological Aspects of the Kore" ([1951b] 1969), 157, 160, 179. Jung's comment in *The Psychology of the Child Archetype* is especially interesting: "An archetypal content expresses itself, first and foremost, in metaphors. If such a content should speak of the sun and identify it with the lion, the king, the hoard of gold guarded by the dragon, or the power that makes for the life and health of man, it is neither the one thing nor the other, but the unknown third thing that finds more or less adequate expression in all these similes, yet—to the perpetual

vexation of the intellect—remains unknown and not to be fitted into a formula" (Jung [1951a] 1969, 157).

9. Jung admits that his is not an exhaustive theory of the functions of dreams. See his "General Aspects of Dream Psychology" ([1948a] 1974), 29–32, 40, 44, 46, 49, and 63; "On the Nature of Dreams" ([1948b] 1974), 70–71; and "The Practical Use of Dream-Analysis" ([1934] 1974), 95–96.

10. See Jung's "General Aspects of Dream Psychology ([1948a] 1974), 24, 27, 41–44; "On the Nature of Dreams" ([1948b] 1974), 92; and *Two Essays on Analytical Psychology* (1966), 46, 131.

11. On the subject of individuation, see also "On the Nature of Dreams" ([1948b] 1974), 78, 100, 108; *Individual Dream Symbolism in Relation to Alchemy* ([1952] 1974), 115, 296–97; *Two Essays on Analytical Psychology* (1966), 59, 80, 110–11, 173–74; and "Psychological Aspects of the Mother Archetype" ([1954] 1969), 95–96.

12. Jung says in "On the Nature of Dreams," "But if dreams produce such essential compensations, why are they not understandable? I have often been asked this question. The answer must be that the dream is a natural occurrence, and that nature shows no inclination to offer her fruits gratis or according to human expectations. It is often objected that the compensation must be ineffective unless the dream is understood. This is not so certain, however, for many things can be effective without being understood. But there is no doubt that we can enhance its effect considerably by understanding the dream, and this is often necessary because the voice of the unconscious so easily goes unheard. 'What nature leaves imperfect is perfected by the art,' says an alchemical dictum" (Jung [1946b] 1974, 80). See also "General Aspects of Dream Psychology" ([1948a] 1974), 33; "The Practical Use of Dream-Analysis" (1934), 101; and *Two Essays on Analytical Psychology* (1966), 73, 88.

13. On the subject of how to approach a dream, see "On the Nature of Dreams" ([1948b] 1974), 69, 73; "The Practical Use of Dream-Analysis" ([1934] 1974), 96; "Individual Dream Symbolism in Relation to Alchemy" (1952), 117–20; "Principles of Practical Psychotherapy" (1935), 17; and "The Aims of Psychotherapy" (1931), 42.

14. "On the Nature of Dreams" notes: "I have mentioned before that dream interpretation requires, among other things, specialized knowledge. While I am quite ready to believe that an intelligent layman with some psychological knowledge and experience of life could, with practice, diagnose dream-compensation correctly, I consider it impossible for anyone without knowledge of mythology and folklore and without some understanding of the psychology of primitives and of comparative religion to grasp the essence of the individuation process, which, according to all we know, lies at the base of psychological compensation" (Jung [1948b] 1974, 76; see also 72); "General Aspects of Dream Psychology" ([1948a] 1974), 45, 64; "The Aims of Psychotherapy" ([1931] 1966), 45; "The Psychologi-

cal Aspects of the Kore" ([1951b] 1969), 189; *Two Essays on Analytical Psychology* (1966), 85; and the whole of "Individual Dream Symbolism in Relation to Alchemy" ([1952] 1974), which makes extensive use of mythological, religious, and alchemical symbolism in the interpretation of an individual's dreams.

15. See Jung's "General Aspects of Dream Psychology" ([1948a] 1974), 27, 35; "On the Nature of Dreams" ([1948b] 1974), 71-72; and especially "The Practical Use of Dream-Analysis" ([1934] 1974), 98, 103.

16. See Jung's "Practical Use of Dream-Analysis" ([1934] 1974), 98.

17. See "The Practical Use of Dream-Analysis" ([1934] 1974), 98; "Individual Dream Symbolism in Relation to Alchemy" ([1952] 1974), 117–20; "Principles of Practical Psychotherapy" (1935), 11; and "The Aims of Psychotherapy" ([1931] 1966), 41.

18. See his *Two Essays on Analytical Psychology* (1966), 65–70; "Concerning the Archetypes, with Special Reference to the Anima Concept" ([1954] 1969), 66–67, 70. There is a great deal of debate currently regarding the neurobiological roots of the archetypes. Anthony Stevens's book *Archetypes: A Natural History of the Self* (1982) gives a strong argument that recent findings in the natural sciences support Jung's account of the archetypes. Don Browning provides a useful review of Steven's book and its place in this debate in *Religious Thought and the Modern Psychologies* (Browning 1987, 161–203).

19. See also Jung's "General Aspects of Dream Psychology" ([1948a] 1974), 52–53.

20. On the dialogical nature of dream interpretation, see Jung's "Practical Use of Dream-Analysis" ([1934] 1974), 94; "Principles of Practical Psychotherapy" ([1935] 1966), 3; "The Aims of Psychotherapy" ([1931] 1966), 49; and *Two Essays on Analytical Psychology* (1966), 25.

21. Jung says in *Two Essays on Analytical Psychology*, "What is true of humanity in general is also true of each individual, for humanity consists only of individuals. And as is the psychology of humanity so also is the psychology of the individual" (Jung [1951a] 1969, 50).

22. "The Psychology of the Child Archetype" says: "For the archetype is an element of our psychic structure and thus a vital and necessary component in our psychic economy. It represents or personifies certain instinctive data of the dark, primitive psyche, the real but invisible roots of consciousness . . . This original form of *religio* ("linking back") is the essence, the working basis of all religious life even today, and always will be, whatever future form this life may take" (Jung [1951a] 1969, 161). For more on the subject of the archetypal roots of religion, see "Individual Dream Symbolism in Relation to Alchemy" ([1952] 1974), 201; and *Two Essays on Analytical Psychology* (1966), 97.

23. See Jung's *Two Essays on Analytical Psychology* (1966), 99.

24. On the persistence of religious elements in the unconscious of modern Westerners, see also Jung's "General Aspects of Dream Psychology" ([1948a] 1974), 62–66; "On the Nature of Dreams" ([1948b] 1974), 83; and *Two Essays on Analytical Psychology* (1966), 71, 94. The latter passage is especially interesting: "Only in the age of enlightenment did people discover that the gods did not really exist, but were simply projections. Thus the gods were disposed of. But the corresponding psychological function was by no means disposed of; it lapsed into the unconscious, and men were thereupon poisoned by the surplus of libido that had once been laid up in the cult of divine images. The devaluation and repression of so powerful a function as the religious function naturally have serious consequences for the psychology of the individual. The unconscious is prodigiously strengthened by this reflux of libido, and, through its archaic collective contents, begins to exercise a powerful influence on the conscious mind. The period of the Enlightenment closed, as we know, with the horrors of the French Revolution."

25. This passage continues on to give a detailed description of the special interpretive measures to be taken with "big" dreams (Jung [1948b] 1974, 76–80). Jung says, "Not all dreams are of equal importance. Even primitives distinguish between 'little' and 'big' dreams, or, as we might say, 'insignificant' and 'significant' dreams . . . We speak on the one hand of a *personal* and on the other of a *collective* unconscious, which lies at a deeper level and is further removed from consciousness than the personal unconscious. The 'big' or 'meaningful' dreams come from this deeper level" (76, 77).

Chapter 6. Content Analysis: Calvin Hall

1. For a good survey of some of the major findings of the content analysis approach to dreams, see Domhoff 1985.

2. Hall also suggests that "contingency analysis" can avoid the problem of distorting a dream by breaking it up into structural elements. A "contingency analysis" involves the investigator looking out for special combinations of elements, combinations that seem to appear more frequently than chance would dictate. For example, Hall says that animal characters and the emotion of aggression frequently appear together in children's dreams. A simple content analysis might pass this combination over, but Hall believes that investigators can be trained to observe, or "struck," by these unusual combinations (see Hall and Nordby 1972, 60–62).

3. See also Hall and Van de Castle: "there are no theoretical concepts in dream reports . . . Concepts are in the mind of the investigator" (Hall and Van de Castle 1966, 30).

4. In *The Individual and his Dreams*, Hall makes a sharp distinction between two different kinds of categories: *empirical* categories and *theoretical* categories. He says, "the categories or classes of elements that have been described in this chapter

are said to be empirical ones because they occur directly in dream reports. There is nothing inferential or theoretical about settings, objects, characters, interactions, and so forth. It is possible, however, to devise classes that are theoretical. A theoretical category is one that is taken from a theory of personality" (Hall and Nordby 1972, 58). Along similar lines, Hall says we must distinguish in dream analysis between *fact* and *inference*: "We started our investigations of dreams without any preconceptions of what we would find. We had no theory that we wished to prove or disprove . . . Throughout this book we have made an effort to distinguish between fact and inference. Unless one is vigilant, it is easy to treat opinion as fact and theory as truth without being aware of what one has done . . . Many inferences can be drawn from the same fact. We must have the facts first, however, and that is what we have tried to provide in this book." (Hall and Nordby 1972, 11, 12). However, it is worth noting that Hall explicitly instructs his subjects on how to report their dreams and on what categories to use in describing the dream: "The handicap of differences in verbal ability [among subjects] can be overcome to some extent by acquainting a person beforehand with the points he should try to cover in his report. We make it a practice of asking a person to include the following information, if possible: the *setting* . . . , the *characters* . . . , the *actions and interactions* . . . , the *objects* . . . , the *emotions* . . . With a little practice, virtually any person can learn to describe a dream" (Hall and Nordby 1972, 13).

We might ask, don't all these instructions influence what appear to Hall as the "facts" of the dream?

5. Hall goes on in this passage to describe "a few basic rules" for interpretation (Hall 1966, 85). First, the "cardinal rule for understanding dreams is that a dream is a creation of the dreamer's mind" (86), i.e., dreams reflect subjective and not objective reality. Second, "nothing appears in a dream which the dreamer does not put there himself" (87). Third, "a dreamer may reveal more than one conception of himself or of another person in a single dream or in a series of dreams" (87); this point emphasizes that dreams may have ambiguous meanings. And fourth, "a dream is an organic whole; one part of a dream should not be lifted out of context and interpreted for itself alone" (88), reinforcing Hall's basic thesis that it is only in the context of a dream series that one can detect objectively valid meanings for any one dream. Another point of interest in Hall's method of interpreting dream series is his notion of "spotlight dreams": "Some dreams of a series are easier to interpret than others. Their meaning is right out on the surface of the dream, and they scarcely need to be interpreted at all. We call dreams of this type *spotlight* or *bareface* dreams. Since these dreams provide us with the easiest avenue into the mind of the dreamer we start with them when we begin analyzing a dream series. We go from the simple to the complex by easy steps so that even the most obscure dream ordinarily divulges its message" (72). In *The Individual and His Dreams*, Hall emphatically states (in a clear slap at Freud and Jung) that dream interpretation does not require any special training or knowledge and, indeed, that it is better *not* to know too much beforehand: "The methods of analysis described here do not require a background of specialized knowledge or technical information. In fact, it is preferable if a person is not too familiar with dream theories so

that he can approach the study of his dreams with an open, receptive, unprejudiced mind. We suggest to the reader that he adopt the attitude of 'reading *out*' of his dreams what is in them instead of 'reading *into*' his dreams what he has learned from books" (Hall and Nordby 1972, 156).

6. Hall goes on to say "In waking life, symbols are used for precisely the same reason. A lion stands for courage, a snake for evil and an owl for wisdom. Likewise, a cross stands for the Christian church, John Bull for England and a hammer and sickle for Soviet Russia" (Hall 1966, 96)

7. In this regard, Hall favorably cites Aristotle's view that dreaming is merely thinking in sleep (see Hall and Nordby 1972, 145).

8. "Why then are there symbols in dreams? There are symbols in dreams for the same reason that there are figures of speech in poetry and slang in everyday life. Man wants to express his thoughts as clearly as possible in objective terms. He wants to convey meaning with precision and economy. He wants to clothe his conceptions in the most appropriate garments. And perhaps, although of this we are not too certain, he wants to garnish his ideas with beauty and taste. For these reasons the language of sleep uses symbols" (Hall 1966, 108). "The function of dreaming as we have said many times is to reveal what is in the person's mind, not to conceal it. Dreams may appear enigmatic because they contain symbols, but these symbols are nothing more than pictorial metaphors, and like the verbal metaphors of waking life their intention is to clarify rather than to obscure thought" (Hall 1966, 215).

9. The passage continues, "When this task is accomplished the mind of man is exposed to public view and becomes an object of scientific study" (Hall 1966, 214).

10. Hall distinguishes between "metaphorical symbols" and "denotational symbols," saying that the latter have "no surplus of meaning" (Hall and Nordby 1972, 63–66). Dreams with only "denotational symbols" are apparently those whose meanings are obvious and require no interpretation; an example of such a dream is on page 37 of the Hall and Nordby work. However, Hall admits that there is no sure way to tell when a symbol is metaphorical and when it is denotational (66).

11. See also Hall and Nordby 1972, 47, 61.

12. Hall goes on in this passage to defend the continuity hypothesis against the objection that we do *not* think or behave in our waking lives like we do in our dreams. He says that the apparent discontinuities "pertain almost exclusively to the impulses of sex and aggression" (Hall and Nordby 1966, 104); these impulses *are* a part of our waking selves, Hall argues, even though we may not consciously acknowledge the fact. Thus, our dreams "often open our eyes to our true feelings, which we close our eyes to when awake" (105). But right here, it seems to me that Hall gives away the game. He apparently formulates the continuity hypothesis in

order to refute Jung's view that dreams *compensate* for the imbalances of waking consciousness; for Jung, dreams present thoughts and behaviors that are *opposite* to the dreamer's waking thoughts and behaviors. Hall disagrees with that idea, but when he admits that dreams reveal our "true feelings" to which our waking consciousness has been blind, he removes any functional difference between his continuity hypothesis and Jung's compensatory theory of dreams.

13. It may be helpful at this point to note briefly what Hall believes these basic human conflicts to be. He claims that one of his major contributions is to show what "normal" people actually dream about—in a sense, providing a "census" of dreams (Hall 1966, 1–2, 21) by letting the dreams "speak for themselves" without any "preconceived ideas" imposed by the investigator (110). What Hall finds in this dream census is that people are beset by five basic conflicts: (1) the Oedipal conflict, (2) a clash between yearnings for freedom and security, (3) a moral conflict between biological instincts and social norms, (4) a conflict over one's appropriate sex role, and (5) anxiety about death.

14. In *The Individual and his Dreams* Hall says that dream study can help us understand social life by "unveiling the psychological meaning of a social institution" (Hall and Nordby 1972, 151). The example he gives is the legal system, involving laws, trials, police, punishments, etc.

15. This passage goes on: "By using his intelligence he has made the world a more comfortable place in which to live. The accomplishments of science and technology are among the most notable achievements of the human mind" (Hall 1966, 233).

16. See Hall: "This resistance against knowledge has been met before in history. The astronomers met it and so have the biologists. At one time it was considered a crime to explore the inner workings of the body or to tamper with the sacred temple of the soul" (Hall 1966, 218).

17. See also Hall and Nordby 1972, 15, 147.

Chapter 7. Neuroscience: J. Allan Hobson

1. Eugene Aserinsky and Nathaniel Kleitman are given credit for first discovering the connection between REM sleep and dreaming. They first published their findings in two papers: "Regularly Occurring Periods of Eye Motility and Concurrent Phenomena During Sleep" (1953); and "Two Types of Ocular Motility Occurring in Sleep" (1955). Hobson gives an excellent account of their discovery in chapter 6 of his book (Hobson 1988, 134–54).

2. Note that Hobson says Joseph's interpretation of Pharaoh's dreams is just like the dream interpretations of psychoanalysis, something that Freud specifically denies in *The Interpretation of Dreams* ([1900] 1965), 128–36.

3. "*The Interpretation of Dreams* was antiscientific because Freud so forcefully dismissed all previous writers that he actually aborted an emerging experimental tradition. Psychiatry and psychology have been in Freud's thrall for almost a century; and even within the modern field of sleep research, the tenacity of psychoanalytic views remains impressively obstructive to integrative theorizing" (Hobson 1988, 50–51). Actually, Hobson claims that Freud's fundamental mistake was to give up the goals of the 1895 *Project*, in which he made an initial attempt at developing a brain-based psychology. While later psychoanalysts dismissed the *Project* as a misguided pursuit, overly influenced by nineteenth-century empiricism, that Freud fortunately abandoned in order to develop psychoanalysis, Hobson turns this judgement on its head: he argues that the *Project* was correct in its aims but lacked adequate knowledge about brain neurology. Thus Freud surrendered to the temptation of filling in the gaps with a "speculative philosophy" that led psychoanalysis further and further away from scientific legitimacy (Hobson 1988, 55). In yet another attack on his scientific credentials, Hobson chides Freud for using "a political organization" (53; see also 64, 67) to promote his ideas rather than the purely rational and nonpolitical arguments by which Hobson apparently assumes scientific knowledge is furthered (Hobson 1988, 53; see also 64, 67). Yet such a view of the progress of scientific knowledge—that its advances are (or ideally can be) pure, logical, and have no taint of political influence—has been persuasively challenged by Karl Mannheim (1936), Thomas Kuhn (1970), Ian Barbour (1974), Paul Feyerabend (1988), Donna Haraway (1984, 1986), Bruno Latour (1987), Richard Bernstein (1988), and Chandra Mukerji (1989).

4. This is a general principle underlying Hobson's research, that we concentrate our efforts on those areas in which we have already developed some knowledge; hence his comment "We know far too little about the brain in any of its functional states to hope to account for the narrative aspects of dreaming. In science we often have to look where the light is." (Hobson 1988, 232). Note also his comment, "The physiological methods are simply not capable of going much farther within this paradigm—at least not yet! But the opportunistic scientist does not grope long for the key in the darkness: one looks where the light is" (Hobson 1988, 227).

5. "The reciprocal-interaction hypothesis proposes that the continuous competition between the excitatory reticular neurons and the inhibitory aminergic neurons is the basic physiological process underlying sleep-cycle alternation. According to this theory, REM sleep and dreaming occur only when the activity in the REM-off aminergic neuronal population has reached a level low enough to allow the REM-on reticular system to escape from its inhibitory control. Then the reticular neuronal population becomes spontaneously active and switches the state of the brain to the REM mode. While this switching process is 'centered' in the brain stem, it is mediated by disinhibition and by consequent excitation of neurons throughout the brain" (Hobson 1988, 184–85).

6. It is important for us to note in passing how Hobson is assuming a REM sleep/dreaming *isomorphism*: the identity of REM sleep patterns in the brain with

the mental experience of dreaming. This is a crucial assumption of many neuroscientists studying dreams, and it has a direct affect on the way they account for the meaning of dreams. See Moffitt and Hoffman (1987) for an excellent critique of this assumption and of the problems it creates in sleep and dream research.

7. Hobson makes this same point more colorfully in his 1977 paper: "Such features as scene shifts, time compression, personal condensations, splitting, and symbol formation may be directly isomorphic with the state of the nervous system during dreaming sleep. In other words, the forebrain may be making the best of a bad job in producing even partially coherent dream imagery from the relatively noisy signals sent up to it from the brain stem" (Hobson and McCarley 1977, 1347).

8. "The physiology that is now in hand best supports the first part of the theory; much more work needs to be done on the synthetic aspects of the process" (Hobson 1988, 204).

9. "The activation-synthesis hypothesis sees the bizarreness of dreams as the unadulterated result of an imperfect integration of internally generated sensorimotor data which is processed under distinctive conditions: the space-time dimensions of the external world are absent; multiple sensory channels are activated in parallel; and attentional processes are impaired" (Hobson 1988, 218).

10. Hobson claims that his notion of the "transparent" meaning of dreams accords with Jung's approach to the meaning of dreams (Hobson 1988, 12, 65).

11. It is worth noting that this is a much softer position than that which Hobson takes in his 1977 paper, where his protestations that he is not denying the meaningfulness of dreams are overshadowed by his conclusion that dreams are merely the mind making the "best of a bad job" (1347), i.e., creating a tiny bit of order out of a mass of disorderly, intrinsically meaningless data (Hobson and McCarley 1977, 1347). And as a recent newspaper article reports, Hobson admits that until recently he believed dreams were meaningless (Blakeslee 1992). In *The Dreaming Brain* Hobson does agree with Freud that dreams are meaningful; however, Hobson rails against Freud's views on how to *interpret* dreams. He says Freud's interpretations are like "speculative literary criticism" (Hobson 1988, 57) which can't be proven (158), which don't allow for closure (274), and which are so excessive that they may be "unhealthy" (11) and "dangerous" (258). Yet Hobson admits (bitterly, it seems) that psychoanalytic interpretations may be more persuasive than his own, for "in such a literary game, the eloquence and mystique of psychoanalysis are likely to win out over the plain talk and common sense of activation synthesis" (222). I must confess that it strikes me as odd to hear a renowned neuroscientist from Harvard Medical School resort to populist rhetoric to support his position.

12. Yet strangely enough, Hobson does say in his conclusion that dreaming "has the function of providing us with an opportunity to understand ourselves better. In this view, dreaming is, after all, a message from the gods in the most prophetic sense" (Hobson 1988, 298).

13. This passage goes on: "Already, for example, it is clear that dreaming comes not from angels, nor from incubi, nor even from wishes, but from the automatic activation of our brains in REM sleep." Hobson also claims at one point that the historical trajectory of dream research "has been from animistic theism—to scientific humanism" (Hobson 1988, 81).

Chapter 8. Lucid Dreaming: Stephen LaBerge

1. Recently LaBerge and Jayne Gackenbach co-edited *Conscious Mind, Sleeping Brain* (Gackenbach and LaBerge 1988) in which they describe some of the many research projects that have been conducted since LaBerge's pioneering work.

2. See Gackenbach and LaBerge 1988 for discussions about the various degrees of consciousness that may be achieved within the dreaming state.

3. For a general audience account of LaBerge's goggles, see "What is This Thing Called Sleep?" by Michael E. Long, *National Geographic* (Dec. 1987), 787–821.

4. "Of course, decision making is only a problem when there is uncertainty about the information involved. Otherwise, the optimal choice is clear-cut. So how might lucid dreams help you to make effective ("correct") decisions under conditions of uncertainty? . . . In our dreams we can draw upon the entire store of our knowledge; we are no longer limited to the tiny portion that we have conscious access to. What I am proposing is that we take advantage of our broadest data base in lucid dreams to assist us in making optimal decisions" (LaBerge 1985, 185–86).

5. "The fact that our laboratory studies have revealed a high correlation between dream behavior and physiological responses presents a rare opportunity for developing an unusual degree of self-control of physiology that might prove useful for self-healing. You could conceivably carry out actions in your lucid dreams specifically designed to have whatever precise physiological consequences you may wish" (LaBerge 1985, 173).

6. "Since health means increased wholeness, psychological growth often requires the reintegration of neglected or rejected aspects of the personality, and this can be consciously and deliberately achieved through the symbolic encounters of lucid dreaming . . . The ability to act voluntarily according to ideals, rather than habits, allows the lucid dreamer consciously to accept, and thereby integrate, previously repressed aspects of the personality" (LaBerge 1985, 174–75).

7. "This is a very important potential of lucid dreaming, since when we 'escape' from a nightmare by awakening, we have not dealt with the problem of our fear or our frightening dream, but merely relieved the fear temporarily and

repressed the fearful dream. Thus we are left with an unresolved conflict as well as negative and unhealthy feelings. On the other hand, staying with the nightmare and accepting the challenge, as lucidity makes possible, allows us to resolve the dream problem in a fashion that leaves us more healthy than before" (LaBerge 1985, 184).

8. See LaBerge 1985, 191–94. Note that the main example LaBerge gives of this "rehearsal" function of dreams is William Dement's dream of smoking, which "changed his life," and made him feel "I was reborn" when he awoke (192). Jeremy Taylor (1991) describes a very similar account of a lucid dream leading a smoker to "kick the habit."

9. LaBerge describes one of his own lucid dreams which had this quality of being a "transcendent experience" in that it revealed to him a state of consciousness far beyond that of ordinary waking life (LaBerge 1985, 270–71).

Chapter 9. Anthropology: Barbara Tedlock

1. "Because most ethnographers are members of Western cultures in which dreaming is either greatly undervalued or else, in artistic inversion, greatly overvalued, the problem of the attitude towards and type or degree of reality accorded to the experience of dreaming by various indigenous peoples is a highly problematical issue in the ethnography of dreaming, and one which we have not as yet properly addressed" (Tedlock 1987, 4).

2. This is also one of Brown's points regarding the Aguaruna dream practices, that they play a role in "the total knowledge system" of the culture" (Tedlock 1987, 156).

3. Tedlock concludes her introduction with this statement: "Thinking about dreaming as a psychodynamic communicative process—instead of examining a single dream or group of dreams as reified objects or written texts to be analyzed solely according to Freud's notion of the dream-work, Hall's content analysis, or Levi-Strauss's structural analysis—entails a major shift in perspective. We feel that such a shift should have important implications for future dream research, whether in the laboratory, the philosopher's study, the clinician's office, or the field" (Tedlock 1987, 30).

Chapter 10. Cognitive Psychology: Harry Hunt

1. See Robert E. Haskell, "Cognitive Psychology and Dream Research: Historical, Conceptual, and Epistemological Considerations," in *The Journal of Mind and Behavior* (1986) for a good, although somewhat dense and abstract, overview of this field. The entirety of this special double issue of *The Journal of Mind and*

Behavior is devoted to the subject of "Cognition and Dream Research" and includes a number of interesting articles on the cognitive psychological approach to dreams.

2. Haskell makes a very persuasive argument for the importance of studying phenomena that may appear only rarely: "The frequency of an event is not a valid index of its significance, as even a cursory reading of the history of astronomy will demonstrate, let alone the history of psychology. The rarity of an event is not necessarily a good index of its importance. In part, its importance may be inversely proportional to the frequency of its occurrence . . . [T]heoretically significant phenomena in science have often been rarely occurring phenomena. An example is optical illusions, which have proved very important in understanding normal perceptual phenomena" (Haskell 1986, 134).

3. "Any cognitive psychology of dreaming must encounter and reconcile two statements: 'the dream is a story' and 'the dream is imagery'. Neither statement is as obvious as it initially appears, because there is no agreement in contemporary cognitive psychology on the ultimate relation between visual-spatial imagery and language. Much evidence and theory supports both the view that a visual-spatial imagistic intelligence rests directly on and creatively reorganizes the processes of perceptions and the view that mental imagery is a surface paraphrase of abstract propositional knowledge, whose deep structure is accordingly far closer to verbal syntax than visual imagery" (Hunt 1984, 159–160).

4. "The contribution of imagery would come mainly from the way it provokes taming and reorganization by propositional knowledge . . . [R]andomization models of creativity ignore repeated demonstrations, involving both scientific discovery and dream psychology, that ostensibly bizarre imagery often directly conveys insights that go qualititatively beyond any previous formulation" (Hunt 1984, 167; see also 163, 168).

5. "There is considerable evidence that dream narrative and novel visual-spatial imagery reflect alternative and potentially independent cognitive processes" (Hunt 1984, 185).

6. See Hunt 1989, 97–101, 108–11.

7. See also Hunt 1989, 86, 218 for Hunt's comments on the effects of modern "mass" society on the experience of dreaming; and also 84 on how people in societies that are becoming "Westernized" tend to dream less.

Chapter 11. The Crisis of Dream Interpretation: Gadamer to the Rescue

1. We should note how Gadamer mentions dreams in relation to the experience of art: "All such ideas as imitation, appearance, irreality, illusion, magic, dream, assume a relationship to something from which the aesthetic is differ-

ent . . . [According to such a view] what was only appearance has now revealed itself, what lacked reality acquires it, what was magical loses its magic, what was illusion is seen through, and from what was dream we awaken. If the aesthetic is mere appearance in this sense, then its power—like the terror of dreams—could last only so long as there was no doubt of the reality of the appearance, and would lose its truth on waking. The shift of the ontological definition of the aesthetic to the sphere of aesthetic appearance has its theoretical basis in the fact that the domination of the scientific epistemological model leads to the discrediting of all the possibilities of knowing that lie outside this new method" (Gadamer 1975, 75).

2. On this count, Gadamer's claim is summarized in this statement: "Is there to be no knowledge in art? Does not the experience of art contain a claim to truth which is certainly different from that of science, but equally certainly is not inferior to it?" (Gadamer 1975, 87).

3. I thank the children of the After School programs at the Laboratory School of the University of Chicago, 1987–92, for instructing me in these subtle nuances of Gadamer's philosophy.

4. "Play does not have its being in the consciousness or the attitude of the player, but on the contrary draws the latter into its area and fills him with its spirit. The player experiences the game as a reality that surpasses him" (Gadamer 1975, 98). See also 262–63, 340, 345, 404, 427–28). Gadamer's discussion of *medial areas* is strikingly similar to D. W. Winnicott's (1971) concept of transitional spaces and transitional phenomena.

5. In this project Gadamer is following in the tradition of Friedrich Schleiermacher and Wilhelm Dilthey, the two great historical figures in modern hermeneutic philosophy. See Gadamer's discussion of Schleiermacher and Dilthey (Gadamer 1975, 153–213).

6. "There is no understanding or interpretation in which the totality of this existential structure does not function, even if the intention of the knower is simply to 'read what is there" and to discover from his sources 'how it really was'" (Gadamer 1975, 358).

7. "To think historically always involves establishing a connection between those ideas and one's own thinking. To try to eliminate one's own concepts in interpretation is not only impossible, but manifestly absurd. To interpret means precisely to use one's own preconceptions so that the meaning of the text can really be made to speak for us" (Gadamer 1975, 358).

8. One of the major problems with the Enlightenment/modern science view is that it assumes that we can know *without* prejudices; as a consequence it is all the harder to bring our remaining false prejudices to awareness. Gadamer asserts that "a person who imagines that he is free of prejudices, basing his knowledge on the objectivity of his procedures and denying that he is himself influenced by historical circumstances, experiences the power of the prejudices that unconsciously domi-

nate him, as a vis a tergo. A person who does not accept that he is dominated by prejudices will fail to see what is shown by their light" (Gadamer 1975, 324).

9. The main focus of Gadamer's argument here is against the pretensions of Enlightenment rationality. Gadamer does, however, also note that the romantic approach to interpretation is equally as flawed. Romantics such as Schleiermacher surrender human reason and agency completely to the old, to tradition, to myth (Gadamer 1975, 242–45, 249–50).

10. On this point, Gadamer develops his concept of 'Wirkungsgechichte' (effective-history). He says, "True historical thinking must take account of its own historicality. Only then will it not chase the phantom of an historical object which is the object of progressive research, but learn to see in the object the counterpart of itself and hence understand both. The true historical object is not an object at all, but the unity of the one and the other, a relationship in which exist both the reality of history and the reality of historical understanding. A proper hermeneutics would have to demonstrate the effectivity of history within understanding itself. I shall refer to this as 'effective-history'. Understanding is, essentially, an effective-historical relation . . . [W]e are always subject to the effects of effective-history. It determines in advance both what seems to us worth enquiring about and what will appear as an object of investigation, and we more or less forget half of what is really there—in fact, we miss the whole truth of the phenomenon when we take its immediate appearance as the whole truth" (Gadamer 1975, 267–68).

11. See Gadamer's critique of the romantic model of interpretation (Gadamer 1975, 169–70).

12. Thus Gadamer rejects the appeal to any supposed "original" meaning of the text: "This is the reason that all understanding is always more than the mere recreation of someone else's meaning. Asking it opens up possibilities of meaning and thus what is meaningful passes into one's own thinking on the subject" (338). He also rejects the appeal to any objective, transhistorical standards: "There is no such thing, in fact, as a point outside history from which the identity of a problem can be conceived within the vicissitudes of the various attempts to solve it . . . The standpoint that is beyond any standpoint, a standpoint from which we could conceive its true identity, is a pure illusion" (Gadamer 1975, 338–39).

13. This is clearly a very conservative standard of truth. We will discuss the problematic aspects of this standard (i.e., how it prevents us from appreciating meanings that deviate radically from our ordinary "relationships of order") in the final chapter of part 3.

Chapter 12. A Hermeneutic Critique of Modern Dream Interpretation Theories

1. The passage goes on: "He [Kracke] is quick to point out, though, that by the time a dream is narratized this imagery has been filtered through a complex,

language-centered thought process which imposes a disjunctive temporal sequencing on to the continuity of dream space" (Tedlock 1987, 22). Kracke's point challenges the popular metaphorical image of a dream as a little internal world. Roger Zelazny's *The Dream Master* (1966) is an award-winning science fiction story that relies upon this image. Zelazny envisions a future in which psychotherapists use a technological device to enter *into* a person's dreams and manipulate them for therapeutic purposes—the basic premise being that a dream is a little world inside the head of the dreamer, a world into which someone else could enter in such a way as to share the dreamer's experiences, like an amusement park. *The Dream Master* was written in those first heady days of sleep laboratory research, when it appeared that scientists were finally "capturing" the dream. However, the recent work of Kracke, Tedlock, and other anthropologists has called this image into question. Their research indicates that the dreaming experience is so thoroughly a product of the dreamer's psychological, linguistic, and cultural structures that another person could not even in theory participate in the experience in a direct, unmediated way. In other words, there is no "inner world" to enter.

2. Allan Bloom's *Closing of the American Mind* (1987) is the most prominent expression of this disgust with the proliferation of "texts" to be interpreted by modern critics. See also Paul Berman, *Debating P.C.: The Controversy Over Political Correctness on College Campuses* (1992).

3. Within these categories, there are many different forms: oral reports in individual therapy, in group therapy, in a family setting, among friends; artistic expression in poetry, prose, painting, dance, music, drama, sculpture.

4. Not that I'm necessarily against quixotic searches. As Wendy Doniger pointed out to me in a conversation, this quest for the "original" dream, the true dream experience behind all the elaborations and revisions, has a powerful mythological dimension to it. Mircea Eliade has written extensively about the human quest for the "time of origins" (see, e.g., *The Myth of the Eternal Return* [1954]). However, in this case I feel compelled to play the role of hard-nosed realist: trying to detect the "original" dream text is like trying to determine the precise geographic location of Eden—an interesting and meaningful pursuit, to be sure, but one that takes us away from our main concerns in this project.

5. Indeed, the idea that the inevitability of conscious mediation in dream reports must rule them out as legitimate texts betrays the influence of the narrow natural scientific model that Gadamer is at such pains to challenge. In the natural sciences the admission that an object of study was influenced by human subjectivity would invalidate the investigation. Gadamer, however, argues that there are many phenomena in the world that are inevitably influenced in this way and yet that still may be studied in such a way that we gain genuine knowledge. This is the whole point of his discussion of historicality and the human sciences: we must recognize that these sorts of phenomena do have meaning. We may learn things from them that we could not from other, more "impersonal" phenomena, and so we must adopt special (i.e., nonnatural scientific) measures to interpret them.

6. "Now I say to you: Give up your abstraction and you will also give up your question" (Marx, 1978, 92).

7. Gadamer says, "The example of the translator, who has to bridge the gulf between languages, shows clearly the reciprocal relationship that exists between interpreter and text, corresponding to the mutuality of understanding in conversation. *For every translator is an interpreter*. The fact that it is a foreign language that is being translated means that it is simply an extreme case of hermeneutical difficulty, i.e., of alienness and its conquest. All 'objects' with which traditional hermeneutics are concerned are, in fact, alien in the same sense. The translator's task of re-creation differs only in degree, not qualitatively, from the general hermeneutical task presented by any text" (Gadamer 1975, 349).

8. Indeed, the same basic point could be made in response to the interpretive standards of Freud, Jung, Hall, Hobson, and Hunt. Each of them claims that without a particular form of specialized knowledge (with Freud, knowledge of psychosexual development; with Jung, knowledge of world religion and mythology; with Hall, knowledge of a series of dreams; with Hobson, knowledge of neuroscience; with Hunt, knowledge of cognitive psychology) the interpretation of a dream cannot be as full as it could be. That is true, undoubtedly. Nevertheless, the point I am trying to make about Tedlock's claim, which also applies to these parallel claims, is that we are *always* dealing with *degrees* of greater or lesser fullness. Thus, the failure to incorporate some form of knowledge into our interpretation of a dream does *not* render our understanding illegitimate. It means our understanding is not as full as it could be and we may continually strive for ever-greater understanding. But the basic point is, we should not labor under the delusion that if we *do* incorporate new forms of knowledge our understanding will at last be complete and exhaustive.

The other, more problematic side of this issue regards the mystifying effect these claims can have on dream interpretation: *only* if you have extensive psychoanalytic training and experience can you interpret dreams; *only* if you have a thorough knowledge of world mythology can you interpret dreams; *only* if you have a huge series of dreams, and plenty of comparative quantitative data, can you interpret dreams; *only* if you know the neuroscientific basis of REM sleep can you interpret dreams; *only* if you know the linguistic and cultural structures of the given social system can you interpret dreams; *only* if you understand the variety of cognitive processes at work in dream formation can you interpret dreams. With each of these claims, the danger is that we push the dream itself farther and farther away from us.

9. The following are some of the passages that support this point: "The moon may be regarded as a condensed symbol of a woman . . . The moon is inferior to the sun, a male symbol. The moon is changeable like a fickle woman while the sun is constant. The moon sheds a weak light which embodies the idea of feminine frailty" (Hall 1966, 97). "If we divide dream settings into two classes, inside a building versus outside, women have more of the former and men more of the latter. This finding is consistent with the belief that men find more satisfaction in

freedom from confinement whereas women prefer the security of enclosed places" (Hall 1966, 26). "Tenderness is the essence of femininity" (Hall 1966, 187).

In chap. 9 of *The Meaning of Dreams*, "The Conflict of Sex Roles," Hall roots the differing nature of men and women in what he sees as their basic biological differences: "In summary then, this is what it means to be a female. It means to have two external structures, vagina and breasts, and two internal organs, ovaries and uterus, a desire to mate with a man and an urge to nourish and rear children. It means being soft, smooth, passive, and submissive. This is what it means to be a male. It means having two visible organs, the penis and testes, and a desire to mate with a woman. It means being hard, rough, active, and aggressive" (Hall 1966, 170). Hall goes on to say that culture has a big influence on the sex roles of males and females. However, he then cautions against cultures trying to "force the individual to adopt a sex role that is at odds with his biological and psychological role as a male or female" (Hall 1966, 171). This occurs, Hall says, when "parents attempt to feminize the boy by deprecating masculinity, by denying him an opportunity to strengthen his muscles through exercise and rough games, and by encouraging him to be passive and obedient . . . Similarly, conflicts are aroused in girls by deprecating the visible emblems of femininity, by ridiculing such activities as playing with dolls, and by encouraging them to engage in strenuous muscle-building games and hard physical work" (Hall 1966, 171).

Hall's gender stereotypes appear directly in his interpretations of people's dreams. In chap. 4, "How Dreams Are Interpreted," Hall illustrates his dream series method with a series of dreams recorded by an eighteen-year-old boy. The entire focus of Hall's interpretation is on the boy's troubles in developing the quality of "manliness" (Hall 1966, 78, 81, 83). The dreams, Hall claims, plainly show that the boy's problem is his inability to take an active, aggressive approach towards sexual relations with women: "For some reason he has not been able to model himself after his father and acquire the confidence and strength necessary to be a dominant and possessive lover" (Hall 1966, 83). Hall makes similar comments in his interpretations of the dreams of two young men, William and Gene: "By contrast with the pallid, passive dream behavior of William, Gene is a vigorous young male animal . . . In waking life Gene is as different from William as they are in their dreams. Gene belongs to that large group of robust young American men who go all out for sports, competition, tinkering with engines, hunting and fishing, and a relatively free sex life, and who shun anything that is intellectual or aesthetic. William is an intellectual aesthete, physically soft, timorous, and tender" (Hall 1966, 37–38).

Carol Schreier Rupprecht has recently criticized Hall on the blatant sexism of his approach to dreams. In "The Common Language of Women's Dreams: Colloquy of Mind and Body," she argues that Hall's claims to objectivity allow him to ignore the gender bias that pervades his work: "Hall's litany of striking contrasts between men's and women's dreams is intriguing, but it makes us skeptical of his methods of collecting and categorizing dream reports. Content analysis with Hall almost invariably confirms central psychoanalytical tenets such as the Oedipus complex and women's inferior superego and ethical capacity, culturally sanctioned roles, and stereotypical behavior and attitudes . . . Hall moves readily from the reporting to the interpretation of his data, which always confirms the theory he supports. The 'fact' that men and women dream differently about aggression and victimization provides confirmation, for Hall, of Freud's theory of different superego functioning in men and women: men take more responsibility for their misfortunes, which they see as arising from something within themselves, while women seek external causes and assign blame outside themselves . . . Many other challenges to Hall leap readily to mind, and yet his data continues to find uncritical acceptance among otherwise insightful, scrupulous dream workers" (Rupprecht 1985, 203, 205, 206).

At the 1991 conference of the Association for the Study of Dreams, G. William Domhoff, one of Hall's leading colleagues, tried to refute Rupprecht's charges in an address titled "The Joys and Surprises of Content Analysis" (delivered 29 June 1991). Domhoff's defense relied on three arguments. First, the content analysis method is a *tool* and is thus neutral; if it is used in a gender-biased way, that is not the fault of the method itself. Second, the statistics on the characteristics of men's and women's dreams are based on content analysis studies that are done across time and in different ethnic groups; this establishes their universal, nonbiased validity. Third, as Hall repeatedly insisted, dreams reflect the preoccupations of the dreamer; thus dreamers who live in a gender-biased society will naturally have gender-biased dreams.

Domhoff's defense fails, I believe, on each of these three points. First, many feminist scholars have argued that the analytic method of breaking phenomena down into structures and categories is a distinctly masculine model of inquiry (see Gilligan 1982; Ortner 1974; Haraway 1984, 1986). Accordingly, the content analysis method is *by its very nature* a male-oriented approach to dreams. Second, the few cross-cultural and cross-temporal content analysis studies that have been conducted, while a good start, are hardly sufficient to support anything like the sweeping claims Hall makes about the "nature" of men, women, and their dreams. Third, if dreams reflect the preoccupations of the dreamer, and if the dreamer's culture can play such an influential role on his or her preoccupations, then the content analysis method as Hall presents it is almost useless for telling us anything about the alleged nature of dreams. Domhoff, by conceding the powerful influence of culture on dream content, completely undercuts Hall's major claim: his method allows us simply to look at the manifest content of a series of dreams, without reference to any associations or any other information, in order to determine the "plain" meanings of those dreams. If we follow the implications of Domhoff's concession, we are led to the conclusion that the content analysis method must be integrated with an anthropological study of the dreamer's culture (something that Hall never does), because without such a study we will consistently confuse the psychological and the cultural sources of a dream's meanings.

And, it should be noted, Domhoff never denies that Hall suffered from strong gender biases that influenced his studies of dreams.

The point of this lengthy discussion of content analysis and gender bias is not to denounce Calvin Hall, for Hall has made some valuable contributions to the modern study of dreams. Nor is it to reject the content analysis method, for it may yield many important insights about the nature and meaning of dreams—*if* it is used with far more self-reflection, humility, and anthropological sensitivity than it has in the past. In short, content analysis must become more *hermeneutically self-aware*.

10. In the interpretation of his "Mozart at the Museum" dream (Hobson 1988, 220–22) Hobson contrasts "the analytic position of the activation-synthesis hypothesis and Freudian orthodoxy" (220). However, he admits that "this dream might have a psychoanalytic 'meaning': I *am* ambitious. I *do* admire Mozart. I *would*, consciously, like to be as brilliant as Mozart" (222). This theme of narcissistic grandiosity is indeed straight out of Freud (Freud, "On Narcissism: An Introduction" [1914]; see also the important work on narcissism by the relatively "orthodox" psychoanalyst Heinz Kohut, *The Search for the Self* [1978]). But Hobson suggests that a Freudian interpretation would have to see the dream figure of Mozart as nothing more than a symbol of Hobson's father—and then Hobson denounces such foolish reductionism.

Later in *The Dreaming Brain*, Hobson analyzes the dream of a subject he calls "the Engine Man" (Hobson 1988, 270–81). He claims that his interpretation of the Engine Man's dream is "broadly psychodynamic without being narrowly psychoanalytic" (271). But what Hobson ultimately finds in the Engine Man's dream are the twin themes of conflicts with authority and desires for nurturance—*classic* psychoanalytic themes that Freud too would certainly identify in this dream.

The main problem here is Hobson's attempt to distinguish a "broadly psychodynamic" approach from one that is "narrowly psychoanalytic." This distinction sounds commonsensical, but it actually serves to mask Hobson's true debt to Freud and psychoanalysis. Freud is the *original source* of a "broadly psychodynamic" understanding of dreams. There have been many advances since Freud and many revisions of his main ideas, but that does not change the fact that all of our "psychodynamic" approaches are thoroughly influenced by Freud. What Hobson in effect does is take all of Freud's good ideas and rename them "broadly psychodynamic"; then he takes all of Freud's bad ideas, labels them "narrowly psychoanalytic," and attacks them for being bad. Not only is this unfair to Freud, but it enables Hobson to ignore the influence of Freud's theories on his interpretations and thus to claim that he has discovered the "plain," "simple," *non*theoretical meaning of dreams.

11. Wendy Doniger challenged LaBerge along these lines in her address at the 1990 conference of the Association for the Study of Dreams: "Lucid Dreaming in the Tales from the Arabian Nights" (delivered 28 June 1990). I have questioned some of LaBerge's views on lucid dreaming and Buddhist thought ("Lucid Dreaming and Ethical Reflection" [Bulkley 1988], "Some Further Thoughts on Lucid Dreaming and Ethical Reflection" [Bulkley 1989b]).

12. It is not Gadamer's intention, I think, to contrast this with the natural scientific method in an absolute sense; the natural sciences surely engage in this "discipline of questioning and research" as well. The crucial difference lies in what the interpretation yields: an explanation that is certain, impersonal, unambiguous, and final, or a meaning that is open, subjectively influenced, ambiguous, and liable to further elaboration.

Chapter 13. The Interpretation of Dreams: Hermeneutic Principles

1. Freud does ultimately say some positive things about art. See the conclusion to *Freud and Philosophy: An Essay on Interpretation* (Ricoeur 1970).

2. For Gadamer's criticism of Plato's view of art and knowledge, see Gadamer 1975, 103.

3. On Freud's life history and its influence on his psychology, see E. Jones 1953–57; Ellenberger 1970; Clark 1980; Gay 1988.

4. I thank Antonio Zadras for bringing this point to my attention at the 1991 conference of the Association for the Study of Dreams.

5. This is one of the grounds for questioning the interpretive approaches of Freud, Hall, and Hobson: they never seem to be *surprised* by what they find. On the contrary, their dream interpretations tend merely to confirm what they already knew. This is also the basis for some of the critiques of LaBerge's approach to lucid dreaming: an excessive focus on manipulating and controlling the dream experience can diminish the surprise, the discovery of the new that so often occurs in dreams.

6. As we discovered in the first pages of this chapter, these distinctive qualities are (1) being sensory-spatial experiences, (2) appearing in different forms (written narratives, oral accounts, private memories, artistic expressions, etc.), (3) changing subtly with time and context, and (4) being influenced by the dreamer's waking consciousness.

Chapter 14. Dora's Dream: The Hermeneutic Principles in Action

1. This particular example suits our purposes for a number of reasons. First, the Dora case is relatively well known. The two dreams at the heart of the case are among the most familiar in psychological literature. Second, Dora's dreams are presented in rich detail, with abundant material on Dora's background, on her associations to the dream, and on Freud's efforts to interpret it. And third, many later psychoanalysts and critics have offered alternative interpretations of Dora's dreams, all questioning the validity of Freud's interpretation. The variety of these alternatives raises the important question of how to decide between different, and often mutually antagonistic, interpretations of the same dream. By far the fullest historical account of the Dora case is Hannah Decker's *Freud, Dora, and Vienna 1900* (1991).

2. See Marcus (1985), Ramas (1985), and Sprengnether (1985) for reflections on Freud's choice of "Dora" as a pseudonym.

3. Freud believes that the use of dreams in such a treatment is "the only practical application of which the art of interpreting dreams seems to admit" (Freud [1905] 1963, 15; see also 114).

4. Freud mentions in a note to the initial text of the dream that "in answer to an inquiry Dora told me that there had never really been a fire at their house" (Freud [1905] 1963, 64)

5. Freud expresses the same motivation later (Freud [1905] 1963, 85-93).

6. Freud says, "the elucidation of the dream seemed to me incomplete so long as a particular requirement remained unsatisfied; for, though I do not wish to insist that this requirement is a universal one, I have a predilection for discovering a means of satisfying it. A regularly formed dream stands, as it were, upon two legs, one of which is in contact with the main and current exciting cause, and the other with some momentous event in the years of childhood. The dream sets up a connection between those two factors—and it endeavors to reshape the present on the model of the remote past. For the wish which creates the dream always springs from the period of childhood; and it is continually trying to summon childhood back into reality and to correct the present day by the measure of childhood. I believed that I could already clearly detect those elements of Dora's dream which could be pieced together into an allusion to an event in childhood" (Freud [1905] 1963, 71). Freud cites his own *The Interpretation of Dreams* as support for these points.

7. On this point, Steven Marcus has commented that the Dora case shows us "Freud the relentless investigator pushing on no matter what. The Freud that we meet with here is a demonic Freud, a Freud who is the servant of his *daimon*. That *daimon* in whose service Freud knows no limits is the spirit of science, the truth, or 'reality'—it does not matter which; for him they are all the same. Yet it must be emphasized that the 'reality' Freud insists upon is very different from the 'reality' that Dora is claiming and clinging to. And it has to be admitted that not only does Freud overlook for the most part this critical difference; he also adopts no measures for dealing with it. The demon of interpretation has taken hold of him, and it is this power that presides over the case of Dora" (Marcus 1985, 85).

8. Another instance of this is his conviction that dreams must always represent the fulfillment of an infantile wish. We have seen that this is an untenable assertion, and thus the legitimacy of Freud's interpretation of Dora's dream is further called into question.

9. However, the Dora case as a whole may well have taught Freud something about transference and counter-transference—which would account for his sense of urgency about writing the case out.

10. Ramas does note that "One can never, of course, disprove a dream interpretation, especially three-quarters of a century after the fact" (Ramas 1985, 167).

Chapter 15. The Concept of Root Metaphors

1. See, for example, Black 1962 and Goodman 1978.

2. Lakoff and Johnson cite the metaphor "time is money" as an example of

this process in modern Western culture (as we discussed briefly in chapter 2). They describe the way that the development of industrialized work in our culture has led us to treat time as a valuable commodity, a quantifiable resource which can be "invested," "saved," "borrowed," "budgeted," and "lost." The treatment of time as money is by no means a natural or universal phenomenon—there are many cultures where time is regarded in a totally different manner (Lakoff and Johnson 8–9, 64–68). But the economic practices of our culture have developed in such a way that the metaphor "time is money" makes *sense* to us—it helps us get along effectively in our culture.

3. "Since the natural dimensions of categories (perceptual, functional, etc.) arise out of our interactions with the world, the properties given by those dimensions are not properties of objects *in themselves* but are, rather, interactional properties, based on the human perceptual apparatus, human conceptions of function, etc. It follows from this that true statements made in terms of human categories typically do not predicate *properties of objects in themselves* but rather *interactional properties* that make sense only relative to human functioning" (Lakoff and Johnson 1980, 163–64).

4. This passage continues: "There are many celebrated examples to show that sentences, in general, are not true or false independent of human purposes:

France is hexagonal.

Missouri is a parallelogram.

The earth is a sphere.

Italy is boot-shaped.

An atom is a tiny solar system with the nucleus at the center and electrons whirling around it.

Light consists of particles.

Light consists of waves.

Each of these sentences is true for certain purposes, in certain respects, and in certain contexts. 'France is hexagonal' and 'Missouri is a parallelogram' can be true for a schoolboy who has to draw rough maps but not for professional cartographers. 'The earth is a sphere' is true as far as most of us are concerned, but it won't do for precisely plotting the orbit of a satellite. No self-respecting physicist has believed since 1914 that an atom is a tiny solar system, but it is true for most of us relative to our everyday functioning and our general level of sophistication in mathematics and physics. 'Light consists of particles' seems to contradict 'light consists of waves', but both are taken as true by physicists relative to which aspects of light are picked out by different experiments" (Lakoff and Johnson 164–65).

5. Thus, for example, in Christianity the metaphors of *creator, governor, and redeemer* have, Browning says, served as "metaphors of ultimacy," representing the nature of humanity's relationship with God; in Buddhism, metaphors of the

void function to portray the most determinative context of experience (Browning 1983, 58).

6. Browning comments, "Whereas Freud's models of constancy and death were based upon metaphors of inertia and resistance to growth, Rogers's model sees life, even the life of troubled and anxious people, through metaphors of forward movement, growth, and expansion" (Browning 1987, 66).

7. Browning argues that "the theory of natural selection as a model for both evolutionary change and learning is also, in the hands of Skinner, a metaphor of ultimacy—a metaphor which accounts for the ultimate context of our experience . . . Not only does it refer to something real, natural selection together with environmental reinforcement *exhaust* the factors that shape and change life; there is for Skinner *nothing but* natural selection and environmental reinforcement" (Browning 1987, 98–99, emphasis in original).

8. I have drawn the term *root metaphors* from McFague's work; she says she draws it from Stephen Pepper's *World Hypotheses* (1942).

9. The deadly effects of idolatry are still very evident today. Salman Rushdie is living under a *fatwa* (death sentence) imposed by certain Islamic authorities for the allegedly blasphemous contents of his novel *The Satanic Verses*. The main passages at issue are the dreams of one of the characters, dreams which reenvision the experiences of Muhammed as he is called by the archangel Gabriel. These dreams are beautiful, moving, deeply spiritual reflections on the heart of the Islamic faith—they are earnest, probing explorations of the root metaphors of Islam. Rushdie is fully aware of the playful, metaphorical character of this exploration, as the refrain "It was so, it was not" is repeated throughout the novel. Sadly, some (but *not* all, it must be noted) Muslims are violently opposed to such playful encounters with their root metaphors and are willing to kill those who question the traditional interpretations.

10. Ricoeur says, "Hermeneutics seems to me to be animated by this double motivation: willingness to suspect, willingness to listen; vow of rigor, vow of obedience. In our time we have not finished doing away with *idols* and we have barely begun to listen to *symbols*. It may be that this situation, in its apparent distress, is instructive: it may be that extreme iconoclasm belongs to the restoration of meaning" (Ricoeur 1970, 27).

11. Ricoeur admits that this teleology is mostly *implicit* in Freud and that Freud does not develop it well; see Ricoeur 1970, 472–93 for Ricoeur's account of Freud's implicit teleology.

12. As noted in chap. 2, root metaphors are in this sense very similar to Paul Tillich's notion of "Ultimate Concern" (Tillich 1948, 1951–63), to David Tracy's account of "limit questions" (1975), and to Mircea Eliade's view of the great symbols of world mythology (Eliade 1957, 1960, 1965).

13. I want to thank Jane White Lewis for bringing this important question to my attention at the 1991 conference of the Association for the Study of Dreams.

14. Adam Kuper (1979, 1983) has done the most extensive work applying structuralist methods to the study of dreams. See Wendy Doniger O'Flaherty (1989) for an excellent critique of structuralism and especially of structuralist approaches to psychological issues

15. We need to make one cautionary point here about root metaphors. This point concerns what the concept of root metaphors is *not*, which is a definition of the "essence" of religion. The history of religious studies is littered with the refuse of such definitions, and we should avoid adding our own work to that ignoble heap. Religion is many, many things, and while I think that root metaphors play an important role in any religious tradition I see no reason for us to assert that root metaphors are *the* essence of religion per se. The virtue of the root metaphor concept for our project is that it enables us to recognize and investigate people's religious beliefs (i.e., their beliefs about the ultimate existential questions of human life), whether those people are church-goers, atheists, or whatever. The concept of root metaphors does, I grant, presuppose that all people are guided by some sort of essentially religious or spiritual belief and that all people are thus in some sense "religious." That is a claim I feel comfortable defending (see Ferre 1963). Indeed, one important potential of the study of dreams and religious meaning is that it can reveal the root metaphors of people who are *not* formally religious or who are *not* fully conscious of their spiritual beliefs. But this is something very different from a grand definition of "religion."

Chapter 16. Flying with Great Eagles and Eating Short Bananas: Examples of Root Metaphors in Dreams

1. The Ojibwa managed to preserve much of their traditional culture into the twentieth century, primarily because their region was not well suited to white settlement. Hallowell does acknowledge the limits of our knowledge of the dream fast: "Many years ago Paul Radin published a sample of dreams from the dream fasts of Ojibwa boys. It should be emphasized, as Radin pointed out, that all the drams of this type which we have on record were told by adults in later life, in some cases, filtered through another person. We have no information whatever on dreams obtained immediately or even after a short time after the dream itself" (283–84).

2. Hallowell argues that the translation of *pawaganak* as "other-than-human being," rather than "supernatural being", is very important to understanding Ojibwa culture (Hallowell 273–79).

3. Hallowell notes that "this account was repeated to me by a man who said he had heard the dreamer narrate it when he was an old man" (Hallowell 1955, 403). Our access to this dream is thus very indirect, to the point where its legiti-

macy as a piece of evidence for our project comes into question. Nevertheless, I believe that our use of this dream account is legitimate for the following reasons: (1) Hallowell says that *all* Ojibwa dream reports are subject to taboo restrictions, so it is unlikely that we could ever get much "closer" to the actual dream experience than we do in this case (Hallowell 1961, 41) and (2) we have enough solid knowledge about the general contours of the Ojibwa dream fast that even if this particular dream report is not perfectly certain (as no Ojibwa dream report ever is), we can still make justifiable claims about the dream fast experiences having the characteristics of root metaphors.

4. This is a primary the concern of existentialist dream interpreters, like Medard Boss (1958, 1977) and Erik Craig (1988), who emphasize the dreams are *real* experiences, and not "mere metaphors" standing for something *else* which is the "really" real meaning.

5. Hallowell says that in this dream "the instability of outward form in both human and other-than-human persons is succinctly dramatized. Individuals of both categories undergo metamorphosis. In later life the boy will recall how he first saw the "master" of the golden eagles in his anthropomorphic guise, followed by his transformation into avian form; at the same time he will recall his own metamorphosis into a bird" (Hallowell 1961, 43).

6. Hallowell also comments in *Ojibwa Ontology, Behavior, and World View* that the dream fast "was the opportunity of a lifetime. Every special aptitude, all a man's subsequent successes and the explanation of many of his failures, hinged upon the help of the 'guardian spirits' he obtained at this time, rather than upon his own native endowments or the help of his fellow *anicinabek*. If a boy received 'blessings' during his puberty fast and, as a man, could call upon the help of other-than-human persons when he needed them he was well prepared for meeting the vicissitudes of life" (Hallowell 1961, 46).

7. Unfortunately, we do not have further information to help us understand what the bananas growing from his hair or the specific differences between the two types of banana might mean.

8. At this point the study of dreams and religion touches on the subject of conversion, a topic of much interest to psychologists of religion. See James [1900] 1958; Starbuck 1899; Leuba 1929; Wulff 1991; Crapps 1986.

9. Mrs. M. has recently engaged in the spiritual exercises of St. Ignatius and is seeking to join a Catholic worship community.

10. Ewing claims that one of the major components of the Sufi initiation dreams is "the iconic relationship of the dream to the dreamer's particular situation and conflicts—that is, its metaphorical representation of them through imagery" (Ewing 1989, 60).

11. Ewing says of Ahmad Sahib specifically that "ultimately, his dream

became the cornerstone of a new self representation and the basis for a new type of relationship with others. He incorporated the dream narrative into a 'story' which served as the framework for a self representation and provided a scenario for his interaction with others as a sufi" (Ewing 1989, 65).

12. On the relationship between dreams and death, see Von Franz 1986 and O'Flaherty 1984. There is an intimate relationship between sleep, dreams, and death in various mythologies; see e.g., *Gilgamesh*, *The Odyssey*, Hesiod's *Theogony*, *The Tibetan Book of the Dead*, and the Hindu epics *The Mahabharata* and *The Ramayana*.

13. These six examples are not, however, to be taken as full interpretations of the dreams. There are certainly many other meanings to these dreams besides the ones we have discussed. Our interest has simply been to understand how these dreams express genuine root metaphors.

14. Levin (1990) has reviewed the recent literature on dream functions and concludes that one of the main functions of dreams is to help humans adapt to new information, experiences, and conditions and to integrate them into our personality.

15. It is worth noting that Mary's was a recurrent dream—suggesting, perhaps, that when the main force of the dream is a more negative rejection of a faith or worldview, without any *new*, positive values and meanings to replace it being immediately apparent, the dreamer is more resistant to accepting the dream, and a repetition of the dream results. Taylor makes a point in his discussion of Mary's dream that is very much in line with our discoveries in this section: "there is a strong tendency for recurrent dreams to be about the deeper layers of the dreamer's personal 'myth'—that essential, archetypal, symbolic story that a person tends to act out, over and over again in various forms, over the course of his or her entire life. Recurrent dreams (particularly recurrent dreams with particularly strong affect, such as Mary's dream of the 'blistering paint'), often turn out to be *concise metaphoric statements of as-yet-unfulfilled aspects of the dreamer's fundamental 'life task', or the 'deepest value conflict' in his/her life*, not just in the moment, but over the entire span of time that the dream has been recurring" (Taylor 1992, 287, emphasis added).

Chapter 17. Root Metaphors and the Eight Paths into the Dream Wilderness

1. This is not, of course, the only concept that could provide us with such an understanding of dreams and religious meaning; it is simply the only one that has, to my knowledge, been presented.

2. Evaluating Jung's ideas is always a difficult matter, because he so frequently makes vague, contradictory statements about subjects that, it must be admitted, do not allow for clear, unambiguous analysis. It is very easy to criticize Jung, but very hard to criticize him *well*. These brief comments do not themselves

accomplish that arduous task but rather suggest the direction in which I believe a fair, balanced critique of Jung might go.

3. These suggestions have been further explored by Gackenbach and LaBerge (1988), Kelzer (1987), and Gillespie (1988a, 1988b, 1990).

4. This leads into ethical considerations, which LaBerge and I have debated in some detail: see Bulkley 1988, 1989b; and LaBerge 1988.

5. Buddhists, however, do address the issue of the relevance of their root metaphors, as they offer additional teachings on the moral virtue of compassion; this checks the ethical anarchy that could result from an unqualified radical idealism (see O'Flaherty 1984). Here the connection with Buddhism works against LaBerge, for unlike Buddhists he fails to consider the problematic consequences of his radical idealism.

6. Rizzuto (1979) and Coles (1990) make this same criticism of Freud as well. Their works make strong arguments for the positive, adaptive value of religious belief, arguments all the more compelling for depending directly upon the psychoanalytic tradition.

7. In particular, Hall's content analysis method can help us explore extremely long and complicated dreams as well as long series of dreams. The content analysis method is *not* a mere tool, untainted by any theoretical or subjective biases; however, it can be a useful guide if its limitations are recognized and accounted for.

8. I make a similar argument in "Interdisciplinary Dreaming: Hobson's Successes and Failures" (Bulkley 1991d).

Chapter 18. Towards Integration: Interpreting "Being Dissected by the Evil Alien"

1. I want to thank Sybe Terwee for bringing this question to my attention at the 1991 conference of the Association for the Study of Dreams, in Chicago.

2. Perhaps the reason why this goal appears so suspicious to some people is because *integrated* often appears to be synonymous with *harmonious*, *serene*, *conflict-free*. But if we are to engage in truly interdisciplinary inquiry, we must reject such connotations. To integrate different approaches towards dreams is *not* to "harmonize" them, to make peace between them, to dissolve their disagreements. Rather, it is to develop an understanding of how their differing and at times sharply conflicting approaches provide us with a richer, broader, more sophisticated view of dreams. Indeed, it is hard to imagine what a "harmonious" theory of dreams would look like. And dreams themselves are usually anything but harmonious.

Our attempt here at an interdisciplinary integration will not seek to eliminate the paradoxes and conflicts that are the very essence of dreams. On the contrary, we will try to achieve a deeper appreciation for the truths these paradoxes and conflicts reveal to us. We are justified, then, in at least taking this risk and attempting an interdisciplinary integration. Whether anything comes of it remains to be seen.

3. Søren Kierkegaard argues in *Concluding Unscientific Postscript* ([1846] 1946) that true religious insight is the ability to perceive the power of the divine in the seemingly ordinary events of our daily lives.

4. This point bears emphasis. Many dream researchers have shown that the majority of dreams are fragmentary, disorganized, and related to only our most mundane and ordinary concerns. Researchers have also found that the vast majority of our dreaming experiences are not remembered—we forget all but the tiniest fraction of our total dreams. These findings would directly challenge a claim that *all* dreams have religious meaning. However, our claim is a much more modest one: it is that *some* dreams *do* have religious meaning and *any* dream *may* have religious meaning. In this regard, Hunt's study (1989) distinguishing the multiple forms of dreaming is very helpful. The research finding that *most* dreams seem to be mundane, ordinary, and religiously meaningless does not preclude the possibility that *some* dreams may be transcendent, extraordinary, and religiously meaningful.

5. These questions do *not*, I want to emphasize, constitute a program for dream interpretation; they do *not* represent a total or complete approach to understanding a dream or dream series. Such questions will, I believe, be most helpful if they are used in conjunction with other, more general approaches to dream interpretation—say, with the approaches presented in Ullman and Zimmerman 1979; Bosnak 1988; Gendlin 1986; Taylor 1983, 1992; Delaney 1979, 1991.

6. There have been numerous studies and books in recent years on the occurrence of powerful dreams during times of crisis and transition: for example, Cartwright et al.'s work (1984) with women going through separations and divorces, Maybruck's study (1989) of dreams during pregnancy, Von Franz's research (1986) on dreams surrounding the experience of death, Bosnak's work (1989) with a man dying from AIDS, O'Connor's analysis (1986) of dreams occurring during the "mid-life crisis," and Siegal's review (1990) of dreams at various "turning points" in a person's life.

7. Presented in this way, Ricoeur would seem to propose a two-stage process: *first* the hermeneutics of suspicion, *then* the hermeneutics of restoration. I believe that in the *practice* of dream interpretation, the process is actually more of a back-and-forth movement between the two hermeneutical strategies—approaching the dream(s) from one direction, then the other, then back again, over and over.

8. All of the dream explorers we have examined have based their research and writings in part (and at times, in large part) on their own dreams. The quality and significance of their findings justifies this turn to autobiographical material. Many fields of scholarship shun autobiography as tainting one's research. Whether or not that is a valid position in other fields, it is certainly a foolish one to take in

the study of dreams. Researchers have gained tremendous knowledge from exploring their own dreams, knowledge they could not have reached if they had strictly bracketed out all of their own personal experiences. Furthermore, a dream research method that uses *only* those dreams collected in the scientifically controlled environment of a sleep laboratory has its own problems and limitations, as Hunt has discussed (Hunt 1989, 42–55). Such a method seems to inhibit the emergence of the many different forms of dreaming experience and thus to narrow artificially the scope of dream research.

9. It's also worth noting that my family had a decidedly cool attitude towards Loren. They were baffled to the point of annoyance by our undefinable relationship, and they did not take kindly to Loren's frequent and unsolicited although usually accurate feminist editorial comments.

10. This is a literary conceit, of course. What follows is *my* belief about what the eight dream explorers might see in the Evil Alien dream. If this section were a *test* of the validity of their positions, I would have to present a far more comprehensive analysis of the dream in order to do justice to their theories of interpretation. However, this is *not* such a test. The point of this section is merely to illustrate the possibilities their methods open up. Insofar as my use of their methods illustrates some of those possibilities, that is all that matters here.

11. In this sense my dream supports one of the most often criticized portions of Freud's theory, namely his account of nightmares. The occurrence of anxiety dreams seems to dispute Freud's claim that a wish underlies every dream, for who *wishes* to be chased, tormented, attacked, etc.? Freud's primary response is that nightmares are a failure of the dreamwork to disguise the undesirable wish effectively enough; the wish is "too hot to handle"; it creates intolerable anxiety, and the dreamer wakes up in self-defense. That is why, Freud argues, so many nightmares end just at the scariest part—the anxiety has become too much to bear, and the dreamer has to wake up. Freud's theory here strikes many people (myself included) as a rather desperate attempt to save his wish-fulfillment theory of dreaming. But I am intrigued by his second response to the problem of nightmares. Some nightmares, Freud says, *are* stimulated by wishes, *masochistic* wishes of punishment. Many dream researchers see this notion as so ridiculous that it is not even worth refuting. I also thought it was improbable, until I began reflecting carefully on my Evil Alien dream. Unlike most nightmares, this dream did *not* end at the scariest part; it continued to a definitive conclusion, suggesting that perhaps I did *not* truly want to escape the torment I was suffering. This observation on the dream's form fits with my understanding of the dream's content, which deals with my ambivalent feelings about leaving my family's world. Part of me, I realize, does *not* want to leave, and believes that I *should* be punished for trying to leave. Although I still disagree with the theory of dreams as wish fulfillments, I believe that Freud is right in arguing that dreams express many, many different kinds of wishes.

12. Jung is often challenged for his seemingly ambiguous stance on the nature of evil. As Andrew Samuels notes, "At different times in his career, Jung was

severely criticized by theologians for his insistence upon the reality of evil and the paradoxical nature of the God-image. We cannot know what good and evil are in themselves, he insisted, but we perceive them as judgements and in relation to experience. He saw them not as facts but as human responses to facts and, therefore, neither, in his opinion, could be regarded as a diminution or privation of the other. Psychologically, he accepted both as 'equally real'. Evil takes its place as an effective and menacing reality in opposition to good, a psychological reality that expresses itself symbolically both in religious tradition (as the devil) and in personal experience" (Samuels 1986, 57). Browning (1987) is one of the most recent theologians to question Jung's view of evil as both relative power and an absolute power in human life. I grant, with Browning and others, that such a view is intellectually inconsistent. But based on my dream experiences, I nevertheless believe that Jung is right. Evil is *both* a relative power that we can overcome and redeem *and* an absolute power that we can no more than try to keep at a distance from us.

13. To be fair to Hall, my series of dreams should be analyzed by someone other than me in order to test the usefulness of the content analysis method.

14. This line of reflection also relates to my association of the Evil Alien's face with a vagina and with breasts: these being primal images of the source of life, creativity, and nurturance, which have been warped, darkened, and perverted into a source of destruction and death.

15. The element of fire in the dream has many interesting symbolic aspects to it. Fire appears in two places in the dream: the knight stands outside on the fire escape, and Scott and I fight in the fireplace. The first is a reference to fleeing from fire, the second to the place where fire occurs in a controlled setting. Fire is one of the great religious and mythic symbols, with a nearly endless array of meanings. Of this vast array, these are the meanings that are particularly striking to me: the ritual use of fire as an agent of transmutation, destroying something in order to purify it and renew it; the "culture hero" myths in which a bold human steals the secret of fire from the gods and as a consequence brings divine wrath down upon himself; and the use of fire imagery to express passion, rage, and lust. The knight standing out on the fire escape represents, I believe, a part of me that wants to break completely with my parents. Perhaps this reflects a fear of their wrath for having sought independence from them; perhaps it also reflects a desire to avoid the painful process of transmuting my relationship with them, of developing a new and better relationship. The fight with Scott in the fireplace seems to express my fight with my own rebellious, anticultural urges. Maybe this fight, although terribly painful and violent, *is* the fire of transmutation; we are *within* the fireplace, our fight itself could be seen as a fire.

16. More specifically, we have found in this example that each of the eight dream explorers has valuable insights to offer about this particular dream and that a dialogue may be generated among their eight different views, a dialogue that yields new insights not achievable from any one perspective alone. The three criteria for a valid interpretation (as outlined in chapter 13) have been met: (1) we

have integrated the various parts of the dream with the dream narrative as a whole; (2) the meanings that emerged fit with the knowledge we have of my life context at the time of the dream, and with the knowledge about dreams we have from the various dream theories; and (3) we have achieved the primary purpose of relating this extremely disturbing dream to my life, creating a bridge between the dream and myself. We should admit, however, that another purpose in exploring this dream has been to validate the principles and methods we have been developing in this work, that is, a purpose that is involved in any dream interpretation used as an example to illustrate a theory or method. In some cases such a purpose may wield an undue influence on the interpretation. In this instance, I feel confident that the meanings that have emerged are no less real or valuable for me than those meanings that would have emerged had I conducted this interpretation in a different context.

17. Disgust is another prominent emotion I feel in the dream. The graphic cutting and dismembering of my body and the numerous food references all contribute to this strong sensation of nausea and sickness. I feel certain that this is related to my long history of stomach sensitivity, which reached a peak some four or five years following the Evil Alien dream. One guess is that this physical disgust reflects the way my encounter with evil disrupts the process of nourishment and growth; my fear of stomach problems, then, would stem from a fear of provoking those evil, destructive powers to return to my life.

18. Erikson expresses this quality of hope very eloquently: "Hope is the enduring belief in the attainability of fervent wishes, in spite of the dark urges and rages which mark the beginning of existence" (Erikson 1964, 118).

19. To the extent that my dream responds to the pressures generated by the conjunction of these three different developmental struggles, it responds to a cultural crisis as well as a personal crisis. Many developmental psychologists (Erikson 1963, Gilligan 1982, Kegan 1982) have argued that contemporary American culture puts an inordinate amount of pressure on late adolescents. By the time they leave school they are supposed to have firm personal identities, to be capable of engaging in intimate, procreative relationships, and to be competent to enter the social and economic world of work. Developmental psychologists claim that our culture does not adequately prepare adolescents to meet these developmental tasks. Erikson in particular refers to the initiatory rituals of other cultures as methods that more effectively guide adolescents through these crises (we saw an example of this kind of ritual with the Ojibwa dream fast in chapter 16). These insights from developmental psychology add to my sense that the Evil Alien dream can be interpreted as a reflection of my unfulfilled need for an initiatory experience.

20. The feeling I have in the dream that there is some sort of "precedent" for this problem is interesting in this regard. My mother experienced a bitter and very painful break with her family soon after she graduated from college; similarly, my father had deep troubles with his family, and he made it a lifelong goal to be completely self-sufficient and independent from them. The "precedent," then, seems

to refer to a pattern of establishing your own identity by sharply separating yourself from your family. I had always wondered, however, about the emotional suffering my parents experienced as a result of their breaks with their families. I had always hoped that we would not have to reach a point where the only way we could get along was to hate each other. But the first scene of this dream makes me realize that we are perilously close to that point. The family tradition is to reject your family. Will I carry that tradition on? If not, how then will I resolve the conflict?

21. This has remained, however, a live conflict for me, as I pursued this desire for understanding in very competitive and success-oriented graduate school programs.

22. Here is where the dream provided an impulse to moral action. Since the Evil Alien dream I have increasingly felt that a better understanding of dreams and nightmares can make a valuable contribution towards the resolution of a variety of our culture's ills. Virtually all of my writings on dreams have addressed moral and cultural questions in some sense, and chapter 20 of this work directly discusses these questions. The challenge of the Evil Alien dream to create a new relationship with my community has impelled me to engage in the moral task of bringing my understanding of dreams to bear on the problems of contemporary culture.

Chapter 19. Why All the Interest Now in the Religious Meaning of Dreams?

1. Although leaders of the Enlightenment like Descartes, Locke, Hume, and Kant tried to find a legitimate place for *some* religious beliefs within their rationalistic philosophies, the overall trend they initiated was one of debunking *all* religious ideas and values.

2. It is true, of course, that religion has not *totally* disappeared in the modern West; in the United States, for example, the vast majority of people still profess adherence to a formal religious institution. See Gary Wills, *Under God: Religion and American Politics* (1990).

3. I am particularly indebted to the work of Peter Homans on the subject of secularization. See his *Jung in Context: Modernity and the Making of a Psychology* (1979) and *The Ability to Mourn: Disillusionment and the Social Origins of Psychoanalysis* (1989).

4. Not all decline theorists are so optimistic; while Marx, Frazier, and Dewey see the decline of religion as positive, Weber, Rieff, Durkheim, and Berger all have their reservations about what has been lost.

5. Secularization theories of both types devote special attention to the *privatization* of religion in the modern West, the trend towards religion's now being a matter of personal, subjective belief, part of the individual's private life rather than of the community's public life. Decline theorists see privatization as further evi-

dence that religion is in retreat, backpeddaling into ever smaller, more constricted, more irrelevant areas of life; transposition theorists see privatization as a positive development, a liberation of religion from the constraints of social regulation and a new opportunity for individuals to discover their own true religious beliefs. Some of the theorists see this as a positive process, while others see it in a negative light.

6. Domhoff's book is, to my knowledge, the only full-length sociological study of dreams. For other important work in this area of dream study, see Breughman 1982; Hillman 1987; Ullman 1987; Dombeck 1991.

7. Lucy Breughman, in *The Rediscovery of Inner Experience*, gives a sociological critique of recent (American) interest in dreams that has some ties to Domhoff's analysis. She argues that recent books on dreams offer a muddled view of dreams: on the one hand, admonishing people to adopt a "trustful receptivity" towards their dreams and yet, on the other hand, encouraging them to manipulate and tinker with their dreams as well. Bruegghman claims that the authors of these books try to "domesticate" the often unpleasant aspects of dreams and stimulate the desire for "magical solutions" to real-life problems. Exactly as Freud, Hall, and Hobson do, she sees this approach to dreams as a holdover of prescientific superstitions: "In fact, much of the self-help literature [on dreams] might well be described as a direct continuation of this ancient folk tradition, with a veneer of psychology added" (Bruegghman 1982, 18).

8. This argument is essentially the same one we made in developing the root metaphor concept—modern Western science is as "religious" as Christianity or Buddhism to the extent that it is fundamentally oriented by certain root metaphors and that it provides people with responses to the ultimate existential questions of human life.

9. This is not to deny, of course, that many people feel perfectly comfortable with the modern West's values. The point is, however, that those people who do *not* feel comfortable with those values are not necessarily "resisting" the truth of those values, and they are not necessarily ignorant, immature, or primitive.

10. Again, as I emphasized in chapter 18, the *practice* of dream interpretation involves a back-and-forth movement between these interpretive methods, rather than a linear, two-step process, as this passage might suggest.

Chapter 20. The Future of the Wilderness of Dreams

1. This claim is supported by the fact that some of the earliest written texts from a number of different cultures have been texts on dream interpretation.

2. I have discussed some of these potentials of dream study for children's education in "Teaching Dreamwork to Children: Helping Them Face a Complex World" (Bulkley 1991b). Calvin Hall also discusses the values of teaching children

about dreams (Hall 1966, 218–20), but unfortunately his reliance on the now-suspect findings of Kilton Stewart on the dream practices of the Senoi render his argument less compelling.

BIBLIOGRAPHY

Abraham, Karl. [1909] 1955. Dreams and Myths: A Study in Folk Psychology. In Clinical Papers and Essays on Psychoanalysis. New York: Basic Books.

Adler, Alfred. 1956. *The Individual Psychology of Alfred Adler*. Edited by Heinz L. Ansbacher and Rowena R. Ansbacher. New York: Harper Torchbooks.

Apuleius. 1960. *The Golden Ass*. Translated by Jack Lindsay. Bloomington: Indiana University Press.

Aristotle. 1941a. *Nicomachean Ethics*. Translated by Richard McKeon. In *The Collected Works of Aristotle*. Edited by Richard McKeon. New York: Random House.

———. 1941b. *On Dreams*. Translated by Richard McKeon. In *The Collected Works of Aristotle*. Edited by Richard McKeon. New York: Random House.

———. 1941c. *On Prophesying by Dreams*. Translated by Richard McKeon. In *The Collected Works of Aristotle*. Edited by Richard McKeon. New York: Random House.

Artemidorus. 1975. *The Interpretation of Dreams*. Translated by Robert J. White. Park Ridge, N.J.: Noyes Press.

Aserinsky, Eugene, and Kleitman, Nathaniel. 1953. Regularly Occurring Periods of Eye Motility, and Concomitant Phenomena, during Sleep. *Science* 118: 273–74.

———. 1955. "Two Types of Ocular Motility Occurring in Sleep." *Journal of Applied Physiology* 8: 1–10.

Augustine. 1961. *Confessions*. Translated by R. S. Pine-Coffin. London: Penguin Books.

———. 1971. *City of God*. Translated by Henry Bettenson. London: Penguin Books.

Barbour, Ian. 1974. *Myths, Models, and Paradigms: A Comparative Study in Science and Religion*. New York: Harper and Row.

Bellah, Robert, Madsen, Richard, Sullivan, William M., Swidler, Ann, and Tipton, Steven M. 1985. *Habits of the Heart: Individualism and Commitment in American Life*. Berkeley and Los Angeles: University of California Press.

Benedict, Ruth Fulton. 1922. The Vision in Plains Culture. *American Anthropologist* 24 (1): 1–23.

Berakhot. 1948. In *The Babylonian Talmud: Seder Zera'im*, vol. 1. Edited by I. Epstein. Translated by Maurice Simon. London: Soncino.

Berman, Paul. 1992. *Debating P.C.: The Controversy Over Political Correctness on College Campuses*. New York: Laurel/Dell.

Berger, Peter. 1967. *The Sacred Canopy: Elements of a Sociological Theory of Religion*. Garden City, New York: Doubleday.

Bernheimer, Charles, and Kahane, Claire, eds. 1985. *In Dora's Case: Freud—Hysteria—Feminism*. New York: Columbia University Press.

Bernstein, Richard. 1988. *Beyond Objectivism and Relativism: Science, Hermeneutics, and Praxis*. Philadelphia: University of Pennsylvania Press.

Bhattacharyya, Pandit Ramesh Chandra, ed. 1970. *Interpretation of Dreams According to the Brahmavaivarta Purana*. Calcutta, India: P. B. Roy, Prabartak Printing and Halftone.

Bible. Revised Standard Version.

Bilu, Yoram. 1979. Sigmund Freud and Rabbi Yehudah: On a Jewish Mystical Tradition of "Psychoanalytic" Dream Interpretation. *Journal of Psychological Anthropology* 2: 443–63.

Black, Max. 1962. *Models and Metaphors*. Ithaca: Cornell University Press.

Blakeslee, Sandra. 1992. Scientists Unraveling Chemistry of Dreams. *New York Times*, 7 Jan., B5.

Bland, Nathaniel. 1856. On the Muhammedan Science of Tabir; or, Interpretation of Dreams. *The Journal of the Royal Asiatic Society of Great Britain and Ireland* 16: 118–71.

Bleicher, Josef. 1980. *Contemporary Hermeneutics: Hermeneutics as Method, Philosophy, and Critique*. Boston: Routledge & Kegan Paul.

Bloom, Allan. 1987. *The Closing of the American Mind: How Higher Education Has Failed Democracy and Impoverished the Souls of Today's Students*. New York: Simon and Schuster.

Blumenberg, Hans. 1983. *The Legitimacy of the Modern Age*. Translated by Robert M. Wallace. Cambridge: MIT Press.

Bonuzzi, Luciano. 1975. About the Origins of the Scientific Study of Sleep and Dreaming. In *The Experimental Study of Human Sleep: Methodological Problems*. Edited by Gabrielle C. Lairy and Piero Salzarulo. New York: Elsevier Scientific Publishing.

Bosnak, Robert. 1988. *A Little Course in Dreams*. Boston: Shambhala.

———. 1989. *Dreaming With an AIDS Patient: An Intimate Look Inside the Dreams of a Gay Man with AIDS by his Analyst*. Boston: Shambhala.

Boss, Medard. 1958. *The Analysis of Dreams*. New York: Philosophical Library.

———. 1977. *I Dreamt Last Night . . .* New York: Gardner Press.

Brennan, John. 1993. Dreams, Divination, and Statecraft in Chinese Poetry and Prose Commentary. In *The Dream and the Text: Essays on Language and Litera-*

ture. Edited by Carol Schreier Rupprecht. Albany: State University of New York Press.

Breton, Andre. [1924] 1965. First Surrealist Manifesto. Translated by Patrick Waldberg. In *Surrealism*. Edited by Patrick Waldberg. London: Oxford University Press.

———. [1927] 1965. Surrealism and Painting. Translated by Patrick Waldberg. In *Surrealism*. Edited by Patrick Waldberg. London: Oxford University Press.

———. [1929] 1965. Second Surrealist Manifesto. Translated by Patrick Waldberg. In *Surrealism*. Edited by Patrick Waldberg. London: Oxford University Press.

———. [1932] 1990. *Communicating Vessels*. Translated by Mary Ann Caws and Geoffrey T. Harris. Lincoln, Nebraska: University of Nebraska Press.

Breughman, Lucy. 1982. *The Rediscovery of Inner Experience*. Chicago: Nelson-Hall.

Brod, Carol. 1991. The Girl Who Was Afraid to Dream: Psychotherapy of an Adolescent. Paper presented at the Eighth International Conference of the Association for the Study of Dreams, Charlottesville, 26 June.

Brook, Stephen, ed. 1987. *The Oxford Book of Dreams*. Oxford: Oxford University Press.

Brown, Norman O. 1969. *Hermes the Thief*. 2d ed. New York: Wiley.

Browning, Don. 1983. *Religious Ethics and Pastoral Care*. Philadelphia: Fortress Press.

———. 1987. *Religious Thought and the Modern Psychologies: A Critical Conversation in the Theology of Culture*. Philadelphia: Fortress Press.

Bubner, Rudiger. 1981. *Modern German Philosophy*. Translated by Eric Matthews. New York: Cambridge University Press.

Bulkley, Kelly. 1988. Lucid Dreaming and Ethical Reflection. *Lucidity Letter* 7 (2): 13–16.

———. 1989a. Salman Rushdie's *The Satanic Verses* (Review). *Dream Network Bulletin* 8 (3): 24.

———. 1989b. Some Further Thoughts on Lucid Dreaming and Ethical Reflection. *Lucidity Letter* 8 (2): 41–43.

———. 1990a. Akira Kurusawa's Dreams (Review). *Newsletter of the Association for the Study of Dreams* 7 (5): 1–3.

———. 1990b. Jacob's Ladder: Dreams and Consciousness, Hollywood Style (Review). *Lucidity Letter* 9 (2): 137–39.

———. 1991a. Telling Stories about Dreaming. *Newsletter of the Association for the Study of Dreams* 8 (1): 6–8.

———. 1991b. Teaching Dreamwork to Children: Helping Them Face a Complex World. *Dream Network Journal* 10 (1): 14–27.

———. 1991c. The Quest for Transformational Experience: Dreams and Environmental Ethics. *Environmental Ethics* 13 (2): 151–63.

———. 1991d. Interdisciplinary Dreaming: Hobson's Successes and Failures. *Dreaming* 1 (3): 225–34.

———. 1991e. Dreaming to Heal the Earth. *Dream Network Journal* 10 (2): 8–10, 55.

———. 1992. Freddy's Dead (Review). *Newsletter of the Association for the Study of Dreams* 9 (1): 1–3.

———. 1993. The Evil Dreams of *Gilgamesh*: An Interdisciplinary Approach to Dreams in Mythological Texts. In *The Dream and the Text: Essays on Language and Literature*. Edited by Carol Schreier Rupprecht. Albany: State University of New York Press.

Burridge, Kenelm. 1960. *Mambu: A Melanesian Millennium*. London: Methuen.

Campbell, Joseph. 1949. *The Hero With a Thousand Faces*. New York: Pantheon Books.

———. 1986. *The Inner Reaches of Outer Space*. New York: A. Van der Marck Editions.

Carroll, Lewis. [1865] 1988. *Alice's Adventures in Wonderland*. New York: Dilithium Press.

Cartwright, Rosalind. 1979. *Night Life: Explorations in Dreaming*. Englewood Cliffs, N.J.: Prentice-Hall.

Cartwright, Rosalind, Lloyd, S., Knight, S., and Trenholme, I. 1984. Broken Dreams: A Study of the Effects of Divorce and Depression on Dream Content. *Psychiatry* 47: 251–59.

Charsley, S. R. 1973. Dreams in an Independent African Church. *Africa: Journal of the International African Institute* 43 (3): 244–57.

———. 1987. Dreams and Purposes: An Analysis of Dream Narratives in an Independent African Church. *Africa: Journal of the International African Institute* 57 (3): 281–96.

Cicero. 1876. *On Divination*. In *Treatises of M. T. Cicero*. Translated and edited by C. D. Yonge. London: George Bell and Sons.

Clark, Ronald W. 1980. *Freud: The Man and the Cause*. New York: Random House.

Coles, Robert. 1990. *The Spiritual Life of Children*. Boston: Houghton Mifflin.

Corbin, Henri. 1966. The Visionary Dream in Islamic Spirituality. In *The Dream and Human Societies*. Edited by G. E. Von Grunebaum and Roger Callois. Berkeley and Los Angeles: University of California Press.

Cott, Nancy. 1977. *The Bonds of Womanhood: "Woman's Sphere" in New England, 1780–1835*. New Haven: Yale University Press.

Coxhead, David, and Hiller, Susan. 1976. *Dreams: Visions of the Night*. New York: Crossroad.

Craig, Erik, ed. 1988. Psychotherapy and Freedom: The Daseinanalytic Way in Psychology and Psychoanalysis. Special Issue of *Humanistic Psychologist*.

Crapanzano, Victor. 1975. Saints, Jnun, and Dreams: An Essay in Moroccan Ethnopsychology. *Psychiatry* 38: 145–59.

Crapps, Robert W. 1986. *An Introduction to Psychology of Religion*. Macon, Georgia: Mercer University Press.

Crick, Francis, and Mitchison, Graeme. 1983. The Function of Dream Sleep. *Nature* 304: 111–14.

Curley, Richard T. 1983. Dreams of Power: Social Process in a West African Religious Movement. *Africa: Journal of the International African Institute* 53 (3): 20–37.

De Ropp, Robert S. 1987. Psychadelic Drugs. In *The Encyclopedia of Religion*, vol. 12. Edited by Mircea Eliade, 46–57. Chicago: University of Chicago Press.

Decker, Hannah. 1991. *Freud, Dora, and Vienna 1900*. New York: Free Press.

Delaney, Gayle. 1979. *Living Your Dreams*. New York: Harper and Row.

———. 1991. *Breakthrough Dreaming: How to Tap the Power of Your 24-Hour Mind*. New York: Bantam.

Descola, Philippe. 1989. Head-Shrinkers versus Shrinks: Jivaroan Dream Analysis. *Man* 24: 439–50.

Devereux, George. 1956. Mohave Dreams of Omen and Power. *Tomorrow* 4(3): 17–24.

———. 1957. Dream Learning and Individual Ritual Differences in Mohave Shamanism. *American Anthropologist* 59: 1036–45.

———. 1966. Pathogenic Dreams in Non-Western Societies. In *The Dream and Human Societies*. Edited by G. E. Von Grunebaum and Roger Callois. Berkeley and Los Angeles: University of California Press.

———. 1969. *Reality and Dream: Psychotherapy of a Plains Indian*. Rev. ed. New York: Doubleday Anchor.

Dewey, John. 1973. *The Philosophy of John Dewey*. Edited by John J. McDermott. Chicago: University of Chicago Press.

Dodds, E. R. 1951. *The Greeks and the Irrational*. Berkeley and Los Angeles: University of California Press.

Dombeck, Mary-Therese. 1991. *Dreams and Professional Personhood*. Albany: State University of New York Press.

Domhoff, G. William. 1985. *The Mystique of Dreams: A Search for Utopia Through Senoi Dream Theory*. Berkeley and Los Angeles: University of California Press.

———. 1991. The Joys and Surprises of Content Analysis. Address given at the Eighth International Conference of the Association for the Study of Dreams, Charlottesville, 29 June.

Dunlop, Charles, ed. 1977. *Philosophical Essays on Dreaming*. Ithaca: Cornell University Press.

Durkheim, Emile. 1915. *The Elementary Forms of the Religious Life*. Translated by Joseph Swain. New York: Free Press.

Dylan, Bob. 1963. Talking World War III Blues. *The Freewheelin' Bob Dylan*. Columbia 8786.

———. 1965. Gates of Eden. *Bringing It All Back Home*. Columbia 9128.

Edelstein, Emma, and Edelstein, Ludwig, trans. 1975. *Asclepius: A Collection and Interpretation of the Testimonies*. New York: Arno Press.

Eggan, Dorothy. 1952. The Manifest Content of Dreams: A Challenge to Social Science. *American Anthropologist* 54: 469–85.

———. 1955. The Personal Use of Myth in Dreams. *Journal of American Folklore*. 68: 445–63.

———. 1957. Hopi Dreams and a Life History Sketch. *Primary Records in Culture and Personality* 2(16): 1–147.

Eliade, Mircea. 1954. *The Myth of the Eternal Return, or, Cosmos and History*. Translated by Willard R. Trask. Princeton: Princeton University Press.

———. 1957. *The Sacred and the Profane: The Nature of Religion*. Translated by Willard R. Trask. New York: Harcourt Brace Jovanovich.

———. 1960. *Myths, Dreams, and Mysteries: The Encounter Between Contemporary Faiths and Archaic Realities*. Translated by Willard R. Trask. New York: Harper and Row.

———. 1964. *Shamanism: Archaic Techniques of Ecstasy*. Translated by Willard R. Trask. Princeton: Princeton University Press.

———. 1965. *The Two and the One*. Translated by J. M. Cohen. Chicago: University of Chicago Press.

Eliade, Mircea, ed. 1987. *The Encyclopedia of Religion*. 16 vols. Chicago: University of Chicago Press.

Ellenberger, Henri. 1970. *The Discovery of the Unconscious: The History and Evolution of Dynamic Psychiatry*. New York: Basic Books.

Emerson, Ralph Waldo. [1844] 1904. Demonology. In *Lectures and Biographical Sketches*. Cambridge: Riverside Press.

Erikson, Erik. 1954. The Dream Specimen of Psychoanalysis. *Journal of the American Psychoanalytical Association* 2: 5–56.

———. 1963. *Childhood and Society*. 2d ed. New York: W. W. Norton and Co.

———. 1964. *Insight and Responsibility: Lectures on the Ethical Implications of Psychoanalytical Insight*. New York: W. W. Norton and Co.

———. [1962] 1985. Reality and Actuality: An Address. In *In Dora's Case: Freud—Hysteria—Feminism*. Edited by Charles Bernheimer and Claire Kahane. New York: Columbia University Press.

Evans, Christopher. 1983. *Landscapes of the Night: How and Why We Dream*, edited and completed by Peter Evans. London: V. Gollancz.

Evans-Pritchard, E. E. 1937. *Witchcraft, Oracles, and Magic among the Azande*. Oxford: Clarendon Press.

Ewing, Katherine 1989. The Dream of Spiritual Initiation and the Organization of Self Representations among Pakistani Sufis. *American Ethnologist* 16: 56–74.

Fabian, Johannes. 1966. Dreams and Charisma: "Theories of Dreams" in the Jamaa-Movement (Congo). *Anthropos* 61: 544–60.

Fahd, Toufy, ed. 1959. *Les Songes et leur interpretation*. Paris: Editions du Seuil.

———. 1966. The Dream in Medieval Islamic Society. In *The Dream and Human Societies*. Edited by G. E. Von Grunebaum and Roger Callois. Berkeley and Los Angeles: University of California Press.

Faraday, Ann. 1972. *Dream Power*. New York: Berkeley Books.

———. 1974. *The Dream Game*. New York: Harper & Row.

Ferre, Frederick. 1968. Metaphors, Models, and Religion. *Soundings* (51): 341ff.

———. 1970. The Definition of Religion. *Journal of the American Academy of Religion* 38: 3-16.

Feyerabend, Paul. 1988. *Against Method*. Rev. ed. New York: Verso.

Firth, Raymond. 1934. The Meaning of Dreams in Tikopia. In *Essays Presented to C. G. Seligman*. Edited by E. E. Evans-Pritchard, Richard Firth, Bronislaw Malinowski, and Isaac Schapera. London: Kegan Paul.

Flannery, Regina, and Chambers, Mary Elizabeth. 1985. Each Man Has His Own Friends: The Role of Dream Visitors in Traditional East Cree Belief and Practice. *Arctic Anthropology* 22 (1): 1–22.

Fosshage, James L. 1983. The Psychological Function of Dreams: A Revised Psychoanalytic Perspective. *Psychoanalysis and Contemporary Thought* 6 (4): 641–70.

Foulkes, David. 1978. *A Grammar of Dreams*. New York: Basic Books.

———. 1982. *Children's Dreams: Longitudinal Studies*. New York: Wiley.

———. 1983. Dream Ontogeny and Dream Psychophysiology. In *Sleep Mechanisms and Functions in Humans and Animals*. Edited by M. Chase and E. Weitzman. New York: Spectrum.

———. 1985. *Dreaming: A Cognitive-Psychological Analysis*. Hillsdale, N.J.: L. Erlbaum.

Fourtier, Millie Kelly. 1972. *Dreams and Preparation for Death*. Ann Arbor, Mich.: University Microfilms.

Frazer, James G. [1890] 1959. *The New Golden Bough*. Edited by Theodor H. Gaster. New York: Mentor.

French, Thomas, and Fromm, Erika. 1964. *Dream Interpretation: A New Approach*. New York: Basic Books.

Freud, Sigmund. [1895] 1954. Project for a Scientific Psychology. In *The Origins of Psychoanalysis: Letters of Wilhelm Fliess, Drafts and Notes: 1887-1902*. Edited by Marie Bonaparte, Anna Freud, and Ernst Kris, translated by Eric Mosbacher and James Strachey. New York: Basic Books.

———. [1900] 1965. *The Interpretation of Dreams*. Translated by James Strachey. New York: Avon.

———. [1901] 1955. The Psychopathology of Everyday Life. In *The Standard Edition of the Complete Psychological Works of Sigmund Freud*, vol. 6. Translated and edited by James Strachey. London: Hogarth Press and the Institute of Psycho-Analysis. Hereafter referred to as *SE*.

———. [1905] 1963. *Dora: Fragment of an Analysis of a Case of Hysteria.* Edited by Philip Rieff. New York: Collier Books.

———. [1907] 1963. Obsessive Acts and Religious Practices. Translated by R. C. MacWatters. In *Character and Culture.* Edited by Philip Rieff. New York: Collier Books.

———. [1908] 1963. The Relation of the Poet to Daydreaming. Translated by I.F. Grant Duff. In *Character and Culture.* Edited by Philip Rieff. New York: Collier Books.

———. [1909a] 1955. Analysis of a Phobia in a Five-Year Old Boy. In *SE*, vol. 10.

———. [1909b] 1955. Notes Upon a Case of Obsessional Neurosis. In *SE*, vol. 10.

———. [1910] 1955. Leonardo Da Vinci and a Memory of his Childhood. In *SE*, vol. 9.

———. [1913] 1955. Totem and Taboo. In *SE*, vol. 13.

———. [1914] 1955. On Narcissism: An Introduction. In *SE*, vol. 14.

———. [1917a] 1966. *Introductory Lectures on Psychoanalysis.* Translated by James Strachey. New York: W. W. Norton and Co.

———. [1917b] 1963. A Difficulty in the Path of Psychoanalysis. Translated by Joan Riviere. In *Character and Culture.* Edited by Philip Rieff. New York: Collier Books.

———. [1918] 1955. From the History of an Infantile Neurosis. In *SE*, vol. 17.

———. [1923] 1963. Remarks Upon the Theory and Practice of Dream Interpretation. Translated by James Strachey. In *Therapy and Technique.* Edited by Philip Rieff. New York: Collier Books.

———. [1925] 1963. *Some Additional Notes on Dream Interpretation as a Whole.* Translated by James Strachey. In *Therapy and Technique.* Edited by Philip Rieff. New York: Collier Books.

———. [1927] 1963. *The Future of an Illusion.* Translated by James Strachey. New York: W. W. Norton and Co.

———. [1930] 1961. *Civilization and its Discontents.* Translated by James Strachey. New York: W. W. Norton and Co.

———. [1933] 1965. *New Introductory Lectures on Psychoanalysis.* Translated by James Strachey. New York: W. W. Norton and Co. (1965).

Frieden, Ken. 1990. *Freud's Dream of Interpretation.* Albany: State University of New York Press.

Friedman, Thomas L. 1990. A Dreamlike Landscape, a Dreamlike Reality. *New York Times* article, 28 October, E3.

Fromm, Erich. 1951. *The Forgotten Language: An Introduction to the Understanding of Dreams, Fairy Tales, and Myths.* New York: Grove Press.

Fuller, Robert C. 1986. *Americans and the Unconscious.* New York: Oxford University Press.

Gackenbach, Jayne, ed. 1987. *Sleep and Dreams: A Source Book.* New York: Garland Publishing Co.

———. 1989. *Control Your Dreams*. New York: Harper & Row.

Gackenbach, Jayne, and LaBerge, Stephen, eds. 1988. *Conscious Mind, Sleeping Brain*. New York: Plenum Press.

Gadamer, Hans-Georg. 1975. *Truth and Method*. Translated by Garrett Barden and John Cumming. New York: Seabury Press.

Gallop, Jane. 1985. Keys to Dora. In *In Dora's Case: Freud— Hysteria—Feminism*. Edited by Charles Bernheimer and Claire Kahane. New York: Columbia University Press.

Gardner, John, and Maier, John, trans. 1984. *Gilgamesh*. New York: Vintage Books.

Garfield, Patricia. 1974. *Creative Dreaming*. New York: Ballantine.

———. 1985. *Your Child's Dreams*. New York: Ballantine.

———. 1988. *Women's Bodies, Women's Dreams*. New York: Ballantine.

Gay, Peter. 1988. *Freud: A Life for Our Time*. New York: Norton.

Gearhart, Suzanne. 1985. The Scene of Psychoanalysis: The Unanswered Questions of Dora. In *In Dora's Case: Freud— Hysterial—Feminism*. Edited by Charles Bernheimer and Claire Kahane. New York: Columbia University Press.

Gendlin, Eugene. 1986. *Let Your Body Interpret Your Dreams*. Wilmette, Ill: Chiron Publications.

Gill, Sam. 1987. *Mother Earth: An American Story*. Chicago: University of Chicago Press.

Gilligan, Carol. 1982. *In A Different Voice: Psychological Theory and Women's Development*. Cambridge: Harvard University Press.

Gillespie, George. 1988a. When Does Lucid Dreaming Become Transpersonal Experience? *Psychiatric Journal of the University of Ottawa* 13 (2): 107-110.

———. 1988b. Lucid Dreams in Tibetan Buddhism. In *Conscious Mind, Sleeping Brain*. Edited by Jayne Gackenbach and Stephen LaBerge. New York: Plenum.

———. 1990. A Look at Mystic Light. *Lucidity Letter* 9 (1): 9–21.

Globus, Gordon. 1987. *Dream Life, Wake Life: The Human Condition Through Dreams*. Albany: State University of New York Press.

Gollnick, James. 1987. *Dreams in the Psychology of Religion*. New York: Edwin Mellen Press.

Goodman, Nelson. 1978. *Ways of Worldmaking*. Indianapolis: Hackett.

Green, Celia E. 1968. *Lucid Dreams*. Oxford: Institute of Psychophysical Research.

Gregor, Thomas. 1981. "Far, Far Away My Shadow Wandered . . . ": The Dream Symbolism and Dream Theories of the Mehinaku Indians of Brazil. *American Ethnologist* 8 (4): 709–20.

———. 1983. Dark Dreams About the White Man. *Natural History* 92 (1): 8–14.

Habermas, Jurgen. 1971. *Knowledge and Human Interests*. Translated by Jeremy J. Shapiro. Boston: Beacon Press.

Hadfield, J. A. 1954. *Dreams and Nightmares*. London: Penguin Books.

Hall, Calvin. 1966. *The Meaning of Dreams*. Rev. ed. New York: McGraw-Hill.

Hall, Calvin, and Van de Castle, Robert L. 1966. *The Content Analysis of Dreams*. New York: Appleton-Century-Crofts.

Hall, Calvin, and Nordby, Vernon J. 1972. *The Individual and His Dreams*. New York: Signet Books.

Hallowell, Irving. 1955. *Culture and Experience*. Philadelphia: University of Pennsylvania Press.

———. 1961. Ojibwa Ontology, Behavior, and World View. In *Culture in History: Essays in Honor of Paul Radin*. New York: Columbia University Press.

———. 1966. The Role of Dreams in Ojibwa Culture. In *The Dream and Human Societies*. Edited by G. E. Von Grunebaum and Roger Callois. Berkeley and Los Angeles: University of California Press.

Hamilton, Mary. 1906. *Incubation; or, The Cure of Disease in Pagan Temples and Christian Churches*. London: Marshall, Hamilton, Kent.

Haraway, Donna. 1984. Teddy Bear Patriarchy. *Social Text* 4(2): 20–64.

———. 1986. Primatology is Politics by Other Means. In *Feminist Approaches to Science*. Edited by Ruth Bleier. New York: Pergamon Press.

Hartmann, Ernest. 1984. *The Nightmare: The Psychology and Biology of Terrifying Dreams*. New York: Basic Books.

Haskell, Robert E. 1986. Cognitive Psychology and Dream Research: Historical, Conceptual, and Epistemological Considerations. *The Journal of Mind and Behavior* 7 (2–3): 131–59.

Hastings, James, ed. 1912. *Encyclopedia of Religion and Ethics*. New York: Charles Scribner's Sons.

Heraclitus. 1987. *Fragments*. Translated by T.M. Robinson. Toronto: University of Toronto Press.

Hesiod. 1973. *Theogony*. Translated by Dorothea Wender. London: Penguin Books.

Hill, Brian, ed. 1967. *Such Stuff as Dreams*. London: Rupert Hart-Davis.

Hillman, Deborah Jay. 1987. Dream Work and Field Work: Linking Cultural Anthropology and the Current Dream Work Movement. In *The Variety of Dream Experience*. Edited by Montague Ullman and Claire Limmer. New York: Continuum.

Hillman, James. 1979. *The Dream and the Underworld*. New York: Harper & Row.

Hobbes, Thomas. [1651] 1968. *Leviathan*. London: Penguin Books.

Hobson, J. Allan. 1988. *The Dreaming Brain: How the Brain Creates Both the Sense and the Nonsense of Dreams*. New York: Basic Books.

Hobson, J. Allan, and Lavie, Peretz. 1986. Origin of Dreams: Anticipation of Modern Theories in the Philosophy and Physiology of the Eighteenth and Nineteenth Centuries. *Psychological Bulletin* 100 (2): 229–40.

Hobson, J. Allan, and McCarley, Robert W. 1977. The Brain as a Dream-State Generator: An Activation-Synthesis Hypothesis of the Dream Process. *American Journal of Psychiatry* 134: 1335–68.

Homans, Peter. 1979. *Jung in Context: Modernity and the Making of a Psychology*. Chicago: University of Chicago Press.

———. 1989. *The Ability to Mourn: Disillusionment and the Social Origins of Psychoanalysis*. Chicago: University of Chicago Press.

Homer. 1951. *The Iliad.* Translated by Richmond Lattimore. Chicago: University of Chicago Press.

———. 1961. *The Odyssey*. Translated by Robert Fitzgerald. New York: Anchor Books.

Hosain, M. Hidayet. 1932. A Treatise on the Interpretation of Dreams. *Islamic Culture* 6(4): 568–85.

Howitt, A. E. 1904. *Native Tribes of South-East Australia*. New York.

Hudson, Liam. 1985. *Night Life: The Interpretation of Dreams*. New York: St. Martin's Press.

Hughes, J. Donald. 1987. Dreams from the Ancient World. in *The Variety of Dream Experience*. Edited by Montague Ullman and Claire Limmer. New York: Continuum.

Hunt, Harry. 1989. *The Multiplicity of Dreams: Memory, Imagination, and Consciousness*. New Haven: Yale University Press.

James, William. [1900] 1958. *The Varieties of Religious Experience*. New York: Mentor Books.

Jayne, Walter. 1925. *The Healing Gods of Ancient Civilizations*. New Haven: Yale University Press.

Jones, Ernest. 1951. *On the Nightmare*. New York: Liveright.

———. 1953–57. *The Life and Work of Sigmund Freud.* 3 vol. New York: Basic Books.

Jones, Richard. 1978. *The New Psychology of Dreaming*. New York: Penguin Books.

Jung, Carl G. [1909] 1974. The Analysis of Dreams. In *Dreams*, edited and translated by R. F. C. Hull. Princeton: Princeton University Press. Hereafter referred to as *Dreams*.

———. [1910–11] 1974. On the Significance of Number Dreams. In *Dreams*.

———. [1931][1966. The Aims of Psychotherapy. In *The Practice of Psychotherapy*. Translated by R. F. C. Hull. 2d ed. Princeton: Princeton University Press. Hereafter referred to as *The Practice of Psychotherapy*.

———. [1934] 1974. The Practical Use of Dream-Analysis. In *Dreams*.

———. [1935] 1966. Principles of Practical Psychotherapy. In *The Practice of Psychotherapy*.

———. [1939] 1969. Psychological Commentary on "The Tibetan Book of the Great Liberation." In *The Collected Works of C. G. Jung*, vol. 11, translated by R. F. C. Hull. 2d ed. Princeton: Princeton University Press (1969).

———. [1948a] 1974. General Aspects of Dream Psychology. In *Dreams*.

———. [1948b] 1974. On the Nature of Dreams. In *Dreams*.

———. [1951a] 1969. The Psychology of the Child Archetype. In *The Archetypes and the Collective Unconscious*, translated by R. F. C. Hull. Princeton: Princeton

University Press. Hereafter referred to as *The Archetypes and the Collective Unconscious.*

———. [1951b] 1969. The Psychological Aspects of the Kore. In *The Archetypes and the Collective Unconscious.*

———. [1951c] 1969. *Aion: Researches into the Phenomenology of the Self.* In *The Collected Works of C. G. Jung*, vol. 9ii, translated by R. F. C. Hull. 2d ed. Princeton: Princeton University Press.

———. [1952] 1974. Individual Dream Symbolism in Relation to Alchemy. In *Dreams.*

———. [1954] 1969. Concerning the Archetypes, with Special Reference to the Anima Concept. In *The Archetypes and the Collective Unconscious.*

———. [1955–56] 1970. *Mysterium Coniunctionis.* Translated by R. F. C. Hall. Princeton: Princeton University Press.

———. 1965. Memories, Dreams, Reflections. Translated by Richard and Clara Winston. New York: Vintage Books.

———. 1966. *Two Essays on Analytical Psychology.* Translated by R. F. C. Hull. Princeton: Princeton University Press.

Kegan, Robert. 1982. *The Evolving Self: Problem and Process in Human Development.* Cambridge: Harvard University Press.

Kelsey, Morton. 1974. *God, Dreams, and Revelation: A Christian Interpretation of Dreams.* Minneapolis: Augsburg Publishing House.

Kelzer, Ken. 1987. *The Sun and the Shadow.* New York: A.R.E. Press.

Kenton, Edna. 1929. *The Indians of North America.* 2 vols. New York.

Kierkegaard, Søren. [1846] 1946. Concluding Unscientific Postscript. In *A Kierkegaard Anthology.* Edited by Robert Bretall. Princeton: Princeton University Press.

Kilbourne, Benjamin. 1987. Dreams. In *The Encyclopedia of Religion*, vol 4. Edited by Mircea Eliade, 482–92. Chicago: University of Chicago Press.

Kluckhorn, Clyde. 1942. Myths and Ritual: A General Theory. *Harvard Theological Review* 35: 45–79.

Kohut, Heinz. 1978. *The Search for the Self: Selected Writings of Heinz Kohut: 1950-1978.* Edited by Paul H. Ornstein. New York: International Universities Press.

The Koran. 1956. Translated by N. J. Dawood. London: Penguin Books.

Krippner, Stanley, ed. 1990. *Dreamtime and Dreamwork.* Los Angeles: Jeremy Tarcher.

Krippner, Stanley, and Dillard, Joseph. 1988. *Dreamworking: How to Use Your Dreams for Creative Problem-Solving.* Buffalo: Bearly.

Kuhn, Thomas. 1970. *The Structure of Scientific Revolutions.* 2d ed. Chicago: University of Chicago Press.

Kuper, Adam. 1979. A Structural Approach to Dreams. *Man* 14: 645–62.

———. 1983. The Structure of Dream Sequences. *Culture, Medicine, and Psychiatry* 7: 153-165.

LaBerge, Stephen. 1985. *Lucid Dreaming.* Los Angeles: Jeremy Tarcher.

———. 1988. Reply to Bulkley. *Lucidity Letter* 7 (2): 17–19.

Lakoff, George, and Johnson, Mark. 1980. *Metaphors We Live By*. Chicago: University of Chicago Press.

Lanternari, Vittorio. 1975. Dreams as Charismatic Significants: Their Bearing on the Rise of New Religious Movements. In *Psychological Anthropology*. Edited by T. R. Williams. Paris: Mouton.

Latour, Bruno. 1987. *Science in Action: How to Follow Scientists and Engineers Through Society*. Cambridge: Harvard University Press.

Laufer, Berthold. 1931. Inspirational Dreams in Eastern Asia. *Journal of American Folk-Lore* 44: 208–16.

LeCerf, Jean. 1966. The Dream in Popular Culture: Arab and Islamic. In *The Dream and Human Societies*. Edited by G. E. Von Grunebaum and Roger Callois. Berkeley and Los Angeles: University of California Press.

Leuba, James Henry. 1929. *The Psychology of Religious Mysticism*. New York: Harcourt, Brace.

Levin, Ross. 1990. Psychoanalytic Theories on the Function of Dreaming: A Review of the Empirical Dream Research. In *Empirical Studies of Psychoanalytic Theories*, vol. 3. Edited by J. Masling. New York: Analytic Press.

Lewis, Naphtali. 1976. *The Interpretation of Dreams and Portents*. Toronto: Samuel Stevens Hakkert.

Lhalungpa, Lobsang P., trans. 1985. *Life of Milarepa*. Boston: Shambhala.

Lincoln, Jackson Stewart. 1935. *The Dream in Primitive Cultures*. London: University of London.

Long, Michael E. 1987. What is This Thing Called Sleep? *National Geographic*, Dec., 787–821.

Lowy, Sameul. 1942. *Psychological and Biological Foundations of Dream-Interpretation*. London: Kegan Paul, Trench, and Trubner.

Luther, Martin. 1945. *Luther's Works*. Edited by Jaroslav Pelikan. St. Louis: Concordia Publishing House.

MacCormac, Earl R. 1976. *Metaphor and Myth in Science and Religion*. Durham, N.C.: Duke University Press.

Mack, John E. 1970. *Nightmares and Human Conflict*. New York: Columbia University Press.

MacKenzie, Norman. 1965. *Dreams and Dreaming*. New York: Vanguard.

Macrobius. 1952. *Commentary on the Dream of Scipio*. Translated by William Harris Stahl. New York: Columbia University Press.

Malcolm, Norman. 1959. *Dreaming*. London: Routledge & Kegan Paul.

Malinowski, Bronislaw. [1927] 1985. *Sex and Repression in Savage Society*. Chicago: University of Chicago Press (1985).

Mannheim, Karl. 1936. *Ideology and Utopia: An Introduction to the Sociology of Knowledge*. Translated by Louis Wirth and Edward Shils. New York: Harcourt, Brace and Co.

Marcus, Stephen. 1985. Freud and Dora: Story, History, Case History. In *In Dora's Case: Freud—Hysteria—Feminism*. Edited by Charles Bernheimer and Claire Kahane. New York: Columbia University Press.

Marx, Karl. 1978. The Economic and Philosophic Manuscripts of 1844. Translated by Martin Milligan. In *The Marx-Engels Reader*. Edited by Robert C. Tucker. 2d ed. New York: W. W. Norton & Co.

Maslow, Abraham. 1964. *Religion, Values, and Peak Experiences*. New York: Viking.

Masson, Jeffrey Moussaieff, trans. and ed. 1985. *The Complete Letters of Sigmund Freud to Wilhelm Fliess 1887-1904*. Cambridge: Belknap Press.

Maybruck, Patricia. 1989. *Pregnancy and Dreams*. Los Angeles: Jeremy Tarcher.

McCaffrey, Philip. 1984. *Freud and Dora: The Artful Dream*. New Brunswick, N.J.: Rutgers University Press.

McFague, Sallie. 1982. *Metaphorical Theology: Models of God in Religious Language*. Philadelphia: Fortress Press.

McGuire, William, ed. 1974. *The Freud-Jung Letters: The Correspondence between Sigmund Freud and Carl G. Jung*. Translated by Ralph Manheim and R. F. C. Hull. Princeton: Princeton University Press.

Meier, C. A. 1967. *Ancient Incubation and Modern Psychotherapy*. Translated by Monica Curtis. Evanston, Ill: Northwestern University Press.

Meltzer, Francoise. 1987. Descartes' Dreams and Freud's Failure, or The Politics of Originality. In *The Trial(s) of Psychoanalysis*. Edited by Francoise Meltzer. Chicago: University of Chicago Press.

Miller, Patricia Cox. 1986. "A Dubious Twilight": Reflections on Dreams in Patristic Literature. *Church History* 55 (2): 153–64.

Milton, John. [1667] 1977. *Paradise Lost*. New York: Viking Press.

Mindell, Arnold. 1982. *Dreambody: The Body's Role in Revealing the Self*. London: Routledge & Kegan Paul.

———. 1985. *Working with the Dream Body*. New York: Mathuen Press.

Moffitt, Alan, and Hoffman, Robert. 1987. On the Single-Mindedness and Isolation of Dream Psychophysiology. In *Sleep and Dreams: A Sourcebook*. Edited by Jayne Gackenbach. New York: Garland Publishing.

Moi, Toril. 1985. Representation of Patriarchy: Sexuality and Epistemology in Freud's Dora. In *In Dora's Case: Freud— Hysteria—Feminism*. Edited by Charles Bernheimer and Claire Kahane. New York: Columbia University Press.

Morgan, William. 1932. Navaho Dreams. *American Anthropologist* 34: 390–405.

M'Timkulu, D. 1977. Some Aspects of Zulu Religion. In *African Religions: A Symposium*. Edited by N. Booth. New York: Nok Publishers.

Muir, John. 1938. *John of the Mountains: The Unpublished Journals of John Muir*. Edited by Linnie Marsh Wolff. Madison: University of Wisconsin Press.

Mukerji, Chandra. 1989. *A Fragile Power: Scientists and the State*. Princeton: Princeton University Press.

Nash, Roderick. 1973. *Wilderness and the American Mind*. New Haven: Yale University Press.

Nashe, Thomas. [1594] 1965. The Terrors of the Night; or, A Discourse of Apparitions. In *Thomas Nashe: Selected Writings*. Edited by Stanley Wells. Cambridge: Harvard University Press.

Obeyesekere, Gananath. 1981. *Medusa's Hair: An Essay on Personal Symbols and Religious Experience*. Chicago: University of Chicago Press.

O'Connor, Peter. 1986. *Dreams and the Search for Meaning*. New York: Paulist Press.

O'Flaherty, Wendy Doniger, trans. 1981. *The Rig Veda*. London: Penguin Books.

———. 1984. *Dreams, Illusion, and Other Realities*. Chicago: University of Chicago Press.

———. 1989. Structuralist Universals versus Psychoanalytic Universals. *History of Religions* 28 (3): 267–81.

———. 1990. Lucid Dreaming in the *Tales from the Arabian Nights*. Address given to the Seventh International Conference of the Association for the Study of Dreams, Chicago, 28 June.

Ohnuki-Tierney, Emiko. 1987. Anu religion. In *The Encyclopedia of Religion*, vol. 1. Edited by Mircea Eliade, 159–61. Chicago: University of Chicago Press.

Olson, Richard, ed. 1971. *Science as Metaphor: The Historical Role of Scientific Theories in Forming Western Culture*. Belmont, Calif.: Wadsworth Publishing Co.

Oppenheim, A. Leo. 1956. The Interpretation of Dreams in the Ancient Near East with a Translation of an Assyrian Dream-Book. *Transactions of the American Philosophical Society* 46 (3): 179–373.

———. 1966. Mantic Dreams in the Ancient Near East. In *The Dream and Human Societies*. Edited by G. E. Von Grunebaum and Roger Callois. Berkeley and Los Angeles: University of California Press.

Ortner, Sherry. 1974. Is Female to Male as Nature is to Culture? In *Women, Culture, and Society*. Edited by Michelle Zimbalist Rosaldo and Louise Lamphere. Stanford: Stanford University Press.

Ovid. 1955. *Metamorphoses*. Translated by Rolfe Humphries. Bloomington: Indiana University Press.

Palmer, Richard E. 1969. *Hermeneutics*. Evanston, Ill.: Northwestern University Press.

Parisi, Thomas. 1987. Why Freud Failed: Some Implications for Neurophysiology and Sociobiology. *American Psychologist* 42 (3): 235–45.

Pepper, Stephen. 1942. *World Hypotheses*. Berkeley and Los Angeles: University of California Press.

Piaget, Jean. 1962. *Play, Dreams, and Imitation in Childhood*. New York: W. W. Norton & Co.

———. 1963. *The Child's Conception of the World*. Paterson, N.J.: Littlefield, Adams.

———. 1973. The Affective Unconscious and the Cognitive Unconscious. *American Psychoanalytic Assocation Journal* 21: 249–61.

Plato. 1961. *The Republic*. Translated by Paul Shorey. In *The Collected Dialogues of Plato*. Edited by Edith Hamilton and Huntington Cairns. Princeton: Princeton University Press.

———. 1961. *Theaetetus*. Translated by F. M. Cornford. In *The Collected Dialogues of Plato*. Edited by Edith Hamilton and Huntington Cairns. Princeton: Princeton University Press.

Radin, Paul. 1936. Ojibwa and Ottawa Puberty Dreams. In *Essays in Anthropology Presented to A. L. Kroeber*. Berkeley and Los Angeles: University of California Press.

Rahman, Fazlur. 1966. Dream, Imagination, and Alam al-mithal. In *The Dream and Human Societies*. Edited by G. E. Von Grunebaum and Roger Callois. Berkeley and Los Angeles: University of California Press.

Ramas, Maria. 1985. Freud's Dora, Dora's Hysteria. In *In Dora's Case: Freud—Hysteria—Feminism*. Edited by Charles Bernheimer and Claire Kahane. New York: Columbia University Press.

Rank, Otto. [1909] 1957. *The Myth of the Birth of the Hero: A Psychological Interpretation of Mythology*. Translated by F. Robbins and Smith Ely Jelliffe. New York: R. Brunner.

Ray, Amy. 1989. Land of Canaan. *The Indigo Girls*. Epic 45044.

———. 1990. World Falls. *Indigo Girls: Indians Nomads Saints*. Epic 46820.

Ricoeur, Paul. 1967. *The Symbolism of Evil*. Translated by Emerson Buchanan. Boston: Beacon Press.

———. 1970. *Freud and Philosophy: An Essay on Interpretation*. Translated by Denis Savage. New Haven: Yale University Press.

———. 1974. *The Conflict of Interpretations: Essays in Hermeneutics*. Edited by Don Ihoe. Evanston, Ill.: Northwestern University Press.

———. 1981. *Hermeneutics and the Human Sciences: Essays on Language, Action, and Interpretation*. Translated by John B. Thompson. New York: Cambridge University Press.

Rieff, Philip. 1966. *The Triumph of the Therapeutic: Uses of Faith after Freud*. New York: Harper & Row.

Rizzuto, Anna-Marie. 1979. *The Birth of the Living God: A Psychoanalytic Study*. Chicago: University of Chicago Press.

Roheim, Geza. 1945. *The Eternal Ones of the Dream: A Psychoanalytic Interpretation of Australian Myth and Ritual*. New York: International Universities Press.

———. 1952. *The Gates of the Dream*. New York: International Universities Press.

Rose, Jacqueline. 1985. Dora: Fragment of an Analysis. In *In Dora's Case: Freud—Hysteria—Feminism*. Edited by Charles Bernheimer and Claire Kahane. New York: Columbia University Press.

Rupprecht, Carol Schreier. 1985. The Common Language of Women's Dreams: Colloquy of Mind and Body. In *Feminist Archetypal Theory: Interdisciplinary Revisions of Jungian Thought*. Edited by Carol Schreier Rupprecht and Estella Lauter.

———, ed. 1993. *The Dream and the Text: Essays on Language and Literature.* Albany: State University of New York Press.

Rushdie, Salman. 1988. *The Satanic Verses.* New York: Viking.

Ryback, David, with Sweitzer, Letitia. 1986. *Dreams that Come True.* New York: Ivy Books.

Rycroft, Charles. 1979. *The Innocence of Dreams.* New York: Pantheon Books.

Sahlins, Marshall. 1972. *Stone Age Economics.* Chicago: Aldine-Atherton.

Saint-Denys, Hervey de. [1867] 1982. *Dreams and How to Guide Them.* Translated by N. Fry. London: Duckworth.

Samuels, Andrew. 1985. *Jung and the Post-Jungians.* Boston: Routledge & Kegan Paul.

———. 1986. *A Critical Dictionary of Jungian Analysis.* New York: Routledge & Kegan Paul.

Schor, Juliet B. 1992. *The Overworked American: The Unexpected Decline of Leisure.* New York: Basic Books.

Seafield, Frank. 1877. *The Literature and Curiosities of Dreams: A Commonplace Book of Speculations Concerning the Mystery of Dreams and Visions, Records of Curious and Well-Authenticated Dreams, and Notes on The Various Modes of Interpretation Adopted in Ancient and Modern Times.* 2d ed. rev. London: Crosby, Lockwood, and Co.

Seligson, Fred Jeremy. 1989. *Oriental Birth Dreams.* Rev. ed. Elizabeth, N.J.: Hollym.

Sendak, Maurice. 1963. *Where The Wild Things Are.* New York: Harper and Row.

Sharma, Jagdish P., and Siegel, Lee. 1980. *Dream Symbolism in the Sramanic Tradition: Two Psychoanalytical Studies in Jinist and Buddhist Dream Legends.* Calcutta: Firma KLM.

Shweder, Richard A. 1982. On Savages and Other Children. Review of *The Foundations of Primitive Thought,* by C. R. Hallpike. *American Anthropologist* 84: 354–66.

Shweder, Richard A., and LeVine, Robert A. 1975. Dream Concepts of Hausa Children: A Critique of the "Doctrine of Invariant Sequence" *Ethos* 3: 209–30.

Siegel, Alan B. 1990. *Dreams That Can Change Your Life.* Los Angeles: Jeremy Tarcher.

Singer, Isidore, ed. 1904. *The Jewish Encyclopedia.* New York: Funk and Wagnalls Company.

Smith, Adam. [1776] 1976. *An Inquiry into the Nature and Causes of the Wealth of Nations.* Edited by Edwin Cannan. Chicago: University of Chicago Press.

Spencer, Baldwin, and Gillen, F. J. 1904. *The Northern Tribes of Central Australia.* London.

Sprengnether, Madelon. 1985. Enforcing Oedipus: Freud and Dora. In *In Dora's Case: Freud—Hysteria—Feminism.* Edited by Charles Bernheimer and Claire Kahane. New York: Columbia University Press.

Starbuck, Edwin D. 1899. *The Psychology of Religion*. New York: Scribner's & Sons.

States, Bert O. 1988. *The Rhetoric of Dreams*. Ithaca: Cornell University Press.

Stephen, Michele. 1979. Dreams of Change: The Innovative Role of Altered States of Consciousness in Traditional Melanesian Religion. *Oceania* 50 (1): 3–22.

Stevens, Anthony. 1982. *Archetypes: A Natural History of the Self*. New York: Quill Press.

Stewart, Kilton R. 1951. Dream Theory in Malaya. *Complex* 6: 21–33.

Sundkuler, Bengt G. M. 1961. *Bantu Prophets in South Africa*. 2d ed. London: Oxford University Press.

Swedenborg, Emanuel. 1986. *Journal of Dreams*. Translated by J. J. G. Wilkinson. Commentary by Wilson van Dusen. New York: Swedenborg Foundation.

Taylor, Jeremy. 1983. *Dream Work: Techniques for Discovering the Creative Power in Dreams*. New York: Paulist Press.

———. 1991. Puff, the Magic Dragon: Kicking the Smoking Habit—One Lucid Dreamer's Experience. *Dream Network Journal* 10 (4): 11–12.

———. 1992. *Where People Fly and Water Runs Uphill: Using Dreams to Tap the Wisdom of the Unconscious*. New York: Warner Books.

Tedlock, Barbara. 1987. *Dreaming: Anthropological and Psychological Interpretations*. New York: Cambridge University Press.

Terry, Patricia, trans. 1965. *The Song of Roland*. Indianapolis: Bobbs-Merrill Educational Publishing.

Thomas, Louis-Vincent. 1987. Funeral Rites. In *The Encyclopedia of Religion*, vol. 5. Edited by Mircea Eliade, 440–49. Chicago: University of Chicago Press.

Thompson, E. P. 1967. Time, Work-Discipline, and Industrial Capitalism. *Past and Present: A Journal of Historical Studies* 38 (Dec.): 56–97.

The Tibetan Book of the Dead: The Great Liberation Through Hearing in the Bardo. 1975. Translated by Francesca Fremantle and Chogyam Trungpa. Boston: Shambhala.

Tillich, Paul. 1948. *The Protestant Era*. Abridged ed. Translated by James Luther Adams. Chicago: University of Chicago Press.

———. 1951–63. *Systematic Theology*. 3 vols. New Haven: Yale University Press.

———. 1952. *The Courage to Be*. New Haven: Yale University Press.

Todorov, Tzvetan. 1982. *The Conquest of America: The Question of the Other*. Translated by Richard Howard. New York: Harper and Row.

Toffelmier, Gertrude, and Luomala, Katherine. 1936. Dreams and Dream Interpretation of the Diegueno Indians of Southern California. *The Psychoanalytic Quarterly* 5: 195–225.

Toksvig, Signe. 1948. *Emanuel Swedenborg: Scientist and Mystic*. New Yaven: Yale University Press.

Tracy, David. 1975. *Blessed Rage for Order: The New Pluralism in Theology*. Minneapolis: Seabury Press.

Turner, Victor. 1969. *The Ritual Process: Structure and Anti-Structure*. Ithaca: Cornell University Press.

———. 1986. Body, Brain, and Culture. *Cross Currents* 36 (2): 156–78.

Tylor, E. B. 1874. *Primitive Culture: Researches into the Development of Mythology, Philosophy, Religion, Language, Art, and Custom*. Boston: Estes and Lauriat.

Ullman, Montague. 1987. Dreams and Society. In *The Varieties of Dream Experience*. Edited by Montague Ullman and Claire Limmer. New York: Continuum Publishing Co.

Ullman, Montague, and Limmer, Claire. 1987. *The Varieties of Dream Experience*. New York: Continuum Publishing Co.

Ullman, Montague, and Zimmerman, Nan. 1979. *Working with Dreams*. Los Angeles: Jeremy Tarcher.

The Thirteen Principal Upanishads. 1931. Translated by Robert Ernest Hume. 2d ed., rev. Delhi: Oxford University Press.

Vande Kemp, Hendrika. 1981. The Dream in Periodical Literature: 1860-1910. *Journal of the History of the Behavioral Sciences* 17: 88–113.

Van Gennep, Arnold. 1960. *The Rites of Passage*. Translated by Monika B. Vizedom and Gabrielle L. Caffee. Chicago: University of Chicago Press.

Von Franz, Marie-Louise. 1986. *On Dreams and Death*. Boston: Shambhala.

Von Grunebaum, G. E. 1966. Introduction: The Cultural Function of the Dream as Illustrated by Classical Islam. In *The Dream and Human Societies*. Edited by G. E. Von Grunebaum and Roger Callois. Berkeley and Los Angeles: University of California Press.

Von Grunebaum, G. E., and Callois, Roger, eds. 1966. *The Dream and Human Societies*. Berkeley and Los Angeles: University of California Press.

Waldberg, Patrick. 1965. *Surrealism*. London: Thames and Hudson.

Wallace, Anthony F. C. 1956. Revitalization Movements. *American Anthropologist* 58 (2): 264–81.

———. 1958. Dreams and Wishes of the Soul: A Type of Psychoanalytic Theory Among the Seventeenth Century Iroquois. *American Anthropologist* 60: 234–48.

Wayman, Alex. 1967. Significance of Dreams in India and Tibet. *History of Religions* 7: 1–12.

Weber, Max. [1904–5] 1976. *The Protestant Ethic and the Spirit of Capitalism*. Translated by Talcott Parsons. London: Unwin Paperbacks.

———. [1919] 1946. Science as a Vocation. In *From Max Weber: Essays in Sociology*. Translated by H. H. Gerth and C. Wright Mills. New York: Oxford University Press.

Wehr, Demaris S. 1987. *Jung and Feminism: Liberating Archetypes*. Boston: Beacon Press.

Wills, Gary. 1990. *Under God: Religion and American Politics*. New York: Harper & Row.

Winnicott, D. W. 1971. *Playing and Reality*. New York: Tavistock Publications.
Wiseman, Ann Sayre. 1986. *Nightmare Help: For Children, From Children*. Berkeley: Ten Speed Press.
Wittgenstein, Ludwig. 1966. *Lectures and Conversations on Aesthetics, Psychology, and Religious Belief.* Berkeley and Los Angeles: University of California Press.
———. 1972. *On Certainty*. New York: Harper Torchbooks.
Woods, Ralph L., and Greenhouse, Herbert B., eds. 1974. *The New World of Dreams*. New York: Macmillan.
Wulff, David M. 1991. *Psychology of Religion: Classic and Contemporary Views*. New York: Wiley.
Zelazny, Roger. 1966. *The Dream Master*. New York: Ace.

INDEX